PATHWAYS:
EXPLORING THE ROUTES OF A MOVEMENT HERITAGE

PATHWAYS:
EXPLORING THE ROUTES OF A MOVEMENT HERITAGE

Edited by Daniel Svensson, Katarina Saltzman and
Sverker Sörlin

With a Foreword by Tim Ingold

© 2022
The White Horse Press, The Old Vicarage, Main Street, Winwick,
Cambridgeshire, UK

Set in 11 point Adobe Caslon Pro and Lucida Sans
Printed by Lightning Source

This work is licensed under the Creative Commons Attribution-Non Commercial-No Derivatives 4.0 (BY-NC-ND) license, which means that the text may be used for non-commercial purposes, provided credit is given to the author. For details go to https://creativecommons.org/licenses/by-nc-nd/4.0
Creative Commons license terms for re-use do not apply to any content (such as graphs, figures, photos, excerpts, etc.) not original to the Open Access publication and further permission may be required from the rights holder. The obligation to research and clear permission lies solely with the party re-using the material.

British Library Cataloguing in Publication Data
A catalogue record for this book is available from the British Library

ISBN   978-1-912186-55-6 (PB)
        978-1-912186-60-0 (ebook)

doi: 10.3197/63787710662654.book

Cover and interior layout by Stefania Bonura Graphics Web & Books
Image re-use may be subject to restrictions.

CONTENTS

List of figures	vii
Author biographies	xi
Acknowledgements	xix
Foreword – *Tim Ingold*	xxi
Introduction Movement Heritage and Path Dependence: Layering the Past – *Daniel Svensson, Katarina Saltzman, Sverker Sörlin*	1
SECTION I – PAST PRECONDITIONS OF PATHS	31
Chapter 1. Footpaths in England: Notes Towards a Radical History – *Paul Readman*	33
Chapter 2. Delineating the Landscape: Planning, Mapping and the Historic Imaginings of Rights of Way in Twentieth-century England and Wales – *Clare Hickman and Glen O'Hara*	56
Chapter 3. Appropriated Heritage? Access Campaigns, Trespass, and Local Rights in Early-twentieth Century Upland England and Austria – *Ben Anderson*	74
Chapter 4. Hefting the Land: A Locative Heritage of Hooves and Feet – *Karen Lykke Syse*	97
Chapter 5. 'Following in the Footsteps of History': Sixteen Multimedia Itineraries through the First World War Sites in the Stelvio National Park and Adamello Park (Italy) – *Stefano Morosini*	114
SECTION II – OFF THE BEATEN TRACKS	129
Chapter 6. Archipelagic Paths: Narratives, Heritage and Community in Public Trail Walking on the Åland Islands – *Susanne Österlund-Pötzsch*	131

Chapter 7. Fusion: Co-created Heritage in Stories from the Camino de Santiago – *Camilla Brudin Borg* 152

Chapter 8. Tracing Memories: The Guided Trail as an Aid to Cultural Memory in Artworks by Janet Cardiff – *Laura Bertens* 167

Chapter 9. Walking and Worlding: Trails as Storylines in Video Games – *Finn Arne Jørgensen* 186

Chapter 10. Attentive Walking: Encountering Mineralness – *Petra Lilja* 201

SECTION III – SEARCHING FOR NEW PATH HERITAGE 219

Chapter 11. Kodagu Walking Trails and Indigenous Heritage Making: A Bioregional Study – *Subarna De* 221

Chapter 12. Heritage Trails: Pathways to Sustainable Development Goals – *John Martin, Joane Serrano, Jacqueline Nowakowski and Dominica Williamson* 240

Chapter 13. Walking on Terrils. Ruderal Ecologies and Toxic Heritage in Wallonia, Belgium – *Daniele Valisena* 264

Chapter 14. Walking, Remembering and Enunciating the Place: Jewish-Israeli Memorial Trails in Nature – *Maria Piekarska* 279

Chapter 15. Walking the Kalderimi: Embodied Knowledge and Heritage Narratives in a Participatory Building Workshop at Zagori (NW Greece) – *Faidon Moudopoulos Athanasiou and Ionas Sklavounos* 295

Chapter 16. Forming Paths within Post-industrial Landscapes – *Benjamin Richards* 316

Index 333

LIST OF FIGURES

Chapter 1

Figure 1. The Kinder Scout Mass Trespass, 24 April 1932.
Figure 2. 'Hiking' (circa 1936), by James Walker Tucker.
Figure 3. The Pilgrims' Way, near Aylesford, Kent, England.
Figure 4: A Public footpath sign in Derbyshire, England.

Chapter 2

Figure 1. Signpost including directions for The Saints Way as well as a Cornwall County Council Rights of Way arrow showing the interlinked typographies of Rights of Way and Trails.

Chapter 4

Figure 1. Accommodation for travellers at Langfjellet, by Johannes Flintoe (1787–1870).
Figure 2. A vertical movement to the mountain dairy in Bergen parish, by Johannes Flintoe (1787–1870).
Figure 3. Milk maid with bell cow, Løken østre, Rudshøgda i Ringsaker.

Chapter 5

Figure 1. The Mount Scorluzzo (3,094 metres) Austro-Hungarian barracks. Recovery and enhancement of the site and interdisciplinary and multidisciplinary research project.
Figures 2 and 3. General description of the project 'Following in the footsteps of history'.
Figures 4 and 5. The Stelvio Pass–Mount Scorluzzo itinerary.

Chapter 6

Figure 1. Map of the Åland Islands.
Figure 2. A boy by the Geta caves, circa 1905. The cave trail has long been a popular walking path. Photograph by Otto Andersson.
Figure 3. The stamp station by the church of Lemland, Åland Islands. Pilgrims on the St. Olav Waterway can collect place stamps in their pilgrim cards in a similar vein to Camino pilgrims.
Figure 4. Uprooted tree left to rot. Messy, or sound forest care?
Figure 5. Building 'stone trolls' is a popular interactive practice among visitors to the cave trail in Geta. Many locals disapprove of this and view it as interfering with nature.
Figure 6. Helping hands – walking as community building. A group of church-walkers on the Lemland trail, Åland Islands.

Chapter 7

Figure 1. 'Roman road', Camino de Santiago de Compostela, Spain.
Figure 2. Material communication at the Camino de Santiago de Compostela, Spain.
Figure 3. Walking and talking at the Camino de Santiago de Compostela, Spain.

Pathways

Figure 4. Early morning at the Iron Cross, Camino de Santiago de Compostela, Spain.
Figure 5. 'Keep going', Camino de Santiago de Compostela, Spain.

Chapter 8

Figure 1. 'Alter Bahnhof Video Walk' (2012), by Janet Cardiff and George Bures Miller. On screen we see several people simultaneously and unexpectedly dropping their suitcases, a direct reference to an earlier remark by the artist: 'Memories are like a different form of travel. It's like filling a suitcase that we pull behind us and we open and close when we need to.'

Chapter 9

Figure 1. Screenshot from *Battlezone* (Atari, Inc., 1980).
Figure 2. Screenshot from *Dear Esther* (The Chinese Room, 2012).
Figure 3. Screenshot from *Firewatch* (Campo Santo and Panic, 2016).
Figure 4. Screenshot from *Red Dead Redemption 2* (Rockstar Games, 2019).
Figure 5. Game map from *Red Dead Redemption 2* (Rockstar Games, 2019).

Chapter 10

Figure 1. Walking in silence.
Figure 2. Mineral bones.
Figure 3. Technofossil silos.
Figure 4. Processed minerals in the shape of buildings clinging on the brink of the quarry.
Figure 5. Pondering the exposed sediment layers.
Figure 6. Encountering mineralness.

Chapter 11

Figure 1. Kodagu walking trails on C.P. Belliappa's coffee estate.
Figure 2. Human trails on Kodagu's forested coffee plantation.
Figure 3. Elephant trails on C.P. Belliappa's estate.
Figure 4. Gunflower bush in Rani Machaiah's coffee plantation.
Figure 5. Kodagu paddy fields and trails.

Chapter 12

Figure 1. Sustainable Development Goals.
Figure 2. Location of Ifugao.
Figure 3. Batad Ifugao community, showing forest, rice field and village.
Figure 4. Youths walking the Nagacadan Ifugao Rice Terraces trails.
Figure 5. One of the stops in the Open Air Museum is a traditional Ifugao house containing artefacts.
Figure 6. Location of Carwynnen Quoit. .
Figure 7. Finding quoit pathways. Left: Celebratory dance under the restored quoit. Right: The discovered Neolithic stone pavement, 2014.
Figure 8. Walking the trail by Fenton-Ia in the Reens. Top: Guest co-developer Brother Petroc stands on the Reens in the summer, reaching the highest point of the trail. Bottom: Co-developers stall on the trail during the autumn to laugh over stories whilst some observe fungi and the view, 2021.

List of figures

Figure 9. Participatory map-making by Fenton-Ia in the Reens. Top: Mapping of land use within the different categories of common land created by Philip Hills. Bottom: Using Green Map Icons to map movement heritage findings, 2021.
Figure 10. Location of Pilgrimage line.

Chapter 13

Figure 1. Liège-Seraing from one of the paths climbing Terril du Gosson, 2015.
Figure 2. Terril du Gosson, 2015.
Figure 3. 'Libellule' by Daniel Steenhaut, Terril du Gosson, 2015.

Chapter 14

Figure 1. The Martyrs' Trail information sign by the Scroll of Fire memorial.
Figure 2. Crossing of trails by the Martyrs' Cave. The green-marked Martyrs' Trail leads towards the Scroll of Fire. The orange-blue-white mark signifies the INT.
Figure 3. The Martyrs' Trail makes a narrow descent towards the Martyrs' Cave.

Chapter 15

Figure 1. A mixture of different techniques, from dry-stone kalderimi (left) to concrete-paved slabs (right).
Figure 2. The architectural drawing of the eastern side of the pathway, showing the remains uncovered during the project. The surviving patches of the nineteenth century paving layer are visible among other structures. The suggested chronologies are preliminary and relative, based on the combination of a) the material culture retrieved from each area, b) archival research and c) oral histories.
Figure 3. Left: imported nineteenth and early twentieth century potsherds from Apulia and Corfu. Right: A material culture assemblage of the so-called Anthropocene.
Figure 4. The small assemblage of coins from Russia, China and Korea.
Figure 5. The eastern edge before (above) and after (below) the intervention.
Figure 6. Left: a coin with the value of 10 Para, printed in year 19 of Sultan Abdulmecit I's reign (1858). Right: the decorative part of the flintlock pistol, partly preserved.

Chapter 16

Figure 1. Desire Path, Rjukan-Notodden World Heritage Site. Photograph by Benjamin Richards.
Figure 2. Paths, Trails and Traces, Rjukan-Notodden World Heritage Site.
Figure 3. Valued and forgotten forms, Rjukan-Notodden World Heritage Site.

AUTHOR BIOGRAPHIES

Daniel Svensson has a Ph.D. in history and is an Associate Senior Lecturer at the Department of Sport Sciences, Malmö University. His research is mainly within the fields of sport history and environmental history, with focus on environmental issues in sport and outdoor recreation. Svensson's dissertation (awarded the International Ski History Association Ullr Award 2017) focused on the scientisation of training methods in endurance sport and meetings between scientific and experiential knowledge in sport during the twentieth century. Svensson lives in the countryside in West Sweden and is proud father of two daughters with whom he loves to go for a walk.

Katarina Saltzman is Associate Professor of Ethnology and Senior Lecturer in the Department of Conservation at the University of Gothenburg, Sweden. In her research she has investigated nature/culture relations and heritage making from an ethnological point of view, often in transdisciplinary collaboration. Her research areas include contemporary vernacular practices such as gardening, rural landscape management and recreational walking, with particular focus on the landscapes where these and other activities are taking place. She has carried out field studies in rural, urban and semi-urban environments, including intensively tended private gardens and agricultural landscapes as well as transitory and temporarily leftover places at the urban fringe.

Sverker Sörlin is Professor of Environmental History at the Division of History, KTH Royal Institute of Technology, Stockholm, where he was also a co-founder with Nina Wormbs of the KTH Environmental Humanities Laboratory (2011). He has a long-standing career as scholar and writer focusing on the science and politics of natural resource extraction and climate change. He has also published widely on representations of landscape and its significance in the formation of national and other identities. His seminal collection on the history of out of doors in Sweden (*Friluftshistoria*, with Klas Sandell) had a second edition in 2008. Increasingly working on 'elemental' Earth-, Cryo- and Atmospheric narratives and histories, his most recent book is *Ice Humanities: Living, Thinking and Working in a Melting World* (Manchester 2022, with Klaus Dodds).

***

Ben Anderson is a Senior Lecturer in Environmental History at Keele University, and author of *Cities, Mountains and Being Modern in Fin-de-siècle England and Germany* (Palgrave MacMillan, 2020). He researches the intersections of modern identities with rural places over roughly the last century, from mountaineering and walking to post-war energy infrastructures, twenty-first century industrial heritage and cultures of ultraviolet light. He is currently working on how co-creative approaches to memory can offer more holistic paths to decommission the vast carbon infrastructures of the twentieth century.

Laura Bertens is assistant professor of Art History at Leiden University, with a Ph.D. in bio-informatics. Her research interests lie in the fields of memory studies, contemporary art and cultural studies. She analyses the construction and functioning of cultural and communicative memories in art, as well as everyday culture. She has published book chapters and articles for peer-reviewed journals such as *Third Text*, *Holocaust Studies* and *German Life and Letters*, on topics ranging from cultural memory in music videos to the Berlin Wall Memorial, Holocaust remembrance in art and the construction of memory through museum audio guides.

Camilla Brudin Borg, Ph.D. in Literature from the University of Gothenburg, specialises in literature, ecocriticism and environmental humanities, studying walking and narratives on the Camino de Santiago de Compostela in Spain by combining literary analysis and ethnographical methods. She is the convener of an international walking-research network focused on interdisciplinary methodological development. She is also the leader the citizen science research project Utopian Stories, which studies visions of a future good life and creative storytelling as a tool for sustainable transformation.

Subarna De is a Landhaus Fellow at the Rachel Carson Center, Ludwig Maximilian University, Munich. She researches transformations of the environment and society, focusing on bioregionalism and indigeneity. Her research is situated at the interface of cultural anthropology, human geography, environmental history and environmental humanities scholarship. She holds a second appointment as a Research Associate at the Ideate Design Studio, New Delhi, where she applies bioregional research to work on field-based environmental, architectural, and conservation practices. Her doctoral thesis (2019), funded by the Central University Doctoral Fellowship (India), focused on the environmental history and ecological practices of Indian coffee plantations and was supported with a research stay at Queen's University, Belfast, UK.

Author biographies

Clare Hickman is Reader in Environmental and Medical History at Newcastle University. She currently leads the Wellcome Trust-funded 'MedEnv: Intersections in Medical and Environmental Humanities' network and the AHRC-funded 'Unlocking Landscapes' network 'History, Culture and Sensory Diversity in Landscape Use and Decision Making'. Clare is also Co-Investigator on the AHRC-funded project 'In All Our Footsteps: Tracking, Mapping & Experiencing Rights of Way in Post-War Britain' and the NERC-funded 'Connected Treescapes' project. Her latest book is *The Doctor's Garden: Medicine, Science, and Horticulture in Britain* (Yale University Press, 2021).

Finn Arne Jørgensen is Professor of Environmental History at University of Stavanger. His research is placed at the intersection of technology and environment, drawing on history, media studies, and science and technology studies. He has published two monographs on environment and infrastructure: *Making a Green Machine* (2011) and *Recycling* (2019). He co-directs the Greenhouse, an environmental humanities initiative at University of Stavanger, with Dolly Jørgensen.

Karen Lykke Syse is an agronomist, ethnologist and holds a Ph.D. in cultural history from the University of Oslo in Norway, where she is Associate Professor at the Centre for Development and the Environment. Her research interests pivot around landscape history, animal studies and the cultural history of food. She has been a member of the Norwegian trekking association (DNT) for many years and has held various positions of trust both within the organisation's Oslo chapter, nationally and by representing its interests politically.

Petra Lilja is an industrial designer, curator and Ph.D. candidate at the University of Arts, Crafts & Design and The Royal Institute of Technology in Stockholm, Sweden. She explores ways to critically examine the contemporary role of the designer in the context of late capitalism, which disconnects design from the origins of material extraction and production. With a special focus on minerals, Lilja explores feminist and critical posthumanities that foreground materialities and more-than-human others that are otherwise backgrounded. Lilja is an affiliated researcher at The Posthumanities Hub and member of Design & Posthumanism.

John Martin, Sustainable Earth Institute, University of Plymouth. John's research focuses specifically on interdisciplinary and co-production approaches to landscape (urban and rural) assessment and monitoring. This includes the mapping and valuation of culture ecosystem services. John uses various mapping techniques ranging from ubiquitous technology tools (Apps, PQGIS) to participatory workshops and remote sensing methods. He has published widely in this area and holds numerous research grants. John is a visiting Professor at the University of the Philippines Open University and a visiting researcher at the University of Gothenburg. In addition to his teaching and research duties, he is also the Head of Research Strategy and Governance.

Faidon Moudopoulos-Athanasiou graduated from the Department of History and Archaeology at the University of Crete in 2013. He completed two MAs, one in Aegean Archaeology at the University of Sheffield (2014) and another in Heritage Management (2016 – joint programme by the University of Kent and the Athens University Business School). From 2017 to 2021 he conducted his Ph.D. research at the University of Sheffield, investigating the archaeology of the early-modern montane Zagori (NW Greece) as a scholar of the White Rose College for the Arts and Humanities (WRoCAH–AHRC) and the A.G. Leventis Foundation.

Stefano Morosini, Ph.D., teaches Environmental history at the University of Bergamo (Italy) and is an associate researcher at the Centre for the History of the Alps (LabiSAlp) – Italian-Swiss University – Mendrisio (Switzerland). He is also the scientific coordinator of heritage projects at Stelvio National Park (Italy). He has been a visiting scholar at the Environmental Humanities Laboratory at the KTH Royal Institute of Technology in Stockholm. His research is dedicated to the economic, social, political, national and environmental characters of mountains, in particular in the alpine area.

Jacqueline Nowakowski, FSA, is a professional freelance archaeologist and educator who has been working in Cornwall for over 40 years and during that time has directed many excavations and landscape projects, working as Principal Archaeologist for Cornwall Archaeological Unit. A keen advocate and practitioner of community archaeology engagements and events, Jacky has been the lead archaeologist on the community projects Carywennen Quoit restoration project, Troon, The Hurlers on Bodmin Moor and Godrevy Warren at Gwthian in West Cornwall. Currently working on Tintagel Castle Research Project for English Heritage, Jacky leads walks, publishes and lectures in the UK and abroad.

Author biographies

Susanne Österlund-Pötzsch holds the Title of Docent (Associate Professor) in Nordic Folklore Studies at Åbo Akademi University. She lives in Helsinki where she works as an archivist specialising in folklore and tradition material. Her research and previous publications focus on food culture, island branding, practices of everyday life, performance and various aspects of mobility, such as migration and everyday walking.

Glenn O'Hara is Professor of Modern and Contemporary History at Oxford Brookes University. A former schoolteacher and journalist, he is the author of a series of books and articles on post-war Britain and a regular commentator on current affairs in *The New European* and *The Guardian*, among others. He is the Principal Investigator on the Arts and Humanities Research Council-funded project 'In All Our Footsteps: Tracking, Mapping and Experiencing Rights of Way in Post-War Britain', and is currently writing a book about the domestic politics of the New Labour government of the UK between 1997 and 2007.

Maria Piekarska is a Ph.D. candidate within the 'Nature-Culture' Interdisciplinary Programme at the University of Warsaw, Faculty of 'Artes Liberales'. Her research interests focus on the spatial, environmental and material dimensions of memory, especially the intertwining of memory practices with the natural environment and the possible fusions between the environmental humanities and the area of memory studies. Her doctoral dissertation in Cultural Studies addresses the development of the Jewish-Israeli memory culture in afforested spaces.

Paul Readman is Professor of Modern British History at King's College London. Author or editor of seven books, he is especially interested in the interrelationship between land, landscape and British national identities, a subject he explored in *Land and Nation in England* (2008) and *Storied Ground* (2018). Since 2013, he has led a major AHRC-funded project on historical pageants in Britain, details of which are available via the *Redress of the Past* project website. He is Co-I on the AHRC-funded network, *Changing Landscapes, Changing Lives*. His essay in this volume derives from his work on this project.

Benjamin Richards is a Ph.D. candidate at the Institute for Culture, Religion and Social studies at the University of South-Eastern Norway (USN). He is a researcher in the field of heritage and sustainability and a member of the research group Cultural Heritage in Use. He has a background in film, heritage studies, ecological economics and border philosophy, with an interest in visual, sensory and phenomenological research methods.

Pathways

Joane V. Serrano is a professor of the University of the Philippines Open University (UPOU). She teaches Environmental Advocacy, Communication of Scientific and Technical Information and Socio-Cultural Perspectives on the Environment. She has a wide array of research interests, including sustainability, socio-cultural perspectives on the environment, development and environmental communication, health promotion, gender and indigenous knowledge, and open and distance eLearning (ODeL). She is currently the editor in chief of the UPOU-managed *Journal of Management and Development Studies*. She has published more than thirty publications and presented at ninety conferences and more than sixty public service engagements. She is part of the Won by Walking Network, Digital Literacy and Intuition Network with Ostfalia University, and Satoyama Initiatives with International Partnership for Satoyama Initiatives and Satoyama Development Mechanism.

Ionas Sklavounos is a Ph.D. Candidate at the University of Antwerp and a researcher within the Marie Skłodowska-Curie Doctoral Network 'TACK – Communities of Tacit Knowledge: Architecture and Its Ways of Knowing'. He graduated in Architecture at the University of Patras and completed his postgraduate studies on the Epistemology of Architecture at the National Technical University of Athens, where he also worked as Teaching Assistant in courses of Architectural Design. He is co-founder of the research collaborative 'Boulouki – Itinerant Workshop on Traditional Building Techniques' which from 2018 has been registered as an Urban Non-profit Company, based in Athens, Greece.

Daniele Valisena, Ph.D. in history of science, technology and the environment. Since October 2021, he has worked as a post-doctoral researcher in environmental humanities at the University of Liège, Belgium, and as a part-time lecturer in history of migration at NYU Florence. His background is in modern history, but his scholarly work delves into migration and heritage studies, environmental humanities and environmental history. Through my research, I focus on the interplay between migration and environmental history, touching also upon themes such as walking as method, rurality and more-than-human storying, post-industrialisation, urban political ecology and critical heritage studies.

Dominica Williamson is an interdisciplinary artist called Ecogeographer, (www.ecogeographer.com) working in the field of sustainable design. New materialism is a strong aspect of her eco-phenomenological approach. She

Author biographies

largely works with co-production methods to empower people and uses abstract mapping methods to communicate ideas. During a Leverhulme Artist-in-Residence Grant at the University of Plymouth she worked with John Martin. They co-developed a transdisciplinary methodology in order to elicit landscape data. This work is simultaneously building on heritage projects. Based in Cornwall, UK, she works with various partners including NGOs, utilising walking, model making and ethnographic fieldwork as primary foci.

ACKNOWLEDGEMENTS

This book is, as most books are, the result of a long and winding walk. It is hard to tell exactly when it started, but it was certainly ongoing already in 2014. Back then, two of us worked together with archaeologist Inga-Maria Mulk in a project on movement heritage in the Swedish mountains. Without the deep knowledge of Inga-Maria, we would not have been able to conduct this research. Building on that project, we teamed up with Peter Fredman, Sandra Wall-Reinius, Annika Dahlberg and Kristin Godtman-Kling in 2016 and 2017 for a project about trails in the mountains of Jämtland, in Mid-Sweden. Through many walks and discussions (with Lennart Adsten, Ola Fransson, Jonas Kråik, Per-Erik Kuoljok, Anna Sarri, Marie Fors, Sven-Olof Arnell, and many others), our interest in issues relating to paths and trails continued to grow.

In 2017, we started a new three-year project about movement heritage in other parts of Sweden and Norway. It was within this project that we developed the idea to compile and edit an anthology on pathways, inviting scholars from many fields to contribute. The book, we thought might be seen as an attempt to assist the formation of an emerging field of interdisciplinary pathway studies. In particular we were interested in the way paths and trails turned into wider landscapes of discreet mobility and how they sometimes matured further into what we had started to call 'movement heritage'. The writing of this book was a collective effort. We held a digital workshop in April 2021, where draft chapters were thoroughly discussed. Apart from all the authors included in this anthology, we also had valuable contributions from Roger Norum, Sonja Laukkanen and Christoph Eggersglüß. Many thanks everyone, for your efforts and perspectives!

We want to thank Sarah Johnson at The White Horse Press, who believed in our idea from the start and has been immensely helpful throughout the process. In addition, the anonymous reviewers at WHP gave us valuable feedback, which has helped us make a better book. We also want to thank the Swedish National Heritage Board, the Swedish Research Council for Sport Science, and the Swedish Environmental Protection Agency for funding the research, which allowed us to initiate and pursue this book project. Ultimately, we owe our gratitude to the many who walked before us. Without them, there would be no pathways.

Malmö, Gothenburg and Stockholm, May 2022, Daniel Svensson, Katarina Saltzman, Sverker Sörlin

FOREWORD

Tim Ingold

When I began my career as a university teacher, I considered myself ahead of the curve. I wasn't just teaching new ideas; I was also using the latest instrumentation to do so. My department had recently acquired a contraption known as an 'overhead projector'. None of my more senior colleagues would touch it, but I was an avid user. I liked to include diagrams in my lectures, and I could prepare by drawing every diagram on a transparent acetate sheet. Placed on the glass of the projector with a powerful light shining below and an inclined mirror above, the diagram would be projected onto a big screen for everyone in the audience to see. I could even write on the sheets with a felt pen, either beforehand or as I spoke. Placing the sheets on top of one another, however, produced an odd effect. As the lower diagrams showed through, the image that appeared on the screen would be a mixed-up jumble of crisscrossing lines. Might this be analogous to the way landscapes are formed?

Observing a landscape, we see a ground likewise crisscrossed with lines of all sorts, including lines of passage like roads, trails, paths and waterways, as well as boundary lines like walls and fences. Some look to be of considerable antiquity, others more recent or even new. Could it be that this line-crossed ground has been assembled in just the same way as the composition on the overhead projector, through the superposition of multiple layers, each marked up with its own inscriptions? Does the history of a landscape stack up, as every present adds its own layer on top of those already laid in the past? Admittedly the lines of old look faint and, compared with more recent ones, are hard to discern. But this, we suppose, is because ground layers are rather less transparent than my acetate sheets. Every additional layer, then, would further obscure its predecessors as the latter sink ever lower in the stack. Nevertheless, as with the projector, the past still *shows through*, albeit dimly, and all the more so under powerful illumination.

This idea of a laminated ground is deeply ingrained in modern sensibilities, as in the scholarship informed by them. We find it, for example, in studies of language and literature, archaeology and architecture. Thus, linguists distinguish the plane of synchrony from the axis of diachrony; on the first is laid out the state of a language at a given time, and along the second the changes it undergoes as one state gives way to the next. Literary theorists describe how new texts and genres overlay old ones, as if on a clean sheet, through which words from the past still remain partially visible, complicating present readings. Archaeologists speak of layers in the occupation of a site, each with its distinctive artefact assemblage, and arrayed in a sequence of strata with the most recent on top and older ones below. Even architects, whose aim is to construct the future rather than to uncover the past, tend to suppose that every new project begins with an immaculate ground on which to build anew.

Behind these examples lies a common premise, namely, that *life is lived in the present*. We, today's people, live in our time; the people of the past lived in theirs. But it is impossible, according to this premise, for descendant lives to prolong ancestral ones, or for ancestral lives to animate their descendants. Social life may be a long conversation but, for linguists, every utterance in the conversation – insofar as it is governed by a structure common to speakers of the language – takes place on the plane of the present. It is like running on one spot. For students of literature, likewise, the text is an expression of its era; in the literary canon, every genre is a generation, and writing goes on within genres rather than in generating those to come. In the archaeological record, artefacts hold fast to the date of their manufacture, while sinking ever further into the past. And in architecture, buildings belong to the centuries of their construction, surviving in the present thanks only to acts of preservation.

This premise, however, is also fundamental to the idea of heritage. Literally, heritage is an inheritance, a legacy that one generation passes on to the next. To be inherited, this legacy – whether of things or ideas, tangible or intangible – must be broken off from the ebbs and flows of life, and from the histories of place and people of which our own life-stories are the continuation. A past that lives on in the present cannot, by the same token, be inherited. Children do not, as a rule, inherit their parents and grandparents. Nor do they inherit the homes or the landscapes in which they were raised. They cannot inherit these persons or things because they comprise the very matrix from which they have grown, and are already constitutive of who they are. But while you cannot inherit your parents or grandparents, you can inherit their property. And while you cannot inherit the home in which you grew up, or the landscape around it, you can inherit the house, and the plot of land on which it stands.

What, then, does it take to turn the past into heritage? It is the same as turning persons into properties, homes into houses and landscape into land. In every case, it means taking the life out of them rather than regarding each as an ongoing nexus of growth and development. With this reduction, the person is but an ensemble of genetic or cultural traits, the home but a building, the landscape but its physical setting. The more life is drained from the past, in its conversion to heritage, the more it is consequently confined to the plane of the present. That's why evolutionary biologists, for example, insist on the distinction

Foreword

between ontogeny and phylogeny. By the former they mean the life-cycle of the individual organism, within a particular environment. By the latter they mean the transfer of resources (genetic, cultural, environmental) from one life-cycle to the next, along a line of descent. Here, ontogeny is to phylogeny as growth to inheritance. One is a life-process, but not intergenerational; the other is intergenerational but not a life process.

Here again, we find the idea that generations are layered over one another, each inhabiting its own slice of time, both separated and connected by the transfers of inheritance. What happens, then, when the object of transfer is a path? That's the central question of this book. It starts from the recognition that paths are worn by the passage of many feet. Just one or two pairs is not enough. A single, bipedal human leaves only footprints, with spaces between them measured by the walker's gait. A quadrupedal animal, such as a horse or dog, leaves a different but equally recognisable pattern of hoof- or pawprints. These are tracks, and you can read much from them about the creature that made them – what it was, when it passed, where it was heading and even how fast it was going. But tracks are not paths. To wear a path, so many feet must pass the same way, whether in one mass movement or in numerous solitary movements over an extended period, that distinct prints are rarely discernible.

In short, when it comes to its formation, the path emerges along with the people who walk it, the homes they inhabit and the landscape in which it is inscribed, as the crystallisation of a collective life process. As such, it carries on through generations. As a child, you may have walked a familiar path with your parents and grandparents, who may have once walked it with theirs, when they were young. It is something that you and they make together. But precisely because it is continually coproduced in the collaboration of generations, the path is not inherited. Perhaps that's why so few paths, even today, are commemorated as vehicles of heritage. In our everyday experience to walk a path is, at the same time, to remember how it goes; it is a vital movement of prolongation that proleptically picks up the past as it anticipates the future. To turn a path into heritage would mean breaking this movement, converting it into an *object* of memory, like a story completed, ready to be handed over like any other heritable property.

To walk a heritage trail, then, is not to carry on a living tradition but to re-enact a past that is already over. To return to my comparison with the overhead projector, it is like placing one acetate sheet upon another that is already marked up with a line, and then tracing the same line on the new sheet. Crucially, in this operation the traced line overwrites the original *without ever making contact with it*. On the heritage trail, we can never walk in the footsteps of our ancestors, as once we walked with our parents and grandparents, since the logic of inheritance has placed us on separate layers whose surfaces can touch but whose lines can never meet. Perhaps this is the source of the peculiar idea that to walk a path is in itself to place a new layer over the ground. It is as if walking along a way of life were like rolling out a carpet. With the walk completed, a new layer is laid, only for the next pedestrian to do the same!

Except under artificial conditions which carefully protect the heritage path from the wear of passing feet, for example by placing it under glass, this is not what happens in practice. On the contrary, far from adding a new layer to the ground, the walker's footprints contribute to its ongoing inscription. Meanwhile the ground surface itself is continually renewed, not through the addition of layers but by way of their removal, through natural processes of erosion. This, finally, is why the analogy with the workings of the overhead projector fails. To explain, let me return to the question of why older paths should appear more faint than recent ones. Long ago, when they were much in use, these ancient ways would have been deeply inscribed in the ground. But, since then, gradual erosion, principally through the effects of weathering, has brought the depths of these inscriptions almost to the surface, soon to disappear altogether. They are scarcely visible. Meanwhile, later paths, yet to suffer prolonged exposure to the weather, have left deeper marks; the most recent deepest of all.

The comparison, in this instance, is not with the overhead projector but with the product of a much earlier technology of writing, with pen on parchment, namely the palimpsest. This is formed when the same parchment is reused, over and over again. Between every round of inscription, the surface is scraped with a penknife, so as to remove as much of the previous traces as possible. But some always remain, casting their shadow on later writing. With the palimpsest, in short, past inscriptions do not lie *beneath* the semi-translucent surface of the present, but rather *rise up* to the surface even as the inscriptions of the present sink down. It is exactly the same in the formation of the ground. Like the writer's parchment, the ground is renewed not by layering but by turning, much as the ploughman turns the soil, bringing up nutrient-rich soil from below while burying the stubble of recent cropping. And this immediately puts it at odds with a discourse of heritage that works on the opposite principle, of renewal by superimposition.

This volume gently nudges us towards a different way of thinking of heritage. It is a way that repudiates the logic of inheritance in favour of what we might call *perdurance*. This is to treat heritage not as a legacy from the past but as an intergenerational life process, in which older and younger generations can once again work together in coproducing the future. It makes no more

Foreword

sense, in this view, to ask how old a path is, than it would do to ask the age of the wind, the river or the mountain. The path never grows older, never recedes from its point of origin, precisely because it is originating all the time, for as long as people of different generations wind along together. Here, generations are not stacked vertically but align longitudinally. Like the twisted strands of a rope, new people enter the weave even as old ones give out. Instead of layering the present over the past, it is by introducing the young into old ways that we can best restore hope of renewal for generations to come.

Aberdeen, June 2022

MOVEMENT HERITAGE AND PATH DEPENDENCE: LAYERING THE PAST

Daniel Svensson, Katarina Saltzman and Sverker Sörlin

Humans are a walking species. We tread on the surface of the Earth. Without this primary mobility we would not be here and even when other means of getting around have become accessible, we don't cease to walk. Our walking leaves traces. This is inevitable. No culture or civilisation or society can escape from this primordial mark-making. Some of these traces cluster and congregate into patterns that remain. They become paths and pathways. With the spread of humans, they have expanded and densified to cover literally the entire planet. From this primary mobility came a primary layer of human planetary signature. This network of paths and its meanings – at once discreet and monumental – is the topic of this book.

Humans added a layer to the earth. Nowadays the patterns of the paths are only one of the multiple signatures humans have left behind. The human footprint on the planet is immense and it has been argued that it is now big and lasting enough to be acknowledged on the geological time scale. It may be helpful, for a sense of continuity, to keep in mind that this imprint of humanity on the Earth and its complex systems in a way started with traces of upright walking people. In more recent millennia, the human footprint expanded, multiplied, overlapped into ever more layers of material blur. This footprint has now reached Anthropocene proportions – a civilisation weighing (in historical sum total) thirty trillion tons,[1] capable of covering the entire world in plastic,[2] and with stratigraphic signatures from nuclear blasts[3] to leaking ammunition alloys[4] to exploding carbon dioxide records.[5]

The subtle scribblings of human feet, although still significant, have become

---

1   Zalasiewicz et al., 'Scale and Diversity of the Physical Technosphere'.
2   Leinfelder and Ivar do Sul, 'The Stratigraphy of Plastics and their Preservation on Geological Records'.
3   Zalasiewicz et al., 'When Did the Anthropocene Begin?'
4   Zalasiewicz and Zalasiewicz, 'Battle Scars'.
5   IPCC, *Summary for Policymakers*.

dwarfed and marginalised, at least relatively speaking and especially as far as the impact on sustainability is concerned. Paths are mostly quite earth-friendly. They sit leisurely and inviting in the landscape and were, in fact, often begun by animals whose treading on the land opened ways for humans to follow. These have been called 'desire paths', referring to human needs to get from a place to the next, but also cow paths, pirate paths, *kemonomichi* (beat trails), donkey paths, *Olifantenpad* (elephant trails), depending on geographical context, but essentially referring to the same phenomenon.[6] But, albeit separate, special, primordial or even clandestine, they belong, when humans make them, essentially within the same overall formation of a tight, mutual and ever-growing material and spiritual human-earth relationship. They are a fundamental feature of it, one that has received too little interest.

In studying paths, we face horizontality and verticality at the same time. The path is a linear way from one point to another. As such, it is quite phenomenal and does tremendous jobs. Above all, it knows more than the walker does. It knows when there is a wet marsh ahead, so the path bends, it knows of a steep cliff and avoids it. 'Who made paths?', the Swedish poet Lars Gustafsson asks in a long and winding poem entitled 'Ballad on the Paths in Västmanland'.[7] His answer: 'Everyone and no one. We make them together.'[8] This is a very Anthropocene, contemporary statement despite being written nearly half a century ago. Paths are forms and features founded by collective effort, and quite often effortlessly, in the sense that they emerge without an original design idea. They are products of a searching for ways.

They are also part of a wider category of remains from time past. By definition, a path requires a past. The number of trampling feet must be reasonably large and frequent, and the purpose of walking just there must have been around for some time. Similarly, the erosion, regrowth and we might say slow closure of an unused path is also a process, gradually sliding into an even slower one, which is oblivion. Paths, in this way, often survive several generations of humans. Still, they are rarely thought about as heritage, or acknowledged as such. This may have to do with their fugitive, linear and somewhat provisional, even precarious, identity. A path is in a very concrete, almost brutal, sense subject to change that is not just local digression. The change is ultimately social and historical. People move, cultivate the land, build cities and roads, cut forests, or give up fishing and thus never walk down to the boathouse anymore. In many ways, paths cease.

---

6   E.g.: Whitridge, 'The Imbrication of Human and Animal Paths'; Moor, 'Tracing (and Erasing) New York's Lines of Desire'. See also chapters in this book by Karen Lykke Syse and Benjamin Richards.

7   Västmanland is a county in Mid-Sweden.

8   Gustafsson, 'Ballad on the Paths in Västmanland'.

Introduction

Perhaps this precariousness becomes less problematic if the linearity of the path is supplemented with a verticality. To begin with, if written into the Anthropocene understanding, all the world's paths immediately take their thin, fugitive but still recognisable place in a human layering of the Earth that has created archaeological and even geological records. Alongside paths, human remains are left, stones are moved and walls have grown. In the so-called Great Acceleration since around 1950 AD, deemed the starting time of the Anthropocene by many,[9] paths are part of the new stratigraphic signal system. Certainly not the strongest signal, but also there and to be counted with, connecting the multiple presents with equally multiple pasts in what may seem a mycelium of mobility that reaches down into the cultural crust of the Earth.

In this volume, both these dimensions of pathways, the horizontal and the vertical, come into play. It extends, we think, the reach of heritage, and the reach of paths into how heritage may be thought and enacted. Heritage is of course a pretentious word, echoing statutes and status, sometimes legislation, but it is also a quite fundamental way of experiencing the relationship between past, present and future. According to a recent book on heritage ecologies, 'heritage has become an indissoluble part of the Enlightenment humanist question of what it means to be human'.[10] Paths are essential, omnipresent, yet fugitive and weakly articulated as part of common heritage, as if their passing horizontal properties have made them less useful material for conventional heritagisation.

In this respect, the vertical layering discourse that has accelerated with the arrival of the Anthropocene may have changed the scene. At least many of the contributors to this book on pathways have, as if attracted by an invisible magnet, been drawn to this kind of thinking around mycelial landscape threads, connecting people and places at the human pace. Layers are seen geologically, in landscapes where pathways pass. They are seen historically, as the forms, features and uses of landscapes are replaced and in palimpsest fashion overwrite each other. They are seen socially and politically, as practices and regulations reform and reshape the conditions of walking and access to land. They are also, culturally and aesthetically, seen as paths which become part of tradition, lore and everyday lives far beyond bare necessity. Paths become an infrastructure of pastime. They acquire, in some cases, design and architecture and they travel into the digital sphere, hence the technosphere, which is yet another in the Anthropocene sequence of spherical layers that paths occupy, from the geosphere and its underground to the lithosphere to the biosphere,

---

9   Zalasiewicz et al., 'When Did the Anthropocene Begin?'
10   Bangstad & Pétursdóttir, *An Ecological Approach to Heritage*, p. 7.

the hydrosphere and the atmosphere. Even near the Earth's summit, there are paths, piled over with waste and dead bodies, sacrifices of vanity but also signals from a culture of hyper-consumption, whose paths reach everywhere.

Artefacts of movement – paths and trails

Already here, only a few pages into this volume, paths are coming forth as a rich topic, one that crosses spatial and disciplinary boundaries, and links the material and the spiritual. It diversifies in multiple directions. As editors, we have embraced this diversifying drift. We think it is as welcome as it is inevitable, ultimately because we need reflexive approaches to different paths for comparison and analysis. Paths as a topic has not been very comprehensively researched and the literature on paths and trails as heritage is especially scarce. There is a need for empirical work, studies rooted in local and regional conditions, to broaden the foundation from which we can draw conclusions.

As editors, we have been searching for ideas and words that can draw things together and, perhaps most importantly, connect paths to other, broader topics where articulations are more established. That ambition also marks this introduction where we try to map the topical and conceptual landscape surrounding paths. We are not proposing that there is a 'theory of paths' – our aim is simply to chart a set of possible approaches that can shed additional light on connections and fault lines between the contributions in this volume. Together, we are on a continued quest to understand this widespread phenomenon and make more sense of it. We are in an early phase of forming what may become a field of research, and it should be a virtue to open things up, rather than pretending that we already have everything in place. To use a congenial metaphor: we will not mark a single route, instead we encourage a search along multiple paths.

Paths and trails exist because there is walking, or at least the trampling of many feet, human and more-than-human. However, their articulation as a distinct landscape and as cultural heritage depends on more than physical movement. Beyond the individual steps, some paths emerge as more than local concerns, and get elevated to a certain significance. Some even acquire names. They turn into trails, drawing on the physical and cultural remains of walking and, with their surroundings, become articulated as a landscape genuinely suitable for movement on foot. They are artefacts of movement, although not much thought has gone into this fact, especially in the agencies and organisations that are supposed to collect, cultivate, and curate culture's past as heritage.

In thinking about this particular form of heritage over a number of years, we found it useful to distinguish between *paths* (in Swedish: *stigar*) and *trails*

Introduction

(in Swedish: *leder*).[11] The former are mainly the result of physical mobility (i.e. walking by humans and their co-species). They appear and disappear organically, depending on local vegetation and soil geography, climate, culture and practice. Trails, on the other hand, are in this rendering designed, managed and maintained with the ambition of attracting walkers, attributed with potential to contribute to tourism, public health, recreation and other positive outcomes.[12] If a path is a result of walking, walking is one of the intended results of trails. Paths and trails are not mutually exclusive categories – they are similar in many ways, and there are probably many hybrid forms. Perhaps they could be seen as *ideal types* in Max Weber's sense. In that spirit, and for the purpose of this introduction, we intentionally make a distinction between the two concepts, although in reality, and in several of the chapters of the book, that distinction may be blurred or not applicable.

Trails and paths are functional in the present, but many of them are also old. This assigns them with yet another function. They are *pathways to the past* – and serve as a physical and cultural infrastructure of human memory and past practices. Walking can be a means of going back, using the oldest possible version of human mobility and visiting places and landscapes where the rates of change occur on different time scales from those where daily life takes place, underscoring Reinhart Koselleck's idea of the co-existence of multiple times.[13] While pathways lead the way forward for anyone out walking, they also point backwards, towards history and into a complex pattern of layered times and meanings.

Acknowledging and enhancing the fugitive and ephemeral

Walking paths have often been neglected by posterity and rarely reached the status of monument or attained official memorability, although they may be deeply remembered in local settings. These subtle landscape features seem to be difficult to handle within established heritage management regimes, partly because of their fugitive and timid nature. However, their uses and impacts have often been decisive and important for individuals and communities across scales. Traces of people's movements can be regarded as a distinct kind of cultural heritage, a 'movement heritage' that is dependent on continuous use or memory work to remain.[14]

---

11   Svensson, Sörlin and Saltzman, 'Pathways to the Trail'.
12   Timothy and Boyd, *Tourism and Trails*; Godtman Kling, Dahlberg and Wall-Reinius, 'Negotiating Improved Multifunctional Landscape Use'.
13   Koselleck, *Historische Semantik und Begriffsgeschichte*.
14   Svensson, Sörlin and Wormbs, 'The Movement Heritage'.

Daniel Svensson, Katarina Saltzman, Sverker Sörlin

In this collection, we will explore possibilities to acknowledge human motion, and traces thereof, as heritage. Today, with increasing interests in local and sustainable connections, and in bodily and spiritual enhancement, we see a growing use of walking tracks, both in landscapes in reach of urban centres and in more remotely located or 'wild' areas. Of course, landscapes understood as wilderness or 'nature' are in most cases distinctly influenced by human actions and movements. While walking trails are typically regarded as pathways to experience nature and as tools to promote public health, they could also be seen and used as routes to culture and history. With the aim of exploring the multiple dimensions of walking, paths, and movement we will engage with and discuss the potential effects of such an expansion of the heritage register.

To walk is universal, yet walking – as pastime, recreation, therapy, pilgrimage or emotional meaning making – is a distinct feature of modern societies. Starting typically as an elite practice in the eighteenth and nineteenth centuries it has spread widely.[15] The rise of slow physical mobility on foot, ski or bike in the landscape can be associated with large trends in modern societies. One is the rise of the nation, the worship of which is to a great extent funnelled through an appreciation of national landscapes, which many have argued should be seen at first hand at close quarters.[16] Religion and the spiritual sometimes come close to worship of the nation, and pilgrimage is part of both. Interest in and concern for nature and the modern 'environment' since the middle of the twentieth century have enhanced interest in walking.[17] Growing wealth and globalisation have made it possible for large masses to reach new walkable venues. An aspect of great importance is health, both public and personal, in turn part of the rise of welfare societies. Walking and paths have thus become instruments of fostering, reinvigorating and curing populations and citizens, and more recently also part of a sustainable, 'good life'.[18] More recently, the COVID-19 pandemic has further increased the importance of landscapes designated for mobility on foot.[19] As tourists and hikers on designated trails, walkers count in the millions annually and the rate of growth has been formidable, outpacing that of tourism in general.[20] The level of organisation and commodification has increased, with maintained paths in literally every

---

15   Amato, *On Foot*; Macfarlane, *The Old Ways*; Moor, *On Trails*.
16   Coates, Moon and Warde, *Local Places, Global Processes*.
17   Warde et al., *The Environment*.
18   Syse and Mueller, *Sustainable Consumption and the Good Life*.
19   Andersson et al., *Idrotten och friluftslivet under coronapandemin*.
20   UNWTO, *Walking Tourism*.

Introduction

community in almost every country, but with considerable variation in spread and frequency.

When looking for connections between walking and heritage, trails have often been interpreted as the routes connecting objects and vistas that are the heritage per se.[21] However, the concept of heritage is itself in motion, and the tendency over the last few decades has been to move away from what heritage 'is', towards what it 'does'.[22] This transition to increasingly emphasise *process* rather than permanence, can perhaps also be described as a move towards what heritage becomes and how it is *becoming*.[23] So, what happens if we try to expand the heritage register a bit, regarding the route itself, the track that walking humans have followed and still follow, *as heritage* too? What happens if we look at walking itself, the physical activity of people moving around in the landscape on foot, *as heritage making*, however fugitive? These questions kept us busy for several years in our research.[24] Ultimately, we thought they were intriguing and important enough to discuss at length with colleagues drawing on pathways knowledge from many fields. The result is this volume.

Tracks and trails, we gradually realised, are formed by human bodies *and* minds in motion, individually and collectively, over time. The footpath evidently connects us, here and now, with those who walked before us and those who might follow our footsteps. Although some old stone roads were made for walking, most paths need to be more-or-less continuously in use to remain. Furthermore, trails need to be maintained through hands-on activities such as cutting back vegetation, removing fallen trees and looking after the subtle infrastructure of signposts, markings, foot-bridges and railings. This mobility work, which must be done by someone and has to be done repeatedly, can be seen as a heritage practice, guided by a specific 'regime of care'.[25] In this sense, the heritage of walking paths and trails is made and constantly remade, quite literally, as part of a complex, historical social effort. The work on, with and for paths and trails has a wider social and political context. This adds dimensions to the horizontality and the verticality. Pathways are social and historical phenomena, finding their ways, connecting and constantly changing.

This *becoming* of trails needs to engage with other-than-human actors:

---

21 E.g. Timothy and Boyd, *Tourism and Trails*; Boyd, 'Editorial: Heritage Trails and Tourism'.
22 E.g. Smith, *Uses of Heritage*; Harrison et al., *Heritage Futures*; Bangstad and Pétursdóttir, *Heritage Ecologies*.
23 Harrison, 'Beyond "Natural" and "Cultural" Heritage', 35; Connolly, *A World of Becoming*.
24 Svensson, Sörlin and Wormbs, 'The Movement Heritage'; Svensson, Sörlin and Saltzman, 'Pathways to the Trail'.
25 Harrison, 'Beyond "Natural" and "Cultural" Heritage'.

water, earth, rocks, plants and many other forms of life – including animals in their path-making and -using. This process can be interpreted as a biosocial becoming.[26] Path-making activities in the landscape also remind us of Rodney Harrison's discussion on how heritage emerges in a dialogue between human and non-human actors 'engaged in keeping pasts alive in the present, which function towards assembling futures', and moves beyond the limitations of categories such as 'natural' and 'cultural' heritage.[27] Paths are both at the same time. Looking at paths *as heritage* inevitably does something to our understanding of paths, but it also seems to do something to our understanding *of heritage*.

Mobility remains

Quite a range of paths, but perhaps mostly the more advanced and arranged trails, have become named, signs of canonisation, but also tools in marketing and place-making. New Zealand has a listed canon into which a trail can be accepted only by decision of the government's department of conservation; there are now ten and an eleventh has been chosen for inclusion in 2022 after a multi-year process.[28] Our approach is different, including more kinds of paths and with a wider register of functions. Yet, despite growing interest, not so many paths have become acknowledged as 'heritage' so far. Perhaps it is no coincidence that there are so few collections of paths, and hardly any museums in their name? Here is a paradox – why is it that such a common, indeed universal human practice with such widespread presence has not merited status and qualification as something to observe systematically, remember collectively, and store and restore to maintain? Or, is precisely the asking of the question a signal that this may no longer be the case? Are we, just in this moment, seeing a change? This book is, also, a way to find this out.

Humans have always *used landscapes* for mobility on the ground. Walking, trekking, tramping, skiing, herding, hunting, collecting, wayfinding and countless other practices have set themselves and material and immaterial processes in motion. Mobility has also *shaped landscapes* that have become what they are because of mobility. Mobility has extended reach and access. Its traces remain, at least for some time, as discreet infrastructures for a vernacular mobility on the ground. Some of these *mobility remains* have gained some kind of permanence

---

26 Ingold, *Prospect*.
27 Harrison, 'Beyond "Natural" and "Cultural" Heritage', p. 28.
28 General information from the Department of Conservation is available at https://www.doc.govt.nz/parks-and-recreation/things-to-do/walking-and-tramping/great-walks/ (accessed 7 Feb. 2022). See also Fagan and Kearns, 'Tramper Perspectives on New Zealand's Great Walks in a Time of Transition'.

Introduction

and status.²⁹ Around the world, there have been efforts to register, analyse and maintain paths and trails and also to protect them. New Zealand is quite an advanced case of centralising authority on canonisation, but many countries (e.g. Scotland, Norway, Sweden, the United States) have institutionalised overview and management, either by government (local or central)³⁰ and/or by civic organisations such as tourism or walking societies. Some paths and trails have gone down in collective memory, some have even had their history written and their importance thoroughly articulated.³¹

Still, the paths that are documented and well-known are only a small fraction of the total. Increasingly, traces of walking may be interpreted as heritage, as part of what we may call a *heritage of vernacular mobility*. This collection asks the question: how do these discreet traces and pathways in landscapes become heritage? Do they at all?

Sustainable mobility – from the ground up

Walking is a common denominator for most human life, though we acknowledge that a certain portion of the human population cannot walk, for a variety of reasons. While other forms of mobility have grown in importance and changed our societies in dramatic ways, most of us still depend on walking in our daily life. The massive number of human steps throughout history has not only created the rich and widespread network of pathways that cross landscapes around the globe. It has also resulted in a vast *immaterial heritage* through literature, art and music about walking. With Paul Readman, we can say that the ground itself has become 'storied'.³² Paths and trails accommodate both the material and the immaterial, and challenge not only conventional heritage management but also the very essence of the nature/culture divide.

When we argue that it makes sense to regard paths as a distinct kind of heritage, a '*movement heritage*', this also points to historical and current forms of land use that are sustainable in the most basic meaning of the word.³³ These activities can be and de facto have been practised over long periods of time without causing large-scale environmental degradation. While walking can

---

29 Svensson, Sörlin and Wormbs, 'The Movement Heritage'.
30 A national trails system was decided by the US Congress in 1968: see Johnson, 'History of the National Trails System'; Berger, Smith and McKibben, *America's Great Hiking Trails*.
31 E.g., Grundsten, *Kungsleden: Walking the Royal Trail*; Bryson, *A Walk in the Woods: Rediscovering America on the Appalachian Trail*; Rhoades and Rhoades, *Santiago de Compostela: Journal of our Camino*.
32 Readman, *Storied Ground*.
33 Svensson, Sörlin and Wormbs, 'The Movement Heritage'.

also affect ecology and place negatively, and while the use of special equipment and clothing with potential negative environmental consequences has grown, few other forms of human mobility can make similar claims to sustainability.[34]

So, while traces and remains from different kinds of movement may be small in their physical scale, and marginalised in the official sense, they are large, literally 'monumental', in their importance for the understanding of how a landscape has been used historically. Traces of mobility form lines that, in Tim Ingold's terms, tie together the life worlds of the past with those of the present.[35] Indeed, walking connects our own bodies to the ground, as our movements are also stored, and storied, in muscle memory, shaping our endurance, gait, health and appearance, associated with a wide range of positive health effects, including improved memory.[36] Movement heritage thus includes traces on the ground, and in ourselves. It puts the historical layers of mobility in landscapes and bodies in focus, and in perspective. It lays in plain sight the interdependence of people and path.

We are aware of the theoretical framework of path dependence and how it has been applied in various disciplines to analyse the impact of historical choices on our current predicament.[37] Charles Tilly summarised it succinctly: 'History matters.'[38] In this volume, we use the concept of path dependence both metaphorically and literally. Humans around the world have been dependent on paths for their everyday mobility, and paths would not exist without people and animals moving. But we can also all see, with our inner eye, the vast mycelial universe of pathways without which humanity as we know it would not exist. That profound dependence is metaphorical, but no less real.

Paths don't stop there. The demand for places suitable for movement, training, events and other bodily activities continues to grow, and hiking trails are a key component in the rise of nature-based tourism, sports such as trail running and mountain biking, and the increasing interest in outdoor life. The COVID-19 pandemic has further propelled these trends. The search for paths to walk has exploded, indicating the potential for a walking revolution and a

---

34   McCullough and Kellison, *Routledge Handbook of Sport and the Environment*.

35   Ingold, *Lines*.

36   E.g., Kelly, Murphy and Mutrie, 'The Health Benefits of Walking'; Olafsdottir et al., 'Health Benefits of Walking in Nature'.

37   E.g., David, 'Clio and the Economics of QWERTY'; Mahoney, 'Path Dependence in Historical Sociology'; van Bottenburg, 'Why are the European and American Sports Worlds so Different?'.

38   Tilly, 'Future History', p. 711.

Introduction

possible new age of transformed mobility.[39] So far, the historical and heritage aspects of these developments have been insufficiently articulated. One example, however, is a project around historical hiking trails, initiated by the Norwegian heritage board together with the Norwegian Tourist Association (*Den Norske Turistforening*, DNT).[40] Similar attempts have been made in Sweden, England and elsewhere, as will be discussed in several chapters in this book.

Literary and artistic accounts also play a role in heritage-making. Historically, travel guides and novels about walking have popularised, even iconised, certain paths and trails, and articulated them as important landscapes for recreational walking, training and spiritual journeys. The 'King's Trail' (*Kungsleden*) in Lapland – arguably Sweden's most well-known trail – was articulated by numerous accounts in the *Swedish Tourist Association Yearbook*, including essays by high-profile citizens such as Dag Hammarskjöld (UN Secretary General 1953–1961).[41] After the publication of the book *Wild* (2012) by Cheryl Strayed, the numbers walking the 4,270-kilometre Pacific Crest Trail along the west coast of the United States and Canada multiplied. Walking literature about pilgrimages has in similar ways popularised the Camino de Santiago de Compostela.[42] These are but a couple of examples of a literary movement that reinforced the walking trend and contributed to the immaterial heritage connected to trails and paths. In an ongoing project, the Swedish-Norwegian border region Finnskogen (*the Finn forest*) has begun the long and winding path towards applying for UNESCO world heritage status. A key ingredient in the argumentation is the walking practices in this area, both historically as a means of moving between the remote and sparsely populated forests, and since the 1990s as the 240-kilometre Finn Forest Trail that has become a magnet for regional and cross-border walking. Pathways of the past have formed historical layers that were articulated by travellers, authors and ethnologists in a series of waves over two hundred years, and ultimately became acknowledge as heritage.[43]

---

39 E.g.: Beery, Olsson and Vitestam, 'Covid-19 and Outdoor Recreation Management'; Monz, Pickering and Hadwen, 'Recent Advances in Recreation Ecology'; Balmford et al., 'A Global Perspective on Trends in Nature-based Tourism'.
40 Riksantikvaren, *Historiske vandreruter*.
41 Hammarskjöld, *Från Sarek till Häväng*.
42 Sánchez-Carretero, *Heritage, Pilgrimage and the Camino to Finisterre*; cf. Brudin Borg in this volume.
43 Svensson, Sörlin and Saltzman, 'Pathways to the Trail'.

Daniel Svensson, Katarina Saltzman, Sverker Sörlin

Conceptual articulations – scapes, scales and faring bodies

Movement heritage is a complex concept and an equally complex, perhaps nebulous, emerging and above all interdisciplinary field of knowledge and inquiry that this collection sets out to explore. It is also a terrain where several existing literatures on heritage, landscape, mobility, and material practices meet and engage. Despite the increasing importance of trails and paths as cultural and natural heritage, neither humanities scholars nor the heritage sector engaged with walking and its discreet infrastructures to any large extent, until quite recently. Important contributions were made in the last decade, not least relating to walking as research methodology,[44] but the potential of trails and paths as heritage still largely remains to be explored.

There is now an extensive body of research on *walking* from geographical, historical, ethnographical, philosophical and sociological perspectives, although only small parts of it are directed toward heritage.[45] There is also a growing literature by geographers and others on 'linear tourism resources and attractions', mainly focusing on management and tourism aspects of trails.[46] Within this research, specific attention has been directed towards *heritage trails*.[47] This body of research tends to frame the actual trail primarily as a tool to reach or experience heritage, rather than as heritage in and of itself. The underlying assumption in much of the research seems to be that trails as such are *not heritage, but merely infrastructure* that enable transport, access and mobility between heritage sites.

However, some notable exceptions, such as pilgrimage trails, show the heritage potential.[48] In Scandinavia, recreational walking has deep historical roots.[49] Some trails evolve into complex 'trailscapes',[50] which can in turn make up interesting dimensions of an ever-richer universe of 'heritagescapes'.[51] Cer-

---

[44] Elliot, Norum and Salazar, *Methodologies of Mobility*.
[45] E.g. Klepp, *På stier mellom natur og kultur*; Solnit, *Wanderlust*; Ingold and Vergunst, *Ways of Walking*; Humberstone et al., *Routledge International Handbook of Outdoor Studies*; Hall et al., *Routledge International Handbook of Walking*; Readman, Bryant and Burns, *Walking Histories*; Readman, *Storied Ground*; Österlund-Pötzsch, *Gångarter och gångstilar*.
[46] Boyd, 'Editorial: Heritage Trails and Tourism', 417.
[47] Timothy and Boyd, *Tourism and Trails*, ch. 2; Boyd, 'Editorial: Heritage Trails and Tourism'.
[48] E.g., Selberg, 'Pilegrimsveien som kulturarv'; Saul and Waterton, 'A Himalayan Triptych'; Øian, 'Pilgrim Routes as Contested Spaces in Norway'.
[49] E.g., Nilsson, *Fjällturismens historia*; Kilander, '*En nationalrikedom av hälsoskatter*'; Ween and Abram, 'The Norwegian Trekking Association'.
[50] Fagence, 'A Heritage "Trailscape"'; Svensson, Sörlin and Saltzman, 'Pathways to the Trail'.
[51] Garden, 'The Heritagescape'.

Introduction

tain strands of human geography and critical heritage studies on landscape, place-making and heritage-making offer useful tools to link mobility, paths and trails as heritage.[52] Geographical and historical analysis of *landscapes* is rich and theoretically astute. Landscape memory was for a long time connected to the strong, and politically problematic, tradition of nationalism and landscape in general was associated primarily with visual qualities.[53] Despite significant critique,[54] the iconic and representational approach to landscape has been important to understand the formation of natural and cultural *value* manifested for example in reserves and parks.

Over the last few decades, *mobilities research* has grown into a productive and dynamic transdisciplinary field, emphasising the 'unstable and ever-changing interrelation of places, persons, technologies and natures connected through performances and practices'.[55] Of particular importance in the context of this book are the ways in which scholars have approached the *body* and the mobility of the individual walker in relation to outdoor environments and 'nature'.[56] It would seem obvious, but it took some time to wield and push the understanding of landscapes into a sophisticated product of *bodily movement*, material practices and immaterial processes.[57] We perceive this approach as kin with a growing pluralism of approaches to landscape. One of its main inroads has been to approach landscapes as parts of 'life worlds', shaped by walking and other forms of 'wayfaring'.[58] These are complex practices of physical mobility, navigation and knowledge gathering. The formation of trails from walking is, hence, an activity that extends in time and space and transgresses boundaries between nature and culture, body and mind.

Environing and becoming – making movement heritage

Acknowledging the need for a heritage literature on paths and trails, this book aims also to search for conceptual and theoretical tools that can be used to approach the diversity of phenomena that extended landscape mobility practices

---

52   E.g., Lowenthal, *The Heritage Crusade and the Spoils of History*; Lowenthal, *The Past is a Foreign Country – Revisited*; Harvey, 'Landscape and Heritage'.
53   Daniels and Cosgrove, *The Iconography of Landscape*.
54   E.g., Rose, *Feminism and Geography*; Mels, *Wild Landscapes*; Olwig, 'Representation and Alienation in the Political Land-scape'.
55   Sheller and Urry, *Mobile Technologies of the City*, p. 13.
56   E.g., Macnaghten and Urry, *Bodies of Nature*; Edensor, *Geographies of Rhythm*; Lorimer, 'Walking'.
57   E.g. Merriman et al., 'Landscape, Mobility, Practice'; Whatmore, 'Materialist Returns'.
58   Ingold, *The Perception of the Environment*; Ingold, *Being Alive*; Olwig, 'Performing on the Landscape Versus Doing Landscape', Hastrup, 'Destinies and Decisions'.

entail. Our primary observation in this regard is that many footpaths represent an extension of human presence into places that hold significant portions of nature. Pathways are as essential to *place-making* and *land holding* as are buildings and other features of human presence. Paths and trails therefore belong in a wider category of human formation of environments. In that vein, we see paths as an outcome of a social process of *environing*.[59] Environing, we posit, is the practices whereby humans enfold nature into society and transform it into hybrid entities, both by design and by making. Paths – and trails – are such hybrid entities, leaning more to the making than the design. They are environmental, hence also products of material and conceptual processes that co-created their dual character and their place in and of the landscape, at the same time culture and nature.[60]

It may also be useful to see the creation of a trail as an element in a wider process of *articulation of territory*, which is essentially a discursive and conceptual dimension of the work of environing.[61] This approach investigates how a landscape is articulated through written, oral, visual or physical means as a place for and of certain activities. A classic is Stephen Pyne's book *How the Canyon became Grand* (1998), which followed explorers, geologists, artists, photographers, journalists, preservationists, politicians, and ultimately the President of the United States, in their work to narrate, story and articulate this place and elevate it into a work of natural wonder, known around the world and protected by federal law.[62] This work, stretching from the eighteenth to the early twentieth century, was not to any large extent a conscious effort to articulate the place. It is our privilege, coming after, to see that this is what they did while they were busy doing other things. Something similar is often the case with paths. Few people, perhaps ever in history, thought about their first probing steps on a piece of ground – moss, gravel, mud, turf... – as the first steps of a path to be. Yet that was what they became. It is a design without an idea, a collective effort provided by an assembly of humans who are not acting together.

Thinking this way has implications for how movement heritage can be delineated. From the outset, we thought about it as a concept meant to cover the broad range of remains linked to landscape movement on foot. Such heritage not only includes physical remains in the landscape, but also ideas about mobility as articulated through concepts, literary and artistic representations,

---

59 Sörlin and Wormbs, 'Environing Technologies'.
60 Macfarlane, *The Old Ways*, pp. 13–14.
61 Sörlin, 'Monument and Memory', Sörlin, 'The Articulation of Territory'.
62 Pyne, *How the Canyon Became Grand*.

Introduction

scientific descriptions, maps and place names.[63] Or, in other words, the full arsenal of environing technologies that comprise the articulation process. Distinct from many of the earlier, organic and evolutionary processes of path-making, modern articulations of territory through man made trails are intentional and instrumental, which means that they are often more elaborate and standardised.

The wider geography of trails is always a product of historical change. It can be just a single path, meandering through a forest or meadow, but it can also be multiple paths, expanded, designed and deliberately connected into the above-mentioned full-fledged 'trailscapes': comprehensive areas, sometimes thematised (history, film, literature, scenery), criss-crossed by paths and trails. While often understood and presented as 'historical', 'wild', 'remote', 'scenic', such areas are today fully environed and articulated spaces, hybrid products of a sequence of material and conceptual interventions and reinterpretations. Although trail-associated landscape changes are usually more discreet than, for example, the large-scale remodelling of mountain landscapes for downhill skiing,[64] trails are nevertheless a form of managed infrastructure for, primarily recreational, mobility. Their historical geographies are more than a sequence of layers of 'uses of history'. More than history is being used, and not all paths are trails. Many paths still uphold everyday functions in communities around the world.

Paths can thus be understood and 'read' as articulations of purposes and values just as much as they are obviously the result of the practice of walking. Their becoming is both material and discursive. The relations of paths and trails to their geographies can be seen as a result of long-term processes of forming complex human-environment relationships – with mobility on the landscape scale as a creative element. This also reminds us that trails offer possibilities to move 'beyond' the nature/culture divide in heritage-making.[65] Trails are nature transformed into culture – yet situated in nature, refusing to abandon their belonging in both (or either). They are also 'environment' in the sense of a man-made *artefact-nature*, which has required 'environing' work. Environing can be material, or it can be conceptual, or both. It can happen by design, or inadvertently, or both.[66] These environed artefact-landscapes will thus 'become' through elaborate processes unfolding in time.[67]

Adopting the idea of paths and trails as central to a movement heritage is

---

63   Svensson, Sörlin and Wormbs, 'The Movement Heritage'; Svensson, 'Skiing through Time'.
64   Anderson, 'The Construction of an Alpine Landscape'; Anderson, *Cities, Mountains and Being Modern in Fin-de-siècle England and Germany*.
65   Harrison, 'Beyond "Natural" and "Cultural" Heritage'.
66   Sörlin and Wormbs, 'Environing Technologies'.
67   Connolly, *A World of Becoming*; Ingold and Pálsson, *Biosocial Becomings*; Lien, *Becoming Salmon*.

at the same time an effort to expand on what paths and trails (and signs, maps, fences, bridges, resting places, lodges, campsites and other *trail elements*) are. Through environing, they are integrated in the realm of human reflection and governance; in essence, a political space and part of a transformative political geography. This is also how paths in some cases turn into trails with a claim on the future too. They are pathways not only because their material remains function as an archaeology, which of course those of paths also always do, but because they were attributed functions and meanings throughout their entire existence. The past they can guide us to is, hence, the situations that occurred when humans used the paths, deliberated over them, or turned them into new modes of existence with new 'uses of heritage',[68] including adoption into the realm of official acknowledgement to serve for their protection. They make up a heritage that does, rather than is.

Pathways through the volume

Perhaps unsurprisingly, we have tried to design the book as a path, or perhaps rather as a hike along a path. It has been, as so often on a hike, a matter of choosing paths at numerous intersections where alternative routes were also possible. On the other hand, we moved with many fellow walkers/authors in what is actually a pathscape, where we were surrounded by a common terrain of concepts, ideas and practices from multiple places and landscapes in many parts of the world but chiefly in Europe, including the Easternmost Mediterranean. Sharing the pathscape, we are confident that we have covered enough ground to be able to make some general observations about the whole – as we do in this introduction – and not just to stick to the lines that each paper has followed.

The book's tripartition into sections is, on the face, of it very basic. We start in section one with the historical roots of paths and trails, long before hikes were invented and anybody had thought about the making of heritage, let alone with paths as part of it. We follow their evolution, meandering all the way into our present, always bringing the social and political along, immersed in mobile conversation between social forms and Earthly conditions. The second section talks of a more mature relationship to pathways in an extended present, now of multiple kinds with very different roles and functions. The diversity has become enormous, which means that there are also diverse narratives and narrative deviations, off the beaten track of the ordinary, into artistic uses and renderings of paths, digital walking, computer games and

68   Smith, *Uses of Heritage*.

Introduction

traces of the COVID-19 pandemic. From this debating the long now, we move in section three into largely uncharted terrain, where existing paths are frail and form loops, sometimes leading nowhere, petering out into the unknown. Chapters here talk of experimental walking and trails as heritage and as tools for sustainable development. They also demonstrate how paths are also part of an ongoing (endless?) co-creation of heritage, as we go, and of a layering of the linear walk in soil and strata.

Section one: Past preconditions of paths

Paths and trails are part of our history. And history is part of all paths and trails. In the first section of this book, all five chapters relate, in one way or another, to historical walking and its ideologies, challenges and practices. They offer historical depth and background. They focus on materiality and the concrete remains of mobility in the landscape, as well as the structures of power and legislation that have governed the role of paths and walking through history. They show a literal path dependence, linking back to historical practices and laws about ownership of the land and who has access to it. This (very old) tradition of ownership is challenged by trespassers, trekkers and others. The historical perspective allows us to spot differences and similarities between places and nations. Looking at the imagery of the chapters from a British context, paths and trails are often clearly delineated by fences. This is a clear difference from Scandinavia, where paths often meander through the landscape without taking much notice of ownership of the land.

In **Paul Readman**'s chapter, we learn more about the deep importance of paths and trails in English history. Indeed, they were instrumental in the articulation of a ruralised Englishness in the country that led industrial development for much of the eighteenth, nineteenth and twentieth centuries. This role of walking and paths is not unique nor unfamiliar. Similar ideas about knowing the land for the sake of loving the nation have been part of nationalistic ideology for centuries. In Sweden and Norway, and many other countries, tourist organisations and other gatherings of intellectual and economic elites argued for the power of outdoor recreation as a means to counter radical socialism and public health decline due to the rapid urbanisation and industrialisation. From this perspective, walking and paths could be seen as a top-down endeavour, designed to keep the people physically active but politically passive. What Readman shows, however, is that paths and trails are also a form of protest, which expands the walking register to include political dimensions with long historical roots and massive impact.

The impact on paths and trails of human naming and characterisation is analysed further by **Clare Hickman and Glen O'Hara**. With the Rights of Way legislation in England and Wales as their case in point, they convincingly argue that remains of human mobility are deeply historical in more ways than the physical dimension. As they argue, history is 'not only found in the creation of the physical track: it is also embedded in how these are legally represented and conceived'. The political and legal dimensions are important for the understanding of many of the paths and trails in the Rights of Way framework, but the individual experiences of walkers should also be considered. Hickman and O'Hara thereby show how mobility – and movement heritage – is co-created by institutions and individuals over time, leaving traces on the ground as well as in personal and institutional memory.

Ben Anderson further builds on the political aspects of walking and paths, through his analysis of how predominantly urban walkers' organisations used trespass as a method to bring the issue of access to local countryside paths onto the national agenda. As Anderson shows, access campaigns achieved a 'reinvention of locally-held, rural resource rights as nationally-held, urban recreational ones'. He argues that trespass had a central role in the re-imagining of rural/local land use and customary mobility as a movement heritage of national importance. Ultimately, trespass was a tool through which growing urban-based communities of walkers could articulate their demand for access to the land for recreational purposes. However, this was not a strictly urban ambition but rather something that was linked to an appreciation of the rural landscape and heritage. Anderson shows how walking, paths and trails have become entangled in a political history of the land. Ultimately, scrutinising ideas about who has a right to move through the landscape also provides significant historical insights on the development of society in general.

In **Karen Lykke Syse's** chapter, we get to know the role of animals in the creation of movement heritage. Norway's longstanding traditions of animal husbandry in remote mountainous landscapes have played a key part in the successive creations of paths throughout the landscape. This concept carries certain meanings and perceptions about the natural world and the actions of animals and humans in it. As Lykke Syse writes, 'from a movement heritage perspective, the sound of animal bells is not just a convenient indicator of people; it is the sound of a cultural and historical continuum of grazing cattle and the people who hung, and still hang, the bell around their necks'. It was this pre-existing network of paths that came to form the backbone of the growing Norwegian nature tourism and outdoor recreation during the late nineteenth and twentieth centuries. This is indicative of how movement heritage is always layered, and how later stages of history may be more easily articulated and thus obscure the

Introduction

long historical roots and more-than-human origins of many paths and trails.

The first section ends with **Stefano Morosini's** chapter about another mountainous region – the Italian Alps. Building on a multidisciplinary research project with a focus on environmental history, the heritage of the mountains and valleys in Stelvio National Park and Adamello Park is analysed, focusing on military heritage from the First World War. Through a blend of walking and digital itineraries, the remains of war on the mountains are articulated as heritage which can be accessed through walking in the footsteps of soldiers. This is a movement heritage which was made through walking, and which requires personal mobility to be experienced. It is a reminder of how mobility has historically been affected by borders and war, and how such factors are still restricting and enabling mobility in many areas of the world. Furthermore, Morosini shows how not only the remains of war can be changed by climate. Warmer winters with less snow and ice have laid bare postings and barracks that were previously inaccessible, but continued warming and mountainside erosion may also threaten the heritage sites.

Altogether, the chapters in section one underline the importance of history in the study of pathways and trails. Whether in densely populated areas of Great Britain, mountainsides in Northern Italy or remote rural landscapes in Norway, historical traces, legislations, practices and ideas affect the possibilities and articulations of current movement heritage. This connects to other historical and currently ongoing struggles for land rights. When indigenous and rural people stand against extractive industries (or over-tourism for that matter), the paths that are a concrete result of experiential, personal knowledge are important. They are explicit evidence of what is in Swedish called *hävd* (literally: claim). This concept refers to ancient traditions of repeated land use, which historically has been associated with a legitimate claim to land rights. Walking is, in a rather corporeal sense, to claim the right to use the land without destroying it. These claims can be made by individuals, groups, organisations, political parties and even nations. In tandem with other forms of claims – juridical, geographical, political, economic – they shape our understanding of paths and trails and who has a right to access them.

Section 2: Off the beaten tracks

The chapters gathered in the second section of the book lead us into a number of present-day examples of path-making and heritage-making activities that each in their own way shed new light on pathways. Here, focus is shifted towards the experiences and stories of walkers and path-makers, and to the narrative elements of walking. History is still an important component, but in these chapters more

Daniel Svensson, Katarina Saltzman, Sverker Sörlin

as a resource for storytelling and heritage-making. Such an interest in impressions and articulations of the past connects to understandings of heritage as a fundamentally contemporary matter. With such a perspective, heritage-making can be understood as a process whereby '[t]he present selects an inheritance from an imagined past for current use and decides what should be passed on to an imagined future'.[69] At the same time, these chapters show that heritage is today regarded as a value of relevance for emerging practices of walking.

Highlighting the narrative aspects of walking and pathways brings intangible aspects of the landscape into focus. While the marks of human feet on the ground may be subtle, they are still concrete, material features. But the making of a path or a trail does not only entail the physical formation of a walkable passage. Pathways are also made and transformed in our thoughts, through immaterial processes that attach meanings and values to the matters that surround us. While threading through physical landscapes, paths and trails are simultaneously finding their ways into our minds, through stories, memories and imagination. And in turn, such immaterial aspects influence how we use, form and change the materiality of specific paths. In order to understand the movement heritage, we believe it is crucial to pay attention to the interplay between matter and mind in the shaping and constant reshaping of pathways. The authors in this section provide guidance in this direction.

In recent years, and not least during the COVID-19 pandemic, we have seen an unexpected rise in the interest in recreational walking.[70] This has also led to an increase in projects to establish new trails and restore old ones, as demonstrated by **Susanne Österlund-Pötzsch**. She shows how the recently increased interest in trail walking has resulted in an array of trail-making activities in small island communities in the Åland archipelago in Finland. With a specific focus on local initiatives and socio-cultural interpretations, she examines the complex interplay between stories, heritage and community. Additionally, she highlights the power of storytelling in projects to promote walking, for example in the establishment of the St Olav Waterway as a route for pilgrimage in the Åland islands. According to Österlund-Pötzsch, narrativity is a key to understand how trails and trail walking are experienced and performed as movement heritage.

Pilgrimage holds a particular place in the heritage of walking paths, and one of the best-known of all pilgrimage trails is probably the one leading to Santiago de Compostela in Spain. The chapter by **Camilla Brudin Borg** examines the

69   Tunbridge and Ashworth, *Dissonant Heritage*, p. 6
70   E.g. Beery et al., 'Covid-19 and Outdoor Recreation Management'.

Introduction

role of literature in the making of the Camino that leads millions of pilgrims to the sacred tomb of Saint James in Santiago de Compostela. In her view, the trail is a storied space, infused with narrative meaning, as well as a material space that is connected into the stories 'along the trail'. A handful of Camino stories by Swedish authors constitute the empirical basis for this chapter, and Brudin Borg uses the metaphor of the palimpsest to detect the layering and co-creation of Camino stories and the topography and worldly conditions of the physical trail. Her chapter also reminds us that, through narratives, it is possible to experience movement along a path without moving our bodies or even being present on the ground.

Some of the chapters in this section foreground various forms of artistic practices in relation to practices and experiences of walking and trail-making. In one of these, **Laura Bertens** invites us to reflect on the possibilities of adding narrative layers to the experience of a walk by using audio guides. Here, two performative artworks by Janet Cardiff – one in Kassel, Germany and one in London – are used as examples of how memories and the act of remembrance can be brought into the experience of a place or a path. Bertens shows how the artist's use of audio guides immerses the participant in a multidimensional soundscape while walking in a physical landscape, in this case an urban landscape. Through the artist's voice historical layers of previous events are added to the walk. In both cases, the artworks evoke an awareness of quite traumatic events that have taken place at the site of the walk. The result is an experience where the past and the present blend seamlessly along the way.

How use of new technology can affect the relationship between walking, pathways and heritage is explored by **Finn Arne Jørgensen**, who uses the virtual worlds of video games as the point of departure to go hiking in digital landscapes. Video gaming is today a major industry and has become important pastime activity for many, not least during the COVID-19 pandemic, with restrained daily routines and reduced possibilities to walk freely. With particular focus on a genre of games called 'walking simulators', this chapter demonstrates how walking trails in the virtual worlds of the games provides a shared space for narratives about movement, landscape and the relationships that evolve through movement. And with recent developments such as the now-widespread use of GPS units, the gap between the virtual and the physical landscape is gradually closing. One of Jørgensen's key arguments is that studies of game-based mobility can help us understand how trails function as media in the landscape.

Petra Lilja takes us on a walk of a different kind. In her chapter, we follow her in silence on a curated walk into a former limestone quarry in southernmost Sweden. There, we are invited to encounter the vibrant materiality of the environment, and of our own bodies, while walking through the layers of time embedded in the limestone and in the remains of the industrial activities connected to the extraction of minerals. Following the path down into the quarry, the author guides us to notice the matters – and in particular the minerals – on their own terms, rather than with an anthropocentric approach to matter as resource. Inspired by theories foregrounding more-than-human agencies, this chapter explores possibilities to 'disrupt our extractive mindsets' and think differently about our being in the world through the simple act of attentive walking.

All the chapters in this section, in one way or another, invite us to follow contemporary pathways that transgress boundaries which used to be seen as given, and to look for connections rather than divisions between, for example, mind and matter, nature and culture, past and present, virtual and physical, human and more-than-human.

Section three – Searching for new path heritage

Talking, as we do in this volume, about the making of a movement heritage as supposedly a new kind of heritage practice, section three searches for possible antecedents, or parallel processes, in cultures outside Europe or the Western world. It also brings together experiences of walking as a method of exploring past and present functions, and indeed agencies, of paths in contexts ranging from national natures to traumatic memories to education and sustainability. **Subarna De** takes us to an Indian mountain district, Kodagu, where coffee planting was introduced in colonial times. The arrival of the plantation economy led to the local population more consciously using the extensive walking paths to maintain memory and knowledge of plants, animals and traditional practices linked to the ecology of the 'bioregion'. This 'Indigenous heritage-making' has been going on, albeit not using precisely that term, since the nineteenth century. Kodagu's trails have kept evolving, as sites of heritage and manifestations of 'cultural continuity'.

Observations of a similar nature are made by **John Martin, Joane Serrano, Jacqueline Nowakowski and Dominica Williamson** in their study of values fostered by paths in the Ifugao Rice Terraces landscape in the Philippines and Carwynnen Quoit, Cornwall, UK. These are two landscapes far apart but at the same time both are in or (Carwynnen) adjacent to a UNESCO World Heritage Site – 'places on Earth that are of outstanding universal value to humanity'. When WHS's are investigated or developed trails are often overlooked. Rather, they are typically identified as tourist-, health', or wellbeing assets. Martin and

Introduction

his colleagues find values in both sites that came from paths and walking and at the same time supported the UN Sustainable Development Goals, suggesting a wider reach of the effects of paths on landscape values and services.

Paths can also serve as productive points of departure for discovering layered histories and landscapes. **Daniele Valisena** applies Michel de Certeau's walking methodology to widen the register of the path to include all senses: smell, sound, taste, vision, the tactile. His area of inquiry, the industrial coal and steel factory landscape in Wallonia, Belgium is rich and scarred. Walking through it, Valisena finds ruderal ecologies and conducts multi-species ethnography that build strata, at the same time geological, toxic and storied. Referring to Stacy Alaimo and Rosi Braidotti, he talks about transcorporeal relations and affections in a narrative that is both about an Anthropocene experience of landscape layering and a revised environmental history of this Belgian mining region.

Also much inspired by de Certeau's *The Practice of Everyday Life* (1984), **Maria Piekarska** explores the intricate dual use of the path as both a memorial tool and a recreational space in Post-WWII Israel. The Martyr's Trail from 2013 is an outgrowth of the planted Martyr's Forest, started in 1951 as an early product of the young Jewish state. The trail combines *en route plaques* of Holocaust victims with intense experience of lush nature, emphasising the modern experience of the Jewish people from suffering to redemption and freedom. It also serves as a vehicle of the old patriotic Zionist tradition used in schools and the military – to 'walk the land' as a sign of possession and gratitude. The path insists, in Piekarska's reading, on its role as an 'enunciation' in de Certeau's terms, a bodily speech-act expressed by the walker as part of the trail while moving on it, an act that transcends its functions as memory and recreation and becomes heritage.

Also walking, **Faidon Moudopoulos Athanasiou** and **Ionas Sklavounos** conduct a revisionist history of the ancient settlement of Aristi in Northwestern Greece. Following not just the official UNESCO cobbled street heritage but also branching out into a wider network of pathways in the village, they identify a multi-layered archaeology of abandoned quarries, prehistoric caves, World War II battlefields and sacred forests. Again, it is a more-than-'literal' engagement that the path approach opens up, captured in sensorial and oral registers and giving memory a vital role in the writing of this reformed archaeohistory. Their new path experience leads them to an articulate critique of the 'historicism embedded in our literate societies' and by implication towards a movement heritage that transcends the path itself and the linear history typically written about it.

The walking methodology can also evoke ideas of how the heritagisation process may unfold. Drawing on fieldwork in southern Norway, **Benjamin Richards** makes a distinction between (already) 'valued trails', where movement is curated for tourism or education, and 'paths of meaning', where meaning is more fluid and appears as we go, or drift, and more subjectively, too. You don't have to make a choice, he argues. Both types exist and speak to the fact that the heritage of paths and trails 'is not a fixed thing, but the process of forming paths', echoing something ongoing, 'across time, across generations and across epochs'. To walk a 'path of meaning' may make us more attentive, but, coming to think of it, even such a path assumes some kind of prearranged 'value', such as being attentive, or just being aware.

There seems to be no escaping this blending of the designed and the inadvertent, the spontaneous desire in a path and its curated directionality, the subjective meaning making and the collective usefulness. In that respect, our exploration of paths speaks to a main feature of recent thinking on heritage-making, which is the capacity of heritage not just to exist, to sit there in a monumental fashion, but also to make. Paths almost quintessentially change, act, and perform in relation to humans (and others). In short, they do things as things are being done with them, mostly walking. As such, they cannot and perhaps should not be harnessed. But they are also a species with many virtues and healing and symbolic functions. They are precious, they are the core of holy spaces. We should take care of them, somehow. One way is to keep walking.

Bibliography

Amato, J., *On Foot: A History of Walking* (New York: New York University Press, 2004).

Anderson, Ben, 'The Construction of an Alpine Landscape: Building, Representing and Affecting the Eastern Alps, c. 1885–1914. *Journal of Cultural Geography* **29** (2) (2012): 155–83.

Anderson, Ben, *Cities, Mountains and Being Modern in Fin-de-siècle England and Germany* (London: Palgrave Macmillan, 2020).

Andersson, K., A. Fabri, P. Fredman, S. Hedenborg, A. Jansson, S. Karlén, J. Radmann and D. Wolf-Watz, *Idrotten och friluftslivet under coronapandemin: Resultat från två undersökningar om coronapandemins effekter på idrott, fysisk aktivitet och friluftsliv*. Mistra Sport & Outdoors, Rapport 2021:2 (Stockholm: Mistra, 2021).

Armiero, Marco, *A Rugged Nation: Mountains and the Making of Modern Italy* (Knapwell: The White Horse Press, 2011).

Aronsson, Peter, *Historiebruk – att använda det förflutna* (Lund: Studentlitteratur, 2005).

Balmford, A., J. Beresford, J. Green, R. Naidoo, M. Walpole and A. Manica, 'A Global Perspective on Trends in Nature-based Tourism', *PLoS biology* **7** (6) (2009): e1000144.

Bangstad, Torgeir Rinke and Þóra Pétursdóttir, 'An Ecological Approach to Heritage', in Torgeir Rinke Bangstadand and Þóra Pétursdóttir (eds), *Heritage Ecologies* (London: Routledge, Taylor & Francis Group, 2021).

Introduction

Beery, T., M.R. Olsson and M. Vitestam, 'Covid-19 and Outdoor Recreation Management: Increased Participation, Connection to Nature, and a Look to Climate Adaptation', *Journal of Outdoor Recreation* 36 (2021): 100457.

Berger, K., B. Smith and B. McKibben, *America's Great Hiking Trails* (New York: Rizzoli, 2014).

Best, Mechelle N. (2017). '"Freedom Footprints: the Barbados Story" – A Slavery Heritage Trail', *Journal of Heritage Tourism* 12 (5) (2017): 474–88.

Billig, M., *Banal Nationalism* (London: Sage, 1995).

Bottenburg, Maarten van, 'Why are the European and American Sports Worlds so Different? Path-dependence in European and American Sports History', in Alan Tomlinson, Christopher Young and Richard Holt (eds), *Transformation of Modern Europe: States, Media and Markets 1950–2010*, pp. 205–25 (London/New York: Routledge, 2011).

Boyd, Stephen W., 'Editorial: Heritage Trails and Tourism', *Journal of Heritage Tourism* 12 (5) (2017): 417–22.

Bryson, Bill, *A Walk in the Woods: Rediscovering America on the Appalachian Trail* (New York: Broadway Books, 1998).

de Certeau, Michel, *The Practice of Everyday Life* (Berkeley, CA: University of California Press, 1984).

Coates, Peter, David Moon and Paul *Warde* (eds), *Local Places, Global Processes* (Oxford: Windgather Press, 2016).

Collins-Kreiner, Noga, 'Hiking, Sense of Place, and Place Attachment in the Age of Globalization and Digitization: The Israeli Case', *Sustainability* 12 (11) (2020): 4548.

Connolly, William E., *A World of Becoming* (Durham, NC: Duke UP, 2010).

Daniels, Stephen and Denis Cosgrove (eds), *The Iconography of Landscape: Essays on the Symbolic Representation, Design, and Use of Past Environments* (Cambridge: Cambridge University Press, 1988).

David, Paul A., 'Clio and the Economics of QWERTY', *The American Economic Review* 75 (2) (1985): 332–37.

Edensor, T., *Geographies of Rhythm: Nature, Place, Mobilities and Bodies* (Farnham: Ashgate, 2010).

Elliot, Alice, Roger Norum and Noel B. Salazar (eds), *Methodologies of Mobility: Ethnography and Experiment* (New York: Berghahn Books, 2017).

Fagan, J. and G. Kearns, 'Tramper Perspectives on New Zealand's Great Walks in a Time of Transition', *New Zealand Geographer* 73 (3) (2017): 66–80.

Fagence, Michael, 'A Heritage "Trailscape": Tracking the Exploits of Historical Figures – an Australian Case Study', *Journal of Heritage Tourism* 12 (5) (2017): 452–62.

Garden, M.C., 'The Heritagescape: Looking at Landscapes of the Past'. *International Journal of Heritage Studies* 12 (5) (2006): 394–411.

Godtman Kling, Kristin, Sandra Wall-Reinius and Peter Fredman, *The Multi-functional Trail: An International Literature Review and the Case of Trails in Southern Jämtland Mountains, Sweden*, Etour Report 2017:1 (Östersund: Mid-Sweden University, 2017).

Godtman Kling, K., A. Dahlberg and S. Wall-Reinius, 'Negotiating Improved Multifunctional Landscape Use: Trails as Facilitators for Collaboration Among Stakeholders', *Sustainability* 11 (13) (2019): 3511.

Grundsten, Claes, *Kungsleden: Walking the Royal Trail: From Abisko to Hemavan* (Hildersley: Carreg, 2009).

Gustafsson, Lars [1980], 'Ballad on the Paths in Västmanland', trans. John Irons. In Lars Gustafsson, *Selected Poems* (Hexham: Bloodaxe Books, 2015).

Hall, Colin Michael, Yael Ram and Noam Shoval (eds), *Routledge International Handbook of Walking* (Abingdon, Oxon: Routledge, 2017)

Hammarskjöld, Dag (posthumous), *Från Sarek till Haväng* (Stockholm: Svenska Turistföreningen, 1962).

Harrison, Rodney, *Heritage: Critical Approaches* (Abingdon: Routledge, 2013).

Harrison, Rodney, 'Beyond "Natural" and "Cultural" Heritage: Toward an Ontological Politics of Heritage in the Age of Anthropocene', *Heritage & Society* (1) (2015): 24-42.

Harrison, Rodney et al., *Heritage Futures: Comparative Approaches to Natural and Cultural Heritage Practices* (London: UCL Press, 2020).

Harvey, D., 'Landscape and Heritage: Trajectories and Cconsequences', *Landscape Research* **40** (8) (2015): 911–24.

Hastrup, Kirsten, 'Destinies and Decisions: Taking the Life World Seriously in Environmental History', in S. Sörlin and P. Warde (eds), *Nature's End: History and the Environment*, eds., pp. 331–48 (London: Palgrave Macmillan, 2009).

Holmberg, Ingrid M., K. Saltzman and S. Andersson, *Att ge plats: Kulturarvssektorn och de nationella minoriteternas historiska platser* (Göteborg: Makadam, 2018).

Humberstone, Barbara, Heather Prince and Karla A. Henderson (eds), *Routledge International Handbook of Outdoor Studies* (London: Routledge, 2016)

Ingold, Tim, *The Perception of the Environment* (London: Routledge, 2000).

Ingold, Tim, *Lines: A Brief History*, new ed. (London: Routledge, 2007).

Ingold, Tim, *Being Alive: Essays on Movement, Knowledge and Description* (Abingdon: Routledge, 2011).

Ingold, Tim, 'Prospect', in T. Ingold and G. Pálsson (eds), *Biosocial Becomings. Integrating Social and Biological Anthropology* (Cambridge: Cambridge University Press, 2013).

Ingold, Tim and Jo Lee Vergunst (eds), *Ways of Walking: Ethnography and Practice on Foot* (Farnham: Ashgate Publishing, 2008).

Ingold, T. and G. Pálsson (eds), *Biosocial Becomings: Integrating Social and Biological Anthropology* (Cambridge: Cambridge University Press, 2013).

IPCC, *Summary for Policymakers*, in V. Masson-Delmotte, P. Zhai, A. Pirani, et al. (eds), *Climate Change 2021: The Physical Science Basis. Contribution of Working Group I to the Sixth Assessment Report of the Intergovernmental Panel on Climate Change* (Cambridge: Cambridge University Press, 2021).

Johnson, Sandra L., History of the National Trails System: The National Trails System is the Network of Scenic, Historic, and Recreation Trails Created by the Act in 1968, (2022): https://www.americantrails.org/national-trails-system/history Accessed 7 February 2022.

Kelly, P., M. Murphy and N. Mutrie, 'The Health Benefits of Walking' *Walking* (Transport and Sustainability, Vol. 9), pp. 61–79 (Bingley: Emerald Publishing Limited, 2017).

Kilander, Svenbjörn, *'En nationalrikedom av hälsoskatter': Om Jämtland och industrisamhället 1882–1910* (Hedemora: Gidlunds, 2008).

Klepp, Ingun Grimstad, *På stier mellom natur og kultur: turgåeres opplevelser av kulturlandskapet og deres synspunkter på vern* (Oslo: Scandinavian Univ. Press, 1998).

Introduction

Kline, Carol, 'Applying the Community Capitals Framework to the Craft Heritage Trails of Western North Carolina', *Journal of Heritage Tourism* **12** (5) (2017): 489–508.

Koselleck, Reinhart, *Historische Semantik und Begriffsgeschichte* (Stuttgart: Klett-Cotta, 1979).

Leinfelder R. and J.A. Ivar do Sul, 'The Stratigraphy of Plastics and their Preservation on Geological Records', in J. Zalasiewicz, C.N. Waters, M. Williams et al. (eds), *The Anthropocene as a Geological Time Unit: A Guide to the Scientific Evidence and Current Debate*, pp. 147–155 (Cambridge: Cambridge University Press, 2019).

Lemky, Kim, 'The Revitalization of a Heritage Travel Route: Canada's Cabot Trail', *Journal of Heritage Tourism* **12** (5) (2017): 526–35.

Lien, Marianne, *Becoming Salmon: Aquaculture and the Domestication of a Fish* (Berkeley, CA: University of California Press, 2015).

Lorimer, Hayden 'Walking: New Forms and Spaces for Studies of Pedestrianism', in T. Cresswell and P. Merriman (eds), *Geographies of Mobilities: Practices, Spaces, Subjects*, pp. 19–34 (Farnham: Ashgate, 2011).

Lowenthal, David, *The Heritage Crusade and the Spoils of History* (Cambridge: Cambridge University Press, 1998).

Lowenthal, David, *The Past is a Foreign Country – Revisited*, Orig. 1985 (Cambridge: Cambridge University Press, 2015).

Macfarlane, Robert, *The Old Ways: A Journey on Foot*, new ed. (London: Penguin, 2012).

MacLeod, Nicola, 'Cultural Routes, Trails and the Experience of Place', in M. Smith and G. Richards (eds), *Routledge Handbook of Cultural Tourism*, pp. 369–74 (Abingdon: Routledge, 2013).

MacLeod, Nicola, 'The Role of Trails in the Creation of Tourist Space', *Journal of Heritage Tourism* **12** (5) (2017): 423–30.

Macnaghten, P. and J. Urry (eds), *Bodies of Nature* (London: SAGE, 2001).

Mahoney, J., 'Path Dependence in Historical Sociology', *Theory and Society* **29** (4) (2000): 507–48.

McCullough, Brian P. and Timothy B. Kellison (eds), *Routledge Handbook of Sport and the Environment* (Abingdon, Oxon: Routledge, 2018).

Mels, Tom, *Wild Landscapes: The Cultural Nature of Swedish National Parks* (Lund: Lund University, 1999).

Merriman, Peter, George Revill, Tim Cresswell, Hayden Lorimer, David Matless, Gillian Rose and John Wylie, 'Landscape, Mobility, Practice', *Social & Cultural Geography* **9** (2) (2008): 191–212.

Miles, Stephen 'Remembrance Trails of the Great War on the Western Front: Routes of Heritage and Memory', *Journal of Heritage Tourism* **12** (5) (2017): 441–51.

Monz, C.A., C.M. Pickering and W.L. Hadwen, 'Recent Advances in Recreation Ecology and the Implications of Different Relationships between Recreation Use and Ecological Impacts', *Frontiers in Ecology and the Environment* **11** (8) (2013): 441–46.

Moor, Robert, *On Trails* (London: Aurum Press, 2016).

Moor, Robert, 'Tracing (and Erasing) New York's Lines of Desire', *The New Yorker*, 20 February 2017.

New Zealand Department of Conservation, 2022: https://www.doc.govt.nz/parks-and-recreation/things-to-do/walking-and-tramping/great-walks/ Accessed 7 February 2022.

Nilsson, Per Åke, *Fjällturismens historia: En studie av utvecklingen i Åredalen* (Östersund: Mitthögskolan, 1999).

Daniel Svensson, Katarina Saltzman, Sverker Sörlin

Øian, Hogne, 'Pilgrim Routes as Contested Spaces in Norway', *Tourism Geographies* **21** (3) (2019): 422–41.

Olafsdottir, G., P. Cloke, A. Schulz, Z. van Dyck, T. Eysteinsson, B. Thorleifsdottir and C. Vögele, 'Health Benefits of Walking in Nature: A Randomized Controlled Study Under Conditions of Real-Life Stress', *Environment and Behavior* **52** (3) (2020): 248–74.

Olwig, Kenneth R. 'Representation and Alienation in the Political Land-scape', *Cultural Geographies* **12** (1) (2005): 19–40.

Olwig, Kenneth R., '*Performing on the Landscape versus Doing Landscape: Perambulatory Practice, Sight and the Sense of Belonging*', in Tim Ingold and Jo Lee Vergunst (eds), *Ways of Walking: Ethnography and Practice on Foot*, pp. 142–60 (Farnham: Ashgate Publishing, 2008).

Österlund-Pötzsch, S., *Gångarter och gångstilar: Rum, rytm och rörelse till fots* (Göteborg: Makadam, 2018).

Pries, Johan and Mattias Qviström, 'The Patchwork Planning of a Welfare Landscape: Reappraising the Role of Leisure Planning in the Swedish Welfare State', *Planning Perspectives* **36** (5) (2012): 923–48.

Pyne, Stephen J., *How the Canyon Became Grand: A Short History* (New York: Viking, 1998).

Readman, Paul, Chad Carl Bryant and Arthur Burns (eds), *Walking Histories, 1800–1914* (London: Palgrave Macmillan, 2016).

Readman, Paul, *Storied Ground: Landscape and the Shaping of English National Identity* (Cambridge: Cambridge University Press, 2018).

Rhoades, Roger and Nancy Rhoades, *Santiago de Compostela: Journal of our Camino* (Linkoln: iUniverse, 2005).

Riksantikvaren, *Historiske vandreruter* (2022) https://www.riksantikvaren.no/prosjekter/historiske-vandreruter/ Accessed 25 February 2022.

Rose, Gillian, *Feminism and Geography: The Limits of Geographical Knowledge* (Cambridge: Polity Press, 1993).

Sánchez-Carretero, Cristina (ed.), *Heritage, Pilgrimage and the Camino to Finisterre: Walking to the End of the World* (Amsterdam: Springer, 2015).

Saltzman, Katarina, *Inget landskap är en ö: Dialektik och praktik i öländska landskap* (Lund: Nordic Academic Press, 2001).

Saul, Hayley and Emma Waterton, 'A Himalayan Triptych: Narratives of Traders, Pilgrims and Resistance in a Landscape of Movements', *Journal of Heritage Tourism* **12** (5) (2017): 431–40.

Selberg, T., 'Pilegrimsveien som kulturarv', *DIN-Tidsskrift for religion og kultur* 1–2 (2011): 120–31.

Sheller, M. and J. Urry (eds), *Mobile Technologies of the City* (New York: Routledge, 2006).

Smith, Laurajane, *Uses of Heritage* (Abingdon, Oxon: Routledge, 2006).

Solnit, Rebecca, *Wanderlust: A History of Walking* (London: Verso, 2002).

Sörlin, Sverker, 'Monument and Memory: Landscape Imagery and the Articulation of Territory', *Worldviews: Environment, Culture, Religion* **2** (1998): 269–79.

Sörlin, Sverker, 'The Articulation of Territory. Landscape and the Constitution of Regional and National Identity', *Norsk Geografisk Tidsskrift – Norwegian Journal of Geography* **53** (2–3) (1999): 103–112.

Sörlin, Sverker and Nina Wormbs, 'Environing Technologies: A Theory of Making Environment' *History & Technology* **34** (2) (2018):101–25.

Introduction

Sundin, Bosse, 'Upptäckten av hembygden: Om konstruktionen av regionala identiteter', in Barbro Blomberg and Sven-Olof Lindquist (eds), *Den regionala särarten* (Lund: Studentlitteratur, 1994).

Svensson, Daniel, 'Skiing through Time: Articulating a Landscape Heritage of Swedish Cross-Country Skiing', in Philipp Strobl and Aneta Podkalicka (eds), *Leisure Cultures and the Making of Modern Ski Resorts*, Palgrave's Global Culture and Sport Series, pp. 93–115 (London: Palgrave, 2018).

Svensson, D., S. Sörlin and N. Wormbs, 'The Movement Heritage – Scale, Place, and Pathscapes in Anthropocene Tourism', in Martin Gren and Edward Huijbens (eds), *Tourism and the Anthropocene*, pp. 131–51 (London: Routledge, 2016).

Svensson, Daniel, Sverker Sörlin and Katarina Saltzman, 'Pathways to the Trail – Landscape, Walking and Heritage in a Scandinavian Border Region', *Norsk Geografisk Tidsskrift – Norwegian Journal of Geography* **75** (5) (2021): 243–55.

Syse, Karen Lykke and Martin Lee Mueller (eds), *Sustainable Consumption and the Good Life: Interdisciplinary Perspectives* (Abingdon, Oxon: Routledge, 2015).

Tilly, C., 'Future History', *Theory and Society* **17** (6) (1988): 703–12.

Timothy, D.J. and S.W. Boyd, *Tourism and Trails: Cultural, Ecological and Management Issues* (Bristol, UK: Channel View Publications, 2015).

Tunbridge, J.E. and G.J. Ashworth, *Dissonant Heritage: The Management of the Past as a Resource in Conflict* (Chichester: Wiley, 1995).

UNWTO, World Tourism Organization, *Walking Tourism – Promoting Regional Development, UNWTO* (Madrid, 2019).

Warde, P., L. Robin and S. Sörlin, *The Environment – A History of the Idea* (Baltimore, MD and London: Johns Hopkins University Press, 2018).

Ween, Gro and Simone Abram, 'The Norwegian Trekking Association: Trekking as Constituting the Nation', *Landscape Research* **37** (2) (2012): 155–71.

Whatmore, S., 'Materialist Returns: Practising Cultural Geographies in and for a More-than-human World', *Cultural Geographies* 13(4) (2006): 600–10.

Whitridge, Peter, 'The Imbrication of Human and Animal Paths: An Arctic Case Study', in Christopher Watts (ed.), *Relational Archaeologies: Humans, Animals, Things*, pp. 228–44 (Abingdon, Oxon: Routledge, 2013).

Widawski, Krzysztof and Piotr Oleśniewicz, 'Thematic Tourist Trails: Sustainability Assessment Methodology. The Case of Land Flowing with Milk and Honey', *Sustainability* **11** (14) (2019): 3841.

Wrede, V. and V. Mügge-Bartolovic, 'GeoRoute Ruhr – a Network of Geotrails in the Ruhr Area National Park, Germany', *Geoheritage* **4** (1) (2012): 109–14.

Zalasiewicz, J. and M. Zalasiewicz, 'Battle Scars', *New Scientist* 225 (2014) (28 March 2015): 36–39.

Zalasiewicz, J., M. Williams, C.N. Waters et al., 'Scale and Diversity of the Physical Technosphere: A Geological Perspective', *The Anthropocene Review* **4** (1) (2017): 9–22.

Zalasiewicz, Jan, Colin M. Waters, Mark Williams, et al., 'When Did the Anthropocene Begin? A Mid-twentieth Century Boundary Level is Stratigraphically Optimal', *Quaternary International* 383 (2015): 196–203.

Section I
Past Preconditions of Paths

CHAPTER 1.

FOOTPATHS IN ENGLAND: NOTES TOWARDS A RADICAL HISTORY

Paul Readman

Winding across field and meadow, through woodlands, along clifftops, up mountainsides and deep into urban areas too, footpaths are a distinctive feature of the English landscape. This essay explores their changing significance from the nineteenth century on. For it was in the nineteenth century that they first became a focus of public debate, in the overlapping contexts of enclosure, the rise of radical land politics, industrialisation and urbanisation, and the emergence of countryside-oriented tourism. Into and through the twentieth century, footpaths remained subject to heated political contestation. As symbols of a popular stake in the landscape, their preservation was not only about preserving a recreational amenity for a largely urban-dwelling people; it was also a means of asserting a demotic claim on the national territory. It helped make possible a ruralised Englishness in the context of industrial modernity.

We are apt to tell the story of footpath preservation as a story of the defence of popular rights. The achievements of early campaigners such as Octavia Hill, Hardwicke Rawnsley and Sir Robert Hunter – the founders of the National Trust – are celebrated now more than ever.[1] In more radical vein, footpath preservation is connected to public protest, much of which has been more-or-less socialist in flavour, with activists breaking down stopped paths, confronting gamekeepers and marching along disputed routes to assert the claim of the common man and woman. The Kinder Scout Mass Trespass of 1932, in the Peak District of Derbyshire, is the example everyone turns to here – and it has attracted more than its fair share of attention from historians.[2] Along with the wider history of access to the countryside, that of footpath preservation is associated with a progressive politics, one congruent with the motivations behind state-created National Parks, long-distance walking trails and the 'right to roam' agenda.

---

1   For broadly positive reassessments of Hill, see Baigent and Cowell, *'Nobler Imaginings and Mightier Struggles'*.
2   D. Hey supplies a revisionist interpretation in his 'Kinder Scout and the Legend of the Mass Trespass'.

Paul Readman

PEAK DISTRICT RAMBLERS IN TROUBLE: WALKING TOWARDS KINDER SCOUT ON THE OCCASION OF THEIR BATTLE WITH THE GAMEKEEPERS.

Figure 1.

The Kinder Scout Mass Trespass, 24 April 1932. Unattributed photograph in the *Illustrated Sporting and Dramatic News*, 30 April 1932. Source: © Illustrated London News Ltd / Mary Evans Picture Library.

Now, I do not wish to dispute this story in any fundamental way. But I do want to give it a bit of a twist. My contention is that the dense network of public footpaths, despite being of high amenity value, is nevertheless compatible with a political economic regime of startling inequality, especially so far as the distribution of property in land is concerned. Although often directed at the grasping landlord who stopped the path of the people, campaigns for the preservation of pedestrian rights-of-way were functionally consistent with support for private property, the wider logic of liberal capitalism, and mainstream understandings of national identity. To flesh out this contention, I need to begin with a brief survey of the place of footpaths in English culture over the last two centuries or so. How and why did they come to be so valued?

1. Footpaths in England

I

The short answer to this question is that they had always been valued. For centuries, footpaths had been one of the main means by which ordinary people got from A to B over the course of their daily lives. As medieval historians have shown, peasants made and used pathways that were quite separate from the routes walked (or ridden) by their lords and masters; the footpath was thus specifically associated with the pedestrian practices of the common man, woman and child.[3] It was how they accessed their places of work and worship; it was a means of recreation, exercise and courtship. But except in the case of disputes over their closure or diversion – which were relatively rare – documentary attestations to the value of footpaths were uncommon until the early nineteenth century.[4]

The enclosure movement changed this. Enabled by the political power of the aristocracy, landowners threw farms together, fenced off commons and extinguished common rights – all in the name of maximising agricultural productivity through capitalist economies of scale. The effects of enclosure on the rural poor have been much discussed by historians; the consensus today is that these effects were generally negative.[5] Ordinary people were denied access to land that had previously been a means of sustaining independent livelihoods: the smallholder economy took a hit from which it never recovered. The poetry of John Clare stands as eloquent testimony to the sense of dispossession. As Clare's poems record, enclosure cut paths as well as stole commons: a whole series of his sonnets had footpaths as their focus.[6] In his *Village Minstrel* (1819–20) he wrote of how

> There once were lanes in nature's freedom dropt,
> There once were paths that every valley wound—
> Inclosure came, and every path was stopt;
> Each tyrant fix'd his sign where paths were found,
> To hint at trespass now who crossed the ground…

It was in this context, towards the end of the enclosure movement, that the first footpath protection societies were set up in the 1820s,[7] their establishment being given added impetus by an Act of 1815 that granted local magistrates the power summarily to close any footpath they deemed unnecessary.[8]

---

3 Kilby, *Peasant Perspectives on the Medieval Landscape*, pp. 59–68.
4 This is reflected in literary references to footpaths, which are scanty in pre-nineteenth-century writing: Taplin, *English Path*, pp. 4–5.
5 See esp. Neeson, *Commoners*.
6 Taplin, *English Path*, p. 7.
7 Taylor, *Claim on the Countryside*, p. 21.
8 'Act as to Closing Footpaths', 55 George III. c. 68, sec. 2 (1815). See Webb and Webb, *English Local Government*, pp. 201–04; Stephenson, *Forbidden Land*, p. 59. The statute was repealed in 1835.

For all that, footpaths were still required to service the post-enclosure economy. Wage labourers needed to get to work, and to church, and because of this many parliamentary enclosure awards explicitly declared paths to be rights-of-way. Some awards even created new such paths. Indeed, the loss of the common and the expansion of large-scale agriculture, with farms extending over many hundreds of acres, made rights-of-way more essential to the functioning of the rural socio-economic order. Since land was now largely held as private property unmoderated by common rights, the footpath did not so much enable public access as define its limits. Literally as well as figuratively, to 'stray off the path' was to transgress, to trespass.

As the nineteenth century progressed, however, the significance of footpaths shifted. They remained unremarked-upon sinews of capitalist agriculture, quietly facilitating the efficient supply of wage labour to farmers' fields. But alongside this, they started to matter in new, more visibly acknowledged, ways. By the 1880s, nearly three-quarters of the population of Britain lived in urban areas; commentators spoke of a 'rural exodus' sapping the nation's health, even its racial 'efficiency', and politicians grew increasingly interested in schemes of allotment, smallholding and other reforms to get people 'back to the land'.[9] Related to this was a concern to maintain a sense of connection to the countryside, and by extension to the English past. Facilitated by cheaper travel, paid and Bank Holidays, and the profusion of tourist guides brought out by John Murray, Adam and Charles Black, Edward Stanford and other publishers, more people saw rural England as offering recreational opportunities. Walking was central to this new interest in the countryside. In the late nineteenth century, walking groups mushroomed: Leslie Stephen's *Sunday Tramps* group of elite metropolitan intellectuals is the best known,[10] but there were many others – from the white-collar Forest Ramblers of Epping Forest to the predominantly proletarian Sheffield Clarion Ramblers.[11] And for all those drawn to countryside walking, whether organised in societies or not, the footpath was central to their recreational practice.

Given their centrality to walking for leisure, the value of footpaths seems obvious. But this is only because we now view such walking as an unalloyed good (except, perhaps, when it contributes to ecological damage such as topsoil erosion). It is worth remembering that, at least insofar as it had any presence in wider culture, purposive walking for leisure – especially long-distance walking

---

9   Marsh, *Back to the Land*; Readman, *Land and Nation*.
10   Whyte, 'Sunday Tramps'.
11   Hill, *Freedom to Roam*, pp. 20–21, 32; Sissons et al., *Clarion Call*.

1. Footpaths in England

– was not widely popular before the later nineteenth century, and not really a fully established element of mass tourism until the interwar period, when it became associated with an increasingly assertive youth culture. One thinks of the Youth Hostels Association (YHA), which was founded in 1930, or the sartorially and behaviourally emancipated young women hikers – many of them members of the YHA – who attracted much public notice in these years. Not all this notice was favourable, of course, but the association between recreational walking and a liberated, progressive modernity was increasingly apparent. It is nicely captured by the then-fashionable stylised realism of *Hiking* (1936), a painting by James Walker Tucker (1898–1972) in which three young women

Figure 2.

'Hiking' (circa 1936), by James Walker Tucker. Tempera on Panel. Source: © Tyne & Wear Archives & Museums / Bridgeman Images.

walkers are depicted as confident, athletic and capable figures, making use of their map to traverse and know the landscape.[12] In 1932, one newspaper article on the 'phenomenon' of hiking wondered 'whether the countryside, especially in the vicinity of the towns, will be large enough to accommodate the ever-increasing hordes of bare-legged, sunburnt boys and girls'.[13]

Before these heady interwar years, however, walking for pleasure was often viewed with suspicion. Trekking for miles cross-country was a thing tramps and vagrants did; it was not an activity for gentlemen, still less for ladies. Despite the peripatetic avocations of Wordsworth and the Lake Poets,[14] recreational walking remained marginal to mainstream culture. Quite why such attitudes shifted repays examination. At one level, walking in the countryside came to be valued because it provided physical and mental benefits. The motto of the Clarion Ramblers was 'A rambler made is a man improved';[15] while at the other end of the social spectrum, the patrician historian and Sunday Tramper G.M. Trevelyan opened his famous 1913 essay on walking with the observation that he had 'two doctors, my left leg and my right'.[16] Increasing Victorian awareness of pollution and other ills of high-density urban living contributed to this perspective: walking conduced to bodily heath. It was also seen as a spiritual balm for a rapidly speeded-up modernity: its slow pace allowed for contemplative observation of nature. It was a context, too, for individual self-reflection, a low-intensity version of the romanticism that had animated Wordsworth and Coleridge and which, by the later Victorian period, had now entered wider culture, if in rather diluted form.

But this was not the whole story. Footpath walking was also an important context for sociability. Indeed, it can be suggested that a desire for social interaction was the dominant germinator of the early twentieth-century efflorescence of pedestrian associational culture. In this interpretation, bodies like the Ramblers' Association, the YHA and the Countrywide Holiday Association were as much about social interaction as anything else.[17] Yet, such a perspective only gets us so far: the activity – walking – that was the raison d'être of these groups mattered, and central to that activity was the footpath.

For those who walked them, footpaths were routes into physical and mental

---

12   For more discussion of this painting, see Matless, *Landscape and Englishness*, pp. 113–14.
13   'Hiking: The Phenomenon of the Post-War Youth', *Sphere* 129 (18 June 1932): 479.
14   Wallace, *Walking, Literature, and English Culture*.
15   Hill, *Freedom to Roam*, p. 32.
16   G.M. Trevelyan, 'Walking', in *Clio: A Muse* (London: Longmans, 1913), p. 56.
17   Thompson, 'Fashioning of a New World'.

1. Footpaths in England

felicity, enablers of self-reflection and sociability, and means of accessing nature. But perhaps most significantly, the affordances of footpaths were historical. They conferred a sense of connection with the past. They were routes into knowing and imagining the past through embodied encounter with the landscape of which history was constituted. To adapt the social anthropologist Tim Ingold, if landscape was 'history congealed', and if the best way of reading landscape was on foot – just as most humans had read it across much of recorded history – then the humble footpath gave as important a means of access to this history as documentary evidence did.[18]

After all, footpaths were themselves evidentiary traces of human experience. Maintained through quotidian use over centuries, they can be seen – to use the helpful category that structures this collection of essays – as a form of 'movement heritage'. For Octavia Hill and her fellow campaigners, footpaths were 'the labourer's heritage in his own parish'; created by the common people, they were 'the common inheritance of Englishmen and women and children'.[19] And the defence of this inheritance was bound up with a popular patriotism, one that was rooted in older traditions of radical Englishness but was also consistent with a modern and democratising idea of nationhood. The crowds who broke down landlord-erected barricades blocking footpaths often marched up the disputed right-of-way singing patriotic songs, such as 'Rule Britannia' or even the national anthem. This is what happened at Latrigg in the Lake District in 1887, for example.[20] And if such behaviour was not generally seen in later access disputes, the undertow of popular Englishness was still present: walking a footpath was a means by which those who did not own land could assert a stake in the national domain and, given the imbrication of landscape and national identity, it was necessarily an activity that could carry a patriotic charge. This was well understood by Hill, who, in appealing to the Commons Preservation Society (CPS) to take up the cause of the protection of footpaths, declared that she thought 'men love a country more when its woods and fields, and streams, and flowers, and lakes, and hills, and the sky that bends over them are visible' – as preserving footpaths as rights-of-way open to the feet of all would help ensure.[21]

---

18   Ingold, *Perception of the Environment*, p. 150.
19   R. Hunter, *Footpaths and Commons and Parish and District Councils* (London: Cassell & Co., 1895), p. 6; O. Hill, 'Footpath Preservation', *Nature Notes* 3 (Oct. 1892): 196; A. Clarke, 'Footpaths and Commons', *Nature Notes* 7 (Jan. 1896): 9–11; *Preservation of Commons: Speech of Miss Octavia Hill at a Meeting for Securing West Wickham Common* (London: Kent & Surrey Committee of the Commons Preservation Society, [1892], [p. 1].
20   *The Times*, 3 Oct. 1887, 7.
21   'Miss Octavia Hill on the Duty of Supporting Footpath Protection Societies', Cumbria Record Office, WDX/422/2/4.

Paul Readman

One later example of how footpath-enabled popular patriotism was mobilised to serve a nationalist agenda is provided by Michael Powell and Emeric Pressburger's 1944 film, *A Canterbury Tale*. Set in wartime Kent near Canterbury, it tells the story of a Land Girl, a British soldier and an American GI getting to know the Kentish way of life. The film begins with narration from the General Prologue to Chaucer's *Canterbury Tales*, accompanied by shots of a procession of medieval pilgrims, then a hawk in flight, then World War II fighter aircraft. The theme is one of continuity with the English past, and the symbol of this continuity is a footpath, and specifically the famous Pilgrims' Way:

> Six hundred years have passed. What would they see, Dan Chaucer and his goodly company today? The hills and valleys are the same. Gone are the forests since the enclosures came. Hedgerows have sprung. The land is under plough. And orchards bloom with blossom on the bough. Sussex and Kent are like a garden fair. But sheep still graze upon the ridges there. The pilgrims' walk still winds above the weald, through wood and brake and many a fertile land.

Figure 3.

The Pilgrims' Way, near Aylesford, Kent, England. Unattributed photograph for the Mustograph Agency, 1950s. Source: Mary Evans Picture Library.

1. Footpaths in England

In the film, contact with Kentish landscape is presented as a way of 'getting close to your ancestors', of accessing 'the old England'.[22]

As this implies, in addition to being valued as popular and patriotic movement heritage, footpaths were also prized because walking the landscape was a means of encountering the past. This had been true for sixteenth- and seventeenth-century antiquaries such as William Camden, whose *Britannia* (1586) had relied heavily on observations made on foot.[23] Their practice had been carried on by later antiquaries such as William Hutton, whose *History of Hadrian's Wall* (1802) was based on a 601-mile pedestrian journey from Birmingham up to Carlisle, along the course of the fortification to Newcastle-upon-Tyne and back, and then home again.[24]

The pedestrian practices of antiquaries survived into the Victorian period. To an underappreciated extent, they were also adopted by professional historians. For E.A. Freeman, 'the finished historian must be a traveller'.[25] Indeed, even when plagued with gout, Freeman was relentless in his commitment to on-foot visits to the places that would feature in his monumental *Norman Conquest* – from the towns and farmland of the Conqueror's native Normandy, to the New Forest of his son William Rufus, to the battlefields of Hastings and Stamford Bridge.[26] Such visits were integral to his method; they were made 'to store my mind', to shed 'new light'.[27] It was a similar story for John Richard Green, who felt that 'History strikes its roots in Geography' and put this insight into practice in his enormously popular *English Social History*, a book suffused with sensitive attention to place and landscape.[28]

Later historians likewise had recourse to the archive of the feet, Trevelyan most famously.[29] Others included the medievalist F.M. Powicke, whose historical sensibility was profoundly influenced by the Lake District, where for much of his life he had a farmhouse in Eskdale. The ineluctably historical quality of landscape inspired Powicke: he was first drawn to the Lakes by work he did

---

22 P. Newland, 'Introduction', in Newland, *British Rural Landscapes on Film*, pp. 2–3.

23 W. Camden, *Britannia*, ed. and trans. E. Gibson, 2 vols (London: R. Ware, 1753 [1586]).

24 W. Hutton, *The History of the Roman Wall* (London: J. Nichols and Son, 1802); W. Hutton, *The Life of William Hutton* (London: Baldwin, Cradock & Joy, 1817), pp. 313–18.

25 E.A. Freeman, *Methods of Historical Study* (London: Macmillan & Co., 1886), pp. 314–15.

26 J. Bryce, 'Edward Augustus Freeman', *English Historical Review* 7 (1892): 499.

27 Letters to Dean Hook, April 1867 and to William Boyd Dawkins, 25 July 1867, in W.R.W. Stephens (ed.), *The Life and Letters of Edward A. Freeman* (2 vols, London: Macmillan & Co., 1895), I, pp. 381, 389.

28 J.R. Green and A.S. Green, *A Short Geography of the British Isles* (London: Macmillan & Co., 1889 [1879]), p. xi; J.R. Green, *A Short History of the English People* (London: Macmillan & Co., 1874).

29 Gange, 'Retracing Trevelyan?'.

for a *Victoria County History* article on Furness Abbey, the sight of the ancient sheepwalks tracking over the fells evoking the monastic life of the past and making a lasting impression on him.[30] And to Powicke's name could be added a host of others, including Eileen Power, A.L. Rowse, Hugh Trevor-Roper, and the whole school of landscape historians inspired by Maurice Beresford and W.G. Hoskins.

The pedestrian footpath-enabled practice of antiquarians and historians was the tip of a larger cultural iceberg. It was the intellectualised expression of a broader desire to connect with the past through embodied experience of landscape. This desire found most obvious expression in recreational culture, with guidebooks aimed at the 'antiquarian tourist' proliferating from the late nineteenth century on. A feature of these publications was the emphasis placed on on-foot exploration. Some were entirely structured around walking tours, detailing how these could give access to the historical associations of landscape. Typical titles included H.H. Warner's *Holiday Tramps through Picturesque England and Wales* (1902), W.H. Burnett's *Holiday Rambles by Road and Field Path* (1889) and Ernest Belcher's *Rambles Among the Cotswolds* (1892). But even more general guides, such as the county handbooks issued by Murray, Black, Stanford and Ward Lock, were filled with suggested walks. And the focus of these was frequently on landscapes whose historical associations were as important as their picturesque or 'natural' beauty (though in the picturesque, of course, visual and historical qualities were often conjoined).

Footpaths, then, were prized as movement heritage in themselves, but their heritage value was also connected to a more widespread engagement with landscape as history: they offered embodied access to the past. As the Yorkshire antiquary Edmund Bogg remarked in his *A Thousand Miles of Wandering Along the Roman Wall*, 'To see … time-honoured remains in situ … is to relive in the past'.[31] Themselves inheritances from the past, footpaths facilitated imaginative historical knowing, which for someone like Trevelyan was key to the poetry of history. As he told his daughter Mary, 'It *is* not – yet it *is*, that world of the Time Past',[32] and the past's simultaneous is- and is-nottedness derived from its tangibility in the places of the present, from the associational value of landscape experienced via footpaths such as one of Trevelyan's favourites, that along the line of Offa's Dyke over the Black Mountains and down off the ridge to the

---

30   Southern, 'Sir Maurice Powicke', 300–02; F.M. Powicke, *Three Lectures, given in the Hall of Balliol College* (London: Oxford University Press, 1947), pp. 71ff.

31   E. Bogg, *A Thousand Miles of Wandering Along the Roman Wall* (Leeds: Edmund Bogg, 1898), p. 13.

32   To Mary, 5 Sept. 1926, Trevelyan papers, Newcastle University: MM 1/4/14/28.

1. Footpaths in England

inn at Llanthony Priory, in the storied landscape of the Welsh borders.[33] To invoke the philosopher of history R.G. Collingwood – whose own historical sense was shaped by on-foot exploration of his native Cumberland – footpaths made possible the 're-enactment' of the past in the mind of the present-day observer.[34] And as Collingwood taught, this is what history is all about. We forget, sometimes, that our understanding of history is derived not only from books and documents, but from what Collingwood called 'the entire perceptible here-and-now'.[35] Footpaths bid us to remember this truth. They provide routes into an embodied form of historical knowing; indeed, as Robert Macfarlane has noted, the English verb 'to learn' is etymologically derivative of a Proto-Germanic word that means 'to follow or to find a track'.[36]

The point here is that, by the late nineteenth century, the historical affordances of footpaths had given them special importance as heritage. It was at this time that a national movement for their preservation got underway, first spearheaded by the National Footpaths Preservation Society (NFPS), then the CPS (precursor of the present-day Open Spaces Society) and later still the Ramblers' Association. And it is surely significant that there was a close relationship between the campaign for the protection of footpaths and that for the preservation of landscape and open space.[37] This relationship found institutional expression in the merger, in 1899, of the NFPS and the CPS: commons, like footpaths, were the inheritances of the people. And at a local level, many footpath societies were involved with efforts to preserve valued landscapes, as well as the footpaths that traversed them. One example is the campaign launched in 1907 by the Reigate and Redhill Open Spaces and Footpaths Preservation Society to raise funds for the purchase of Colley Hill in Kent, then threatened with housebuilding. A shilling fund was launched, which generated £1,250 from 13,000 donors. Further monies were raised by an historical pageant, which involved a procession of costumed performers along the ancient route of the Pilgrims' Way, on the slope of Colley Hill itself.[38]

Many similar campaigns were waged in the late nineteenth and early twentieth centuries, the successes won indicating a recognition of the heritage value of footpaths and the landscapes to which they gave access. The factual story of

33   Trevelyan, 'Walking', pp. 72–73.
34   Collingwood, *Idea of History*, esp. pp. 282ff.
35   Ibid., p. 247.
36   Macfarlane, *Old Ways*, p. 31.
37   Hinrichs, 'Out for a Walk'.
38   T. Winter (ed.), *The Pilgrims' Pageant, Reigate* ([Reigate]: Reigate and Redhill Open Spaces and Footpaths Preservation Society, 1913), pp. 9–10.

Figure 4.

A Public footpath sign in Derbyshire, England. Photograph by Phil Sangwell. CC BY-2.0.

1. Footpaths in England

state intervention to improve and regulate public access to the countryside is a familiar one and does not need repeating here. Landmarks included the 1949 National Parks and Countryside Act and a long string of access legislation, from the generally ill-regarded 1939 Access to Mountains Act through to the post-war measures of 1981 and 1990, and finally the Countryside and Rights of Way Act of 2000.[39] Public footpaths are now marked on maps, regulated by law and overseen by local government.

II

Many accounts of the story I have just told might stop here. Despite a recent flurry of concern about vanishing footpaths,[40] it is a happy story for those of a liberal mindset. Footpaths, once shut willy-nilly by tyrannical aristocrats, are now regulated by the state, the neat green signs (and green dotted lines on OS maps) making it clear that the walker has a right to be there, to walk the path (see Figure 4). The rambler need not fear the thuggish gamekeeper or irate farmer; her stake in the national domain that the footpath embodies is recognised in law. Footpaths give the English – and I do mean the *English* particularly – a powerful sense of quasi-proprietorial connection to the green and pleasant land of home. They have contributed to ensuring the centrality of the English landscape to mainstream constructions of national identity. This is because it is largely by means of footpaths that the landscape, and the history of which it is constitutive, remains accessible through embodied experience.

In performing this function, footpaths have done conservative cultural work. I don't mean by this that they did so because they supported constructions of national identity in which the countryside loomed large. After all, rural preoccupations of all kinds – from esteeming the art of Constable to agitating for land reform, to allotment gardening, youth hostelling, botanising, hiking, preserving open spaces and footpaths, and very many other things besides – are in no way necessarily indicative of political or cultural conservatism. As the work of David Matless and others has suggested, cultural ruralism – even in its nationalistic iterations – was not antonymous with urban-industrial modernity; it is better seen as a function of this modernity.[41]

What I mean, rather, is that footpaths performed conservative work through

---

39 Shoard, *This Land is Our Land*; Shoard, *Right to Roam*.
40 See e.g., K. Rushby, 'Ramble On: The Fight to Save Forgotten Footpaths', *Guardian*, 7 Aug. 2019; 'Love it. Save It: Don't Lose your Way', https://www.ramblers.org.uk/dontloseyourway (accessed 2 April 2021).
41 Matless, *Landscape and Englishness*; Readman, *Storied Ground*.

providing a popular sense of territorial connection to the landscape – and the continuous national history that was constituted by this landscape and was so important a component of Englishness – without challenging a political-economic system that concentrated actual landownership in the hands of a few. As Henry, Lord Thring, told a CPS meeting in June 1888, while introducing a speech by Octavia Hill,

> Preserve your footpaths … and you convert England into one great park. The poorest man in the land, if the footpaths are preserved, can enjoy as richly the pleasures and the beauty of English scenery as if he were the possessor of the soil.[42]

Thring's use of the hypothetical conditional is important here: 'as if he were the possessor of the soil'; the point is, of course, that he (or she) was not. Footpaths were a key means through which ordinary people established affective ties with the countryside in a context in which, by the 1870s, approximately 75 per cent of the land area of Britain belonged to about 5,000 people, a little over 700 of whom owned one-quarter of England and Wales.[43] Footpaths conferred a sense of possession without the reality of ownership. In the preface to one of his popular walking guidebooks, E.S. Taylor quoted the poet Edwin Arnold to the effect that 'Everyone is a landed proprietor who has enjoyed … those quiet bypaths which reveal delights unknown to rail and road, and reserved only for the pedestrian'.[44] In these and similar publications, the happy memories deriving from such walking excursions were presented as 'precious treasures', as possessions 'which neither moth nor rust doth corrupt, and into which no thief can break through and steal'.[45]

Whether or not this was a good thing depended upon one's ideological perspective. From that of the land nationaliser or communist, it likely was not. But it was a different matter for liberal-radical defenders of footpaths as the poor man's inheritance, or – as Octavia Hill put it – 'the great common inheritances to which as English people they are born'.[46] It is right to view Hill and her CPS comrades as progressives rather than reactionaries.[47] But in common with most people in Britain across the nineteenth and twentieth centuries,

---

42   'Miss Octavia Hill on the Duty of Supporting Footpath Protection Societies'.

43   Cannadine, *Decline and Fall*, pp. 54–56; D. Spring, 'Introduction', to J. Bateman, *The Great Landowners of Great Britain and Ireland* (5th ed., Leicester: Leicester University Press, 1971 [1883]), p. 12.

44   Walker Miles [pseud. E.S. Taylor], *Field Path Rambles (Canterbury and Kent Coast Series)* (London: R.E. Taylor & Son, 1904), p. xii.

45   H. Evans, *The London Rambler and Footpath Guide to the Surrounding Districts* (London: H. Vickers, 1884), p. 87.

46   'Miss Octavia Hill on the Duty of Supporting Footpath Protection Societies'.

47   For readings of Hill as progressive, see Baigent and Cowell, *'Nobler Imaginings'*.

1. Footpaths in England

on the political left as well as the right, they did not support any wholesale redistribution of real property rights, let alone land nationalisation. And since a substantial re-ordering of landed property was seen as practically impossible, even if it were desirable, then the value of footpaths was great indeed. For the liberal Sir Robert Hunter, a leading member of the CPS and a founder of the National Trust, footpaths helped 'make the whole country one open space'.[48]

The merits of footpaths were also apparent to conservatives, for whom the provision of regulated access to land without challenging property rights had considerable appeal. From its foundation in 1884, the NFPS drew support from liberals and radicals, but conservatives too were prominent among its membership.[49] The society's first president, Thomas Taylour, the Earl of Bective, was a Conservative MP, and other scions of landed families served as vice-presidents, their names adorning the society's official letterhead – among them prominent Tory and unionist politicians such as Lord Randolph Churchill, the 4th Earl of Onslow, and the Marquess of Hartington.[50] Its patron was Hugh Lupus Grosvenor, the Duke of Westminster, one of the wealthiest landowners in the country.

Patrician backing for footpath preservation did not go unnoticed. Significantly, it drew the attention of the *Field*, the self-described 'country gentleman's newspaper', which welcomed the foundation of the NFPS as a body that might do much to spread awareness of the law relating to rights-of-way, so obviating controversies that could spill over into disruptive protests.[51] The *Field* was not disappointed in these hopes, writing in 1892 to commend the NFPS for defending public rights while at the same time 'consistently discourage[ing] illegal trespass'. For the paper, proof that 'the landowners of England are not the rapacious personages' radicals presented them as could be found in 'a glance through the list' of the society's 'leading supporters'.[52]

As the *Field* implied, landlord support for footpath preservation was part of a wider effort to rebut the liberal-radical critique of 'landlordism', then gathering pace and driving proposals for land reform as well as mounting hostility to the aristocracy-dominated House of Lords.[53] The blocked footpath was a

---

48 *Proceedings of the General Meeting of the Commons and Footpaths Preservation Society*, 7 May 1913, National Trust Archives 4/1.

49 For a list of early members of the NFPS, see Malchow, *Agitators and Promoters*, p. 252. Of those whose political affiliations can be determined, 29 were Liberal or radical and 22 Conservative or Liberal Unionist; of those members who were also vice-presidents, the equivalent figures were 9 and 13.

50 Examples of such nobility-encrusted stationery can be found in NFPS correspondence, for instance that relating to Lake District footpaths, e.g. Cumbria Record Office, DSO/24/7/3.

51 *Field*, 28 Nov. 1885, 777.

52 *Field*, 12 March 1892, 380.

53 Readman, *Land and Nation*; also Taylor, *Lords of Misrule*.

potent symbol of the pettifogging territorial tyranny of the landed elite, and it was one that had traction with public opinion – especially since footpath closure impinged not only on the pleasures of the ordinary inhabitants of the countryside, but also those of the increasing numbers of largely middle-class tourists for whom the pedestrian excursion was an important holiday activity.

Along with support for the voluntary provision of allotments, agricultural co-operatives and various rural charities,[54] aristocratic and gentry involvement in footpath preservation sprang from a desire to demonstrate that the established socio-economic order conduced to the welfare of ordinary people. It expressed a demotic social conservatism, one that acknowledged a popular stake in the land – and the popular movement heritage of footpaths – while refusing to countenance any significant challenge to the claims of private property. It was, in short, a technology of control; it helped define the bounds of the permissible so far as walking the land was concerned; it made clear who was, and who was not, a trespasser. For its exponents, it implied an assumption of the responsibilities of stewardship, an idea nicely caught in a short story by Rudyard Kipling, which was published in 1909 just as anti-landlord sentiment approached its climax. In the story, a wealthy American couple – George and Sophie – move to England, take up residence in the country, and as Lords of the Manor learn the duties of benevolent paternalism. Strolling over their land one Sunday, the couple fall into conversation:

> 'D'you see that track by Gale Anstey?'
> They looked down from the edge of the hanger over a cup-like hollow. People by twos and threes in their Sunday best filed slowly along the paths that connected farm to farm.
> 'I've never seen so many on our land before,' said Sophie. 'Why is it?'
> 'To show us we mustn't shut up their rights of way.'
> 'Those cow-tracks we've been using cross lots?' said Sophie forcibly.
> 'Yes. Any one of 'em would cost us two thousand pounds each in legal expenses to close.'
> 'But we don't want to,' she said.
> 'The whole community would fight if we did.'
> 'But it's our land. We can do what we like.'
> 'It's not our land. We've only paid for it. We belong to it, and it belongs to the people—our people they call 'em. ...
> They passed slowly from one bracken-dotted field to the next – flushed with pride of ownership, plotting alterations and restorations at each turn.[55]

---

54   For some examples, see W.H. Onslow, 4th Earl of Onslow, *Landlords and Allotments* (London: Longmans & Co., 1886); F. Impey, 'Lord Tollemache, the labourer's lord', *New Review* 9 (Sept. 1893): 299–313; H.A. Russell, 11th Duke of Bedford, *A Great Agricultural Estate* (London: J. Murray, 1897), ch. 7.

55   R. Kipling, 'An Habitation Enforced', in *Actions and Reactions* (New York: Doubleday, Page & Co., 1909), pp. 36–37.

1. Footpaths in England

Kipling wrote this before the First World War, often seen as a decisive moment in the decline of the old rural order, many young heirs meeting bloody ends in the mud of Flanders. Yet, the landed elite survived the war and still survives today: very large territorial estates remain an enduring feature of British economic life.[56] At the time of writing about one-third of the land area of Britain is in aristocratic hands, with 24 dukes alone owning more than four million acres.[57] And indeed, throughout the twentieth and into the twenty-first century, the defenders of the agrarian status quo did not abandon support for the public footpath as a technology of control.

At least until the Second World War, they were assisted in this by the preservationist movement, many of the leading voices in which remained focused on footpaths and open spaces rather than supporting more general rights of access to uncultivated land. The long-serving secretary of the CPS, Sir Lawrence Chubb, was an important figure here. Chubb distanced the CPS from the Kinder Scout trespassers, publishing a letter condemning them in the *Field*; privately, he told the Secretary of the Ramblers' Association that the arrested hikers deserved prosecution.[58] Chubb's influence was also a key factor behind the limited nature of the 1939 Access to Mountains Act, which – had it come into force – would have restricted access rights to tightly defined areas.[59]

The 1939 Act was nevertheless a landmark of sorts, pointing the way for more substantial state intervention in the regulation of recreational land use – not least the creation of National Parks.[60] But while the agency of the state did certainly work to improve public access to the countryside, it was also a means through which this access could be regulated. For all that they tended towards politically conservative views, farmers and landowners were not averse to state intervention to achieve this. If pedestrian recreation in the countryside was a modern phenomenon, the expression of a modern (and largely urban) national culture, their instinct was to impose order on this modernity. If the hordes of hikers from the towns could not be prevented from exploring rural England, their activities could at least be disciplined. In a 1938 article on 'The Trespassing Public', the *Field* expressed this point of view in urging that footpaths be made more visible, not least by the provision of local authority-supplied signposting. This would 'do a very real service to landowners in ensuring that at least

---

56   Christophers, *New Enclosure*; Shrubsole, *Who Owns England?*
57   Hayes, *Book of Trespass*, p. 218.
58   Hill, *Freedom to Roam*, p. 77.
59   Stephenson, *Forbidden Land*, pp. 165–81.
60   Sheail, 'Access to Mountains Act 1939'.

the public enter their land on the correct paths ... Each footpath ... should be signposted at all junctions from end to end. Each branch from the public path should be marked private. A notice should be erected in woods where there are pheasants that game is preserved...'. The message was clear: through such measures, the property rights of landowners might more effectually be protected, since any trespassing that did then occur would be done knowingly and so could be dealt with by the full 'severity' of the law.[61]

If anything, in fact, the apparatus of the modern state made the footpath more potent as a means of shoring up the claims of property. Some powers over footpaths had been granted to parish councils, which had been created in 1894. But local authority control over their creation, maintenance and regulation was greatly extended by the 1949 National Parks and Countryside Act, under the provisions of which county councils were instructed to oversee surveys of all footpaths and bridleways under their jurisdictions, determine which of these were rights-of-way, and mark them on official 'definitive' maps. Given the significant presence of landowners in rural local government, this was not a process that involved any revolutionary extension of the people's rights.[62] The determination of paths as rights-of-way was largely intuitive, and subject to landowner influence; and those paths that were defined as rights-of-way in turn defined the limits of public rights over the land, restricting future opportunities for challenge. *Country Life* understood this well, welcoming the measure as 'a sort of Domesday Book of Rights of Way'.[63] For such commentators, the definition of what was and what was not a right-of-way would help ensure property rights were respected. It was in this spirit that the same magazine welcomed the publication of the first OS map to show county-council mandated footpaths in May 1960: the document, it felt, would 'deprive some people of an excuse to trespass'.[64]

Indeed, the utility of publicly defined footpaths in this respect explains the dissatisfaction expressed by landowner and farming opinion at the slow rate of progress in the creation of the maps. In truth, the delays were primarily a function of practical difficulties: determining rights-of-way imposed considerable administrative burdens on often under-resourced local authorities. But this did not prevent both *Country Life* and the *Field* from voicing concern about the apparent tardiness of local authorities in discharging their statutory duty, the latter complaining in one 1961 editorial that only 22 of 61 counties

---

61   R. Davey, 'The Trespassing Public', *Field*, 24 Sept. 1938, 732.
62   Shoard, *This Land is Our Land*, pp. 271–73.
63   'Rural Footpaths', *Country Life*, 29 April 1949, 978.
64   'Footpaths on the Map', *Country Life*, 26 May 1960, 1172.

1. Footpaths in England

had prepared definitive maps.[65] This, the paper made clear, did not serve the landowner any more than it did the rambler, since it rendered less legible the behavioural 'conventions' to which the 'desire for healthy recreation' ought to be subject. Local authority-sanctioned rights-of-way defined the parameters of this recreation, preventing it from overstepping its proper bounds: 'To the extent that the establishment of well-defined footpaths regulates the behaviour of visitors, they are an inducement to respect the farmer's land'.[66]

This understanding of the use-value of footpaths persisted into the late twentieth century. Of course, there remained landowners and farmers who closed or deliberately neglected paths that tracked across their land. But the typical landowner was not brusquely heedless of statutory public rights over his property. He (or less frequently she) did not need to be. And he did not need to be because these rights – as embodied in footpaths – were limited by those same footpaths. Hence, by the 1970s, we have the spectacle of *Country Life* reporting on efforts by farmers and landowners to maintain footpaths, preventing them from becoming overgrown and clearing them of debris. As an editorial in January 1971 saw it, well-looked-after footpaths protected the landowners' proprietorial interests: 'The weekend invaders from the towns are bound to go somewhere, so it is in everyone's interest that they should walk on designated footpaths rather than over crops or among livestock. The wise landowner will regard footpath clearance not as a nuisance but as an activity to be encouraged'.[67] To an extent, it was ever thus. More than a hundred years earlier, the American radical Elihu Burrit, in his *Walk from London to John O'Groats*, had noted how many footpaths in England crossed cultivated fields. But 'so far from obstructing them', the farmer 'finds it good policy to straighten and round them up, and supply them with convenient gates or stiles, so that no one shall have an excuse for trampling on his crops, or for diverging into the open field for a shorter cut to the main road'.[68]

III

A generalised right of access to land remains elusive: the Countryside and Rights of Way Act 2000 applied to just ten per cent of England and Wales.[69]

---

65   'Footpaths and their Proper Uses', *Field*, 19 Jan. 1961, 101.

66   Ibid.

67   'Footpath Explosion?', *Country Life*, 28 Jan. 1971, 170.

68   E. Burritt, *A Walk from London to John O'Groats* (2nd ed., London: Sampson Low, Son, & Marston, 1864), pp. 9–10.

69   Shrubsole, *Who Owns England?*, p. 288.

Public rights over rural land thus remain to a significant extent confined to and defined by public footpaths. As I have argued, these footpaths constitute an important element of British movement heritage, providing embodied connection to history as congealed in the landscape. They have supported an enduring sense of rural Englishness in a country whose population has long been concentrated in urban areas. But while this Englishness is popular, of the people, the language of patriotism that underpins it is a conservative demotic – conservative with a small if not necessarily a large 'C'. And it is conservative not least because of the support it gives to an inherited political economy of astonishing inequality insofar as the distribution of real property is concerned. Public footpaths are compatible with this system of inequality. Now regulated by the state rather than subject to the discretion of paternalist landlords, they are consistent with a liberal-capitalist order that the heads of still-mighty aristocratic families, rich businessmen and faceless corporations find equally congenial. As Nick Hayes has written, 'Every pathway that is secured by law further strengthens the fence between us and the land either side of it', the legally protected footpath being 'a causeway of legitimacy while all around the land has been washed away into a sea of private ownership'.[70]

One response, of course, is to trespass, and it is the one advocated by Hayes in his stimulating recent book. He gives plenty of examples from his own experience. One woodland encounter with 'wild-eyed and unpredictable' red deer is the kind of thing he feels 'is only available off the path … I would swap a hundred nice walks along a pretty Right of Way for this one moment of magic'.[71] On another occasion, having escaped the confines of the 'Wilderness' music festival to 'roam free through the ancient Wychwood, dabbing at a small bag of MDMA', he and his trespassing friends climb a fallen tree to loll about like tactile, loved-up big cats in its branches. Revelling in his transgressive idleness, Hayes muses that 'This is what Octavia Hill was talking about when she wanted to turn the cemeteries and waste ground of inner-city London into "open-aired sitting room" – very simply: to be at home in nature'.[72]

Octavia Hill – who was nothing if not strait-laced – probably would have disapproved of the behaviour of Hayes and his pals. But that her example can now be invoked in support of a radical position – albeit one riffing on an Ecstasy-fuelled reverie – is suggestive. Hill may not have endorsed trespass, but many other nineteenth-century advocates of rural walking certainly did

---

70 Hayes, *Book of Trespass*, pp. 90, 91.
71 Ibid., pp. 81–82.
72 Ibid., pp. 296, 297.

1. Footpaths in England

and, in a sense, Hayes is following in their footsteps. Leslie Stephen's Sunday Tramps used habitually to indulge in what Stephen called 'a little trespassing' in their walks in the countryside around London.[73] If challenged by gamekeepers, they would repeat in unison a formula devised by one of their members, the eminent jurist Sir Frederick Pollock: 'We hereby give you notice that we do not, nor doth any of us, claim any right of way or other easement into or over these lands and we tender you this shilling by way of amends'. As *The Times* reported, when chanted by the assembled politicians, men of letters, artists and other assorted members of the intellectual aristocracy that comprised the Tramps, 'the effect on the gamekeeper must have been devastating'.[74]

Most of us, however, have not the cultural capital or social status of Leslie Stephen and his Sunday Tramps; we lack the resources to project such confidence in a gamekeeperly direction. Neither, alas, are we all possessed of the assertive righteousness of a Nick Hayes. We shy from confrontation with authority; we don't want to break the law and face prosecution, by so doing risking our jobs and livelihoods. Although the penalties for transgression were far greater for him than for us, our perspective retains some affinity with that of John Clare in the 1830s:

> I dreaded walking where there was no path
> And prest with cautious tread the meadow swath,
> And always turned to look with wary eye,
> And always feared the farmer coming by;
> Yet everything about where I had gone
> Appeared so beautiful, I ventured on;
> And when I gained the road where all are free
> I fancied every stranger frowned at me,
> And every kinder look appeared to say,
> 'You've been on trespass in your walk today.'[75]

Prey to such sentiments as these, most English people tend to keep to the path, the modern-day legal status of which hardens the line between public and private. In doing so they pay homage both to the genuinely popular movement heritage that footpaths embody, while also acknowledging – and implicitly accepting – the limited extent of their inheritance in the land.

---

73   L. Stephen, 'In Praise of Walking', *Monthly Review* 4 (Aug. 1901), 98–114, at 111.
74   'The Sunday Tramps', *The Times*, 18 July 1930, 11.
75   J. Clare, 'I dreaded walking where there was no path' (c. 1832–37).

Acknowledgements

The research presented here draws on work undertaken as part of my involvement in the AHRC research network, 'Changing Landscapes, Changing Lives' (AH/T006110/1); I am grateful to the AHRC for their support.

Bibliography of secondary sources

Baigent, E. and B. Cowell (eds)., *'Nobler Imaginings and Mightier Struggles': Octavia Hill, Social Activism, and the Remaking of British Society* (London: Institute of Historical Research, 2016).

Cannadine, D., *The Decline and Fall of the British Aristocracy* (New Haven & London: Yale University Press, 1992).

Christophers, B., *The New Enclosure* (London: Verso, 2018).

Collingwood, R.G., *The Idea of History* (Oxford: Oxford University Press, 1946).

Gange, D., 'Retracing Trevelyan? Historical Practice and the Archive of the Feet', *Green Letters* **21** (2017): 246–61.

Hayes, N., *The Book of Trespass* (London: Bloomsbury, 2020).

Hey, D., 'Kinder Scout and the Legend of the Mass Trespass', *Agricultural History Review* **59** (2011): 199–216.

Hill, H., *Freedom to Roam* (Ashbourne: Moorland, 1980).

Hinrichs, J. 'Out for a Walk: Pedestrian Practices and British Preservationism, c.1850–1950', Unpublished Ph.D. dissertation, University of St Andrews, 2020.

Ingold, T., *The Perception of the Environment* (London: Routledge, 2000).

Kilby, S., *Peasant Perspectives on the Medieval Landscape* (Hatfield: University of Hertfordshire Press, 2020).

Macfarlane, R., *The Old Ways* (London: Hamish Hamilton, 2012).

Malchow, H. LeRoy, *Agitators and Promoters in the Age of Gladstone and Disraeli* (New York and London: Garland, 1983).

Marsh, J., *Back to the Land: The Pastoral Impulse in England, from 1880 to 1914* (London: Quartet, 1982).

Matless, D., *Landscape and Englishness* (2nd ed., London: Reaktion, 2016).

Neeson, J.M., *Commoners: Common Right, Enclosure and Social Change in England, 1700–1820* (Cambridge: Cambridge University Press, 1993.

Newland, P. (ed.), *British Rural Landscapes on Film* (Manchester: Manchester University Press, 2016).

Readman, P., *Land and Nation in England: Patriotism, National Identity and the Politics of Land 1880–1914* (Woodbridge: Boydell & Brewer, 2008).

Readman, P., *Storied Ground: Landscape and the Shaping of English National Identity* (Cambridge: Cambridge University Press, 2018).

Sheail, J., 'The Access to Mountains Act 1939: An Essay in Compromise', *Rural History* **21** (2010): 59–74.

Shoard, M., *A Right to Roam* (Oxford: Oxford University Press, 1999).

1. Footpaths in England

Shoard, M., *This Land is Our Land* (London: Paladin, 1997 [1987]).

Shrubsole, G., *Who Owns England?* (London: William Collins, 2019).

Sissons, D. et al., *Clarion Call: Sheffield's Access Pioneers* (Sheffield: Northend Creative Print Solutions, 2017).

Southern, R.W., 'Sir Maurice Powicke 1879–1963', *Proceedings of the British Academy* **50** (1964): 275–304.

Stephenson, T., *Forbidden Land* (Manchester: Manchester University Press, 1989).

Taplin, K., *The English Path* (2nd ed., Sudbury: Perry Green, 2000 [1979]).

Taylor, A., *The Lords of Misrule: Hostility to Aristocracy in Late Nineteenth and Early Twentieth Century Britain* (Basingstoke: Palgrave Macmillan, 2004).

Taylor, H., *A Claim on the Countryside* (Edinburgh: Edinburgh University Press, 1997).

Thompson, S., 'The Fashioning of a New World: Youth Culture and the Origins of the Mass Outdoor Movement in Interwar Britain', unpublished Ph.D. dissertation, King's College London, 2018.

Wallace, A.D., *Walking, Literature, and English Culture* (Oxford: Clarendon, 1994).

Webb., S. and B. Webb, *English Local Government: The Story of the King's Highway* (London: Longmans, Green & Co., 1913).

Whyte, W., 'Sunday Tramps (act. 1879–1895)', *Oxford Dictionary of National Biography* (Oxford: Oxford University Press, 2007).

CHAPTER 2.

DELINEATING THE LANDSCAPE: PLANNING, MAPPING AND THE HISTORIC IMAGININGS OF RIGHTS OF WAY IN TWENTIETH-CENTURY ENGLAND AND WALES

Clare Hickman and Glen O'Hara

Introduction

The interlinked network of rights of way that crisscross the English and Welsh landscape perhaps appear at first glance to be ahistorical elements of near-invisible infrastructure, or even just simple means of transit. As Timothy Earle has argued in his work on how different routes move through many distinct terrains, they 'capture the different ways that movement is significant and becomes etched in the landscape'.[1] Their perceived antiquity and course following natural contours of the land perhaps adds to this impression. This is reflected in much of the scholarly literature, where the focus is often less on what is underfoot than on the experience of movement by walkers and others, including the way in which trails allow human and nonhuman animals to connect with the surrounding landscape. In this, the literature perhaps reflects historiographical trends overall, summing up the workaday nature of most human experience as 'the everyday', permitted and underpinned by little-noticed but commonplace systems. Recent work including Joe Moran's 2009 book *On Roads*, or Matthew Gandy's 2014 volume *The Fabric of Space* on water geographies, are just two examples.[2]

It can be very easy, given these trends, to emphasise transitory human experience, not the interaction between people and physical space. The extreme age of many paths on the one hand, and very brief experiences of moment-by-moment walking on the other, can lead to a condition Marcus Colla has recently framed as 'presentism' – a 'dissolution of both ... temporal and spatial coordinates'.[3] There are however notable exceptions to this 'presentism' in terms of pathmaking

---

1   Earle, 'Routes', p. 269.
2   Moran, *Roads*; Gandy, *Fabric*.
3   Colla, 'Spectre', esp. 124–25.

2. Delineating the Landscape

history, which includes recent work by Spooner and collaborators on rights of way in Norfolk from the 1930s onwards.[4] In some historical works, it therefore becomes clear that tracks themselves are inherently historical features that have always been named, characterised and sorted into different types by humans, as well as actually being created via movement. More ancient examples have been created by generations of human and nonhuman animal movement, but the important point is deep historicity of all paths – and the role of human language, understanding and imagination as key parts of their very existence.[5] What is also required, therefore, is research that focuses on the interaction between humans and the landscape, not on either the immediate experience of following trails or the perceived 'deep history' of some long-lasting paths. Such work could bring out the impermanence and contingency of how we understand movement in the landscape. As Earle has also argued: 'paths ... should be considered no more permanent than the patterns of household movements ... paths, trails, and roads are the physical imprint of repeated economic and sociopolitical interaction'.[6]

Such an emphasis on the human use of space can take us in new directions, away from the more common heroic stories of time-hallowed trails or long-distance treks, and towards men's and women's movement in quite humdrum settings that still might be thought of as simply 'everyday'. In many and often literally 'edgelands' between and within urban and suburban areas, the most obvious paths have usually been – and still are – 'lines of desire' crisscrossing planned spaces, in defiance of their designers' wishes. The poets Paul Farley and Michael Symmons Roberts have recognised these 'as the kinds of paths that begin over time, imperceptibly, gathering definition as people slowly recognise and legitimise the footfall of their peers'. They can become ubiquitous in newly planned spaces such as Britain's New Towns or Green Belt: but they can also be 'as old as the earlier transhumance, as the first drovers and movers of livestock, or even older'.[7]

In order to explore how different histories are mobilised in the often 'ordinary' spaces between grand narratives and individual experiences, this chapter attempts to uncover how rights of way were understood and delineated. As a secondary and more specific aim, it will furthermore consider the various ways in which 'historical' narratives have been assembled as part of the attempts to pin down rights of way in an authoritative series of county maps serving post-war England and Wales. Despite paths and other tracks often moving in response

---

4 Gregory and Spooner, 'Public Rights of Way and Countryside Access in Norfolk 1880–1960'.
5 Bates, 'Track Making', 21–28.
6 Earle, 'Routes', 255.
7 Farley and Roberts, *Edgelands*, p. 24.

to changing needs, desires, economic circumstances and landowners' behaviour, the twentieth and early twenty-first centuries have witnessed an ongoing attempt to create definitive legal maps in order to preserve these etched lines of access running across the countryside. The 1949 National Parks and Access to the Countryside Act is only one, and perhaps the most famous, statutory example of these efforts. However, the 1932 Rights of Way Act replicated and permitted the continuance of a complex process of local negotiation under which any route could be defined as a public path if the public could show twenty years of use, though landowners could challenge that length of use and the onus was on path users to prove it.[8]

'History' is, therefore, not only found in the creation of the physical track: it is also embedded in how these are legally represented and conceived. As Natural England commented in 2008, 'there is a legal principle, "Once a highway, always a highway". All public Rights of Way are highways, so that once a right of way exists it remains in existence unless and until it is lawfully closed or diverted.'[9] This legal principle however brings with it other issues, particularly the status of rights of way that have fallen into disuse or dispute. This was evident at the start of the post-war period, as in the Hobhouse Report of 1947 (the report that paved the way towards the 1949 Act) which already argued that 'in spite of the maxim "once a highway, always a highway" it is a fact that a very large number of rights of way are being lost through disuse'.[10]

Based on the recommendations in the Hobhouse Report, the 1949 Act required 'the council of every county in England or Wales … not later than the expiration of three years after [the commencement of the Act] … [to] prepare a draft map of their area'.[11] These would be marked on draft maps which could be challenged, and then captured as Rights of Way which could either be given protection or extinguished from the record. As Lewis Silkin, Minister for Town and Country Planning in 1949, noted when bringing the Bill before parliament, 'it requires the county councils to make a survey of existing rights of way within three years. It requires that, wherever possible, the district councils and parish councils should be used in making this survey … District councils and the parishes would have a much more detailed knowledge of the existing rights of way than a county council.'[12]

---

8   Hodson, 'Ordnance Survey', 105–07; Feldman, 'Property', 39.
9   Natural England, *Guide*, p. 2.
10 Cmnd. 7207, *Report of the Special Committee*; see Cullingworth and Nadin, *Planning*, pp. 272–73.
11 Geo. 6 Ch. 49, National Parks and Access to the Countryside Act 1949 (27) (1), https://www.legislation.gov.uk/ukpga/Geo6/12-13-14/97/enacted (accessed 23 March 2021).
12 *House of Commons Debates*, vol. 463, cols. 1461–568, Debate on the National Parks and Access to the Countryside Bill, 31 March 1949.

2. Delineating the Landscape

English and Welsh local government had, however, nowhere near the capacity or organisation to conduct this work even as their other duties grew very quickly between the late 1940s and the later 1960s, and indeed the Labour government of 1945–51 had been riven with debate over how to reform it.[13] Both countries were divided into a patchwork quilt of hundreds of overlapping jurisdictions: in the 1960s, England for instance was divided into 79 county boroughs, 49 counties and 1,086 county districts.[14] Parish councils numbered 11,175 in 1951, before a wave of mergers saw parish councils' number fall to under 10,000 in 1960.[15]

Throughout the second half of the twentieth century, the attempt to draw up a definitive map of English and Welsh rights of way did therefore make the relationship between historic use and present rights of access more evident. The Ramblers Association, then as now a powerful organisation with a large membership and strong contacts in organised politics, mobilised the concept of historical use in their argument for what constituted a right of way in relation to the legal process of mapping. This was quickly embedded in advice developed by them and their allies.[16] As the Ramblers put it at the time, stressing minor and routine paths in a way strikingly similar to the recent literature on this question:

> Paths which were originally used only by farm or estate workers, and were known as accommodation paths, are said to have been wrongly included on the county council maps. The truth is that a track which originated as an accommodation path may, with lapse of time, have become a legal right of way. Thus, a path could have started, perhaps two hundred years ago, as leading from a farm to a village; later a second path from the same farm might be trodden to another village. Both paths were originally accommodation paths, but farmers were not likely to object to people using them as a link between the two villages. Eventually, the path could have been used by the public for a sufficiently long time without interruption for it to have been established as a public right of way. In that event, irrespective of the origin of the path, it was the duty of the county council to record it on their map.[17]

The most important element determining inclusion of routes on the map was their actual use. Therefore, if a right of way needed to be defended, the debate

---

13 Chandler, *Local Government*, e.g., pp. 170–78.
14 Cmnd. 4040, *Royal Commission*, p. 2, ft. 1; Local Government Information Unit, 'Local Government Facts and Figures: England', https://lgiu.org/local-government-facts-and-figures-england/ (accessed 6 March 2021).
15 Poole and Keith-Lucas, *Parish Government*, p. 189. We are grateful to Justin Grigg, of the National Association of Local Councils, for this information.
16 'Notes of Guidance for Honorary Path Advocates' as sent out from CROW in 1952/3, Museum of English Rural Life, Reading, Berkshire (hereafter MERL), SRC CROWC/B.
17 Ramblers Association, *Footpaths*, MERL, SR CPRE C/1/131/1.

centred on who was currently using it, as well as on who might be using it in the future – with witnesses defending paths on both grounds in local cases.

The work of the Central Rights of Way Committee set up in 1950 (in part to monitor the 1949 legislation) shows how a renewed emphasis on historical use meant that different forms of imagining the past – historically-informed ways of making meaning – came to the fore. In this analysis, we adopt a three-fold typology: history in the law, embodied in the making and the practice of the 1932 and 1949 Acts; history as constant negotiation and grassroots controversy under those Acts, most obviously in terms of local footpaths and bridleways used for such supposedly prosaic activities as dog walking, horse-riding or going to the shops; and, third and last, a 'constructed history' of large-scale narratives which attempted to boost tourism, ideas of amenity and the use of access as leisure.

History and the law

In the period before the 1949 Act, cases and redress in the courts were the main method of making decisions about access to the land. In this respect, the construction of English and Welsh rights of way resembled Victorian and Edwardian attitudes to pollution, whether of the air or of rivers and estuaries: so-called 'riparian rights', to receive but also not to interfere with clean air or water, could be built up and tested on a case-by-case basis.[18] Similarly, although landowners could not simply treat rights of way as they pleased, their legal responsibility was to the local users of paths or byways – not to a general 'right' of access. What is notable, and perhaps surprising, is the initially small role longer-term history played in conflicts over rights of way. The law at this time understood 'historic' access as describing access in the previous twenty to forty years, not the deep past. It is an interesting reflection on an era during which Prime Minister Stanley Baldwin's emphasis was on the deep-seated nature of 'Englishness' rooted in long occupation of the land.[19]

The use of a set length of time that paths had been commonly traversed in order to create rights to general use – such as the twenty to forty years stipulation of the 1932 Act – went back to nineteenth century legislation. Sir Lawrence Chubb, Secretary of the Commons, Open Spaces and Footpaths Preservation Society, appealed directly to the precedent of the 1832 Prescription Act in order to justify the Rights of Way Act in the early 1930s. Chubb made clear that types of oral history had to play a role here:

18   See e.g. Rosenthal, *River Pollution*, pp. 35–38.
19   Daunton, *Wealth*, p. 66.

2. Delineating the Landscape

> Hitherto there has existed no simple rule on this point for the guidance of local authorities or landowners, and litigation with regard to disputed rights of way tended to become ever more complicated and expensive as well as more uncertain in its results. It was essential, for instance, to bring to Court the oldest men and women of the district, regardless of the fact that the ordeal of a long and trying examination might prove detrimental to their health. That will not be necessary in the future, because in normal circumstances the evidence need not go back further than about 20 or 40 years.[20]

There was however an obvious potential tension between what individuals might say about a path and its designation on any extant maps, or what we might call a distinction between history 'in use' and in documentation. It was these contradictions that the 1932 Act was designed to some extent to simplify, though it was obviously not thought to be enormously successful, given the passing of the 1939 Access to Mountains Act – though the latter never came into force, superseded in its turn by the 1949 Act. As Chubb also made clear, in guidance prepared for members of his Society at the time of the 1932 Act and reissued in 1938, anyone seeking access to a path on a map that had been created by custom had, if challenged, to prove that a path had at some point been 'dedicated' as a public right of way. This remained the case even if 'their antiquity and utility are often testified to by references in the Court Rolls of a Manor or by the Tithe map or by even earlier maps and records'.[21]

The role of maps was also altered by mid-century legislation, as were the types of map acceptable as historical evidence. As Chubb discussed when he advised his members about 'Maps as Evidence', 'very strict rules' had previously applied to such documentation: 'Maps or records (such as Inclosure Awards) prepared under express statutory authority have always been admissible', while in legal decisions such as the 1914 Folkestone vs Brockman case before the House of Lords, tithe maps and awards were also permissible.[22] But none of the best modern maps, such as the work of Ordnance Survey, were allowed: a situation that the 1932 Act rectified.[23] Even so, these reforms did not make the problems of delineating paths from either oral or cartographic evidence go away. Such issues were still a problem according to the Ramblers in the 1960s, and

---

20   From Chubb, 'History', p. 3. Available at https://www.ramblers.org.uk/-/media/Resources/Public%20resources/Blue%20Book%20Extra/BBR05%20Definitive%20maps%20historical%20at%2020130731.ashx (accessed 29 July 2021).

21   Chubb, 'History', p. 5; Geo. 5 Ch. 45, 'Rights of Way Act 1932' (3) https://www.legislation.gov.uk/ukpga/1932/45/pdfs/ukpga_19320045_en.pdf (Accessed 8 March 2021).

22   For a case study on the use of both enclosure awards and tithe records, see Breen, 'Public or private?', 56-8.

23   Chubb, 'History', p.22; Geo. 5 Ch. 45, 'Rights of Way Act 1932' (3), https://www.legislation.gov.uk/ukpga/1932/45/pdfs/ukpga_19320045_en.pdf (Accessed 8 March 2021).

they discussed these difficulties at the time in the context of evidence needed for footpath claims not on any of the draft maps – of which 5,000 had been submitted. Some claims were accepted without question, but many had to go to hearings held by persons appointed by county councils: 'local people, who would declare in private that there was a right of way, could seldom be persuaded to appear as witnesses. Inclosure awards, tithe maps and old guidebooks had to be combed for supporting evidence.'[24]

In their published reaction to the Government's 1966 White Paper, *Leisure in the Countryside*, the Ramblers invoked one judgement which ignored historical evidence even though the landowner had not contested the existence of a path on their land: Caernarvon Council, for instance, refused to add a right of way over the Carneddau mountains. The Welsh Office also dismissed the claim, even though there was evidence in favour from *The Gossiping Guide to Wales* published in 1882, as well as Aber Parish council's claim that the path had been in uninterrupted use for fifty years. Even historical evidence used commonly by the Ramblers was in many cases not given weight. Rather, because the landowner might have objected had they known about this access, the Minister felt obliged to uphold Caernarvon Council's decision.[25] Maps, paths and access were all in flux, and were still slanted towards landowners' property rights in the present rather than historical rights, regardless of whether those rights were contained in maps or oral testimony.

The passing of the 1949 Act, and in reaction the creation of the CROW Committee by the Open Spaces Society and the Ramblers, was supposed to change this piecemeal 'system' (or lack of it) fundamentally. As CROW's 1957 Report put it:

> The Central Rights of Way Committee was set up in 1950 to keep a watch on the progress of the Survey of Public Rights of Way ... to advise local authorities and societies on the value of evidence in support of claims of public rights of way; to assist in the presentation of claims; and to negotiate with County Councils and the Ministry of Housing and Local Government on general points of importance arising from the operation of the Survey Provisions of the Act.[26]

The Committee's importance and perceived utility grew as attempts to settle the survey proved more difficult than the Government had imagined.

Much of CROW's work involved attempts to codify how and when rights of way should be defended, and the legal use of both oral and documentary

---

24   RA, *Footpaths*, MERL, SR CPRE C/1/131/1.
25   Ibid.
26   Central Rights of Way Committee, 'Report on the Committee's Work in 1957', MERL, SR CPRE C/1/131/1.

2. Delineating the Landscape

evidence. For example, in the 1950s they called for people to act as 'Honorary Path Advocates'. They envisaged that the ideal person for this role was 'someone with either some local knowledge or experience of rights of way, and presumably retired or with sufficient leisure to undertake such investigations'. By 1953 they had received 83 offers from people willing to take up the role and those who showed interest were sent notes of guidance on what the position entailed. From these we can see how witnesses would be used to challenge legal arguments for the exclusion of select rights of way, as well as check over the draft maps for accuracy. One of the key elements, as well as visiting the right of way itself and understanding the history of the path, was the collection of oral testimonies. As the guidance stated: 'investigation will almost certainly involve visiting the locality and questioning some of the oldest inhabitants, agricultural workers, the Clerk of the Parish Council, possibly the vicar, and in some cases, landowners...'[27]

This idea of witness testimony became further codified and developed when in 1965 CROW considered draft notes for non-expert representatives at public enquiries. This guidance was aimed at resisting the extinguishment and diversion of public paths instituted under the 1959 Highways Act (containing a 28-day period for objections, after which the Minister might call a public enquiry). If this did happen, path advocates were advised to walk the path and note its features, but also select witnesses for the hearing with care. The notes recommended calling on six or seven witnesses and stated that 'the very best type of witness is someone who uses the path regularly to go to work or take children to school'. They went on to say: 'do not forget that if a school is near, children who go by themselves can often be very good witnesses and if, as is sometimes the case these days, part of the alternative route involves walking along a busy vehicular road, this can be strong evidence in favour of keeping the path'. Elsewhere, the strong influence of agriculture was still evident. The notes stated that local authorities were likely to call farm owners and farmworkers: 'it would be useful to ask a farm labourer who has testified that he's only seen four people on the path in five years, what hours he works'.[28]

History as local negotiation

Despite CROW's work, and the efforts of its constituent parts, the three years that Silkin had imagined would be enough for the definitive map had, by 1957,

---

27 Letter from R.V. Vernede, Honorary Secretary of CROW to A.J. Drake, Hon Sec of the R.A. North Gloucestershire Committee, 24 Feb. 1953, MERL, SR 2CROWC/B.

28 CROW minutes, 6 Jan. 1965, Appendix B on Extinguishment and Diversion of Public Paths, MERL, SR CPRE C/1/49/130.

proved hugely inadequate. As that year's CROW report continues:

> It was thought, at the time when the Committee was set up, that the Survey would take three years; it will be seen from ... this report how far the estimate has fallen short of the time actually taken. The practical problems arising throughout the country have been so unexpected and so varied that the work undertaken by the Committee in 1957 has reached proportions which could never have been expected in 1950, bearing in mind the fact that it is now five years since the estimated date for the completion of the Survey.[29]

Those 'practical problems' were manifold and demonstrated how the reality of a system now based more squarely on national legislation still relied – perhaps necessarily – on the historicity of paths. One difficulty was the amount of time spent conducting hearings, which might again reduce the historical usefulness of any evidence by the sheer passage of time. By this stage in the mapping process, Kent had only conducted half of its hearings, so there was a fear expressed by CROW that 'when published, Kent's Definitive Map will be at least ten years out of date: the Committee therefore feels that many paths shown on the map are likely to be closed or diverted'. The use and status of maps also continued to be deeply contested. In Somerset, delays were also used by some unscrupulous farmers and other landowners physically to block such rights of way.[30]

There was also the issue of change of use over time, both in terms of where the path itself now ran on the ground and as regards what access was possible in any year or season. In 1953, the Clerk to Cheltenham Rural District Council wrote to CROW to complain that 'the maps have been marked to show footpaths which, though probably in use as public rights of way for a long time ... in fact are not now physically in existence'. The example he gave was of a footpath marked on the map which took its route across the lawn and vegetable garden belonging to a house built fifty years before. Cheltenham's clerk therefore argued that 'the path across this route has not been usable for about 50 years, because when the house was erected and the grounds laid out, fences, walls and the cultivated garden created obstructions of which apparently no notice has ever been taken'. He continued by pointing out that people had been using a diverted route without any issues, and then asked CROW to take account of these cases.[31]

Overall, less had changed under the 1949 Act than its advocates and makers had intended. 'History' was still constantly evoked, but still remained simply

---

29 Central Rights of Way Committee, 'Report on the Committee's Work in 1957', MERL SR CPRE C/1/131/1.
30 Appendix A: Report (for CROW meeting, 6 Jan. 1965?), MERL SR CPRE C/1/49/130.
31 Letter from W.A.G. Acocks, Clerk, Cheltenham Rural District Council to CROW, 10 Jan. 1953, MERL, SR 2 CROWC/B.

2. Delineating the Landscape

one element deployed among many in a series of local debates and conflicts. At the 1975 Annual General Meeting of the Commons, Open Spaces and Footpath Preservation Society, one motion for debate (though covering roads, and not paths) still ran thus: 'that this Society do encourage all those who are concerned with Reclassification of RUPPs ["Roads Used as Public Paths"] to consider the long term objective of conserving the character of the countryside and protecting age-old carriageways, cart tracks and green lanes from plough and bulldozer, by seeking in such cases byway status…'[32] 'History' was being evoked here in a preservationist frame, to defend and protect those characteristics of the landscape which were thought to contain or embody the past.

Many paths had been preserved by appeal to longstanding use or physical existence, but many had not. This was to some extent due to the very different situations reflected in battles over, and ideas about, each right of way in turn. Here there was very little administrative infrastructure to guide local decision-makers, and strategic planning remained virtually impossible. The highly localised governance of whole swathes of the country involved not just parish councils, but fissiparous and powerful land management organisations such as the armed forces, the highways authorities and River or Drainage Boards.[33] Most footpaths always felt 'owned', not by large-scale representative groups, but by local people and their memories.[34] In this sense, the rise and ubiquity of maintained, formal trails can be exaggerated. Paths were still usually workaday links between determinedly 'normal' activities, rather than sites of leisure and commemoration – but they usually (and organically) still generated historical meanings.

Constructed history and long-distance trails

The idea of long-distance trails was included in the 1949 Act, which argued that 'the public should be enabled to make extensive journeys on foot or on horseback along a particular route'. The National Parks Commission was granted very wide powers of discretion not only to advise on the condition and upgrading of existing routes so as to make something longer by joining them together, but to create new routes, and even to advise about ferries, accommodation and food along the way. The first category of recommendations listed was the 'maintenance and improvement of existing paths' – foreshadowing

---

32 Commons, Open Spaces and Footpath Preservation Society AGM Minutes, 14 June 1975, MERL SR2CROWC/A/2.
33 O'Hara, *Water*, e.g. pp. 66–67, 89.
34 On 'ordinary' walking, see e.g. Lorimer, 'Walking', 20–21.

many years of joining together sequential rights of way so that they made up a single route with one identity.[35] From the 1960s and 1970s onwards, as they became established, those conscious 'ways' often became planned and managed sites of leisure, heavily signposted and interpreted heritage trails which saw walkers strongly governed and directed. The sense of place involved was often flattened and homogenised – in terms of the Pennine Way, for instance (completed in 1965), or the South West Coast Path (finished in 1978), both of which passed through areas with their own very distinct identities not captured by the phrases 'the Pennines' or 'the South West'.[36]

As such, many of these long-distance routes are part of the highly commodified tourist culture of the post-Fordist economy: an entire industry exists to attract walkers to these routes, and to assist them while they are there. Numerous glossy guidebooks tell consumers about exactly that handful of 'great walks' they should take before they die.[37] A whole industry of trail guides has hugely expanded the colour, coverage and detail of the National Trails that have been constructed since the 1960s (though walking guides themselves can be dated well back into the nineteenth century). These are termed 'The Great Walking Trails' in the publicity material covering England and Wales, or 'Scotland's Great Trails' for that country.[38] Other states have their own versions, for instance New Zealand's ten 'Great Walks'.[39]

The idea of what eventually became fifteen 'Ways' or 'Paths' across England and Wales came, more often than not, to mean important paths, trails that might be long in terms of distance, historically 'important' or revealing of a key moment of change or historical note – of local or regional import, perhaps, as well as national. This was in contrast to many formal and official arguments for the creation of long-distance trails. When in 1967 the Ministry of Housing consulted on proposed routes for The Ridgeway Walk that included a novel footpath along the Chiltern escarpment, the proposed new route was declined on the basis that the Icknield Way was preferred. This, the CROW minutes reveal, was thought to offer a 'broad unmetalled track of historic interest and

---

35 Geo. 6 Ch. 49, National Parks and Access to the Countryside Act 1949 (51) (1)-(5), https://www.legislation.gov.uk/ukpga/Geo6/12-13-14/97/enacted (Accessed 23 March 2021).

36 See the radical views of Peter Howard and David Pinder, focusing on ideas of social class encoded in 'heritage', as well as tourist car use and access: Howard and Pinder, 'Cultural Heritage', esp. 63–66.

37 For instance Watkins and Jones, *Unforgettable Walks*.

38 'National Trails – The Great Walking Trails', https://www.nationaltrail.co.uk/en_GB/trails/ (Accessed 20 Jan. 2021); 'Scotland's Great Trails', https://www.scotlandsgreattrails.com/ (Accessed 20 Jan. 2021).

39 'Great Walks of New Zealand', https://www.newzealand.com/uk/feature/great-walks-of-new-zealand/ (Accessed 20 Jan. 2021).

2. Delineating the Landscape

giving good and unobstructed views all along the way over the Oxfordshire Plain'.[40] Here a preservationist rather than historicist ideology was to the fore. Although the minutes suggest that only part of the Icknield Way was on the Definitive Map at that point, it was the influence of views taking in the historic countryside that took priority.

Here there were clearly debates around historical importance, but those in the end prioritised amenity and beauty, related to – but not necessarily always part of – the historical character of these trails themselves. The vistas offered, presumably for the benefit of the leisure walker, were given as much weight as the historical importance of the footpath. On many occasions, too, different meanings of 'history' and 'heritage' are attached to trails of different length. Many shorter local paths possessed heritage value, but it was only to the longer 'national' routes that the highest heritage status was attached and historical interest could trump access to wide open rural spaces. Personal, national or political events and monuments, for instance, often boosted longer walks that could be very strongly defined as 'historical' – in the case, for instance, of the Hadrian's Wall Path, Offa's Dyke, or Glyndŵr's Way.[41]

Many of the more formal long-distance trails popular with planners and tourist authorities since the Second World War can – perhaps in part for these reasons – seem actually like an imposition rather than a more imaginative or creative experience. Many of Britain's long-distance trails have been experienced as an old-new experience akin to those artefacts the tourism writer David Brown calls 'genuine fakes': Cusack's work on St Cuthbert's Way, through Scotland and the North-East of England, is a good example of writings that interrogate the meaning of such simulacra of the past. On St Cuthbert's Way, for instance, the walker is directed via a diversion to Dryburgh Abbey, a mid-twelfth-century foundation seemingly unconnected to the seventh-century St Cuthbert.[42] The actual experience of such trails can feel quite synthetic. When in the early 2000s Iain Sinclair began his walk out of London to follow John Clare's famous nineteenth-century path 'home' to North Cambridgeshire, he found the managed trail out to the Great North Road worryingly one-dimensional: 'our route is dispiriting: too much has been invested by outside parties. Noticeboards offer bubblegum cartoons of local history'.[43]

---

40   Central Committee on Rights of Way Committee Meeting Minutes, Appendix E, 5 July 1967, MERL SR CPRE C/1/49/130.

41   Victoria Bell has interestingly contrasted the formal 'heritage' of Hadrian's Wall with very complex personal travels to, around and by the side of it: Bell, 'Heritage', esp. 175–84.

42   Cusack, 'Saint Cuthbert's Way', 12.

43   Sinclair, *Edge*, p. 141.

Figure 1.

Signpost including directions for The Saints Way as well as a Cornwall County Council rights of way arrow showing the interlinked typographies of rights of way and trails. Photograph by Clare Hickman, 2019.

2. Delineating the Landscape

Another example of these created historic narratives to tie a series of smaller footpaths together with one overarching historic narrative is the Saints Way in Cornwall (Figure 1).

Running for 27 miles from Padstow to Fowey, this Way is signalled as having historic significance through its distinctive Celtic cross way marking signs. Despite many claims, including the idea on the British Pilgrimage Trust's website that it 'follows the probable route of early Christian travellers making their way from Ireland and Wales to Brittany and the European mainland', even the Trust admits that the Way itself was really constructed as a coherent trail only in the 1980s.[44] The local men involved were Cliff Townes and Alf Fookes from Luxulyan, who, in 1984, 'uncovered a number of elaborate granite stiles near the village and interested the Co-operative Retail Services Community Project in carrying out clearance work in the parish'.[45] The role of the local council with an eye on tourism, and the use of community project funds for leisure-based projects, are all evident in the foreword to the booklet describing the Way published in 1991. In this the Chairman of the Transport Services Sub-committee, W.R. Husking, stated that:

> Long-distance paths, such as this, are never complete. They continue to develop over the years as they are 'discovered' by more and more people and their routes are improved and altered with changing circumstances and opportunities. The County Council is committed to a policy of providing an expanding network of recreational paths throughout the county ... The path is now there to be enjoyed by one and all.[46]

There is of course the argument that the route goes past many ancient and religious sites in the county and the Bishop of Truro in a preface to the same booklet was happy to expand on this to create his own religious meaning for the route: 'pilgrimaging, as the Celtic Saints who came here from Wales, Brittany and Ireland knew, was the experience of and for a lifetime ... hidden behind it all is the mystery of St Petroc and his followers down the ages who beckon us to tread in their footsteps, and see the things that they saw.'[47] Again we can see the creation of a historical narrative which argues for a deep spiritual idea

---

44   British Pilgrimage Trust, 'Cornish Saints' Way', https://britishpilgrimage.org/portfolio/cornish-saints-way/?gclid=CjwKCAiA4rGCBhAQEiwAelVti1J8rCO6txMVNci3aFpCfHst4ZcoG9_BmGmqc-qKdldp364jxzlTGWhoCKPAQAvD_BwE (accessed 23 March 2021).

45   Also published in 'Saints Way', *Magazine of the Cornwall Wildlife Trust* 73 (Summer 1997): 25, available at https://www.chycor.co.uk/wild-cornwall/sum97/page3.htm (accessed 23 March 2021).

46   Ibid.

47   Ibid.

of following in the footsteps of others and the development of a story that connects together a series of disparate paths running across the land.

Many people find deep meaning in the so-called 'constructed' historic trail. The emphasis we place here on their deliberate creation is not intended to specify their nature too closely, still less to engage in pejorative rhetoric about such trails when compared to others. Ursula Martin has written about her contemplation of life with a cancer diagnosis, very slowly traversing the 224-mile-long Severn Way from Shrewsbury to Bristol. The Severn Way is an unassuming, low-key path along canals and rivers, across fields and hills, and through small towns. It does not involve dramatic sweeps through the landscape, or a very strong atmosphere that can be attached to a particular history. 'Constructed' histories can blend together these cadences, while walkers themselves add others.[48] Perhaps the best example of this trend in pathway writing is the bestselling work of Raynor Winn, who reacted to being made homeless by walking England's South West Coast Path. For Winn, as for Martin, the point of the walk was not the 'historic' nature or infrastructure on or around the National Trail, but the effect of being immersed in process: 'our feet instinctively followed the path, drawn west on the dusty umbilical cord that was allowing us to grow, unseen, in our strip of wilderness'.[49]

Conclusions

Experiencing English and Welsh rights of way in the middle years of the twentieth century certainly did not emphasise pathmaking as historical curation, still less make it part of the more recent and commodified heritage boom. Instead, the practical, the local, the voluntary and the collective were to the fore – creating a number of fascinating crosscurrents that help us to understand what rights of way were supposed to mean at that time. These delineations once more point backwards in time, as well as forwards. There had been collective, 'national' markers of intentional government policy since at least the nineteenth century, when the propaganda of the Commons Preservation Society and individual Parliamentarians all called for the emblematic River Thames – which *The Times* called 'a national pleasure-ground' – to be bordered by a free towpath along its entire length. The National Footpaths Preservation Society (later one of CROW's founders) had in 1888 already called on civic society, in the words of the social reformer and co-founder of the National Trust Octavia Hill, 'to preserve for our countrymen and women and their children one of the great common inheritances to which they as English citizens are born – the

48 Martin, *One Woman*, pp. 27, 31, 33.
49 Winn, *Salt Path*, pp. 119, 125.

2. Delineating the Landscape

footpaths of their native country'.[50]

In this chapter, we have explored the manifold, overlapping and unstable ideas that informed this pluralistic effort at planning both old and new pathways. Legal forms, precedent, historical use (including oral and cartographic evidence), formal heritage and ideas about 'history' ranging from constant use to national and regional 'identity' all played a role – but just as much as the practical problems of drawing up a formal definitive map, they also demonstrated the persisting, confusing dilemmas involved in situating rights of way. This was another reason why CROW's efforts were frustrated, though they allow us a precious insight into how rights of way were perceived. The categories we have chosen here are hardly definitive, and could be joined by many others that overlap and intermix: one might for instance distinguish between analyses issuing out of physical planning, pluralist negotiation, amenity or consumerism. There are likely many more ways to investigate both personal and organisational memories and archives.

Many rights of way may have become ordered, guided and in some places marketised. But as the debates illuminated in this chapter demonstrate, their meanings are always contested and in flux. They can draw their meaning from the very recent legal past; emerge from contest and argument, sometimes involving fierce debate; or (more recently) can be constructed by planners as part of the leisure economy. That still allows a space for the embodied and embedded body in movement, allowing users to become more reflective and reflexive – just as pilgrims on the Santiago de Compostela can closely approach some of the teachings of St Augustine as they toil along their way, imagining past, present and future together.[51] These histories are plural, rooted not only in the legal and political but in individuals' use and experience as they interact with any path, as Martin's and Winn's works demonstrate.

Academics' recent attention has therefore rightly been focused on the ways in which these three meanings are blended. Morag Rose's practical work unpacking experiences of the 'everyday' urban landscape, critically matching perhaps its multifaceted post-capitalist nature, is but one example.[52] As Christopher Tilley has commented, introducing the work of Mark Edmonds on movement in and across the Lake District:

> The temporalities of landscape are multiple and scaled. They reside in mountains and hills, rivers and forests, roads and paths, people and activities and events, monuments and

---

50   Readman, *Storied Ground*, pp. 282–84, 125.
51   See Slavin, 'Santiago de Compostela', esp. 5–6.
52   Rose, 'Pedestrian Practices', pp. 211–29.

memorials, interpretations and reinterpretations ... Landscape histories are entangled, messy, contested and directly implicated in contemporary struggles for access and rights to use and enjoy the land.'[53]

It is clear that, similarly, there is much more to say about the historical meaning of English and Welsh rights of way in the modern era – using their creation and management to open up questions of legal, political and individual understandings of national, regional and personal history.

Acknowledgements

This work was supported by the United Kingdom's Arts and Humanities Research Council [grant reference AH/V00509X/1].

Bibliography

Bates, G.H., 'Track Making by Man and Domestic Animals', *Journal of Animal Ecology* **19** (1) (1950): 21–28.

Bell, V.R., 'Experiencing Heritage at a World Heritage Site: Personal Encounters with Hadrian's Wall', *Annals of Leisure Research* **13** (1–2) (2010): 167–190.

Breen, T., 'Public or Private? An Analysis of the Legal Status of Rights of Way in Norfolk', *Landscapes* **18** (1) (2017): 55–70.

Chandler, J.A., *Explaining Local Government: Local Government in Britain since 1800* (Manchester: Manchester University Press, 2007).

Chubb, L., 'Its History and Meaning', in The Commons, Open Spaces and Footpaths Preservation Society, *The Rights of Way Act, 1932* (London: Open Spaces and Footpaths Society, 1938 rev. edn.).

Cmnd. 4040, *Royal Commission on Local Government in England, 1966–69; Volume I: Report and Maps* (London: HMSO, 1969).

Cmnd. 7207, *Report of the Special Committee on Footpaths and Access to the Countryside* (London: HMSO, 1947).

Colla, M., 'The Spectre of the Present: Time, Presentism and the Writing of Contemporary History', *Contemporary European History* **30** (1) (2021): 124–35.

Cullingworth, B. and V. Nadin, *Town and Country Planning in the UK* (London: Routledge, 13th edn, 2002).

Cusack, C.M., 'History, Authenticity, and Tourism: Encountering the Medieval while Walking Saint Cuthbert's Way', in A. Norman (ed.), *Journeys and Destinations: Studies in Travel, Identity and Meaning* (Newcastle upon Tyne: Cambridge Scholars Publishing, 2013), pp. 1–22.

Daunton, M.J., *Wealth and Welfare: An Economic and Social History of Britain 1851–1951* (Oxford: Oxford University Press, 2007).

Earle, T., 'Routes through the Landscape: A Comparative Approach', in J.A. Darling, C.L.

---

53   Tilley, 'Introduction', 26.

2. Delineating the Landscape

Erickson and J.E. Snead (eds), *Landscapes of Movement: Trails, Paths and Roads in Anthropological Perspective*, pp. 253–70 (Philadelphia, Pa.: University of Pennsylvania Press, 2011).

Farley, P. and M.S. Roberts, *Edgelands: Journeys into England's True Wilderness* (London: Vintage, 2012 edn).

Feldman, D., 'Property and Public Protest', in F. Meisel and P.J. Cook (eds), *Property and Protection: Legal Rights and Restrictions*, pp. 31–60 (Oxford: Hart Publishing, 2000).

Gandy, M., *The Fabric of Space: Water, Modernity and the Urban Imagination* (Cambridge, Mass.: MIT Press, 2014).

Gregory J. and S. Spooner, 'Public Rights of Way and Countryside Access in Norfolk 1880–1960', *Journal of Historical Geography* **74** (2021), 10-27.

Hodson, Y., 'Ordnance Survey and the Definitive Map of Public Rights of Way of England and Wales', *The Cartographic Journal* **39** (2) (2002): 101–24.

Howard, P. and D. Pinder. 'Cultural Heritage and Sustainability in the Coastal Zone: Experiences in South-West England', *Journal of Cultural Heritage* **4** (1) (2003): 57–68.

Lorimer, H., 'Walking: New Forms and Spaces for Studies of Pedestrianism', in T. Cresswell and P. Merriman (eds), *Geographies of Mobilities: Practices, Spaces, Subjects* (Farnham: Ashgate, 2011), pp. 31–46.

Martin, U., *One Woman Walks Wales: A 3,700 Mile Journey Round, Through and Across Wales* (Dinas Powys: Honno Press, 2018).

Moran, J., *On Roads: A Hidden History* (London: Profile Books, 2009).

Natural England, *A Guide to Definitive Maps and Changes to Public Rights of Way* (London: Natural England, 2008).

O'Hara, G., *The Politics of Water in Post-War Britain* (Basingstoke: Palgrave Macmillan, 2017).

Poole, K.P. and B. Keith-Lucas, *Parish Government 1894–1994* (London: Local Government Association, 1994).

Ramblers Association, *Footpaths and Bridleways: A Plea for their Protection* (London: Ramblers' Association, c.1967).

Rosenthal, L., *The River Pollution Dilemma in Victorian England: Nuisance Law Versus Economic Efficiency* (Farnham: Ashgate, 2014).

Sinclair, I., *Edge of the Orison: In the Traces of John Clare's 'Journey Out of Essex'* (London: Penguin Books, 2006 edn).

Slavin, S., 'Walking as Spiritual Practice: The Pilgrimage to Santiago de Compostela', *Body and Society* **9** (3) (2003): 1–18.

Readman, P., *Storied Ground: Landscape and the Shaping of English National Identity* (Cambridge: Cambridge University Press, 2018).

Rose, M., 'Pedestrian Practices: Walking from the Mundane to the Marvellous', in H. Holmes and S.M. Hall (eds), *Mundane Methods: Innovative Ways to Research the Everyday* (Manchester: Manchester University Press, 2020), pp. 211–29.

Tilley, C., 'Introduction: Identity, Place, Landscape and Heritage', *Journal of Material Culture* **11** (1/2) (2006): 7–32.

Watkins, S. and C. Jones, *Unforgettable Walks to Take Before You Die* (London: BBC Books, 2008).

Winn, R., *The Salt Path* (London: Penguin, pb. edn, 2019).

CHAPTER 3.
APPROPRIATED HERITAGE? ACCESS CAMPAIGNS, TRESPASS, AND LOCAL RIGHTS IN EARLY-TWENTIETH CENTURY UPLAND ENGLAND AND AUSTRIA.

Ben Anderson

Introduction

In 1908, recreational access to rural space came before no less than three European Parliaments. In Britain, Liberal MP Charles Trevelyan (1870–1958) revived James Bryce's Access to Mountains Bill, broadening it to England and Wales. In the newly-democratised Austrian House of Deputies, Social Democrats called to end path closures in Alpine territories; and in the Bavarian Chamber of Deputies, representatives of the conservative *Deutsche und Oesterreichische Alpenverein* and socialist *Touristenverein 'Die Naturfreunde'* (*Naturfreunde*) demanded that State Forest Officials prioritise tourists and paths over hunters and quarry.[1] All three bids to upend the land-use of Europe's uplands failed, but the British and Central-European movements were strikingly similar in other ways too. They were both formed of predominantly male walkers, climbers and trespassers, from relatively diverse social backgrounds, led by organised outdoor leisure movements. Both built on existing traditions of rural transgression and protest, but argued for a relatively new right of recreation located in the urban and national. Both faced entrenched hunting interests with significant connections to political processes and inherited landed interests, opposed through acts of both individual and organised trespass.[2] Both offered – in the Scottish/British Access to Mountains Bills since James Bryce's 1884 original, the 1924 Law of Property Act, and Arthur Löwy/Lenhoff's *Der Verbotene Weg* [The Forbidden Path] – carefully constructed legal methods to solving the access

---

1   Hansard: HC Deb 15.05.1908 vol. 188 cc1439-523; 'Der Verbotene Weg [The Forbidden Path]', *Der Naturfreund: Mitteilungen des Touristen-Vereins "Die Naturfreunde' in Wien* [The Friend of Nature: Newsletter of the Rambling-Club 'The Friends of Nature' in Vienna] **12** (4) (1908): 83–84; 'Der Alpenverein in der bayrischen Kammer der Abgeordneten [The Alpine Club in the Bavarian Chamber of Deputies]', *Mitteilungen des Deutschen und Oesterreichischen Alpenvereins* [Newsletter of the German and Austrian Alpine Club] **34** (11) (1908): 153–54.

2   On Kinder Scout, see Hey, *Peak District*, pp. 273–309. On Austria, see G. Aigner, 'Ein vereiteltes Wegverbot [A Thwarted Path Closure]', *Naturfreund* **13** (6) (1909): 131–32 (131); 'Der verbotene Weg', *Naturfreund* **16** (1912), 246.

3. Appropriated Heritage?

problem, methods which prioritised recreational resources over both existing agricultural production and the rights of rural communities.[3]

How access campaigns achieved this reinvention of locally-held, rural resource rights as nationally-held, urban recreational ones is the subject of this chapter.[4] It argues that trespass had a central role, as a form of protest that enabled largely urban-based communities of walkers and climbers to assert a claim to heritages of rural land use, resistance and custom that might justify public, urban access for recreation. Yet at least some trespassers also sought an understanding of local environments, politics and culture with whom they felt a close connection. They embodied the tensions of access campaigns that advocated for the recreational rights of a largely urban population, but could only be successful by working alongside rural communities and their differing priorities.

This chapter examines the ambivalent position of trespassers and access campaigners towards the local people whose rights and heritage they drew on to assert their claims.[5] In England, this provides a counterpoint to histories stretching through the mid-nineteenth century and foregrounding urban political space and resources alongside recreational access.[6] Urban campaign groups supported locally-led popular protests with roots in older traditions of enforcing customary rights, or acted for subaltern groups whose lives on the urban periphery included the use of nearby land for entertainment, liaison and politics.[7] As Anthony Taylor has demonstrated, rural landscape concerns intersected with largely-urban political difference – a pattern we can find repeated amongst turn-of-the-century outdoors organisations.[8] In this earlier period, access campaigns integrated practices, objectives and traditions that cannot be reduced to either 'urban' or 'rural'.[9] Yet, by the late-nineteenth century at the latest, the city was

---

[3] 'A Bill to Secure to the Public Access to Mountains and Moorlands in Scotland', *Parliament: House of Commons* **122** (London, 1884); L. Chubb, 'The Law of Property Act, 1925. (Provisions for the Protection of Commons.)', *Journal of the Commons, Open Spaces and Footpaths Preservation Society* **1** (1) (1927): 7–13 (8–9); A. Lenhoff-Löwy, 'Der Verbotene Weg. Ein juristische Versuch [The Forbidden Path: A Legal Commentary', *Naturfreund* **13** (7–8) (1909): 144–52 and 177–82. See Readman, 'James Bryce', pp. 287–318. Many thanks to Dr. Katrina Navickas for her help.

[4] See Bradley, 'Green Belt', 629–701; McDonagh and Griffin, 'Occupy!', 1–10. For other uses of common land in the late-nineteenth century, see Howkins, 'English Commons', 107–32; Howkins, *Death of Rural England*, pp. 104–11.

[5] See also chapters by Readman and O'Hara and Hickman in this volume.

[6] Navickas, *Protest and the Politics of Space and Place*.

[7] Cowell, 'Berkhamsted Common, 145–61; D. Killingray, 'Knole Park', 63–79; Baigent, 'Religion, Theology and the Open Space Movement', 31–58. Navickas, *Protest and the Politics of Space and Place*; Readman, *Storied Ground*, pp. 154–94.

[8] Taylor, '"Commons-Stealers"', 383–407. See Anderson, *Being Modern*, pp. 26–30.

[9] Taylor, *Claim on the Countryside*, p. 5; Navickas, *Protest and the Politics of Space and Place*, p. 304.

a core element of rambling identity – it was urban work patterns, urban living standards and urban environments that walkers routinely hoped to escape; it was urban modernity that walking in the countryside was often understood as supporting, and urban forms of organisation that dominated its movements.[10] A distinctly *urban* identity, in other words, was a core element of both organised walking and access campaigns by the late-nineteenth century and, by the early-twentieth, much of the material they produced carefully avoided rooting itself in these earlier histories of protest, even as it sought to instrumentalise heritages of commons and public rights.[11] However complex and relational difference was on the ground, walkers, climbers and campaigners wove distinctions between 'urban' and 'rural' into the fabric of outdoors leisure culture and, for this reason, the place of rural inhabitants in that culture requires closer analysis.

In Austria, it might be expected that these relations were even more pronounced. The rapid growth of Vienna in the late-nineteenth century, combined with the railway connectedness of its Alpine hinterlands, meant that personal connections between Alpine villages and the capital were more likely, though this was, to be sure, true of almost every part of the Empire.[12] So too, Austria's peasantry had good reason to celebrate the 1848 revolutions, whose most significant permanent social policy was the *Bauernbefreiung*, ending the last vestiges of feudal relations in areas such as the Alps. Yet there are few signs of anything like the alliances or integration of urban and rural in protest movements that we find in England. Austrian farmers may have benefited from the politics of 1848, but they largely refused to support the revolution. Instead, the politics of the Eastern Alps rapidly came to be driven by the national identities disappointed by 1848, and a conservative Catholicism wary of external influence.[13] Perhaps for these reasons, a significant element of what might be termed 'rural protest' in the Eastern Alps of c. 1900 was directed at the newly-built infrastructure of tourism itself, and only continuing traditions of poaching 'rebels' point to continuing rural claims on communal land resources.[14]

In both England and Austria, the legal position of rights of way ensured a

10   See Baigent, 'Religion, Theology and the Open Space Movement', 40.
11   For example, P. Barnes' well-received pamphlet, *Trespassers will be Prosecuted* (Sheffield: Barnes, 1934), pp. 3–4, dated the beginning of the access movement in the Peak District to 1912, specifically aimed the pamphlet at 'ramblers from Southern districts where the same problem does not arise', and characterises the region as a 'wild, unspoilt' area surrounded by 'industrial England'.
12   Steidl, 'Migration Patterns', pp. 71–76, 82–86.
13   Goetz and Heiss, 'Nation vom Rande aus gesehen', 150–71. See also Morosini, *Sulle vette della Patria*, pp. 72–84; Judson, *Guardians*, pp. 141–77.
14   Anon., 'Zerstörung von Wegtafeln [Destruction of Path-markers]', *Naturfreund* 11 (5) (1907): 96. For poachers, see 'Huetteneinbruch [Hut break-in]' *Naturfreund* 8 (4) (1904): 48; Girtler, *Wilderer*.

3. Appropriated Heritage?

central role for local people, their institutions and history, and access campaigners from further afield had little choice but to work within this reality, a perspective that contributes to a growing 'legal turn' in the history of landscape.[15] Access campaigns forced recreational walkers to engage with the politics, heritage and environmental contexts of rural lives in ways unparalleled in England, and only surpassed in the Eastern Alps by the vast construction of high-Alpine tourist infrastructure.[16] Yet weaving purported urban rights into the fabric of rural land use patterns, customs and history was a complex business, and neither access campaigners nor trespassers are easily reduced to caricature. While some acted with a barely-concealed contempt for the local cultures they encountered, others offered a remarkable sensitivity to the challenges of rural upland agriculture and environmental inequalities in the landscapes through which they moved. In appropriating rural heritage for urban claims, trespassers and campaigners often developed a new sensitivity to rural needs and interests.

Access heritage

Trespass might be a practised assumption of commonality, a refutation of the boundaries imposed by property rights, or a reassertion of personal sovereignty. It was a form of protest that might speak to longer traditions of conflict, collective rights, or the 'trespasses' of landowners over communities that once relied on enclosed land. In the early years of the twentieth century, G.H.B. Ward (1876–1957), a Sheffield-based metalworker set the tone and content for a generation of 'respectable', militant, socialist and 'manly' walkers.[17] His *Clarion Club Ramblers*, and its pocket-sized *Handbook* became a recognised part of trespass culture by 1914, typified by antiquarian research, tales of trespass and rural anecdotes that offered an accessible narrative to the struggle for access:

> We'll beat the track, the old historic track, the Bradfield Gate 'Road' which the record band of ninety-two boys and girls trod upon the blessed blithesome day just twelve months ago.

---

15 Houston, 'People, Space and Law', 48. See also Brosnan, 'Law and the Environment', 513–52. In England, establishing a right of way required either demonstration of continuous use for as much as 75 years, or (and sometimes in addition), the designation of a right of way on, for example, enclosure acts or other cadastral records often held in parish records, or even physical evidence of ancient usage. Gathering such evidence – and then asserting a claim – often required collaboration of local people and parish authorities. In Austria, the principle of *Ersitz* followed a similar logic, but required only 30 or 40 years usage. For a path to be declared 'public', however, a local *Gemeinde*, or community, the smallest political unit in Austria, would need to make the claim, and write the path as such in the locally held land-register. See Lenhoff and Loewy, *Verbotene Weg*.

16 Anderson, *Being Modern*.

17 Tebbutt, 'Manly Identity', 1125–53; Tebbutt, 'Landscapes of Loss', 115–20.

> I think of these old rights-of-way which climb the highest, breeziest hills; and sometimes my soul is filled with madness. Men who are possessed of 'culture' and also of the wild, now half useless moorlands of the Peak, often dare to deprive their fellows of the simple right of enjoyment of these 'enclosured' and often unbought, shooting lands; to use their eyes and exercise their town-stiffened and tramcar-blighted legs upon the heights of Good Health. Verily, there is an English form of culture which may be labelled **German**.[18]

This passage was written shortly after the beginning of the Great War, and Ward used this opportunity to connect the land question to patriotism. Yet he also offered a heritage of historic roads and old rights-of-way, since lost to enclosure, now to be reclaimed for the health of urban bodies through trespass, here imagined reviving similarly lost rural customs of beating the bounds. In Ward's writing, such slippages between past and present, rural and urban, rendered trespass a connection between these worlds, and a way for campaigners to assert urban rights as both the inheritance of rural custom and the necessary modernisation of land for the good of a new, urban and public nation. Trespass constituted a repossession of 'our one-time waste moorland commons' as one 1923 article discussing a 'no trespassers' sign put it.[19]

While access rights had not been – and still were not – a purely urban campaign, urban demands and requirements gradually came to dominate from the late-nineteenth century. Early campaigns for access to the broad sweep of moorlands between Manchester and Sheffield had certainly been led by locals, and this included that for the famous Snake Pass path between Hayfield and Ashopton. This was initiated in the late 1870s by a small group of largely-local residents in the 'Hayfield, Kinder Scout and District Ancient Footpaths and Bridlepaths Association'. According to Ward's narrative, this group 'stepped in' to mediate between landowners bent on closing local rights of way, and 'excursionists' whom the Association blamed for causing 'considerable annoyance'. While the organisation did find some success in ensuring access to a series of local paths, it failed to open the 'Snake', and folded in the early 1880s. By 1894, the 'Snake' became the target of a new organisation, the 'Peak District Footpaths Preservation Society', based substantially in Manchester with funds sufficient to mount a legal challenge to the Duke of Devonshire's estate. The Duke offered a shockingly one-sided counterproposal; he would grant access via a new path, but on condition that the public renounce all claims over all other paths on the area, comprising much of Hayfield. Now the Peak District Footpath Preservation Society sought to pressurise Hayfield members and the

---

18   G.H.B. Ward, in *Sheffield Clarion Ramblers' Handbook* (1915–16): 7.
19   Anon., 'Another Notice Board', *Sheffield Clarion Ramblers' Handbook* (1923–24): 11; G.H.B. Ward, 'Ancient Ways Across Win Hill', *Sheffield Clarion Ramblers' Handbook* (1923–24): 118–30 (118–19).

3. Appropriated Heritage?

local parish council to accept the compromise as the best possible outcome, despite 'putting in jeopardy the right to travel over a great portion of the footpaths in the neighbourhood'. The parish council and locals refused, and eventually the full route over the pass opened in 1896.[20]

Although the ceremonial opening of the path, much like similar festivities in the Eastern Alps, sought to smooth over what had been a fraught relationship, this was not so much a victory for the Peak District Footpath Preservation Society as for local people in Hayfield, who ensured the protection of both the 'Snake' route and other rights of way in the locality.[21] The episode was nevertheless indicative of the increasing dominance of urban walkers, whose priorities were not necessarily shared by locals.[22] By the early-interwar period, Lawrence Chubb, the leader of what was now the 'Commons, Open Spaces and Footpaths Preservation Society' could cite the preservation 'of open spaces for public use and enjoyment' as the organisation's singular aim. He celebrated the 1924 legislation that enshrined a right only of recreational access to commons, and offered landowners a means to deal with the 'gypsy nuisance' in return for recreational access.[23] Increasingly, the role of such organisations was limited to the protection of what was widely now called 'amenity', a term that included aesthetic landscape beauty and recreational access, but did not protect informal resource rights, or rural communities from urban demands for water, energy or construction resources.[24]

In England, a rhetoric of 'returning' commons to public use encompassed a slippage from the local to the national that turned such landscapes into a resource for urban recreation before rural production, as Chubb's victorious description of the 1924 Law of Property Act explained. In Austria and Germany, similar claims were run through with the national and confessional identities of politics in the Eastern Alps. Speaking in the lower house of the Austrian parliament in 1887, the *Deutsche Nationalbewegung* (German National Movement) member, and later founder of the *Deutsche Nationalpartei* (German National Party), Otto Steinwender (1847–1921) appealed to 'old German law'

---

20 See J. Garside and G.H.B. Ward, 'The History of the Right of Way under Kinder Scout', *Sheffield Clarion Ramblers' Handbook* (1927–28): 153–62.

21 Garside and Ward, 'Kinder Scout', 153, 161.

22 For example, in campaigns over the Doctor's Gate path from Glossop to the Snake pass, which saw many ramblers join demonstrations from Manchester and Sheffield, only one inhabitant of Glossop joined. G.H.B. Ward, 'James Grove – the Glossop Rambler', *Sheffield Clarion Ramblers' Handbook* (1927–28): 163.

23 Chubb, 'Law of Property Act', 7–13.

24 T. Boulger, 'News for Ramblers – Footpaths Preservation', *Sheffield Clarion Ramblers' Handbook* (1927–28): 117–23 (118, 119–21).

which, he claimed, had allowed for both unlimited open access and hunting rights across German 'forests and wildernesses'.[25] Steinwender was, first, able to narrate a more recent loss of customary, place-based rights through the *Bauernbefreiung* as one of lost public rights connected to nation. Second, he rooted that loss in a wider *völkisch* history that co-opted the culturally-complex Alpine borderlands as unproblematically German, and even located their threat in 'Roman' – ie. Italian – law.[26] At a 1916 meeting of path access campaigners, Steinwender finally sought to divert blame from the nobility, asserting that 'this really has nothing to do with the old established dynasties', but rather 'those people who have become rich in the present circumstance ... certain men who have huge wealth, and want to express this by, for example, going deer hunting (laughter)'. If the implication here was not enough, Steinwender's last joke relied on the assumption that Jewish people did not actually hunt: 'Even if he doesn't shoot, he at least wishes to be invited to shoot (applause and laughter).'[27] For Steinwender, the loss of 'ancient' patterns of landholding in the mountains could be explained by appealing to fears of a small minority of mainly-Viennese residents who, until recently, had been excluded from property ownership entirely.

The 'heritage' that emerged, like the rhetoric of 'commons' access in England certainly drew upon local languages of lost rights and, according to Roland Girtner, a documented history of hunting rights controlled at a local level, whose memory was still closely embedded in the poaching cultures of the mountains.[28] Yet, Steinwender and his associates did not intend to restore locally-held rights. Theirs was instead a modernist project of nation-building that was anathema to many communities in the diverse and fragmented borderlands of the Eastern Alps. While rarely as extreme as Steinwender's, such 'improving' projects and 'cultural missions' were a staple of urban-based Alpine

---

25 O. Steinwender, in *Stenographische Protokolle des 163. Sitzung des X. Session des Abgeordnetenhaus am 23. Mai 1887* [Stenographic Minutes of the 163rd Sitting of the X. Session of the House of Deputies on 23 May 1887], pp. 6002-6012 (pp. 6010-6011). See Bodner, 'Verbotene Weg', 363-365. According to Roland Girtler, this was indeed the legal situation in Germany before the advent of Roman law: Girtler, *Wilderer*, p. 22.

26 On the cultural complexity of Alpine borderlands and the problematic role of tourist organisations, see Anderson, *Being Modern*, pp. 222-230; Keller, *Apostles*, pp. 47-66; Morosini, *Sulle vette della Patria*, pp. 72-84; Judson, *Guardians*, pp. 141-77; Cole, 'Emergence and Impact', 31-40; Peniston-Bird, Rohkrämer and Schulz, 'Glorified, Contested and Mobilized', 141-158.

27 Bodner, 'Verbotene Weg', p. 364; 'Naturschutz und Wegefreiheit: Eine Rundgebung der Touristen [The Protection of Nature and Path Freedom: A Public Meeting of Mountaineers]', *Neues Wiener Tagblatt* **16** (16 Jan. 1916), 15-16 (16); 'Naturschutz und Wegerecht [The Protection of Nature and Path Rights]', *Österreichische Touristenzeitung* **36** (3) (1916): 32-39 (37).

28 Girtler, *Wilderer*, p. 22.

3. Appropriated Heritage?

Clubs in Germany and Austria, irrespective of their other political positions.[29] As the general secretary of the Austrian Association for *Heimatschutz* pointed out, the closure of Alpine paths by landowners might best be understood as the 'robbery of colonies from their colonisers'.[30]

Yet as the growing anti-semitism of German-speaking tourism in the early-twentieth century suggests, there were already other exclusions at work. The most visible period of access campaigning by the *Naturfreunde* coincided with the male enfranchisement of Austria's poorest communities in 1907, a renewed attack on recreational access in hunting regions and the de-facto exclusion of the poor from the huts of most Alpine organisations, led by the *Deutsche und Oesterreichische Alpenverein*. All this was accompanied, from the early years of the twentieth century, with increasingly vociferous discussions of 'Alpine Knigge' [Alpine etiquette], which included complaints about a new absence of deference amongst mountain guides under the influence of urban mountaineers who viewed them as social equals.[31]

Similar concerns emerged in English texts. 'We are', Ward wrote in 1929, 'being blamed largely for the faults of a few hundreds of noisy juveniles who, now following in the wake of the youngest Clubs, are of a class who, 25 years ago, would scarcely have had the wit to proceed beyond the suburbs of the city.'[32] Though Ward sought to empathise with those criticised in the wider media, both he and other organisations such as the Clarion's less militant counterparts, the *Manchester Ramblers' Federation*, nevertheless called for increased punishment, criminal prosecutions and systems of surveillance by the late 1920s, in an attempt to control increased numbers of visitors to the Peak District, and mould them into the 'manly', and 'civilised' image of the rambler.[33] 'A few of the larrikins', Ward wrote in 1928, 'who are "coming out" and may become men in a while, are doing thoughtless damage and the rambler who sees it should not hesitate in dealing with them severely.'[34] Indeed, it was often the 'manliness' that Ward and his club sought in the hills that was judged lacking in such behaviour. Young boys or women, he contended, did not have the

---

29 Anderson, *Being Modern* pp. 116–19. See, for example, J. Szombathy, 'Die Touristenwege am Schneeberg [The Mountain Paths on the Schneeberg]', *Oesterreichische Touristenzeitung* [Austrian Mountaineering Times] **16** (14) (1896): 169–70.

30 'Naturschutz und Wegerecht', 34.

31 Anderson, *Being Modern*, pp. 70–83.

32 G.H.B. Ward, 'Chiefly about Ramblers and Other People', in *Sheffield Clarion Ramblers' Handbook* (1928–29): 133–47 (136).

33 G.H.B. Ward, 'Fun in the Hills', *Sheffield Clarion Ramblers' Handbook* (1928–29): 119–25 (123); Anderson, 'Liberal Countryside', 96–100.

34 Ward, 'Fun in the Hills', 123.

requisite toughness, denoted by a 'brown, and hair-covered body' to survive on the moors without adequate protection.[35] Class was also relevant to such critiques, with Ward citing *from experience* that most damage to fields came from the actions of 'school children and young hooligans' in agricultural areas 'near the slum districts'.[36]

Ward was repeating the typical tendency of tourists to distinguish themselves from other tourists by ascribing moral and behavioural standards on their activities. Here though, his concern for the impacts of 'larrikins' from the peripheral and informal districts of urban settlements on nearby rural places separated his access campaigns from those connected to the radical politics, urban poor and protest cultures of mid-nineteenth century North-West England.[37] The solution proffered (and actioned) by him and other campaigners sought to regulate behaviour on the moors, and while these 'respectable' ramblers protested at the comparison, to an outside observer there might well appear little difference between their 'warden guides' scheme and the keepers of public parks, with their restrictions and bye-laws.[38]

In both England and Austria, the increasing obsession amongst club leaderships with behaviour in the outdoors also aligned with conciliatory approaches to hunting interests. Justifications for path closures, when not centred on the safety of walkers themselves, often turned on the 'disturbance' of game, despite ample evidence for the increasing numbers of grouse, pheasants, chamois and deer in hunting preserves during the same period.[39] Such criticisms were taken to heart, and censure of such behaviour became a staple of an Alpine press that sought to be the voice of 'respectable' outdoors leisure. This was true above all of the *Deutsche und Oesterreichische Alpenverein*, whose membership extended into the upper elites of German society. The 'unnecessary noise' of 'alpine Wildlinge', whose warnings of potentially fatal rockfall 'disturb the wonderful atmosphere' wrote the Alpinist and landscape photographer Fritz Benesch (1864–1949) in the *Deutsche und Oesterreichische Alpenverein*'s annual journal of 1898, 'leads in the end to friction with the hunting personnel, and

---

35 Ward, 'Other People', 135.
36 Ward, 'Other People', 145. On another occasion, however, he blamed 'hangers-on and unregulated imitators of the Boy Scout movement': G.H.B. Ward, 'Notes for Ramblers', *Sheffield Clarion Ramblers' Handbook* (1930–31): 172–75 (174).
37 Navickas, 'Popular Protest', 93–111.
38 Anderson, 'Liberal Countryside', 96–100.
39 See, for example, Szombathy, 'Schneeberg', 169–71; Ward, 'Other People', 142–43.

3. Appropriated Heritage?

thus to harsher path closures'.[40] For members of 'respectable' rambling clubs or middle-class mountaineers in Germany and Austria, the new codes of behaviour meant an importation of urban middle-class values into the mountains. As such, attempts to mollify upper-class and noble hunting interests meant imposing urban, middle-class values and conduct onto an outdoors space, and critiquing or excluding those, including locals, who transgressed the new 'commandments'.[41] Campaigners for access rights who were sensitive to criticisms raised of outdoor leisure participants in local and national newspapers sought to distance themselves from such behaviour, and supported attempts to regulate the outdoors in the name of freedom.[42]

Practising trespass

At its most basic, trespass operated as a performative counterpart to the languages of access lobbies, a practised assumption of commonality and refutation of the boundaries imposed by property rights which drew on older practices of resistance – poaching especially. The placing of bodies in environments where they were not allowed to be also forced their owners to engage with the landscape and its inhabitants in new, and unpredictable ways. Trespassers did not merely use their bodies to act out thoughts, frustrations or politics, but rather as a tool for forming and thinking those ideologies in the first place. In the case of those described in this chapter, those ideologies might be of rural/urban difference, identification with nature or, as we will examine in the following section, with the plight of rural inhabitants.

English ramblers and mountaineers relished near-encounters with gamekeepers, supposedly relying on what the librarian and access campaigner E.A. Baker (1869–1961) called the 'well-known frailties of the game-keeper', and taking advantage of the terrain. This was a common trope of writing, albeit with different inflections, from the masculinist, militarist metaphors employed by Ward to the sorts of vaguely comedic references common to 'respectable', middle-class ramblers. In such texts, keepers were understood as stupid, slow, and corrupt. In one oft-repeated anecdote, Leslie Stephen's 'Sunday Tramps' club chanted a legalistic verse as they walked over private land, apparently in the

---

40   Fritz Benesch, 'Die Raxalpe und der Wiener Schneeberg [The Raxalpe and the Viennese Schneeberg]', *Zeitschrift des Deutsche und Oesterreiche Alpenvereins* [Journal of the German and Austrian Alpine Club] **29** (1898): 214. See Bodner, 'Verbotene Weg', 356–57. See also Szombathy, 'Schneeberg', 170–71.

41   F. Friedensburg and C. Arnold, 'Die zehn Gebote des Bergsteigers [The Ten Commandments of Mountain Climbers]', *Mitteilungen des Deutsche und Oesterreichische Alpenvereins* **23** (3) (1907): 33–34.

42   Anderson, 'Liberal Countryside'.

hope of confusing gamekeepers.[43] Ward was sometimes more complimentary, but this did not prevent him publishing stories with titles such as 'Fun with a Gamekeeper', or 'Diddling the Longshaw Gamekeepers', and occasionally praising violence towards them.[44] The minor novelist Halliwell Sutcliffe claimed the 'game' of trespass had 'strict rules' and 'delicately shaded rules of etiquette', that turned basic countryside politeness into an exercise in the types of sportsmanship, character and fairness familiar to historians of colonial cricket and football – though even these could be overcome in extreme circumstances, such as being a little late.[45] By the 1920s, the popular philosopher C.E.M. Joad recounted techniques of 'keeper-baiting', each of which relied on obfuscation and confusion.[46] Far from members of rural communities exploited by landowners or potential allies in access campaigns, gamekeepers served as the physical symbol of the authority of the landowner, their 'frailties' metaphors of a backward and traditional rural power structure easily overcome by urban intelligence or manliness.

Such trespassers occupied a triple role. They carried both ancient customary rights and democratic modernity into moorlands currently occupied by unscrupulous and corrupt landowners, *and* performed a theatrical game of hunter and hunted marked with imperial fantasy. 'I have spent whole days in the innermost recesses of game forests', remarked the sponsor of successive Access to Mountains Bills, Charles Trevelyan at a dinner meeting of rambling clubs in 1925, 'and it is a very good game – one of the best in the world – keeping out of the way of gamekeepers'.[47] The 'game' of trespass could also be usefully paralleled to hunters, whose own heritage trespassers denied by pointing to the sheer efficiency, brutality and ease of modern hunting practices. Albert

---

43   G.H.B. Ward, 'How the Sunday Tramps Go A-Trespassing', *Sheffield Clarion Ramblers' Handbook* (1930–31): 177–78.

44   'The Tramp' [G.H.B. Ward], 'Fun with a Gamekeeper', *Sheffield Clarion Ramblers' Handbook* (1915–16): 61–64; G.H.B. Ward, 'Diddling the Longshaw Gamekeepers', *Sheffield Clarion Ramblers' Handbook* (1927–28): 62–64. G.H.B. Ward, 'The Story of Baslow's "Big Moor" or Bridleways and Moormen's Ways, in History Topography and Anecdote', *Sheffield Clarion Ramblers' Handbook* (1927–28): 78–129 (125–26); anon., 'How they "Keep" on a Derbyshire Mountain', *Sheffield Clarion Ramblers' Handbook* (1927–28): 164–65; Ward 'Fun in the Hills'; G.H.B. Ward, 'How to Test the Law of Trespass', *Sheffield Clarion Ramblers' Handbook* (1936–37): 103–04 (103).

45   H. Sutcliffe, *A Benedick in Arcady* (London: John Murray, 1906), quoted in *Sheffield Clarion Ramblers' Handbook* (1914–15) and in Sissons and Smith, *Right to Roam*, p. 12.

46   See also G.H.B. Ward, 'Several Derbyshire Peak District Stories (Sheffielders at Eyam and Chatsworth and Natives of Eyam, Ashopton and Hathersage)', *Sheffield Clarion Ramblers' Handbook* (1936–37): 114–18 (117–18).

47   'The Joy of the Rambler: Mr C.P. Trevelyan and the Access to Mountains Bill', *Yorkshire Post* 14 Dec. 1925, in *Sheffield Clarion Ramblers' Handbook* (1927–28): 44–45 (44).

3. Appropriated Heritage?

Blattmann encountered a company of drivers sitting on the summit of Pyhrgas in 1903, and while he was 'impressed by their excellent climbing':

> We were disgusted by the behaviour of the 'noble' huntsmen, to which we must bear witness. It probably is enjoyable to dangerously follow the track of a fleeing deer, and to be victorious in an honorable struggle, but this mass murder of sweet, charming creatures was a crude juxtaposition to the previously undisturbed quiet of the mountains.[48]

The same claims about the decline of hunting as a 'manly' pursuit can be found in England, where the emphasis is on driven grouse shooting, in which grouse were made to fly, in great numbers, in front of the hunters, resulting in astonishingly large 'bags'. Ward compared such 'deteriorated and lazy sportsmen' to older examples of, for example, Scottish deerstalkers who 'loved the hills, and also the hardships and exposure of the chase', or, during the First World War, pointedly described modern hunting practices as 'the *sit and slaughter* of today'.[49] Ward's emphasis on the word 'sit', descriptions of laziness and criticisms of immobile hunting techniques all recalled walkers' antipathy towards 'sedentary' urban cultures, and accused hunters of having abandoned the connection to both the terrain and its pasts implied by hunting on foot or horseback. Alongside claiming one heritage for themselves, trespassers and heritage campaigners sought to deny hunting's own claims on both past and landscape.

Though not imbued by the same public-school traditions, or emphasis on imperialism, those same qualities can be found in trespasses in Austria before World War One. Much as the upland plateau of Kinder Scout provided an iconic forbidden landscape in the Peak district of Northern England, the Blühnbachtal came to symbolise the conflict between walkers and hunting interests in the Eastern Alps. This long Alpine valley near Salzburg, running to the German border in Berchtesgaden, became the possession of Crown Prince Franz Ferdinand in 1908. He immediately closed the whole valley to all visitors, censored access and ownership information, worked in combination with local mountain guides to remove nearby paths and constructed a vast hunting residence complete with state-sponsored police force. Over the next six years, the valley witnessed an intensive campaign, combining local actors with mountaineers from both the *Naturfreunde* and *Oesterreichische Touristenklub*. These groups collaborated in individual and mass trespass, use of the newly-democratised Austrian parliament to allow censored material to be published

---

48 A. Blattmann, 'Eine Überschreitung des Hallermauerngrates [A Crossing of the Hallermauer Ridge]', *Naturfreund* 9 (3) (1905): 25–29 (27).

49 G.H.B. Ward, 'The Deer, the Forest, and the True Sportsman', *Sheffield Clarion Ramblers' Handbook* (1928–29): 25–28 (28). G.H.B. Ward, 'Bamford Lodge and Bradfield Game', *Sheffield Clarion Ramblers' Handbook* (1915–16): 19–20 (20), emphasis in original.

and press coverage both in the powerful German-language Alpine literature and mainstream liberal newspapers such as the *Münchner Neueste Nachrichten*.[50] A mountaineer from Vienna, J.V. Kastner, emerged as the most vocal and lyrical exponent of accessing the valley, and celebrated the accompanying *Wildererstimmung* ['poacher-spirit'] in his description of a 'resistance game' in the valley:

> The mountaineer on forbidden paths, who expects to see a hunter around every corner, feels like an Indian on the warpath. Eyes and ears continuously trained on the features and sounds of the wilderness, the attention to every small twig that might break under one's foot, traversing across clearings, looking with your peepers at the terrain with a view to possible hiding places – all of these are pleasures that have been denied us peaceful, civilised Europeans for millennia. If respect for law and property means that we observe footpath closures, the perfidious justifications given by landowners have actually provided me with a licence [to enjoy these pleasures].[51]

In both Britain and the Eastern Alps, those who risked trespass on closed or blocked paths brought themselves into closer contact with the mountain terrain. 'Nature is still, and I am still, standing concealed amongst trees, or moving cautiously through the dead russet bracken', William Hudson wrote in 1911, 'I am on forbidden ground, in the heart of a sacred pheasant preserve, where one must do one's prowling warily.'[52] In contrast to the open grouse moors, in Southern England and Austria, terrains of thick forest also meant that those on forbidden paths were more likely to be heard than seen – most reports of trespass note the silence that accompanied them, enforced by the act of avoiding detection.[53]

Some exploited this heightened connectivity to nature to reflect on a more-than-human approach to environmental awareness. Ward reproduced an extraordinary quote from the working-class novelist Lionel Britton's *Hunger and Love* (1931):

> As you pass along the hedge you cast your eye at the hanging things. The fierce free things of life. The stoats hanging from the twigs, the wire biting into the throat, maggots crawling out of the eyes. The fierce free things of nature: warning to them: warned

---

50   See Pils, *"Berg Frei!"*, pp. 56–59; 'Jagd und Touristik [Hunting and Mountaineering]', *Münchener Neueste Nachrichten* [Newest Munich Reports] **411** (14 Aug. 1912): 6.

51   J.V. Kastner, 'Trutzpartie: Zeitgemäße Erinnerungen eines Bergsteigers [Resistance Game: Timely Memories of a Mountaineer', *Naturfreunde* (1913): 11. 'Trutzpartie' could also be translated as 'resistance party' or 'group' – the multiple meanings are probably intentional. See also Gustav Jurek, 'Eine Bergfahrt im Watzmanngebiet: Ersteigung des Höchsten Watzmannkindes (2260m) auf theilweiser neuer Route [A Mountain Trip in the Watzmann region: Ascent of the Highest Watzmannkind (2260m) Via a Partly New Route', *Naturfreund* **5** (10) (1901): 89–90 (89); Benesch, 'Raxalpe', 228.

52   W.H. Hudson, *Afoot in England* (London: Hutchinson, 1911), p. 79.

53   See Jurek, 'Bergfahrt', 89; A. Riegler, 'Eine Herbstliche Bergfahrt im Sengsengebirge [An autumn mountain trip in the Sengsengebirge', *Naturfreund* **9** (12) (1905): 165–66 (165).

3. Appropriated Heritage?

off the earth. This is our land. We own the earth. Trespassers will be prosecuted. No thoroughfare. Freemen till! Breathes there the man (with soul so dead, who never to himself has said; this is my own my native land?) The fierce free things of nature. Britons never, never, never! And the stoat could not read.[54]

The identification of reader with Britton's protagonist, Arthur, with a dead stoat – a fierce, free thing of life – and their juxtaposition with a breathing, but dead gamekeeper recruited the more-than-human world to questions of freedom, access and nationhood. Here, trespassers did not emulate poachers so much as the wildlife hunted to near-extinction in the hunting preserves of Britain – a notion of landscape desolation that Ward clearly felt appealing. In Kastner's writing, too, trespass created room for reflection on the equal rights of ants to the space of the mountains, or the benefits of educating people in and through the mountain environment. As such, while a culture of rural-urban difference pervaded a significant proportion of encounters between trespassers and their gamekeeper foes, where trespass moved bodies from the safe, controlled space of the path and placed them instead in a responsive and recalcitrant environment, walkers and mountaineers soon developed alternative languages, ideas and rhetorics for their experiences. That these also transformed, on some occasions, into nuanced and complex appreciations of rural ecologies and society is the subject of the last section of this chapter.

Access and environmental injustice

In an important sense, walkers and mountaineers understood themselves as already the victims of environmental injustice, and argued – with some truth – that rural places could in some way alleviate the unjust environmental relations of the city. 'Thousands of young people from busy factories and offices, mean streets and dreary suburbs, could enjoy here the healthiest recreation and exercise', access campaigner Phil Barnes wrote of the Peak District in 1936.[55] Refrains like this had become a staple of rambling and mountaineering by the last years of the nineteenth century across Europe.[56] It was hardly surprising, then, that they emerged as central arguments of access campaigns. Yet a minority of access campaigners, and trespassers in particular, also identified forms of social harm in the landscapes that they traversed that would now be understood

---

54   L. Britton, *Hunger and Love* (London: Putnam, 1931), quoted in *Sheffield Clarion Ramblers' Handbook* (1936–37): 24.
55   Barnes, *Prosecuted*, p. 3.
56   Anon., 'Der Verbotene Weg', *Naturfreund* 12 (4) (1908): 83–84 (84). See Anderson, *Being Modern*, pp. 25–64.

as 'environmental injustice' – that 'the heaviest environmental burdens [fall] upon marginalized, disadvantaged, and less powerful populations'.[57]

Trespass contained the potential for a more nuanced and complex appreciation of the role of the environment in the poverty of upland communities, particularly when socialist ideologies informed the narrative of landscape appreciation.[58] In the *Naturfreunde*, the clandestine experience of trespass rapidly became a central aspect of the organisation's distinctly 'social hiking' as it emerged before World War One, but many of the same ideas can be found amongst socialists in Britain, including Ward's *Clarion Ramblers*.[59] Trespass was an essential aspect of this wider engagement with a landscape of environmental inequality. Ramblers from both organisations delivered socialist newspapers, talked directly to local people about both socialism and their everyday struggles, and investigated local examples of inequality rooted in the landscape and its heritage. As early as 1899, leaving the path became a performative and rhetorical metaphor for the other resistive aspects of social hiking, and played on an imagination of local people as victims of exploitation hidden away in the forbidden areas of the Alps and other regions.

For some socialist walkers and mountaineers, connections between recreational access and rural poverty were evidence of a imagined solidarity with rural communities. As early as 1899, Leopold Happisch (1863–1951), a co-founder of the *Naturfreunde*, editor of its journal and leader of the organisation's Vienna branch, indicated how 'sometimes even a train journey can turn contented people into the discontented' by encouraging an imagination of landscape rooted in labour:

> You are a tiny little thing, but there outside, where you are passing over, smoke climbs from a high, sooty pit. There too, there are people working hard, and they think like you. And there in the bowels of huge mountains, they dig and hammer for ore and coal. And all those who labour deep underground think as one with you. The farmer, who carries out his dangerous work on steep banks, the logger who grasps his axes with brawny fist, they all sigh of the same pressures, and wish their day was over: over them, high over the awe-inspiring mountains over their beautiful home, the sun of freedom rises![60]

Within the *Naturfreund* journal that Happisch edited, however, analyses of

---

57 Holifield, Chakraborty and Walker, 'Introduction', p. 1.
58 Examples of this tendency elsewhere: E.A. Baker, *The Highlands with Rope and Rucksack* (London, H. F. & G. Witherby, 1923), pp. 1–10; F. Kordon, 'Touren im Bereiche des Malteinthales [Routes in the region of the Malteinthales]', *Zeitschrift des deutsche und oesterreichische Alpenvereins* **26** (1895): 201–58 (221); L. Reichenwallner, 'Winke zur Abwehr rechtwidriger Wegverbote [Hints for Defence against Unlawful Path Closures]', *Oesterreichische Touristenzeitung* **33** (7) (1913): 97–100.
59 Williams, *Turning to Nature*, pp. 67–104; Hasenöhl, 'Nature Conservation', 131–32.
60 L. Happisch, 'Unser Ausflug nach Zell am See [Our Excursion to Zell am See]', *Naturfreund* **3** (10) (1899): 74–75.

3. Appropriated Heritage?

social and environmental justice were rare before World War One, and historians of the *Naturfreunde* have disagreed as to whether such social engagement in rural affairs was core to the movement from its founding, or emerged only after 1918.[61] Certainly, the above article does little to support the idea – promoted by *Naturfreunde* members immediately after 1918 – that the organisation self-censored accounts of its activities, though we at least know that some members habitually distributed socialist newspapers.[62] Much of the argument has focused on questions of 'when', rather than 'how', with the result that the complex practice of Social Hiking either seems to have emerged, fully formed, from World War One, or since the beginning of the movement, as an inevitable result of the application of socialism to countryside leisure.[63]

There is good evidence to suggest that social hiking emerged from activities related to the *Naturfreunde* campaigns for access and the protection of recreation in the Alps – objectives that, as John Alexander Williams has noted, *were* central to its ideology from the beginning, and summarised by the greeting 'Berg Frei'.[64] Happisch's 1899 article bore seemingly no relation to the other narratives of the *Naturfreunde*'s trip to Zell am See, but it certainly did to its preceding article, 'Capital and Natural Monuments', also written by Happisch. This covered a dispute regarding the *Mirafaelle*, a waterfall and beauty spot near Vienna, whose landowner, Oskar von Rosthorn, planned a hydroelectric plant. For Happisch, permission to build the plant meant prioritising individual profit over local livelihoods. In threatening both the closure and permanent destruction of the waterfall if members of the *Naturfreunde* and *Oesterreichischer Touristenklub* continued their opposition, von Rosthorn forced walkers to link their own access disputes to rural environmental inequalities.[65] Other leaders of the movement also made this connection. The teacher and socialist educational reformer Georg Schmiedl (1855–1929), who co-founded the *Naturfreund* in 1896, implored its members 'to find time to consider the people themselves, who live out their days in the shadow of mountain giants'. Schmiedl described the growing control of giant 'feudal landowners', whose insistence on hunting led to 'boundary disputes, game disturbance suits, the closure of old forest paths and pasture drives [and] the destruction and removal of water and fishing rights'.

---

61   For example, Williams, *Turning to Nature*, pp. 67–104; Hasenoehl, 'Nature Conservation'; and Günther, *Sozialismus*, pp. 11–14.
62   Gunter, *Sozialismus*, p. 13; Birkert, *Von der Idee zur Tat*, p. 28.
63   On Social Hiking, see Williams, *Turning to Nature*, pp. 78–91.
64   Williams, *Turning to Nature*, pp. 78–79.
65   L. Happisch, 'Capital und Naturschönheiten [Capital and Natural Monuments]', *Naturfreund* 3 (10) (1899): 73–74.

Remaining communal woodland was insufficient and so overexploited, and railways only hastened depopulation. In connecting local rights, and persecution, to the rights to 'free mountains' that the *Naturfreunde* proposed, Schmiedl made rare common cause with the inhabitants of the Alps.[66]

Through access – and trespass in particular – *Naturfreunde* members found common ground with rural populations that evaded them elsewhere. This was made most apparent by the one full-length treatment of 'Social Hiking' produced before the First World War – a short book by the pioneer investigative journalist and associate of the *Naturfreunde*'s leadership, Max Winter (1870–1937), entitled *Soziales Wandern*.[67] Like Happisch, Winter advised that the walker should not aim to 'bring home the number of completed kilometres, but rather deeper insight into the multifaceted lives of the people', gently critiquing the irrelevance of competitive climbing for social progress.[68] In Winter's narrative, leaving the path served as a moment of social and cultural, as well as legal, resistance. In his first anecdote, he recounted a conflict between an anonymous tenant farmer and landowner in which deer were eating crops.[69] In trespassing, Winter was thus able to reveal the trespasses of hunting landowners against their tenants, and so expose the hypocrisy of property rights that protected hunting domains from the poor, but not the poor from hunting. After revealing further aspects of Winter's impression of rural poverty – overcrowding, the emergence of work-discipline, drunkenness and Catholic superstition – his narrative was complete: 'and once again, the gurgling, murmering stream and again the path'.[70] Later in the book, he repeated the same social investigation constituted through literary and physical trespass and punctuated by returns to normative tourism. 'And again the road and again the stream and again the path', he wrote after his searing critique of the condition of miners in Bad Hallenberg.[71]

There was never a formalisation similar to 'Social Hiking' in the England, but, where socialism and access campaigning met, similar practices emerged. These were most obvious in the publications of the Clarion Ramblers. Although he never provided a methodology, Ward's walking often included extensive research, limited not just to the archival and antiquarian interests typical to

---

66 F. Bauer (=G. Schmiedl), 'Die Kehrseite der Medaille [The Other Side of the Coin]', *Naturfreund* **4** (1) (1900): 3–4.

67 M. Winter, 'Soziales Wandern [Social Hiking]', in Josef Luitpold Stern (ed.), *Die Junge Welt* [The Young World] **2** (1911).

68 Winter, 'Wandern', p. 1.

69 Winter, 'Wandern', pp. 6–8.

70 Winter, 'Wandern', p. 17.

71 Winter, 'Wandern', pp. 24–29.

3. Appropriated Heritage?

many of his peers, but also relying heavily on interviews with local people, ad-hoc conversations and the environmental attributes of the landscapes through which he walked and trespassed.[72] His writing integrated all these concerns, but wove them around anecdotes drawn from rural communities. It is difficult to know how faithfully he recounted these stories, but they routinely punctured contemporary clichés about rural life, and rarely romanticised either people or livelihoods.[73] 'Farmers, like ramblers, are not Angels,' he wrote in 1930, while in a discussion of the 'depopulation of the [Peak District's] Longdendale Valley'. Though Ward devoted most attention to sheep farmers and shepherds who had been forced from their homes by early-nineteenth century moorland enclosure acts, he insisted on the role of 'economic questions, market values, and other considerations' in farmers' decision making. These were rational small-businessmen, not survivals from a previous age.[74]

Indeed, much as Austrian mountaineers sought to connect the purchase and closure of high Alpine pastures for hunting to the 'meat shortage' of the years before World War One, so Ward insisted on the necessity to the national economy of productive landscapes. In both cases, access campaigners turned social elites' own languages of 'improvement' and productivity against them – after all, it could hardly be maintained that hunting preserves were an efficient way to feed the population.[75] If rural farmers appeared every bit as modern as the ramblers in Ward's writing, so too did he puncture stereotypes of other relevant rural characters. He recounted, for example, a story based on the credulity of 'the tribe called ramblers' to accept rural stereotype by acting out a conversation between wily poacher and corrupt gamekeeper.[76] Poachers in particular emerged as anti-heroes. At times, they were the moral protesters of moorland enclosure, at others wily operators whose attempts to fool gamekeepers Ward's ramblers might attempt to reproduce. Yet, in Ward's writing, poachers were rarely far from more organised and violent criminality linking countryside and city – a point historians only arrived at this century.[77] Ward even avoided generalisations about

---

72   See G.H.B. Ward, 'Ashopton and Ashop Woodlands', *Sheffield Clarion Ramblers' Handbook* (23–24): 84–91 (91); G.H.B. Ward, 'The Mystery of Edale Cross and Other Crosses, or a Peep into the Past', *Sheffield Clarion Ramblers' Handbook* (1928–29): 63–90 (66–67).

73   Sometimes this was explicit: see G.H.B. Ward, 'Derwent and Ashop Woodlands and the Monks, etc.', *Sheffield Clarion Ramblers' Handbook* (1923–24): 95–103 (103); Ward, '"Big Moor"', 79–80.

74   G.H.B. Ward, 'Derbyshire Moorlands and the Production of Food', *Sheffield Clarion Ramblers' Handbook* (1930–31): 109–17 (112).

75   For example, Ward, 'Food', 109; Reichenwallner, 'Wegverbote', 97–100.

76   G.H.B. W[ard] and W.H. Whitney, 'The Poacher and the Gamekeeper', *Sheffield Clarion Ramblers' Handbook* (1927–28): 73–78.

77   See Osborne and Winstanley, 'Poaching', 187–212.

gamekeepers: some stories tell of collusion between gamekeepers and poachers, others of the violence – including implied sexual assault – meted out on trespassers, others of reasonableness and friendly understanding.[78] The gamekeeper certainly did appear as a witless figure; but Ward also republished Richard Jefferies' effusive assertion of their 'vitality of early manhood', and celebrated at least one gamekeeper with whom he and other walkers had become friends.[79]

Ward's concern was not, it seems clear, to draw the kinds of cultural lines between rural and urban, backward and modern, that underscored so much of the writing about trespass amongst his male, middle-class contemporaries, and formed the basis for preservationist 'order' in the countryside.[80] Instead, his writing unearthed the myriad social costs of the environmental desolation wrought by enclosure and the emergence of vast hunting tracts where there had once been sheep droves. His heritage was one not of a lost, tranquil and peaceful countryside, but instead of the abuses and poverty he saw written into the landscape around him. This helps to explain, for example, why he published a contemporary description of how poaching gangs dominated Peak District rurality in the 1830s.[81] His objective was not to denigrate poachers, but rather to show what he considered to be the decline and desperation wrought on the countryside by outside hunting interests and the 1830 'game laws' – a tradition of critique for which he found plenty of evidence from Sheffield-based writers and popular cultures of the mid-nineteenth century. As we have seen, for Ward, the poaching practices that inspired much of his activity in the Peak district were one result but, crucially, Ward was also alive to both the violence that sometimes accompanied such practices, and the other environmental injustices wrought on upland communities, referencing, like Kastner, the tendency of hunters' quarry to feed on nearby marginal croplands, or the tree cover that protected such soils.[82]

---

78 G.H.B. Ward, 'Carl Wark and a Friendly Gamekeeper', *Sheffield Clarion Ramblers' Handbook* (1928–29): 51; Ward, 'Fun in the Hills', 119–25.

79 R. Jefferies, 'The Guide to Good Health – By a Gamekeeper', quoted in *Sheffield Clarion Ramblers' Handbook* (1915–16): 28–30. On the importance of manliness within the Clarion Ramblers, see Tebbutt, 'Manly Identity'; G.H.B. Ward, 'Stanage Cottage', *Sheffield Clarion Ramblers' Handbook* (1915–16): 50–53; Ward, 'Fun in the Hills', 125.

80 Matless, *Landscape and Englishness*.

81 J. Thomas, 'A Story of the Poachers of Grenoside and Ecclesfield', in John Thomas, *Walks in the Neighbourhood of Sheffield* (Sheffield, 1830), quoted in *Sheffield Clarion Ramblers' Handbook* (1915–16): 13–16. See also H. Oliver, *The Laurel Wreath or Rhymes of Youth* (Sheffield: Clowes and Company, 1888), quoted in *Sheffield Clarion Ramblers' Handbook* (1923–24): 12; G.H.B. Ward, 'Poaching in the Old Days', *Sheffield Clarion Ramblers' Handbook* (1923–24): 90.

82 Ward, '"Big Moor"', 85, 123. Ward, 'Other People', 143. B. Gilbert, *Old England: A God's Eye View of a Village* (London: W. Collins Sons & Company, 1921), quoted in *Sheffield Clarion Ramblers' Handbook* (1936–37): 34–35.

3. Appropriated Heritage?

Conclusion

Trespassers were only one of many voices within access lobbies. The same tensions emerged explicitly elsewhere, such as during the famous negotiations over the Snake Pass footpath in the Peak District, when access campaigners attempted to force a deal with the landowner that would have meant the permanent closure of other paths important to locals. The Commons, Open Spaces and Footpaths Preservation Society celebrated its 'long fight for the preservation of the ancient playgrounds of the Nation', after the Law of Property Act of 1925 'at last ... recognised that commons as public open spaces have a value far exceeding their use as grazing grounds'. The Act did more than this, in fact – it formed, effectively, a bargain with owners of rural commons, who could render what Chubb termed the 'Gipsy nuisance' illegal in return for allowing public recreational access. Such priorities relied on ramblers' insistence on some ancient rights but not others, and on their own ownership and authority over those rights – rather than the local people to whom many actually applied.

How 'appropriated' this heritage was, is nevertheless open to question. Footpaths and, for limited activities, commons, *were* open to all under the customary rights that access campaigners claimed to uphold, in all parts of both Britain and the Eastern Alps. Access campaigners might also be more closely connected to rural places than their urban residences and ethos suggests – in a period of high rural to urban migration, large populations of cities such as Manchester or Vienna had been born in rural places, and it was in these cities that campaigns often emerged first. Yet these were not ex-rural residents reclaiming their lost local rights to resource use or grazing. Few urban people travelled into the mountains or traversed the moorlands to forage, collect wood or tend to their cattle, and access campaigners neither focused their energies on their home villages, nor understood their campaign as one for the restoration of rights similar to those their rural ancestors might have enjoyed. Instead, these campaigns and trespassers subverted heritages of customary rights, and used their moral force to justify a campaign aimed only at asserting *national* rights to rural paths and commons for recreational use by a population now imagined as urban (and, often, sedentary). While many walkers, trespassers and campaigners may have had a legitimate claim to this heritage, they nevertheless 'appropriated' it, in the sense that, in asserting their claim, the heritage was made to do work that largely sidelined the problems faced by people still living in Europe's impoverished rural communities.

Acknowledgements

Many thanks to: Dr Katrina Navickas for helpful comments, and Sonja Laukkanen for reading my extremely rough draft. Particular thanks also to the *Naturfreunde* office in Vienna for their help and hospitality.

Bibliography

Anderson, B., 'A Liberal Countryside? The Manchester Ramblers' Federation and the "Social Readjustment" of Urban Citizens', *Urban History* **38** (1) (2011): 84–102.

Anderson, B., *Cities, Mountains and Being Modern in* Fin-de-siècle *England and Germany* (London: Palgrave Macmillan, 2020).

Baigent, E., '"God's Earth will be Sacred": Religion, Theology and the Open Space Movement in Victorian England', *Rural History* **22** (1) (2011): 31–58.

Birkert, E., *Von der Idee zur Tat: Von der Ortsgruppe zum Weltverein und zur Naturfreunde-Internationale* (Stuttgart: Touristenverein 'Die Naturfreunde', 1970).

Bodner, R., 'Der verbotene Weg: Ein kulturgeschichtliche Versuch [The Forbidden Path: A Cultural-History Commentary]', in M. Achrainer et al. (eds), *Hoch Hinaus: Wege und Hütte in den Alpen* [Aiming High: Paths and Huts in the Alps], pp. 347–71 (Cologne: Böhlau Verlag, 2016).

Bradley, Q., 'Public Support for Green Belt: Common Rights in Countryside Access and Recreation', *Journal of Environmental Policy and Planning* **21** (6) (2019): 629–701.

Brosnan, K.A., 'Law and the Environment', in A.C. Isenberg (ed.), *The Oxford Handbook of Environmental History* (Oxford: Oxford University Press, 2014), pp. 513–52.

Cole, L., 'The Emergence and Impact of Modern Tourism in an Alpine Region: Tirol, c. 1880–1914', *Annali di San Michele* [Annals of San Michele] **15** (2002): 31–40.

Cowell, B., 'The Commons Preservation Society and the Campaign for Berkhamsted Common, 1866–70', *Rural History* **13** (2) (2002): 145–61.

Girtler, R., *Wilderer: Rebellen in den Bergen* [Poachers: Rebels in the Mountains], 4th edition (Cologne: Böhlau, 2003).

Goetz, T. and H. Heiss, 'Die Nation vom Rande aus gesehen: Nationale, konfessionelle, regionale Konfliktlinien in Tirol, 1848/49 [The Nation Viewed from the Margins: National, Confessional and Regional Conflict in the Tirol, 1848/49', in C. Jansen and T. Mergel (eds), *Die Revolution von 1848/49: Erfahrung – Verarbeitung – Deutung* [*The Revolution of 1848/49: Experience – Analysis – Meaning*], pp. 150–71 (Göttingen: Vandenhoeck & Ruprecht, 1998).

Günther, D., *Wandern und Sozialismus: Zur Geschichte des Touristenvereins 'Die Naturfreunde' im Kaiserreich und in der Weimarer Republik* [Rambling and Socialism: The History of the Mountaineering Club 'The Friends of Nature' in the German Empire and the Weimar Republic] (Hamburg: Verlag Dr. Kovac, 2003).

Hasenöhl, U., 'Nature Conservation and the German Labour Movement: The *Touristenverein Die Naturfreunde* as a Bridge between Social and Environmental History', in G. Massard-Guilbaud and S. Mosley (eds), *Common Ground: Integrating the Social and Environmental in History*, pp. 125–48 (Newcastle-upon-Tyne: Cambridge Scholars Publishing, 2011).

Hey, D., *A History of the Peak District Moors* (Barnsley: Pen and Sword, 2014).

3. Appropriated Heritage?

Holifield, R., J. Chakraborty and G. Walker, 'Introduction: The Worlds of Environmental Injustice', in R. Holifield, J. Chakraborty and G. Walker (eds), *The Routledge Handbook of Environmental Justice*, pp. 1–12 (London: Routledge, 2018).

Houston, R.A., 'People, Space and Law in Late Medieval and Early Modern Britain and Ireland', *Past and Present* **230** (2016): 47–89.

Howkins, A., *The Death of Rural England: A Social History of the Countryside since 1900* (London: Routledge, 2003).

Howkins, A., 'The Use and Abuse of the English Commons, 1845–1914', *History Workshop Journal* **78** (2014): 107–32.

Judson, P.M., *Guardians of the Nation: Activists on the Language Frontiers of Imperial Austria* (London: Harvard University Press, 2006).

Keller, T.S., *Apostles of the Alps: Mountaineering and Nation Building in Germany and Austria, 1860–1939* (Chapel Hill: University of North Carolina, 2016).

Killingray, D., 'Rights, "Riot" and Ritual: The Knole Park Access Dispute, Sevenoaks, Kent, 1883–85', *Rural History* **5** (1) (1994): 63–79.

McDonagh, B. and C.J. Griffin, 'Occupy! Historical Geographies of Property, Protest and the Commons, 1500–1850', *Journal of Historical Geography* **53** (2016): 1–10.

Morosini, S., *Sulle vette della Patria. Politica, Guerra, e nazione nel Club alpino italiano (1863–1922)* [On the Peaks of the Fatherland: Politics, War and Nation in the Italian Alpine Club (1863–1922)] (Milan: Francoangeli, 2009).

Navickas, K., 'Moors, Fields, and Popular Protest in South Lancashire and the West Riding of Yorkshire, 1800–1848', *Northern History* **46** (1) (2009): 93–111.

Navickas, K., *Protest and the Politics of Space and Place 1789–1848* (Manchester: Manchester University Press, 2015).

Osborne, H. and M. Winstanley, 'Rural and Urban Poaching in Victorian England', *Rural History* **17** (2) (2006): 187–212.

Peniston-Bird, C., T. Rohkrämer and F.R. Schulz, 'Glorified, Contested and Mobilized: The Alps in the "Deutscher und Oesterreichischer Alpenverein" from the 1860s to 1933', *Austrian Studies* **18** (2010): 141–58.

Pils, M., *"Berg Frei!" 100 Jahre Naturfreunde* [Mountains Free! 100 Years of the Friends of Nature] (Vienna: Verlag für Gesellschaftskritik, 1994).

Readman, P., 'Walking and Environmentalism in the Career of James Bryce: Mountaineer, Scholar, Statesman, 1838–1922', in C. Bryant, A. Burns and P. Readman, (eds), *Walking Histories, 1800–1914*, pp. 287–318 (London: Palgrave Macmillan, 2016).

Readman, P., *Storied Ground: Landscape and the Shaping of English National Identity* (Cambridge: Cambridge University Press, 2018).

Sissons, D. and R. Smith (eds), *Right to Roam: A Celebration of the Sheffield Campaign for Access to Moorland* (Sheffield: J.W. Northend, 2005).

Steidl, A., 'Migration Patterns in the Late Habsburg Empire', in G. Bischof and D. Rupnow (eds), *Migration in Austria* (Innsbruck: Innsbruck University Press, 2017), pp. 69–86.

Taylor, A., '"Commons-Stealers", "Land-Grabbers" and "Jerry-Builders": Space, Popular Radicalism and the Politics of Public Access in London, 1848–1880', *International Review of Social History* **40** (1995): 383–407.

Taylor, H., *A Claim on the Countryside: A History of the British Outdoor Movement* (Keele: Keele University Press, 1997).

Tebbutt, M., 'Landscapes of Loss: Moorlands, Manliness and the First World War', *Landscapes* **2** (2004): 114–27.

Tebbutt, M., 'Rambling and Manly Identity in Derbyshire's Dark Peak, 1880s–1920s', *The Historical Journal* **49** (4) (2006): 1125–53.

Williams, J.A., *Turning to Nature in Germany: Hiking, Nudism and Conservation, 1900–1940* (Stanford: Stanford University Press, 2007).

Matless, D., *Landscape and Englishness* (London: Reaktion, 1998).

CHAPTER 4.

HEFTING THE LAND: A LOCATIVE HERITAGE OF HOOVES AND FEET

Karen Lykke Syse

Charles Boileau Elliot was a member of the Royal Geographical Society who was exploring Norway in the 1830s. Elliot and his four companions were caught in wet and stormy weather when they followed a pack horse path across the mountain to find an undescribed route over Hardangervidda. Fortunately, they found a tiny milking hut in which they could seek shelter.

> The stones forming the hut, if such a title it could merit, were rudely and irregularly put together. A hole in the center let out the smoke and admitted the fresh air. The former had no other exit; the latter had free entrance on every side. Four women and three children were lying on two litters which nearly filled the hut. The intermediate space was occupied by a calf. Ranged round the sides were bowls of milk and cream, the produce of a herd of cows, whose lowing indicated an unaccustomed intrusion. The smell and filth were almost intolerable; but our minds were braced to the encounter. Three horse-blankets were laid on the wet ground, and our feet were turned towards the smoking embers of the fire. Thus, wrapped in cloaks, we slept a little; but the rain beat in so violently that it was not possible to repose for any length of time.[1]

The weather was extreme, and so perhaps were the material and social conditions they encountered. Nevertheless, the paths led these visitors to a mountain dairy, providing safe, if not too comfortable, accommodation.

This passage encapsulates how the first tourists, trekkers and ramblers in Norway found their way and navigated the paths that ran through pastures, forests and mountains, along rivers and streams, over running brooks and frozen lakes. Needless to say, these paths were there before the visitors, and so were the people and animals who had created the paths and knew the places within and between them. This chapter seeks to explore who made the paths you can walk in the dark, and ask if we can reach a deeper understanding of the habitual movements that created the paths, if we include the history of the pack horses, cows, sheep, goats and the people who tended to them? Can the stories of dairymaids and shoeless shepherds and the animals with whom

---

1   Elliott, *Letters from the North of Europe*, p. 119.

Figure 1.

Accommodation for travellers at Langfjellet, by Johannes Flintoe (1787–1870). Source: National Museum Oslo, object NG.K&H.B.06352, CC BY 4.0.

they cohabited add to our understanding of how the paths came to be, and how they changed with changing movement practices and technologies? The hoof- and footsteps of people and animals can be found in between the lines and as afterthoughts in travel accounts, from which we can learn how people and animals co-created and maintained a material movement heritage in the nineteenth century, and can add to our understanding of how, and by whom this heritage is maintained today.

Locating a Norwegian movement heritage

According to Robert McFarlane 'Paths are habits of a landscape. They are acts of consensual making. It is hard to create a footpath on your own'.[2] The paths the first visitors to Norway walked on, and indeed the paths we still use today,

---

2 Macfarlane, *The Old Ways*, p. 17.

4. Hefting the Land

were created by hooves and feet, walking habitually, going about everyday or seasonal labour, everyday or seasonal grazing, transporting people and things from place to place; from one farm to the next; from farm to outfields; to rough grazing grounds and to shielings;[3] from farm to market town, and back.

From the mid-1700s until about 1900, several hundred books about Norway and the Norwegians were published.[4] The very first explorers mainly came from England, Germany, France and the other Nordic countries. Norway was like other Nordic countries, considered to be in the periphery of Europe, both geographically and culturally.[5] Visitors from both within and beyond Norway often had a scientific purpose for their explorative rambles, however this was soon to change. Up until the 1830s, visitors from abroad had been few and far between, then, during the next decade or so, an avalanche of people with an interest in rugged and wild landscapes came to Norway.[6] They described the routes they journeyed, the paths they followed and the peculiar rural culture they saw. Half a century after Elliot's account quoted above, the British tourist William Mattieu Williams described the wild and untouched landscapes of Norway with breath-taking views and awe-inspiring waterfalls: 'There is a path to the Mongefoss, free of course, though closed by a cattle gate; but this fall is nearly as well seen where its waters pass under a bridge of the road.'[7] What visitors like Williams experienced as unexplored territory was obviously a place in which there was a path, were cattle were kept on one or the other side of a grid, where there was a bridge, and even a road.

Edward Casey argues in *Remembering* how movement in a particular place allows the body to integrate its emplaced 'past into its present experience: its local history is literally a history of locales'.[8] Michel de Certeau adds a perspective to this by labelling modern historiography *heterography*, or 'a discourse about the other', because the past becomes an *object* of knowledge rather than an integrated part of history itself'.[9] Following David Harvey's call to 'look towards the intangible and performative entities' and to integrate this without supporting 'an exclusivist, elitist and even racist discourse of heritage and landscape',[10] this chapter will seek to integrate and incorporate the non-human animals in

---

3   A shieling is an upland or mountain dairy used within transhumance.
4   Schiøtz, *Utlendingers reiser i Norge* and Pettersen, *Udlændingers reiser i Norge*.
5   Oslund, *Iceland Imagined*, p. 7
6   Rogan, *Det gamle skysstellet*.
7   Williams, *Through Norway with Ladies*, p. 252.
8   Casey, *Remembering*, p. 194
9   De Certeau, *The Writing of History*, p. 3.
10 Harvey, 'Landscape and Heritage', 920.

the historiography of movement, heritage and landscape. Such a processual methodologically opens for a study of the past 'as well as the emerging present ... engage[ing] critically with the future.'[11]

Everyday lives in exceptional landscapes

When tourists and visitors opened the cattle gate and followed the path towards their perception of wild, untouched nature, they entered a sphere that was unfamiliar to them. A heterogeneous group including local farmers, peasants, semi-professional pilots, milkmaids and shepherds, and finally the animals themselves, facilitated and enabled visits to this sphere. Understanding the heritage of movement requires a diverse exploration of the available written sources, and combining these sources with the material and embodied culture of the land and the animals. Places we encounter in these sources are still there, and some are still within the same systemic context as they were at the time of writing – thus still part of a functional and living cultural system.[12]

The temporality and rhythms of the agricultural year and the logic of utilising natural resources like grazing and fodder harvest are still possible to see and understand in the present. In some areas and for some farms, grazing patterns still run from the farms and lower valleys to the grazing and shielings of the higher grounds and mountain regions. Communications between farms and shielings are still connected by paths, and shielings are connected to other shielings through paths. A crisscrossing network of paths within the land ties places and people together, personalising this land and – in Braudel's terms – providing structure to everyday life. There are a few problems with exploring everyday lives in the past through texts created in a setting which encompasses the dichotomy of everyday life versus the extraordinary and adventurous. For one thing, the mundane might be described as extraordinary. Whether it was the folklorist Peder Christian Asbjørnsen who collected fairytales, a social scientist like Eilert Sundt surveying social conditions, English tourists bagging summits, or Norwegian students amassing adventures, they were all in a different mode from the people who lived in these places.[13] They were pursuing the Norwegian landscape rather than the land.

---

11   Ibid., 920.

12   Schiffer, *Behavioral Archaeology*; Schiffer, *Formation Processes of the Archeological Record*; and Johnson, *Ideas of Landscape*.

13   Asbjørnsen, 'Indberetning om en i 1851 med Reisestipendium fra 1849 foretagen Reise i Østerdalen osv. for at samle Folkediktninger, Eventyr, Sagn osv'.

4. Hefting the Land

Embracing the land and landscape

The words land and *landskap* both have a long history of use in the Scandinavian countries, denoting geographical and political boundaries within them. According to Kenneth Olwig, landskap was used to denote 'a unit of territory identifiable with a folk'.[14] The meaning of the word landskap changed in Norwegian, however. In the first dictionary of the Norwegian language[15] compiled by Ivar Aasen in 1850, the terms *lende* and *lendt* are defined as derivations of *land*.[16] The latter denotes roughly the same as the English word 'land'. The word lende, however, is a noun denoting ground, or terrain[17] and lendt – used as a suffix for an adjective – is used to explain how suitable or unsuitable the land is for a particular use, like movement, for instance. We have the word *brattlendt*, meaning steep-grounded, *våtlendt* meaning wet-grounded, or simply *ulendt*, a negation meaning unsuitable or difficult for movement.[18] In the same dictionary, use of the word *landskap* is explained as rare, and the words *landskapnad* or *landskikkelse* are provided as more common synonyms. Their Danish translation is '*et Lands Udseende eller Skikkelse*' [the look or shape of the land].[19] In English, the word landscape was imported along with Dutch landscape art in 1598,[20] while in Norway (as in some other countries) the word's meaning was revised and gained more traction as a framing concept used within the arts, and later as a scholarly term used for land management and governance. Although the concept landscape arguably balances between matter and ideas, and can conceptually and theoretically bridge these,[21] its general use conveys the land statically and from a distance. Lende describes its practical, embodied experience, conveying a closeness between the subject and the land.[22] Conceptually and analytically, lende allows for an emic approach while landskap/landscape allows for an ethic approach.[23]

While the Norwegian term lende rings foreign to all but Norwegians, there is an obvious English equivalent that is still is use within agricultural parlance.

---

14 Olwig 'The "Natural" Landscape and Agricultural Values', 27.
15 Up to this point, and because Norway for centuries had been ruled by Denmark and later Sweden, Norwegians had used Danish as their written language.
16 I. Aasen, *Ordbog over det norske Folkesprog* (Kristiania: Werner & Comp. 1850), p. 276.
17 W.A. Kirkeby *Norsk-Engelsk ordbok stor utgave* (Oslo, Kunnskapsforlaget, 1993), p. 700.
18 Lykke Syse, *Lende og landskap*.
19 Aasen, *Ordbok over det norske Folkesprog*, p. 260
20 http://www.merriam-webster.com/dictionary/landscape
21 Saltzman, *Inget landskap är en ö: Dialektik och praktik i öländska landskap*, pp. 38–39.
22 Lykke Syse, *Lende og landskap*, p. 92.
23 Goodenough, 'Describing a Culture'; Harris, 'The Epistemology of Cultural Materialism'.

Karen Lykke Syse

The term 'land' is used to describe the solid part of the surface of the earth, or a portion of the earth's solid surface distinguished by boundaries or ownership. It is also a word used by the people who labour the land to describe it. 'Land' will often be redefined or specified in other terms such as hills and fields, bogs and woods, and all these places are connected and intersected by paths. In this chapter, the word 'land' will be used alongside landscape, to explain the analytical positioning. Firstly, 'land' is a suitable English translation of the Norwegian word 'lende', which connotes a tactile, processual relationship with the soil or terrain, and which has an agency of its own.[24] Lende – or its English translation land – has been in use for a long time and is still in use. A fairly recent historical account of the mountain lodge Spiterstulen exemplifies this:

> The mountain road follows the land. Around a hill, over a crag, carefully turning around a thicket pine, it seeks carefully forward from bridge start to bridge end. No bulldozers have ravaged it – it is Jo and Ola who have shoveled meter by meter using pick-axe and spade. (Henriksen, *Spiterstulen gjennom 150 år*, p. 45, author's translation.)

Secondly, using this term allows for an integration of sensations in a cultural context, following Howes 'sensescapes'.[25] 'Land' encapsulates the terrain understood by all the senses. Christopher Tilley shows the importance of integrating the perception of the whole body in his phenomenological approach to studying landscapes.[26] The land, hills and fields can be touched, heard and smelt, allowing one to receive and structure information.[27] *Land* is a place of labour or chores, and the conceptual predecessor both to terms like *sensescape* and anthropologist Tim Ingold's concept *taskscape* merging the words 'task' and 'landscape'.[28] *Land* is concrete; hands on.[29]

If landscape were inclusive enough a concept to encompass all of the above, such specifications would be less relevant. The archaeologist Matthew Johnson argues, however, that since the word 'landscape' entered the English vocabulary,

---

24 Lykke Syse, *From Land Use to Landscape*; Lykke Syse, 'Expert Systems, Local Knowledge and Power'; Lykke Syse, *Lende og landskap*.

25 Howes, 'Sensation in Cultural Context', 143.

26 Tilley, *Handbook of Material Culture*, p. 161; and Tilley, *A Phenomenology of Landscape*.

27 Lykke Syse, 'Expert Systems, Local Knowledge and Power'; Feld, 'Places Sensed, Sensed Placed'; Rodaway, *Sensuous Geographies*.

28 Ingold, *The Temporality of the Landscape*.

29 I learnt through fieldwork among Norwegian foresters (Lykke Syse, *Lende og Landskap*) that they would use the word 'lende' to myself and amongst one another when talking about the land, the terrain, its suitability for various utilitarian tasks both in the past, using horses, and in the present, using heavy machinery. Once they talked about official management plans, biodiversity issues and other 'official' topics, they slipped into using the word landskap. Farmers in Scotland used the term 'land' in a similar way (Lykke Syse, *Land Use and Landscape*).

4. Hefting the Land

a panoramic or distant way of regarding nature has become a perspective many scholars choose to use to analyse and interpret the land, implicitly requiring a certain disconnection from that which is described. Its revised meaning has emigrated along with internationalisation and emphasis on English as the lingua franca of scholars. In many contexts, landscape became a concept describing land that could be framed by a map, drawing, camera or chart, thereby allowing it to be brought into an office or library for further perusal.[30]

The way in which we have mapped, counted, drawn, measured and archived nature has been an important part of the civilising process of controlling the land and its people.[31] Most of the sources this chapter leans on are guilty of objectifying both landscapes, humans and non-human animals by visualisation and representation through sight, pen or paintbrush, and thereafter projecting and analysing for others to see. A methodological challenge is moving from this ethical stance to the emic, seeking to understand what is said between the lines and images created in the past, representing inhabited historical landscapes. This is where we can find the land and the paths between places and seek to understand those that lived and worked there.

Even with a reflexive use of emic and ethic perspectives, attempts to include more dimensions, senses and agents will always just be subjective and suggestive. How can we understand the perspective of another subject? One way is to ask oneself what other perspectives could potentially be possible. Although this can never be clear or unambiguous, it facilitates and suggest other interpretations. The ethnologist Terje Planke shows how actions, perspectives and intentions can be reconstructed using material culture as a starting point. Intentions and actions are closely connected and, for Planke, the most challenging issue is understanding what the meanings or intentions were behind actions resulting in objects. Planke has researched and reconstructed past actions through material culture, and argues that these actions can be suggested by using analogies from the present to the past.[32] The renowned historian Keith Thomas applied a similar methodology to approach the written sources in his pivotal work *Religion and Decline of Magic* and in *Man and the Natural World*.[33] Thomas applied perspectives from anthropology and sociology to suggest and explain the reasoning behind actions, subjects and objects within his historical written sources. My argument is that separating the noun 'land' and the concept 'landscape' enables

---

30   Johnson, *Ideas of Landscape*.
31   Scott, *Seeing like a State*, p.11.
32   Planke, 'Feltarbeid og redselen for nærhet'.
33   Thomas, *Religion and The Decline of Magic*; Thomas, *Man and the Natural World*.

the researcher to combine these methodologies, as the land was and is material while the understanding or interpretation of landscape that is projected through the sources might need re-evalutation.[34] Some of the landscapes portrayed and projected through the sources as wild and inhospitable were not wild at all, but were places where people farmed, mowed and tended to their domestic animals. Rough grazing areas and shielings were perhaps what Thomas Hardy would define as 'far from the madding crowd', but they were still very much populated and used by people and herds of grazing animals.

Locating the paths connecting places

Whether tourists were ascending mountains, hunting, fishing or trekking, exploring Norwegian nature was both means and end in their activity, and there was an idea that something natural and unsoiled, a pure Northern European peasantry, could still be found in Norway.[35] Part of exploring Norway was exploring its 'natives', thus trying to understand what the tourists' own countries had been before modernity and industrialisation. Norway was on the periphery of Europe, where industrialisation and urbanisation had happened later and at a smaller scale than in some other countries. According to Charles Boileau Elliot, Norway in the 1830s was 'in a state of demi-civilization, a century behind Sweden, which is a century behind Denmark, and at least another century behind France and England'.[36] Thomas Malthus described Norwegians as 'nature children' when he visited in 1799, and throughout the 1800s visitors still described rural Norwegians as healthy, uncorrupted and innocent.[37] Travel accounts shows how land and landscapes in Norway were arenas where foreign visitors met native people going about their everyday lives, harvesting grass, foliage and moss, while native animals were transforming the same into manure, meat and dairy. The economic worldview of the peasants and small-scale farmers came up against a romantic view of nature as an exotic, awe-inspiring arena for adventure, in which the local people were perceived to lead a picturesque and primitive life that was both ornamental and curious.

In the early 1800s, there were no marked trails that made it self-evident to a visitor which route to choose. Nevertheless, the land was organised and structured in routes in a manner which was both legible and obvious to those who lived there. Farms, inns and the local manse mediated the routes by pro-

---

34 Lykke Syse, *Land Use and Landscape*, pp. 52–53.
35 Fjågesund and Symes, *The Northern Utopia*.
36 Elliot, *Letters from the North*, p. 153.
37 Malthus, *Reisedagbok fra Norge*, p. 71.

4. Hefting the Land

Figure 2.

A vertical movement to the mountain dairy in Bergen parish, by Johannes Flintoe (1787–1870). Source: National Museum Oslo, object NG.K&H.1994.0589.

viding accommodation, and the country roads that ran between them allowed for a certain coaching system for travellers.[38] The paths that connected buildings belonging to each farm were systematic, if not formalised. There were hay barns in the lower lands, with paths leading to them and between them. A more complex system was that of the multifarious paths connecting systems of shielings to the farms on lower ground. Larger farms often had as many as three shielings.[39] The need for such was evident: envision springtime in a cold climate. As the snow gives way to sun, the grass first returns in the lower areas on the valley floor. Days and weeks of sunshine do their job and the frost pulls back up the mountains. A green curtain of grass slowly returns, first in the valley, then creeping further and further up the mountainside. Once the farm grass in the valley has been grazed, the dairy maid takes the cows, goats,

---

38   Rogan, *Det gamle skysstellet*.
39   Solheim, *Norsk Sætertradisjon*.

sheep and the occasional pig with her up to the lowest dairy where the grass is lush. Meanwhile, the warmth of spring lets the grass reappear after winter in the second and finally the top dairy, and the dairy maid can move her two and four-legged companions along at the same pace as the grass ripens.

The paths were created by this annual movement of hooves and feet year after year, decade after decade, century after century, and have an inner logic of movement that connects building structures as safe havens to one another both vertically and horizontally through the yearly cycle.

Vertically, the paths allowed and maintained communication and transport from the farm up to the dairy, but the dairies of different farms were also connected to one another horizontally. A complex communication system running from farm to dairy, between dairies, from dairies to rough grazing areas, was maintained year after year and connected valleys to mountain plateaus and even some mountain tops. Material remains, such as the farms, byres, dairies, fanks, fences and bothies and indeed the paths that tie them all together, are systems of place making; a cultural heritage of movement between shelter. Whether consisting of stone huts, a log notched shed or grander timber structures, they were safe havens for both dwellers and the odd passing traveller, and they provided the amenities needed to traverse mountains and hills in the 1800s.

When the Norwegian Trekking Association (DNT) was established in 1868, it had a clear sense of priorities: its first yearbook called for procuring or building cabins and marking paths. This might seem curious, as the articles in this first volume describe treks that DNT members explain in detail, following the pattern explained above: they go from shieling to shieling, and they refer to paths between them. In other words, the paths and the shelter were already there. One such route description explains that accommodation of a 'tolerable' sort can be found at any shieling, and that the shielings' inhabitants in this case will simply budge and find a bed at a neighbour's shieling or in the byre. He then explains that if more than two people trek together, they will need to distribute their need for beds among two or more shielings.[40] Another trekker tells his fellow members that, 'One can always find rest in a byre, the cattle lie outdoors philosophising in the moonshine on the grass outside, and only a patient might be indoors in its stall, but its monotonous rumination does not disturb us in our sleep.'[41] In short, what the Norwegian Trekking Association did was to expand, label, formalise and take ownership of a material movement heritage that habit had already created.

---

40 G.C. Krefting, in *Den Norske Turistforening Aarbog for 1868* (Christiania: Det Steenske Bogtrykkeri, 1868), p. 80.

41 L. Grønstad, in *Den Norske Turistforening Aarbog for 1868*, p. 33.

4. Hefting the Land

The feet and hooves that made the paths: a continuous movement heritage

Travellers' accounts also introduce us to the relationship between human and non-human animals in the landscape. Sir Arthur De Capell Brooke described a particularly filthy inn he visited. He couldn't stand the flea-ridden bed longer than absolutely necessary and tried searching for his manservant. But he opened the wrong door, and:

> [O]n opening the door, a scene both curious and strange to my eyes presented itself. In five or six wooden cribs near twenty persons of both sexes, perfectly naked, were lying together in heaps. Several large pigs were enjoying the sweets of repose, and responding with drowsy grunts to the snores of, I might almost say, their fellow swine.[42]

Such cohabitation might seem hard to believe but it is not singular.[43] People and animals often shared a house in rural Norway, and milkmaids and the younger generations on the farm would often sleep in the warm byre. The human-animal relationship was multisensory and embodied. Animals were friends and companions; it was even common for animals to be blessed, christened, and given personal names.[44] Several sources describe this close relationship, and foreign visitors noted that the animals themselves were particularly tame.

> The cows are remarkably inquisitive; they followed me along the road, peeped into my knapsack and pockets, and licked my shoulders and back. The horses exhibited a similar docility. This tameness and absence of fear among the cattle is a safe indication of a kindly disposition of the people.[45]

Although the cattle described above might have been looking for salt to lick rather than companionship, their eager meeting with this traveller probably indicated that they regarded people as beneficent rather than a threat.

> Hitterdal will look more smiling than ever when you return at eventide and meet the country-girls sitting astride on the goats as they milk them; others carrying home the dairy produce in chip boxes painted all over flowers, and driving before them pigs with high bristling manes, surmounted by wooden yokes.[46]

Emily Lowe's aestheticisation of everyday life in the quote above both exemplifies and illustrates methodologically how we can read the animals in between

---

42 Brooke, *Travels Through Sweden, Norway and Finmark*, p. 118–19.
43 Sundt, *Om renlighets-stellet i Norge*; Lykke Syse, 'Griseliv og grisedød i Norge før og nå'.
44 Visted and Stigum, *Vår Gamle Bondekultur*, p. 162.
45 Williams, *Through Norway with a Knapsack*, p.164.
46 Lowe, *Unprotected Females in Norway*, p. 249.

the lines in other sources.[47] Animals and humans touched one another, both emotionally and physically, but they also imprinted their relationship on the land, and the traces of their presence can be found beyond the lines and pages of books, and not just between them. We can read the physical traces of these historical animals through the ridges their hoofs have imprinted in the land today. The animals themselves have conveyed these patterns to one another since the land was first grazed. Cow to calf, ewe to lamb, movements to particular places are ingrained in their bodies and through their hooves, and also ingrained in the land. They have an agency of their own, and have in fact created a network of routes, a non-human heritage of movements. The ethnologist Ragnar Pedersen carried out an extensive fieldwork on transhumance in Hedemark in Mid-Norway in the late 1960s. He explains the systematic use of all the grazing areas, showing paths and routes between them, and mentions how the sheep would usually follow the cows out to graze. 'The cows had their steady movement patterns and followed the terrain, near brooks and valleys in particular. Often the shepherd would just follow the herd ...'[48] Animals and people make paths in a manner that Macfarlane labels the 'habitual' or 'consensual', and this particular example shows how the animal movement has created continuity and anchored grazing actions to the land. Traces such as paths, ridges, fanks, fencing and cairns show the continuity of use, and the systematic context of this movement heritage has been maintained many places, not just through the patterns of movement, but also through sightlines.

Sightlines do not necessarily show you how to move, but where to go. Elements in the land itself can provide such sightlines, but they can also be created by people to be visible, as with cairns. You might attach your gaze to a mountain top or a cairn, and let your feet follow a path that zig-zags towards it. In many cases, hoofs made marks that became paths before feet followed – habitually. Grazing animals have populated the mountains since the ice pulled back after the ice age. We find evidence of this through physical elements set up to aid the people who either hunted them (in the case of reindeer) or tended to them (in the case of sheep, goats and cows).[49]

Pulling away from the visual sightlines again, the land can also be heard.

---

[47] See Baker, *Picturing the Beast*; Holloway, 'What a Thing, Then, Is This Cow...'; Lykke Syse, 'Stumbling over Animals in the Landscape'.

[48] Pedersen, *Seterbruket på Hedmarken*, p. 96.

[49] A cairn by Hellevassbu at the mountain plateau Hardangervidda was recently rebuilt and, unlike most old cairns, the stones on this one were without trace of lichen on the inside of stones. It was most probably built in the centuries after the ice withdrew (8500 BC) by reindeer hunters, as lichen was well established on the stones facing outwards. The first sign of grazing animals from the same area is from 3500 BC. (Personal communication)

4. Hefting the Land

Figure 3.

Milk maid with bell cow, Løken østre, Rudshøgda i Ringsaker. Source: https://digitaltmuseum.no, object HHB-01981, CC pdm.

The sound of wood being chopped for firewood, cows lowing, sheep bleating, dairy maids calling the livestock home and, last but not least, bells tinkling, all indicate a populated place. These sounds assist the tired traveller in finding his or her path back to shelter:

> The tinkling bells of cattle struck the hour of rest; tired, weary, as they, we pulled up at a farm, and reposed for the night; to-morrow morning I will tell you how.[50]

The tinkling of bells that called Miss Emily Lowe to rest in the quote above, was probably particularly helpful in fog, rain or bad weather. It indicated safe havens and shielings. But from a movement heritage perspective, the sound of animal bells is not just a convenient indicator of people; it is the sound of a

---

50   Lowe, *Unprotected Females in Norway*, p. 199.

cultural and historical continuum of grazing cattle and the people who hung, and still hang, bells around their necks.[51]

The cow or goat wearing the bell would be chosen by the dairy maid and was often her favourite,[52] elected among the others in her flock for intelligence, kindness and wisdom – words that repeat in the source material. The bell cow would know the way to the best pasture. The *reason* she knew is because she once followed another bell cow as a calf and heifer.[53] The rest of the flock would follow the bell cow, and the bell itself would and will – be passed on down the line of animals, generation after generation.[54] Meanwhile, the younger cows have been taught where the best grass is, where the easiest paths leading from one grazing area to the next are, thus creating and maintaining the paths themselves through their walking, by following the bell cow. These animals are 'hefted' to the land;[55] they know where to go because they have embodied this heritage of movement throughout their lives.

Hefting the heritage of the land

Today, trekking has become Norway's favourite kind of outdoor recreation; the Norwegian Trekking Association, established by an elite in 1868, has more than 300,000 members today[56] – quite significant in a country with only 5.3 million people. Paths going up to popular vistas and mountain tops suffer from widening and soil erosion, while other paths have surprisingly enough almost disappeared. In the past, people followed the needs of animals in order to fulfil their own needs; thus grazing patterns created the system of transhumance and shielings. People adapted themselves to animals' movement and grazing needs, because the animals provided them with their living. With the global trade in animal fodder and quest for efficiency in modern agriculture, grazing

---

51   Meyer, *Norges lyder*.
52   Dairy maids usually pose alongside their bell cow on formal photos in Norway, and the Digital Museum shows many such photos from all over the country.
53   Cows would live 20 or more rather than 4 or 5 years back then, which is also relevant to the argument.
54   Interview with a dairy maid during ethnographic fieldwork in a mountain dairy.
55   The English hill farmer and author James Rebanks uses the word 'hefted', explaining the word as a Norse import: 'HEFT Noun: 1) *(Northern England)* A piece of upland pasture to which a farm animal has become hefted. 2) An animal that has become hefted thus. Verb: *Trans. (Northern England and Scotland) of a farm animal, especially a flock of sheep*: To become accustomed and attached to an area of upland pasture. Adj.: Hefted: describing livestock that has become thus attached. *(Etymology: from the Old Norse hefð, meaning 'tradition')'* Rebanks, *The Shepherd's Life*, p. xi. In modern Norwegian 'hevd' is also a legal term for habitual use of the land 'hevd'. For a thorough explanation and contextualisation of these customary rights, see also Olwig, 'Heritage as common(s)', 97–98.
56   https://www.dnt.no/om/ (accessed 31 Aug. 2021).

4. Hefting the Land

outfields have decreased and only fifteen per cent of Norwegian cows are still brought out to graze outfields like shielings. Brushwood encroachment in heritage landscapes has become a problem.[57] Quoting Macfarlane again, 'Paths are consensual, too, because without common care and common practice they disappear: overgrown by vegetation, ploughed up or built over ... Like sea channels that require regular dredging to stay open, paths NEED walking.'[58]

A recent study shows that, although people have stopped using some of the paths that were created – consensually – through an ancient agricultural practice now under threat, the animals that are still allowed to graze the outfields have not. Cows belonging to the unbroken line of animals hefted to the land maintain their practice. By attaching a GPS to each bell cow, scientists could trace the movement patterns of the cows throughout the grazing season.[59] When they downloaded the bell-cows' movement routes onto old aerial photos and maps, the scientists had a eureka moment. Digital movement patters revealed that the cows sought fields surrounding old dairies that are long gone. These places had a higher biodiversity and a wider and probably more interesting selection of herbage to graze. In fact, they would even follow the old paths between them, although these were difficult to actually see. 'In a manner, they read the history in the landscape.'[60] Animals co-create movement heritage and are also stewards of it, and their agency could be acknowledged in heritage management. According to the editors of this volume, '[w]hereas a path is an unintended result of walking, walking is one of the intended results of trails'.[61] Following this, we owe both our movement heritage and its resulting *trailscape*[62] to our non-human companions. Their hooves have habitually embodied the movement heritage of the land.

Bibliography

Asbjørnsen, P. Chr., 'Indberetning om en i 1851 med Reisestipendium fra 1849 foretagen Reise i Østerdalen osv. for at samle Folkediktninger, Eventyr, Sagn osv', in *Norske Universitets- og Skole-Annaler*, 2. rekke VII (Christiania, 1857), pp. 83–103.

Baker, S., *Picturing the Beast: Animals, Identity, and Representation* (Manchester, New York: Manchester University Press, 1993).

Brooke, Arthur de Capell, *Travels Through Sweden, Norway and Finmark* (London: Rodwell & Martin, 1823).

---

57 Stensgaard, 'Hvordan står det til på setra?'
58 Macfarlane, *The Old Ways*, p.17.
59 Tuv (ed.), *Prosjekt Levande stølar*.
60 Ibid., p. 37.
61 Svensson, Sörlin and Saltzman 'Pathways to the Trail'.
62 Fagence, 'A Heritage "Trailscape"'.

Karen Lykke Syse

Casey, E. S., *Remembering: A Phenomenological Study* (Bloomington: Indiana University Press, 1987).

De Certeau, Michel, *The Writing of History* (New York: Columbia, 1988).

Elliott, Charles Boileau, *Letters from the North of Europe; or a Journal of Travel in Holland, Denmark, Norway, Sweden, Finland, Russia, Prussia, and Saxony* (London: Colburn and Bentley, 1832).

Fagence, M., 'A Heritage "Trailscape": Tracking the Exploits of Historical Figures – an Australian Case Study', *Journal of Heritage Tourism* **12** (5) (2017): 452–462.

Feld, Steven. 'Places Sensed, Senses Placed', in David Howes (ed.), *Empire of the Senses: the Sensual Culture Reader* (Oxford: Berg, 2005).

Fjågesund, Peter and Ruth A. Symes, *The Northern Utopia. British Perceptions of Norway in the Nineteenth Century* (New York, Amsterdam: Rodopi, 2003).

Goodenough, Ward, 'Describing a Culture', in *Description and Comparison in Cultural Anthropology*, pp. 104–19 (Cambridge: Cambridge University Press, 1970).

Grønstad, Laurits, In *Den norske Turistforening Aarbog for 1868* (Christiania: Det Steenske Bogtrykkeri, 1868).

Harris, Marvin, 'The Epistemology of Cultural Materialism', in *Cultural Materialism: The Struggle for a Science of Culture*, pp. 29–45 (New York: Random House, 1980).

Harvey, David, 'Landscape and Heritage: Trajectories and Consequences', *Landscape Research* **40** (8) (2015): 911–24.

Henriksen, Vera (ed.), *Spiterstulen gjennom 150 år* (Otta: Engers boktrykkeri, 1986).

Holloway, L., '"What a Thing, Then, Is This Cow...": Positioning Domestic Livestock Animals in the Texts and Practices of Small Scale "Self-Sufficiency"'. *Society & Animals* **11** (2) (2003): 145–65.

Howes, David (ed.), *Empire of the Senses: The Sensual Culture Reader* (Oxford: Berg, 2005).

Ingold, T., 'The temporality of the landscape', *World Archaeology* **25** (2) (1993): 137–284.

Johnson, M., *Ideas of Landscape* (Malden, Mass.: Blackwell, 2007).

Lowe, Emily, *Unprotected Females in Norway, or The Pleasantest Way of Travelling There, Passing through Denmark and Sweden* (London: Routledge, 1857).

Macfarlane, Robert, *The Old Ways: A Journey on Foot* (London: Hamish Hamilton, 2012).

Malthus, Thomas [1799], ed. Patricia James *Reisedagbok fra Norge [The Travel Diaries of Thomas Robert Malthus]* (Oslo: J.W. Cappelens Forlag, 1968).

Meyer, Frank, *Norges lyder* (Oslo: Norsk lokalhistorisk institutt, 2018).

Olwig, Kenneth, 'The "Natural" Landscape and Agricultural Values', in NIKU Temahefte 4, *Landskapet som historie*, pp. 24–31 (Oslo: NIKU, 1997)

Olwig, Kenneth, 'Heritage as Common(s) – Commons as Heritage: Things We Have in Commons in the Political Landscape of Heritage', in H. Benesch, I.M. Holmberg, F. Hammami, and E. Uzer (eds), *Heritage as Common(s): Common(s) as Heritage*, pp. 89–115 (Gothenburg: Makadam, 2015).

Oslund, Karen, *Iceland Imagined: Nature, Culture, and Storytelling in the North Atlantic* (Seattle: University of Washington Press, 2013).

Pedersen, Ragnar, *Seterbruket på Hedmarken: Fra system til oppløsning* (Oslo, Universitetsforlaget, 1974).

Pettersen, Hjalmar, *Udlændingers reiser i Norge' Utg* (Christiania: Cammermeyer, 1897).

Philo, Chris and Jennifer Wolch, 'Through the Geographical Looking Glass: Space, Place and Human–Animal Relations', *Society and Animals* **6** (2) (1998): 103–18.

4. Hefting the Land

Planke, Terje. 'Feltarbeid og redselen for nærhet'. *Dugnad* 2 (1999): s 39–61.

Rebanks, James, *The Shepherd's Life: A Tale of the Lake District* (London: Penguin, 2015)

Rodaway, Paul, *Sensuous Geographies: Body, Sense and Place* (London: Routledge, 1994).

Rogan, Bjarne, *Det gamle skysstellet* (Oslo: Samlaget, 1986).

Saltzman, K., *Inget landskap är en ö: Dialektik och praktik i öländska landskap* (Lund: Nordic Academic Press, 2001).

Schiffer, M.B., *Behavioral Archaeology* (New York: Academic Press, 1976).

Schiffer, M.B., *Formation Processes of the Archeological Record* (Albuquerque: University of New Mexico Press, 1987).

Schiøtz, Eiler H., *Utlendingers reiser i Norge* (Oslo: Universitetsforlaget, 1986).

Scott, J.C., *Seeing Like a State: How Certain Schemes to Improve the Human Condition Have Failed* (New Haven: Yale University Press, 1998).

Solheim, Svale, *Norsk Sætertradisjon* (Oslo, Aschehoug, 1952).

Stensgaard, Kari, 'Hvordan står det til på setra? Registrering av setermiljøer i perioden 2009–2015'. *NIBIO rapport* **3** (88) (2017).

Sundt, Eilert, [1869] *Om renligheds-stellet i Norge* (Oslo: Gyldendal, 1975).

Svensson, D., S. Sörlin and K. Saltzman, 'Pathways to the Trail – Landscape, Walking and Heritage in a Scandinavian Border Region', *Norsk Geografisk Tidsskrift – Norwegian Journal of Geography* (2021).

Syse, Karen Lykke, *Lende og landskap: en analyse av skogens fysiske landskap og landskapspersepsjon i Nordmarka fra 1900 til 1999* (Oslo: Universitetet i Oslo, 2000).

Syse, Karen Lykke, *From Land Use to Landscape: A Cultural History of Conflict and Consensus in Argyll*. (Oslo: Unipub 2009).

Syse, Karen Lykke, 'Expert Systems, Local Knowledge and Power in Argyll, Scotland', *Landscape Research* **35** (4) (2010): s. 469–84.

Syse, Karen Lykke, 'Stumbling over Animals in the Landscape: Methodological Accidents and Anecdotes', *Nordic Journal of Science and Technology Studies* **2** (2) (2014): s 20–26

Syse, Karen Lykke, 'Griseliv og grisedød i Norge før og nå', *Arr Idéhistorisk Tidsskrift* **32** (3) (2020): 15–29.

Thomas, Keith, *Religion and The Decline of Magic* (London: Penguin, 1991).

Thomas, Keith, *Man and the Natural World: Changing Attitudes in England 1500–1800* (London: Penguin, 1984).

Tilley, Christopher, *A Phenomenology of Landscape: Places, Paths and Monuments*, Explorations in Anthropology (Oxford: Berg, 1994).

Tilley, C., *Handbook of Material Culture* (London: Sage, 2006)

Tilley, Christopher, 'Introduction: Identity, Place, Landscape and Heritage', *Journal of Material Culture* **11** (1) (2006): 7–32.

Tuv, Kjell Håvard (ed.), *Prosjekt Levande stølar* (Skjetten: Det kgl. selskap for Norges vel, 2002).

Visted, Kristoffer and Hilmar Stigum, *Vår Gamle Bondekultur*, Vol. 2 (Oslo, Cappelen, 1952).

Williams, W. Mattieu, *Through Norway with a Knapsack* (London: Smith, Elder & Co, 1859).

CHAPTER 5.

'FOLLOWING IN THE FOOTSTEPS OF HISTORY'. SIXTEEN MULTIMEDIA ITINERARIES THROUGH THE FIRST WORLD WAR SITES IN THE STELVIO NATIONAL PARK AND ADAMELLO PARK (ITALY)

Stefano Morosini

There are many traces of the First World War in Northern Italy's mountain areas, above all in the Stelvio National Park and the Adamello Park, where fighting took place. These are beautiful places at an average altitude of between 2,000 and 3,000 metres above sea level, where extraordinary natural scenes starkly contrast with the tragic nature of the events that occurred in this extreme environment. To promote this priceless patrimony, the ensuing essay will present the recovery and enhancement of an Austro-Hungarian barracks located on top of Mount Scorluzzo (3,094 metres), by means of an interdisciplinary and multidisciplinary research project. The essay will also describe the creation of sixteen themed itineraries using innovative, zero environmental impact technologies. These experiential itineraries give visitors a new, participatory and interactive approach to these sites and explain (in Italian, English and German languages) the events that took place here during the First World War. Using a georeferenced and accessible to everyone App, visitors can encounter fragments of history and details on natural surroundings, taking a step back in time. These projects aim to help new generations understand what Europe went through before becoming a largely peaceful and borderless multinational space.

The white war

The earliest studies of alpine warfare were products of reverence for the beauty of the scenery combined with fear resulting from the inclement harshness of the climate. Temperatures as low as −50°C; blizzards and avalanches in autumn, winter and spring; powerful thunderstorms during the remaining months, when, after 'white death' had already taken a heavy toll, lightning bolts came to claim more lives. All of this led to a romanticised description of alpine warfare,

5. 'Following in the Footsteps of History'

an excellent example of which is Mario Mariani's 1915 poetic description of fighting at the Stelvio National Park territory:

> It was a war of chamois hunters, of alpine patrols concealed in ambush or climbing up the inaccessible peaks on the offensive, armed with craftiness and patience, with crampons and ice axe, war of bandits and daredevils, scattered over airy suspended trails, hidden amongst the glaciers' crevasses, under the rocks' brushwood, inside every grotto, inside every cavern, a war that cannot be followed, a war in which to prevail one had to be an actor too.[1]

A great contribution to the study of alpine warfare was made by personal memoirs released by several Italian and Austro-Hungarian officers in the interwar period.[2] High altitude warfare then became a topic of interest for historians by passion, but not by training; these sources contain a wealth of information, but lack academic rigour and in many cases this implies heroic tones and sometimes nationalist accents.[3] Archive-based studies realised in the past decades have shed a more historically accurate and unbiased light on high-altitude warfare.[4] This theme has also progressively become of great interest to environmental history, a fertile field of cutting-edge interdisciplinary analysis.[5] Indeed, natural sciences have also proved indispensable for an all-round understanding of the complex realities of First World War battlefields.[6] Analysis of historically relevant phenomena through the lens of the natural sciences has also been made in relation to alpine warfare.[7]

Contemporary analyses of the First World War at high altitude have definitely abandoned not only romanticised (or heroic, or nationalist) interpretations, but also the resulting excessive focus on the 'bare-handed man versus nature' narrative. This had long downplayed the highly technological and modern

---

1   Mariani, *Sulle Alpi e sull'Isonzo*, p. 153. Quote translated by the author.
2   von Lempruch, *Der König der Deutschen Alpen*; Fiocca, *Come occupammo lo Stelvio*; von Ompteda, *Bergkrieg*; Robbiati and Viazzi, *Guerra d'Aquile*; Martinelli, *La guerra a 3000 metri*; Fettarappa Sandri, *La Guerra sotto le Stelle*; Robbiati and Viazzi, *Guerra Bianca*; Flores, *La Guerra in Montagna*.
3   Schaumann, *Schauplätze des Gebirgskrieges*; von Lichem, *Gebirgskrieg 1915–1918*; Martinelli, *Guerra alpina sull'Adamello*; Viazzi, *La guerra alpina sul fronte Ortler-Cevedale*.
4   David, *Stilfserjoch-Umbrail 1914–1918*; Jordan, *Krieg um die Alpen*; Thompson, *The White War*; Keller, 'The Mountains Roar'; Camanni, *Il fuoco e il gelo*; John, *The Italian Army and the First World War*; Labanca, 'The Italian Front'; Leoni, *La guerra verticale*; Cimbolli, *Al di là delle trincee*; Sigurtà, *Montagne di guerra*; Segesser, 'Fighting'.
5   Hughes, *An Environmental History of the World*, p. 4; McNeill, 'Observations on the Nature', p. 6; Isenberg, 'Introduction'; Daly et al., 'Landscapes of War', p. 3.
6   Pirc et al., 'Remains of World War I'; Souvent et al., 'Pollution Caused by Metallic Fragments'; Baba et al., 'Effect of Warfare Waste on Soil'; Bausinger et al., 'Environmental Remnants of the First World War'; Van Meirvenne, 'Could Shelling in the First World War'; Meerschman, 'Geostatistical Assessment of the Impact of World War I'; Thouin et al., 'Characterization and Mobility of Arsenic and Heavy Metals'.
7   Angetter, 'Über den Minierkrieg in hochalpinen Fels'.

Figure 1.

The Mount Scorluzzo (3,094 metres) Austro-Hungarian barracks. Recovery and enhancement of the site and interdisciplinary and multidisciplinary research project. Source: © Stelvio National Park.

character of high-altitude warfare and the considerable successes achieved by anthropic aggression against the mountains. A fitting example of these is the cableway, which Austro-Hungarian troops had built by November 1915 in the Ortles-Cedevale area. It linked the valley floor with the Dreisprachenspitze (2,843 m) and consisted of two incredible single-span segments, one of which was 2,500 metres in length. In little less than an hour, supplies travelled 1,245 m in altitude and the cableway operated 22 hours a day, constituting the sole means to resupply the forward high-altitude positions during wintertime, when roads could be buried under as many as ten metres of snow.

This paragraph presents the theme, scope and core methodological aspects of the interdisciplinary and multidisciplinary research project activated in 2019 to study an Austro-Hungarian artificial barracked cave originally built in the summer of 1915 at 3,094 metres above sea level on the top of Mount Scorluzzo. The mountain is part of Stelvio National Park and belongs to the Ortles-Cevedale range, whose highest summits reach up to almost 4,000 metres, which stretches between the Italian regions of Lombardy and Trentino-

5. 'Following in the Footsteps of History'

Alto Adige/Südtirol and borders Switzerland. Mount Scorluzzo was key to the defence of the Stelvio Pass itself. It directly overlooks the pass and has a commanding position over the nearby valleys and lower lands. At the beginning of the war, it was in undisputed Italian territory, right at the crossroads between the Austro-Hungarian Empire, the Kingdom of Italy and the Swiss Confederacy. Italian troops refrained from active military actions on the Stelvio front during the first months of the war and Mount Scorluzzo was given no permanent garrison.

On 4 June 1915, the personal initiative of a Merano Gendarmery Rittermeister, Andreas Steiner, led to the Austro-Hungarian conquest of Mount Scorluzzo.[8] Being fully aware of the strategic position they had just acquired, Imperial troops immediately began fortifying it and did so to such an extent that, notwithstanding several Italian attempts to recapture the summit, Mount Scorluzzo and its twin lower peak, Scorluzzino (2,990 metres) remained consistently in Austro-Hungarian hands until the very end of the war. The conquest of Mount Scorluzzo received enthusiastic celebration in the Austro-Hungarian and German press: the first 3,000-metre peak in the history of warfare had been conquered. What is more, as Jewish Austro-Hungarian journalist Alice Schalek wrote, recalling the words of an ecstatic Austro-Hungarian officer: 'we have our front line on enemy territory; we have Monte Scorluzzo'.[9] Since then, Mount Scorluzzo has become known both amongst Italian and Austro-Hungarian troops as the 'mountain of blood and iron'.[10]

The recovery of the Mount Scorluzzo barracked cave began in 2017. One hundred years after its construction, climate change had caused such a retreat of the glaciers that it became conceivable to excavate and retrieve the barrack. Yet, its entire surface was sealed in sixty cubic metres of ice and its location made recovery operations possible only during the summer months. The first surveys started in 2015–2016, when the upper strata of the ice were melted to reveal the barrack's wood structure (deck, supporting pillars, wood plank walls and ceiling). During the month of August in 2017, 2018 and 2019 the remaining ice was removed, approximately one third at a time with pressure washers, thanks to the voluntary effort of the staff of the White War Museum located in Temù (Brescia). More than 300 disparate artefacts were recovered (munitions, provisions, uniforms, stoves, lanterns, personal items, documents and books, etc.). Finally, in August 2020, a high-altitude engineering team

---

8   Jordan, *Krieg um die Alpen*, p. 231.
9   Schalek, *Tirol in Waffen Kriegsberichte*, p. 23.
10   Fettarappa Sandri, *La Guerra sotto le Stelle*, p. 26; Springensch, *Unter dem Tiroler Adler*, p. 25; von Lempruch et al., *Ortles*, p. 36.

proceeded to disassemble the entire wood structure, catalogue it and transport it via helicopter to the nearby town of Bormio, as well as to structurally reinforce the cave through micro-piling. The barrack will be rebuilt in a new museum that will open in Bormio in 2022–2023, containing all recovered artefacts. A replica of the original barrack will be set up on the top of Mount Scorluzzo, provided with lighting and information boards and open to visitors during guided tours following the multimedia war itineraries.

Figures 2 and 3.

General description of the project 'Following in the footsteps of history'. Source: © Stelvio National Park.

5. 'Following in the Footsteps of History'

The project is rooted in the methodology of environmental history, but the group of more than twenty researchers belong to a range of disciplines: botany, chemistry, ecology, epidemiology, genetics, glaciology, geology, geomorphology, history, microbiology, palynology, topography, zoology, escaping disciplinary hierarchies. The Scorluzzo project has attracted unprecedented international attention since it was covered in May 2021 by *The Guardian* in its online and printed editions. The news was reported widely across the globe and, most notably, the *New York Times* also covered the project in both online and printed editions.[11]

The unique recovery and enhancement of the Mount Scorluzzo barracks is not the only project that the Stelvio National Park has dedicated to the historical traces of the First World War in its territory. This particular mountain front has guaranteed the specific conservation of many signs of the presence of the two armies on these peaks. In partnership with the Adamello Natural Park, the 'Following in the footsteps of history' project and its sixteen itineraries want to offer historical and environmental contents without setting up and managing info boards, which could be considered as an element of negative impact on the landscape. The aim of the project is to describe places, events and artefacts linked to the First World War, bringing out hitherto unknown aspects of the war and, above all, remembering that the history of the White War, like that of the Great War as a whole, is a story of unimaginable suffering on both sides.

Moving along the sixteen itineraries, users receive mobile phone notifications as they reach points of interest. A map of the area appears automatically, giving the opportunity to activate an audio description in Italian, English or German and performed (in the Italian version) by the Oscar-winning actor Giuseppe Cederna. The use of headphones is recommended to remain focused on the route during the walk. Besides audio information, the App also shows a series of historical images. During the vocal description, users will find a selection of quotes from letters, diaries, and books of Italian and Austrian soldiers. The App aims to be accessible for a wide audience in both ways: in its usability, and in the ease of understanding its historical and environmental contents. In fact, paths are easy to walk for a large public of hikers and have no mountaineering difficulties. Seven of the sixteen itineraries are also accessible to people with disabilities by the use of a 'Joelette', and one is accessible for people in wheelchairs. The hope is that users of this App will undertake a beautiful walk

---

11   Giuffrida, 'Melting Ice Reveals First World War Relics'; Fortin, 'Melting Glaciers Have Exposed Frozen Relics of World War I'; Squires, 'Melting Alpine Glacier Reveals Hidden WW1 Tunnels and Bunker'; Suliman, 'Historians Found a WWI Bunker "Frozen in Time" in the Alps'. Overall more than 40 media outlets from 18 different nations covered the Scorluzzo project, writing in 13 different languages.

Figures 4 and 5.

The Stelvio Pass–Mount Scorluzzo itinerary. Source: © Stelvio National Park.

5. 'Following in the Footsteps of History'

in a spirit that is respectful not only of nature but first and foremost of the memory of the men who were obliged to fight here. A different, and higher, aim is dedicated to the European unification process. This project aims to help new generations in the understanding of what Europe tragically endured before becoming a peaceful and borderless multinational space.

The itinerary from Passo dello Stelvio to the peak of Mount Scorluzzo follows path number 13, a straightforward footpath with an altitude gain and loss of around 336 metres and an average ascent time of around one hour. Along this short and easy itinerary, users come across four points of interest: artillery positions on the ridge to the south of Passo dello Stelvio; remains of trenches in the moonscape at Passo delle Platigliole; trenches and positions dominating Passo dello Stelvio at Mount Scorluzzino; and, lastly, to the south, the front-line positions on the peak of Mount Scorluzzo.

Until just before the war, Passo dello Stelvio was guarded by a small number of Italian and Austrian soldiers. A few hours before the formal beginning of the war, set at zero hour on 24 May 1915, the Italian squad received an order to abandon the pass and withdraw to the valley as no shelters or supply routes invisible to the Austrian army had been set up. A small squad of *Alpini* occupied the peak of Mount Scorluzzino. This almost inevitable withdrawal had a significant impact on later military action in this area. In fact, all subsequent Italian attempts to capture Passo dello Stelvio were blocked by stubborn Austrian resistance facilitated by dominant positions on Mts Scorluzzo and Scorluzzino.

Just after leaving Passo dello Stelvio, hikers come across certain artillery positions carved out of the rock on the small ridge above it. Looking westwards it is clear that these positions enabled the Austrians to control the entire upper Braulio valley and consequently a large part of the Stelvio road on the Italian side. When war broke out, Austria had been fighting ultra-fierce battles on the Russian Front in Galicia for nearly a year. To defend the new front with Italy, Austria had only very limited resources, mainly *Standschützen*, local divisions made up of civilians outside military conscription age but enrolled at the shooting ranges, which were then very common in the Austro-Hungarian Empire. They were excellent marksmen and knew the area very well indeed.

These cave positions were built by Austrian soldiers in 1916 when the front line had been stabilised after small-scale fighting in the summer of 1915. Prior to digging these cave positions, the Austrians had set up open air positions just behind the ridge and only a few digging traces and slight stone parapets remain of these. This position took the name of Ferdinandstellung, in honour of the hotel nearby destroyed by Italian artillery in autumn 1915.

At that time, the ridge remained above the area's permanent snowfields only for a few weeks in summer. In a book about First World War in the Alps, Austrian historian Heinz von Lichem described the strategies employed on this section of the front very well

> The Italians continued vainly to attack the natural fortresses, strenuously defended by the Austrians. It should be said to the credit of the Italians and the fighting spirit of the Alpini soldiers: if the Italians had managed to occupy the ridges first, the Tyroleans and the Austrians would equally have thrown themselves uselessly against rock and ice walls. The conformation of the terrain meant that the Italians were forced to attack from below on open ground towards dominant strategic positions, an entirely thankless and ultimately pointless military enterprise.[12]

The footpath to the peak of Mount Scorluzzo deviates from the road and climbs up a scree slope. Looking from north to south, the landscape shows evident signs of the work of the ancient glaciers. The different formations of the rocks around it are also easily visible. On the pass, they are limestone, the outcome of sedimentation in an ultra-ancient ocean, while Mount Scorluzzo is made up, for the most part, of metamorphic schists.

During First World War the highest rocks of the whole Passo delle Platigliole emerged from the perennial snow fields for only a few weeks per year, linking up to the ridge which continues to the higher Nagler Spitze (Cima del Chiodo) and subsequent Punta del Naso. On these rocks the Austrians built an advanced defence line with machine gun positions directed at Valle dei Vitelli. Protected walkways and trenches were carved out using metal cages filled with stones. Today what has survived the passage of time in this quasi-lunar landscape, almost always windy, gives us an insight into the lives of the soldiers of the day, with snow over ten metres thick for many months a year. This defensive line was guarded by the Standschützen battalion *Prad-Stilfs-Taufers* for the whole duration of the war. It is interesting to remember certain peculiarities of the *Standschützen*: this peculiar Tyrolese defence militia – integrated in the Austro-Hungarian army since 1871– whose members were enlisted in local shooting ranges could enlist marksmen from seventeen to over fifty years of age and elect their own junior officers and their captain in command. They also had their own division flag. At the outset of the war, with no access to army logistical supplies, which were still not present in the area, their wives and mothers provided directly for getting the necessary food to them from their valley hometowns.

Approximately halfway between Passo delle Platigliole and the peak of Mount Scorluzzo, there is a rocky spur at 2,995 metres, commonly called Scorluzzino. This rocky bastion juts out northwards like a terrace with a direct

---

12   von Lichem, *Gebirgskrieg 1915–1918*, p. 76. Quote translated by the author.

5. 'Following in the Footsteps of History'

view over Passo dello Stelvio. It was in these very rocks, without stable shelters or the chance for rapid supplies, that the soldiers of Tirano Alpini Battalion attempted to establish an approximate defensive line in the first days of the war, from 24th May to early June 1915. However, in the first days of June 1915, the captain of the Austrian gendarmes, Andreas Steiner, commanding a squad of soldiers, attacked the Italian frontline and occupied it. The defenders withdrew to Mount Scorluzzo, whence they were immediately obliged to withdraw. From that moment, the Austrians occupied the whole ridge from Passo dello Stelvio to Mount Scorluzzo with small divisions and, to the west, the rocky ridge as far as Nagler Spitze. This guard was progressively reinforced with a number of wooden barracks for the troops and firing positions for rifles and machine guns. Later on, certain caves were carved out as soldiers' shelters. A spotlight was placed in the cave to light up the area around Passo dello Stelvio and thus head off potential night attacks from Valle del Braulio. Colonel Carlo Fetterappa Sandri described the Austrian attack:

> Optimally supported by short range but certain fire from the Gold See battery, on 7th June a detachment made up of soldiers from the Gendarmeria, Guardie di Finanza, Landstürmer and Standschützen reached the great Mount Scorluzzo via Eben Ferner and Scorluzzino. In actual fact, all that remained on the peak was a sort of distant back line guard made up of just a few men who withdrew to join the bulk of the large platoon which had descended some time earlier.[13]

Given the altitude of nearly 3,000 metres, the severe weather conditions and terrain reduced to bare rock and debris, it is somehow surprising to find plants here. The vegetation no longer manages to fill whole areas but is limited to small isolated green patches. These are the high altitude 'specialists' such as Alpine rock jasmine – dense cushions of little leaves with small pink flowers – or yellow flowering *Geum reptans*. Given the difficulty of producing seeds in these extreme conditions, it produces red stolons, which stretch out from the mother plant to colonise the surrounding space. And there is the *Glacier Crowfoot*, the Alpine plant with the altitude record. On the Bernese Alps in Switzerland, it has been found at altitudes of 4,275 metres.

The final item in this multimedia itinerary is located at the peak of Mount Scorluzzo, at an altitude of 3,094 metres. On a clear day, the views across the horizon are truly majestic, and the beauty of the high-altitude environment is astonishing. In this area, it is frequently possible to encounter groups of chamois early in the morning and also to see Golden Eagles – the park's symbol – or Bearded Vultures in flight. Since being reintroduced to the Alps, this latter is

---

13   Fettarappa Sandri, *La Guerra sotto le Stelle*, p. 112. Quote translated by the author.

now the most majestic of the Alpine birds with females, the largest, reaching a wingspan of 2.8 metres. Its diet, made up, for the most part, of the bones of dead animals, is also unusual. On the peak of Mount Scorluzzo and the rocky ridges, which descend southwards and westwards from it, the remains of what was once the most important Austrian fortress over Passo dello Stelvio can be seen. After occupation in early June 1915, the Austrians built a great many rifle and machine gun positions on this peak, as well as shelters for troops, and placed Mountain guns here both in the open air and in caves. As Colonel Carlo Fetterappa Sandri wrote:

> This Stelvio defensive pillar, this unequalled observation point, was now in enemy hands and, immediately realising the importance of its easy conquest, the latter did not hesitate to reinforce Mount Scorluzzo and supply it with a few guns.[14]

These high-altitude positions were visited on 16 September 1917 by no less than Austro-Hungarian Emperor Karl I. Comfortably protected in a trench behind the Swiss border, just a little below Cima Garibaldi, the emperor observed the defensive line as far as Mount Scorluzzo. A strange situation which developed near Cima Garibaldi is worthy of mention: in the large, almost flat space to the north called Gold See, the Austrians built an army village equipped with shelters for the troops, warehouses and open-air artillery positions. This army guard would have been an easy target for the Italian artillery positioned in Valle del Braulio but, as any shells would have passed through Swiss air space, violating its neutrality, the Italian command forbade fire in this direction.

The Italians attempted to recapture the peak on more than one occasion: one attack was launched on 26 June 1915 by the 46th Company of the Alpini Battalion Tirano, by climbing up from Rese and Filon dei Mot, but the Austrians successfully defended their positions. Other attacks were made by the Val D'Orco Alpini Battalion in May and June 1916, but these were also unsuccessful. No further attacks on Mount Scorluzzo are documented but the peak was a constant target of Italian artillery fire for the whole duration of the war.

From up here, Austrian soldiers had full visibility over the whole upper Braulio valley and to Platigliole and dominated the whole Filon dei Mot crest with their artillery too, with an Italian circular advanced position that visibly stands out on the rocky ridge from the peak. If you are very careful you can visit the remains of Austrian buildings and defensive positions made with metal cages here, a clear sign of the huge effort made to adapt the mountains to their needs for shelter and defence. It is up to us to take these signs of history on board and remember the young men on both sides who fought on these mountains.

---

14   Ibid.: 145. Quote translated by the author.

5. 'Following in the Footsteps of History'

Conclusions. Paths between first world war heritage

The Italian framework legislation on protected areas, approved in 1991, states in the first article that parks have to promote the integration between humans and environment through the conservation of anthropological, archeological, historical and architectural heritage and through the conservation of traditional agro-silvo-pastoral activities. The recovery, conservation and evaluation of the First World War sites in this peculiar alpine area provide an interesting case study in a comparative analysis of movement heritage and are entirely consistent with the purposes of two parks, the Stelvio National Park and Adamello Park. Walking inside original trenches and coming inside artificial caves dug between 1915 and 1918 is an interesting way to directly live a historical experience and to savour cultural and sustainable tourism. It also helps new generations understand what Europe went through before becoming a largely peaceful and borderless multinational space. First World War sites like Mount Scorluzzo and the other places described in the sixteen multimedia itineraries give a direct experience of how soldiers, but also women, children and animals, shaped these paths and help to understand wartime experience in an extreme environment. It is not only hiking or mountaineering in a beautiful alpine scene, but also a remembrance activity that can be practised without causing large-scale environmental degradation.

These mountains are also a clear representation of climate change. In this alpine sector, landscape is not only a scene of war, but also an Anthropocene representation. Every summer, the dramatic retreat of glaciers and the dropping of their surface make new artefacts and relics of the First World War emerge. This huge phenomenon makes this heritage accessible and permits the recovery and conservation of cultural patrimony: for this reason it could be considered a positive consequence of global warming but, on the other hand, the huge transformation of the mountain landscape and the risk of collapse of structural elements of the historical sites due to the melting of ice and permafrost areas are extremely dangerous and worrying.

Bibliography

Angetter, D. and J-M. Schramm , 'Über den Minierkrieg in hochalpinen Fels- und Eisregionen (1. Weltkrieg, SW-Front, Tirol 1915–1918) aus ingenieurgeologischer Sicht', *Geo.Alp* **11** (2014): 135–60.

Baba, A. and O. Deniz, 'Effect of Warfare Waste on Soil: A Case Study of Gallipoli Peninsula (Turkey)', *International Journal of Environment and Pollution* **22** (2004): 657–75.

Bausinger, T. and J. Preuß, 'Environmental Remnants of the First World War: Soil Contamination of a Burning Ground for Arsenical Ammunition', *Bulletin of Environmental Contamination and Toxicology* **74** (6) (2005): 1045–52.

Bausinger, T., E. Bonnaire and J. Preuss, 'Exposure Assessment of a Burning Ground for Chemical Ammunition on the Great War Battlefields of Verdun', *Sciences of the Total Environment* **382** (2007): 259–71.

Camanni, E., *Il fuoco e il gelo. La grande guerra sulle montagne* (Bari: Laterza, 2014).

Cimbolli, P. (ed.), *Al di là delle trincee: territori e architetture del Regno d'Italia al tempo della prima guerra mondiale: atti del congresso internazionale* (Roma: Quasar, 2017).

Daly, S., M. Salvante and V. Wilcox, 'Landscapes of War: A Fertile Terrain for First World War Scholarship', in S. Daly et. al. (eds), *Landscapes of the First World War* (New York: Springer International Publishing, 2018).

David, A., *Stilfserjoch-Umbrail 1914–1918: Dokumentation. Kampf in Fels, Schnee und Eis nahe der Schweizergrenze* (Bern: Militärische Führungsschule, 2004).

Fettarappa Sandri, C., *La Guerra sotto le Stelle. Episodi di Guerra Alpina: Stelvio, Ortles, Cevedale, San Matteo, 1915–1918* (Milano: Mursia, 2012).

Flores, I., *La Guerra in Montagna* (Milano: Mursia, 2021).

Fiocca, A., *Come occupammo lo Stelvio e giungemmo a Bolzano* (Milano: Fratelli Cristofari Editori, 1925).

Fortin, J., 'Melting Glaciers Have Exposed Frozen Relics of World War I', *New York Times*, 8 May 2021, www.nytimes.com/2021/05/08/world/europe/italy-glacier-wwi-artifacts.html (accessed 15 November 2021).

Giuffrida, A., 'Melting Ice Reveals First World War Relics in Italian Alps', *The Guardian*, 4 May 2021, www.theguardian.com/environment/2021/may/04/melting-ice-reveals-first-world-war-relics-in-italian-alps (accessed 15 November 2021).

Hughes, J.D., *An Environmental History of the World: Humankind's Changing Role in the Community of Life* (London: Routledge, 2001).

Jordan, A., *Krieg um die Alpen. Der Erste Weltkrieg im Alpenraum und der bayerische Grenzschutz in Tirol* (Berlin: Duncker & Humblot, 2008).

John, G., *The Italian Army and the First World War* (Cambridge: Cambridge University Press, 2014).

Keller, T., 'The Mountains Roar: The Alps during the Great War', *Environmental History* **14** (2) (2009): 253–74.

Isenberg, A.C., 'Introduction: A New Environmental History', in A.C Isenberg (ed.), *The Oxford Handbook of Environmental History*, pp. 1–14 (New York: Oxford University Press, 2014).

Labanca, N., 'The Italian Front', in J. Winter (ed.), *The Cambridge History of the First World War. Part II*, pp. 266–96 (Cambridge: Cambridge University Press, 2014).

Leoni, D., *La guerra verticale. Uomini, animali e macchine sul fronte di montagna (1915–1918)* (Torino: Einaudi, 2015).

Mariani, M., *Sulle Alpi e sull'Isonzo: dalla fronte nei primi quattro mesi della nostra guerra, 23 maggio–26 settembre 1915* (Milano: Società editoriale italiana, 2015).

Martinelli, V., *Guerra alpina sull'Adamello: 1915–1917* (Pinzolo: D. & C. Povinelli, 1998).

Martinelli, U., *La guerra a 3000 metri: dallo Stelvio al Gavia: 1915–1918* (Chiari: Nordpress, 2009).

McNeill, J.R., 'Observations on the Nature and Culture of Environmental History', *History and Theory* **42** (2) (2003): 5–43.

Meerschman, E., L. Cockx, M.M. Islam, F. Meeuws and M. Van Meirvenne, 'Geostatistical

5. 'Following in the Footsteps of History'

Assessment of the Impact of World War I on the Spatial Occurrence of Soil Heavy Metals', *AMBIO. A Journal of Environment and Society* **40** (2011): 417–20.

Pirc, S. and T. Budkovič, 'Remains of World War I Geochemical Pollution in the Landscape', in M.L. Richardson (ed.), *Environmental Xenobiotics*, pp. 375–418 (London: Taylor & Francis, 1996).

Robbiati, P. and L. Viazzi, *Guerra d'Aquile. Ortles, Cevedale, Adamello, 1917–1918* (Milano: Mursia, 1996).

Robbiati, P. and L. Viazzi, *Guerra Bianca. Ortles, Cevedale, Adamello, 1915–1916* (Milano: Mursia, 2019).

Schalek, A., *Tirol in Waffen Kriegsberichte von der Tiroler Front* (München: H. Schmidt, 1915).

Schaumann, W., *Schauplätze des Gebirgskrieges in 5 Bänden* (Cortina d'Ampezzo: Ghedina & Tassotti, 1973).

Segesser, D.M., 'Fighting Where Nature Joins Forces with the Enemy', *The Hungarian Historical Review* **7** (3) (2018): 568–93.

Sigurtà, D., *Montagne di guerra, strade in pace: la prima guerra mondiale dal Garda all'Adamello: tecnologie e infrastrutturazioni belliche* (Milano: FrancoAngeli, 2017).

Springensch, K., *Unter dem Tiroler Adler: vier Erzählungen* (Stuttgart: Franckh, 1938).

Souvent, P. and S. Pirc, 'Pollution Caused by Metallic Fragments Introduced into Soils because of World War I Activities'. *Environmental Geology* **40** (3) (2001): 317–23.

Squires, N., 'Melting Alpine Glacier Reveals Hidden WW1 Tunnels and Bunker', *The Telegraph*, 8 November 2021, www.telegraph.co.uk/world-news/2021/11/08/melting-alpine-glacier-reveals-hidden-ww1-tunnels-bunker/ (accessed 15 November 2021).

Suliman, A., 'Historians Found a WWI Bunker "Frozen in Time" in the Alps. Climate Change Makes it a Bittersweet Discovery', *The Washington Post*, 13 November 2021, www.washingtonpost.com/world/2021/11/13/climate-change-italy-alps-world-war-one/ (accessed 15 November 2021).

Thompson, M., *The White War: Life and Death on the Italian Front 1915–1919* (New York: Basic Books, 2009).

Thouin H., L. Le Forestier, P. Gautret, D. Hube, V. Leperche, S. Dupraz and F. Battaglia-Brunet, 'Characterization and Mobility of Arsenic and Heavy Metals in Soils Polluted by the Destruction of Arsenic-containing Shells from the Great War', *Science of the Total Environment* 550 (2016): 658–69.

Viazzi, L., *La guerra alpina sul fronte Ortler-Cevedale, 1915–1918* (Milano: Mursia, 2012).

Van Meirvenne, M., T. Meklit, S. Verstraete, M. De Boever and F. Tack, 'Could Shelling in the First World War Have Increased Copper Concentrations in the Soil around Ypres?'. *European Journal of Soil Science* **59** (2) (2008): 372–79.

von Lempruch, M.E.F., *Der König der Deutschen Alpen und seine Helden (Ortlerkämpfe 1915/1918)* (Stuttgart: Belser, 1925).

von Lempruch, M.E.F. and G.F. von Ompteda, *Ortles. La guerra tra i ghiacci e le stelle*. A cura di P. Pozzato, P. Volpato (Bassano del Grappa (Vicenza): Itinera, 2009).

von Lichem, H., *Gebirgskrieg 1915–1918. Ortler-Adamello-Gardasee*, 3 vols (Bozen: Athesia, 1980).

von Ompteda, G.F., *Bergkrieg* (Berlin: Verlag Tradition W. Kolk, 1932).

Section II
Off the Beaten Tracks

CHAPTER 6.

ARCHIPELAGIC PATHS: NARRATIVES, HERITAGE AND COMMUNITY IN PUBLIC TRAIL WALKING ON THE ÅLAND ISLANDS

Susanne Österlund-Pötzsch

The island of Sottunga in the Åland Islands archipelago is approximately five kilometres long but still offers almost fifteen kilometres of hiking trails. Sottunga is the smallest municipality in Finland, consisting of four inhabited islands with a total population of just under ninety people. The newly marked Sottunga walking trails are indicative of the current interest in hiking on Åland. In recent years, many new trails have been cleared while older paths have received maintenance and improved waymarking.

As pointed out by the editors of the present volume, walking constitutes both material and immaterial heritage. Trails are concrete inscriptions in the landscape and physical evidence of activity. However, trails are also characterised by intangible aspects such as practices, tacit knowledge and narrativity. 'Narrative', here, is employed in its most generous sense, as a framework covering coherent stories as well as tropes, meta-narratives and proto-narratives.[1] Based on ethnographic material, I want to examine what role heritage, community and storytelling play in the practice of trail walking in a small island context.[2] My contention is that narratives (and narrative elements) are central to how we experience and understand trails and trail walking, and, moreover, to how we perform trails as heritage.

The Åland Islands

The province of the Åland Islands is an autonomous region of Finland with its own government and parliament.[3] It is an archipelago community consist-

---

1   See e.g. Fludernik, *Towards a 'Natural' Narratology*; Klein, 'Introduction'.
2   Interviews with hikers, pilgrimage-guides, tourist board representatives and voluntary trail workers on the Åland Islands 2020–2021. My warmest thanks to all contributors.
3   Åland and Finland were part of Sweden until the war of 1808–1809, when Finland (along with Åland) was ceded to the Russian Empire. When Finland gained independence in 1917, the public opinion on Åland was to seek reunion with Sweden, something that was rejected by the Finnish government. The question was deferred to the League of Nations, which decided in 1921 that the

Susanne Österlund-Pötzsch

Figure 1.

Map of the Åland Islands. Source: Wikimedia Commons / © Sémhur / CC BY-SA 3.0.

ing of over 6,500 islands and skerries, connected with the Åboland (Finnish: *Turunmaa*) archipelago in the east. Åland is divided into sixteen municipalities: the town Mariehamn and nine countryside municipalities on the main island and six archipelagic municipalities east of the main island. The population is approximately 30,000, of whom most live on the main island of Åland. Due to its autonomous status, Åland has many markers of local identity such as

islands would remain under Finnish sovereignty but would be granted autonomy as a demilitarised region and have Swedish as their official language.

6. Archipelagic Paths

its own flag, postage stamps and vehicle license plates. Regional citizenship is required in order to own land, set up a business and have the right to vote in local elections.[4]

As is the case with many island communities, tourism is a vital part of the local economy. The majority of tourists come from the neighbouring countries, primarily from the mainland of Finland and Sweden, followed by the other Scandinavian countries and Germany. The main tourist attraction is the archipelago landscape, but Åland is also promoted for other aspects of 'islandness'[5] – a theme that goes beyond the geographical fact of being an archipelagic community.

Narratives and trails

Narratives are ubiquitous in human life: they are how we make sense of the world, bestow meaning on events and give coherence to experiences.[6] There is an inherently narrative structure to a trail walk in that it has a beginning, a middle (including stops along the route) and an end. Every walk is different in rhythm and character, and tells its own story. However, trails are connected with narratives in myriads of ways. In fact, stories were at the heart of one of the first deliberate nature tourist projects. In the 1830s, the war veteran and passionate walker Claude Denecourt published his guide to the Fontainebleau Forest outside Paris. His idea of making the forest accessible to even the most inexperienced of nature walkers established a new form of tourism – by colour coding and clearly demarcating the multitude of paths, visitors did not risk getting lost and could choose walks of preferred length and character. In order to further enhance the attraction of the area, Denecourt employed storytelling. Specific spots, stones and trees were given suggestive names, and thus gained a sense of particularity. Through anecdotes and legends, many of which Denecourt embellished or simply made up, the landscape was romanticised and historicised.[7] Thanks to good railway connections, Fontainebleau soon became a favourite place for Sunday walks and recreational activities for residents in the Paris region and beyond. Denecourt's dramatic interpretation of the forest

---

4 The regional has citizenship also had a concrete influence on nature protection in that it controls the number of summer homes erected in the fragile archipelago landscape: see https://finlandsnatur.naturochmiljo.fi/artiklar/miljogifter/article-91885-69557-landsk-vildmark-med-spar-av-historien/ (accessed 2 April 2021).

5 Ronström, *Öar och öighet*.

6 See e.g. Dolby-Stahl, 'A Literary Folkloristic Methodology', 45–69.

7 Green, *The Spectacle of Nature*; Schama, *Landscape and Memory*.

paths of Fontainebleau was a decided success. The stories, maps and coloured lines to follow invited visitors to read and fully experience the landscape, which today is firmly established as model behaviour for the nature tourist.

A similar, but in several respects different, trail-making project to that of Denecourt was enacted in the 1990s by schoolteacher Kjell Andersén in the municipality of Geta situated in the north of the main island of Åland. Instead of finding stories for places, Andersén located the places for existing stories. Andersén had become aware of local legends that had never been documented in print. Wishing to preserve the oral tradition as living heritage, he decided that, rather than publishing them in book form, he would connect the stories with their places along a trail. The foundation of the trail was an old well-used path leading from the top of the Geta hills to a set of caves, which also happened to be the setting for several legends. Andersén extended the existing path and made it into a circular route, incorporating beautiful vistas and places connected with local stories along the way. He put up signs with place stories and white arrows to make the trail easier to follow. The initiative and vision behind the project were Andersén's own, but he underlines the low level of bureaucracy and positive Ålandic attitude to enterprise as factors making the process easier: 'That's what's great about Åland', he comments.[8] The so-called cave trail (*grottstigen*) had long been one of Åland's most popular trails for both tourists and local visitors. The local legend project gave visibility to an old path already conceived as heritage-as-practice, but also provided it with additional heritage layers in terms of narratives and local stories that further increased its appeal.

In the wake of a flourishing interest in outdoor activities, health and wellbeing as part of holidaymaking, there have been renewed efforts to promote walking and walking facilities on Åland also at a more official level than Andersén's initiative. A destination developer at the Ålandic tourist board, Visit Åland, explains that, although there were already many hiking trails on Åland, they were 'invisible': 'The nature and the presence of the sea are the main reasons why people visit Åland – that's what we want to showcase, and that's how the push to improve already existing trails came about.'[9] Several of the restoration projects have been financed by EU-grants through LEADER-applications for rural development. The aim was an overall improvement of the trails and the infrastructure surrounding them. On the municipal level, much of the work was carried out by voluntary efforts. In some municipalities, trail maintenance

---

8   SLS 2357_ljud_1. (All reference codes from The Language and Tradition Collection at The Society of Swedish Literature, Helsinki)
9   SLS 2245_av_1.

6. Archipelagic Paths

Figure 2.

A boy by the Geta caves, circa 1905. The cave trail has long been a popular walking path. Photograph by Otto Andersson. Source: The Society of Swedish Literature in Finland, object SLS105b_foto_048, CC BY 4.0.

became a dedicated community endeavour. In connection with the mapping and marking, some of the old trails were re-routed, sometimes for practical reasons but mostly from the point of view of serving visiting walkers by incorporating scenic spots and places of interest. The project organisers' ambition was to offer a good and varied experience by taking the walk through different terrains and sites. Furthermore, an important element of the Ålandic restoration project was to storify all trails, i.e. to produce short texts for websites and information boards about what makes each trail special and worthwhile. The trail guide writers' task was to highlight how walking a particular trail is an exciting way to experience different features of heritage, landscape and nature.[10]

Apart from beautiful scenery, an aspect wished for in Ålandic trails is proximity to water. Several of the people involved with trail marking that I spoke with explained that a common reason for re-routing older trails – and thus changing their 'script' – was to incorporate more sea-views. 'Walking close to

10   SLS 2245_av_1.

the sea appeals, and both we [Ålanders] and visitors want to do that', one trail project organiser concluded.[11] The view, sound, smell and feel of the sea testify to the islandness of Åland – a key element for Ålandic place identity and an attraction for visitors. The feeling of remoteness is another sought-after quality in trails that is intrinsically connected with the idea of islandness. Ethnologist Owe Ronström observes that, along with boundedness, smallness and isolation, remoteness has become a hallmark of islandness to the degree that ascribing remoteness to a place is an effective way to island it. Remoteness is a relational concept produced in various contexts, and, as such, works as a frame for experiences of time and place.[12] Notably, avoiding habitation is often a main concern for trail-making. For example, Kjell Andersén took great care to maintain the impression of undisturbed nature in order to align with a trail-walking ideal:

> One troublesome stretch [that needed to be re-routed] is where you can see Viktor's cabin from the trail. There's a house in the middle of the wilderness. That felt totally wrong! The people who are walking in the wilderness and are in that ambience should not suddenly be faced with a house, and then have to worry about whether they are trespassing.[13]

The theme of islandness as a narrative framework for Åland trail walking is further supported by trail features emphasising their historical authenticity, unique micro-flora and other perceived island qualities.[14]

Trail heritagisation

The power of storytelling for communicating messages is widely employed in marketing to strengthen personal identifications with brands and lend products distinguishable identities. Stories constantly inform our perception and have an impact on how we experience given environments. This is evident in the process of heritagisation, a fundamental part of which is to make claims of uniqueness and value from the past for the present and the future. Regina Bendix notes that, even though heritage is singled out in the intersections of politics, markets, social networks and value systems, the specific power relations involved are easily glossed over.[15]

What 'works' as heritage is dependent on context. While walking paths are as ancient as human existence, they have generally not carried any significant cultural value. Within present day value regimes, it makes sense to view trails

---

11   SLS 2245_av_1.
12   Ronström, 'Remoteness, islands and islandness', 271–72.
13   SLS 1357_ljud_1.
14   See Ronström, *Öar och öighet*.
15   Bendix, *Culture and Value*, p. 105.

6. Archipelagic Paths

in terms of heritage. However, in order for heritage to have efficacy it needs social recognition. Storytelling, names, maps and signposts are all concrete ways to direct our attention and create interest. For a tourist organisation like Visit Åland, promoting public trails offers the possibility of making heritage sites visible. A project developer describes it as a question of focusing appreciation: 'Museums can be combined with the walking and ancient monuments can be highlighted so that they get more value. The nature reserves already have a significant cultural value – the importance of preserving nature.'[16]

Heritagisation tends to take place on many different levels simultaneously. For example, in the case of present day pilgrimage, the interconnected dimensions of tangible and immaterial heritage reinforce each other. The designation of the Routes of Santiago de Compostela as World Heritage increased the already growing number of Camino pilgrims.[17] A similar effect was observed when the St Olav Ways leading to Nidaros Cathedral in Trondheim were certified as a 'Cultural Route of the Council of Europe' in 2010.[18] The popularity of pilgrimage reflects many current concerns such as new forms of spirituality, being in nature, walking as a form of wellbeing, adventure tourism and personal engagement with cultural heritage.[19] As pointed out by Bowman, Johanssen and Ohrvik, the transformation of remote footpaths into heritagised spaces often relies on local and individual activism, but the work is still taking place within the structures of larger institutions.[20] This interplay between macro- and micro-structures characterises the international St Olav Waterway project. The aim of the project (2016–2020), predominantly financed by the EU INTERREG Central Baltic Programme, was to mark and map the route from Turku cathedral through the Finnish south-eastern archipelago and the Åland Islands to connect with the St Olaf Ways in Sweden. An important objective was to get the route certified as a Culture Route of the European Council, which was achieved in 2018. After the conclusion of the project, the association St Olav Way in Finland was founded to oversee the continued maintenance of the route. The Finnish association, in turn, is a member of the International Association for the Route of St Olav Ways (ACSOW). However, for the Ålandic part of the route, there is no central organisation to coordinate the work. Ester Laurell, who has worked with the St Olav Waterway both as an information officer for

---

16 SLS 2245_av_1.
17 See e.g. Parga-Dans, 'Socio-Economic Impacts of the Camino to Finisterre'.
18 Johannsen & Ohrvik, 'How to Be a Pilgrim', 509–10, 513.
19 See Brudin Borg, this volume.
20 Bowman, Johannsen and Ohrvik, 'Reframing Pilgrimage in Northern Europe'.

Central Baltic and as a private activist, notes that the lack of coordination and macro perspectives is a challenge that is somewhat mitigated on the micro level by a network of local enthusiasts and volunteers doing all the ground work.[21]

The St Olav Waterway was a separate project from the LEADER-projects run by Visit Åland; however, the trails sometimes converge, although with different markings. The local trails are marked with white, while the St Olav Waterway route is marked with the official logo and red colour of the St Olav Ways. At times, this has become a bone of contention, as different types of perceived heritage collide. The rights of landowners have traditionally been strong on Åland and their consent is required for a trail to cross their lands. When volunteers marked the St Olav Waterway with red paint, some landowners objected that they had not been asked specifically for permission and that the red colour competed with the white colour of the local hiking trail. Consequently, the St Olav marking had to be removed for some stretches.[22] Individual landowners' attitudes to having walkers traversing their lands have had a decisive influence over the course of the trails. In many cases, the proprietors have been happy to give their permission or the issue has been solved in other ways. For example, Kjell Andersén's project of creating a trail connected to local legends had the benefit of incorporating a popular and well-established path, and the new section of the trail could be drawn in such a manner that it did not directly cross properties but ran along their borders.[23] The St Olav Waterway trail on the other hand, could not always be realised according to the wishes of trail activists. The idea was to incorporate as many old trails and historical forest roads as possible, but the permission to do so was not always secured, as activist Ester Laurell explains: 'The route across Åland runs for large parts along country roads because of this. Of course, the country roads are also old, and traditionally [the pilgrimage] went along existing roads. But, if one can get access to the old forest trails and walk along them it would give an added value.'[24]

When it comes to trail-walking, the aura of heritage adds to the experience and the inclusion of older paths is therefore often preferred when creating new trail entities. Still, heritage can be invested in many ways, for example through association with a landmark, a local narrative or a historical person of note. Several of the Ålandic trails have names that connect them to some form of recognised heritage, such as the Middle Ages Trail and the Kungsö Artillery

---

21   SLS 2357_av_1.
22   Ibid.
23   SLS 2357_ljud_1.
24   SLS 2357_av_1.

6. Archipelagic Paths

Figure 3.

The stamp station by the church of Lemland, Åland Islands. Pilgrims on the St. Olav Waterway can collect place stamps in their pilgrim cards in a similar vein to Camino pilgrims. Photograph by Susanne Österlund-Pötzsch.

Battery trail. Naming a trail gives it the status of constituting a space in its own right, being more than a means of transportation between sites. In the St Olav Waterway, heritage is already alluded to in the name harking back both to a historically significant figure (Saint Olav) and a historically significant practice (pilgrimage). The multitude of heritage narratives have a cumulative effect: The fact that the route continues along traditional paths, traverses heritage sites and natural heritage can be inferred from, but also strengthens, the overall notion of heritage associated with pilgrimage routes.

Grand narratives and values

As noted above, the concept of value occupies a central place in heritage discourses.[25] On the one hand, heritage is selected based on sets of values. On the other hand, being appointed heritage lends value to a phenomenon. The importance of heritage values can be found along the whole macro-micro continuum when it comes to trail work. At the macro level, favoured values tend to be broad and abstract in order to act as umbrella concepts for a large number of actors and concerns. In this vein, the Association for the Route of St Olav Ways (ACSOW) prominently states that it is based on the democratic values of the European Cultural Routes. The European Council programme, in turn, connects the identified routes to a set of supranational ambitions and ideas: 'The Cultural Routes of the Council of Europe are an invitation to travel and to discover the rich and diverse heritage of Europe by bringing people and places together in networks of shared history and heritage.'[26] The statement continues by identifying particularly European values, '[The Routes] put into practice the values of the Council of Europe: human rights, cultural diversity, intercultural dialogue and mutual exchanges across borders.'[27]

Being an official part of the 'European Cultural Route' brand not only connects the St Olav Waterway with a larger administrative structure, but also with a grand narrative of a European cultural, democratic and intellectual heritage. As pointed out by Barbro Klein, we are constantly surrounded and influenced by grand narratives.[28] They shape both our everyday experiences and how we tell stories about our experiences. Grand narratives, thus, intertwine with small everyday narratives. For example, the alleged Nordicness of walking in nature

---

25 See e.g. Bendix, *Culture and Value*
26 https://www.acsow.org/wp-content/uploads/2019/08/Brochure-ACSOW.pdf (accessed 3 April 2021)
27 Ibid.
28 Klein, 'Introduction', 7.

6. Archipelagic Paths

can be viewed as type of grand narrative.[29] The backdrop for the link between nature and nationality in the Nordic countries can be traced to international trends emerging in the late eighteenth century.[30] In the Nordic countries, walking in nature became a component in a broad nation-state consolidation project and was regarded as an expression of love for one's country. During the late nineteenth century and early twentieth century, it was, for example, common that school classes in Finland spent their summer holidays hiking in the countryside with the purpose of collecting folklore, getting to know the flora, and, most importantly learning to appreciate the beauty of the nation.[31] Outdoor life became established as a key ingredient of being Nordic.[32] Although rambling is also associated with national identity in many other nations, notably Great Britain and Germany, Nordic popular practices and traditions such as the Right of Public Access have contributed to cementing the connection between national identity and outdoor life in Scandinavia. Accordingly, the Right of Public Access is frequently described in terms of heritage in official presentations.[33] Despite neither having the same content in different Nordic countries nor being unique to the region, the Right of Public Access was identified in a report issued by the Network of Outdoor Organisations in the Nordic Countries in 2018 as part of Nordic cultural heritage and a fundamental value of *friluftsliv* [outdoor life]. The report strongly recommended incorporating the Right of Public Access into the UNESCO heritage list.[34]

Many outdoor guides, trail activists and keen walkers seem to agree that the Nordic outdoor tradition is an important foundation for the current enthusiasm for pilgrimage and trail-walking in the Nordic countries. However, although the Right of Public Access is seen as symbolically important, the availability of clearly signposted and mapped trails was deemed vital for a growing group of urbanites who want to walk in nature but do not have much experience of roaming freely.[35] A further incentive to improve the marking of trails on Åland is that the Right of Public Access is somewhat more restricted there than in the rest of the Nordic countries. Marked trails are seen as a feasible solution

---

29   The connection between nature and nation is deeply rooted also in many other countries, see e.g. Nash, *Wilderness and the American Mind*.

30   See e.g. Readman, this volume; Williams, *Turning to Nature in Germany*.

31   Österlund-Pötzsch, *Gångarter och gångstilar*, pp. 65–79, 101–103.

32   See e.g. Löfgren, 'Människan i naturen'; Sandell and Sörlin (eds), *Friluftshistoria*.

33   Österlund-Pötzsch, 'Walking Nordic', 33–35.

34   https://svensktfriluftsliv.se/wp-content/uploads/2018/04/2018-01-24-report-from-joint-nordic-project-recommendations.pdf (accessed 3 April 2021).

35   SLS 2245, SLS 2357_ljud_1, SLS 2357_av_1.

for encouraging outdoor life in a way whereby walkers neither walk freely over private properties nor cause damage to the fragile archipelago environment.[36]

Although most walkers might not reflect over whether their stroll in nature is subsumed under a specifically Nordic identity or a set of European values, various overarching value narratives act as a definite incentive for many pilgrimage activists. One St Olav Ways pilgrim explains:

> It is important because it is genuine. It is based on something authentic, something real. Not because Olav walked here – no, he was whoever he was. I don't care about the Olav myth as such. *But* he was a real person and these are important cultural and historical facts. I see this as a shared path. And it is a certified European Cultural Route, which I find incredibly powerful. A truly important status. It is not made up, there is an actual history behind it, actual culture, memories.[37]

As elucidated by Bendix, authenticity stands out as a persistent, but slippery, value designator for heritage.[38] The concept is replete with divergent contextual interpretations and connotations. In the quote above, the pilgrim distinguishes between St Olav as myth and pilgrimage as traditional popular practice. The feeling of participating in something authentic constitutes a significant motivation for many pilgrims.[39] The narrative sphere surrounding pilgrimage imbues the activity with meaning and purpose.[40] Heritage, here, encapsulates both the roads and the movement towards the goal.

Pilgrims testify that walking the same routes that have been walked by people for hundreds of years creates a tangible sense of being part of a heritage.[41] The act of doing, of walking the trail oneself, seems to align the pilgrim with UNESCO's principle of not merely preserving but safeguarding intangible cultural heritage.[42] Safeguarding heritage puts the emphasis on ensuring a tradition remains relevant so it will continue to be practised. 'Grand' heritage narratives may also generate meaning and relevance for individual walking narratives. While the act of walking on one level is the same whether one walks as a pilgrim to Nidaros Cathedral or as an everyday commuter heading for work, on another, decisive, level, they are widely differing experiences belonging to separate narrative realms.

---

36 SLS 2245_av_1.
37 See e.g. SLS 2357_av_1.
38 Bendix, *Culture and Value*.
39 Österlund-Pötzsch, *Gångarter och gångstilar*, pp. 183–86.
40 See Johannsen and Ohrvik, 'How to Be a Pilgrim', 515; see also Bendix, *Culture and Value*, p. 20.
41 SLS 2357_av_1.
42 https://ich.unesco.org/en/safeguarding-00012 (Accessed 7 April 2021).

6. Archipelagic Paths

Local history, local heritage, local tourism

> I had read Paolo Coelho's *The Pilgrimage*, but I did not want to walk the Camino. I did not want to walk in Spain. I felt that we also have a Nordic heritage. I didn't know too much about it but was aware of the St Olav Ways. I wanted to start my pilgrimage in the Nordic countries – this is my cultural heritage. My heritage is here. Why cross the stream to fetch water?[43]

The quote above by a St Olav pilgrim, echoes a wish expressed by several Nordic pilgrims and hikers to explore 'their own' landscapes and trail heritage.[44] While there are certainly strands of the national romantic 'know your country' endeavours to be found in such sentiments, there are also clear influences from current concerns about sustainable tourism, ecological footprints and the wish to experience cultural heritage through personal involvement.[45]

Despite the tourism angle of the recent trail renewal projects on Åland, the projects were also seen as doing something positive for local communities. In connection with heritage work, Bendix notes that, for many actors, 'economic value is not separate but intertwined with other kinds of value'.[46] One project leader observed, 'On [the island municipality of] Kumlinge it was all hands on deck. They know that it is something they can offer their visitors, Ålanders in general and those who live on Kumlinge – it wasn't just for tourists but for us who live here.'[47] The Corona pandemic with resulting lockdowns boosted an already growing interest in trail walking on Åland. A trail guide observed, 'There are trails in all municipalities, it has been a huge success. People have been out walking, walking and walking. Families have walked, well, everyone has walked – and that's just fantastic!'[48]

Trail walking has become a popular form of everyday local tourism and staycation activity. One interviewee commented, 'I think Corona has contributed to a new form of movement. Sure, we have always walked a lot, but I think people have become aware of how much great stuff there is here on Åland to see and experience.'[49] Another active walker noted the reactions of

---

43   SLS 2357_av_1.
44   SLS 2245: 166.
45   Johannsen and Ohrvik note that walking the St Olav ways is a very different experience from walking the Camino de Santiago, due to 'the physically much more challenging topography, the harsher climate, and the historic narrative of a Viking king that unified the country by becoming a martyr' ('How to Be a Pilgrim', 510).
46   Bendix, *Culture and Value*, p. 5.
47   SLS 2245_av_1.
48   SLS 2357_ljud_2.
49   SLS 2245_av_1.

Ålanders who had walked the St Olav Waterway across the Åland Islands: 'They say, Wow, I've never been here before! Well, that's how we grow to love our home region and the environment, when you have an experience you would never have had otherwise, and it is so close – you don't need to go far to get a compelling, genuine, experience.'[50]

The 'discover-while-walking' philosophy was a pronounced part of the trail restoration projects. The underlying presumption is that walking the trail is not only a good way to learn about a place, but that having a story (e.g. about a local landmark) also makes walking the trail more enjoyable. Many municipalities have therefore created new information boards for hikers. The texts on the boards succinctly convey something about the local history or various landscape features. Typically, the short narratives portray the trail acting as a local guide, dispensing information to the walker about the community's history, social life and nature. Here, the trail will not only take the visitor on a walk in place but also through time. The capacity of trail-walking to involve many layers of history has often been observed.[51] The aspects of history actualised in trail walking transcend historical monuments and may be recent, incidental or ephemeral. For Ålanders, a poignant example of present history is the visible and widespread damage caused by the storm Alfrida, which devastated Åland in early 2019. Many trails were destroyed by the storm, and some stretches had to be re-routed due to fallen trees and open roots. Whereas some forest sections have been cleared, fallen trees have been left in many places for ecological reasons – something that has led visiting walkers to register complaints with Visit Åland about the forests looking 'messy and unkempt'.[52] In cases like this, urban aesthetics and expectations may clash with forestry practices and represent conflicting narrative spheres.

History, as pointed out in the introduction, not only inhabits, but has also created the trails as objects. The very existence of trails and paths implies walking in the footsteps of previous users. Stories become attached to places and proliferate the layers of heritage creating a textual 'thickness'.[53] For people, who have repeatedly walked the same paths themselves, memories and observations may become personal place stories, adding to the complex and constantly changing clusters of narratives surrounding trails.

---

50   SLS 2357_av_1.
51   See e.g. Macfarlane, *The Old Ways*.
52   SLS 2245_av_1.
53   Cf. Honko, 'Thick Corpus and Organic Variation'.

6. *Archipelagic Paths*

Figure 4.
Uprooted tree left to rot. Messy, or sound forest care? Photograph by Susanne Österlund-Pötzsch.

Figure 5.

Building 'stone trolls' is a popular interactive practice among visitors to the cave trail in Geta. Many locals disapprove of this and view it as interfering with nature. Photograph by Susanne Österlund-Pötzsch.

Walking and community

Walking is a physical connection of points. A trail, consequently, reads as a joining of geographically separate places. There is a clear symbolic significance in an official route such as the St Olav Waterway, connecting the Åland Islands both with the Finnish mainland in the east and the Swedish mainland in the west. As such, it is a project demanding a great deal of transborder co-operation. Trails, as well as trail walking and trail maintenance, provide points of connection in many respects, not least through the social aspects of trail work. The project leaders and volunteers for the Ålandic trail restoration project described it as 'joint work together' involving both institutions and grassroots efforts. The appeal of walking together is also apparent. Several interviewees commented on the rise of walking groups during the pandemic. While there was already an abundance of outdoor societies on Åland, a great many new Facebook groups

6. Archipelagic Paths

dedicated to various types of walking appeared during the Corona lockdown.[54]

The pilgrim parson Maria Widén was one of the initiators of a walking group that organises hikes to the Ålandic churches, along nature trails. The popular church hikes are social events but parts of the walks are always undertaken in silence for personal meditation. 'You don't need to go abroad to do a pilgrimage, you can do it to your own church', Maria Widén comments and adds that many of the walkers are not members of the church but view the forest as 'their cathedral of peace'.[55] The tendency to perceive nature as a spiritual space has often been linked to the growing popularity of hiking and trail-walking.[56] A closely related perspective affirms the benefits for wellbeing and health of spending time in nature. Stories and reports on meditation and self-improvement through forest walking are ubiquitous in traditional and social media.[57] There is an expanding selection of courses and workshops on Åland offering 'forest bathing' and other mindful activities.[58] The attraction of visiting nature for restorative purposes is reflected in Visit Åland's portrayal of the islands a as a sanctuary of peace and wellbeing.[59] Not surprisingly, images of 'the remote island' are frequently evoked in this context.[60]

Wellbeing is also linked to feelings of connectedness to other walkers. Many of the active group walkers point out that companionship is a large part of the appeal of the organised walks. The social aspect of walking extends beyond physically walking together. In Facebook groups, such as 'Walkers on Åland', 'Walking with children', 'Pilgrims on Åland' and 'Church walks on Åland', keen walkers ask each other for advice, discuss trails, and share photos and stories from their own walks. The sharing of walking narratives has become a feature on other social media as well, for example, Visit Åland's #hikingaland, and the browser tab 'Stories' on the St Olav Waterway home page.[61] Notably, the sense

---

54   SLS 2245_av_1.
55   SLS 2357_ljud_3.
56   See e.g. Thrift, 'Still Life in Nearly Present Time'; Thurfjell, *Granskogsfolk*; also Österlund-Pötzsch, *Gångarter och gångstilar*, pp. 94–95.
57   Wilke, 'Wohlbefinden durch "Hinspüren"'.
58   See e.g. 'Sinnesvandring i tystnad', https://www.natur.ax/evenemang/sinnesvandring-tystnad (accessed 11 Aug. 2021).
59   Under the headline 'Places to Breathe', various spots on Åland are singled out and recommended: 'a calm and relaxing environment', 'it cannot get more peaceful than this', 'a tranquil and unique atmosphere that inspires reflection and serenity', 'The longest sand beach on Åland offers hundreds of metres of contemplation by the sea'. https://www.visitaland.com/en/do/outdoor-life/places-where-you-can-just-breathe/ (downloaded 11 Aug. 2021).
60   Cf. Ronström, 'Remoteness, Islands and Islandness', 271.
61   https://stolavwaterway.com/berattelser/ (accessed 10 Aug. 2021).

Figure 6.

Helping hands – walking as community building. A group of church-walkers on the Lemland trail, Åland Islands. Photograph by Susanne Österlund-Pötzsch.

6. Archipelagic Paths

of community through walking is not only synchronic but also diachronic: many walkers, especially pilgrims, mentioned the feeling of timelessness in walking, and of being connected to the numerous walkers throughout time who have traversed the same trails.

Conclusion

Trails and trail walking are immersed in narratives. When looking at narrative elements in connection with trail walking in a small island context such as the Åland Islands, a complex interplay between stories, heritage and community emerges. Attracting visitors is an important incentive behind much of the recent trail maintenance work. Nature tourism is an important economic niche for Åland. Trail walking promoted and motivated by storytelling has created opportunities of encouraging sustainable tourism and for small municipalities to showcase their historical and natural heritage without large costs. However, through the way they are routed, trails inevitably also tell stories about local circumstances such as landownership and traditional place connections.

Today, the interest in outdoor life and walking has given rise to many grassroots forums where information and stories are exchanged, simultaneously creating new communities of walkers. Walking is increasingly practiced within narrative generated ideals such as spiritual and physical wellbeing, or as means of individual interaction with the nature, history or culture of a place. Walking traditional trails brings a physical and personal element to engagement with history, in which the walking itself becomes a performance of heritage and its values – consequently making heritage (more) affective and compelling. In this respect, performance, as a powerful means of persuasion and authentication, makes trail heritage 'feel genuine'. The heritagisation process of Ålandic trails stems from a wide array of motives where heritage is not necessarily the overarching aim, but something that offers a convenient framework. Heritage narratives inform the tourist experience but might also be important for Ålanders' understanding of islandness, local tradition and history. Movement heritage is constantly framed through narrativity in a multitude of ways, in effect communicating cultural ideologies while engendering socio-cultural interpretations and experiences.

Susanne Österlund-Pötzsch

Bibliography

Archive material

The Society of Swedish Literature in Finland, Helsinki
The Language and Tradition collection
SLS 2245, SLS 2357

Literature

Bendix, Regina, *Culture and Value. Tourism, Heritage, and Property* (Bloomington: Indiana University Press, 2018).

Bowman, Marian, Dirk Johannsen and Ane Ohrvik. 'Reframing Pilgrimage in Northern Europe. Introduction to the Special Issue', *Numen* **67** (2020): 439–52.

Dolby-Stahl, Sandra. 'A Literary Folkloristic Methodology for the Study of Meaning in Personal Narrative', *Journal of Folklore Research* **22** (1) (1985): 45–69.

Fludernik, Monika, *Towards a 'Natural' Narratology* (London: Routledge, 1996).

Green, Nicholas, *The Spectacle of Nature. Landscape and Bourgeois Culture in Nineteenth-Century France* (Manchester: Manchester University Press, 1990).

Honko, Lauri (ed.), 'Thick Corpus and Organic Variation. An Introduction', in *Thick Corpus. Organic Variation and Textuality in Oral Tradition*, pp. 3–28 (Helsinki: Finnish Literature Society, 2000).

Johanssen, Dirk and Ane Ohrvik, 'How to Be a Pilgrim. Guidebooks on the Norwegian St Olav Ways and the Heritagization of Religion', *Numen* **67** (2020): 508–36.

Klein, Barbro, 'Introduction. Telling, Doing, Experiencing Folkloristic Perspectives on Narrative Analysis', in Annikki Kaivola-Bregenhøj, Barbro Klein and Ulf Palmenfelt (eds), *Narrating, Doing, Experiencing Nordic Folkloristic Perspectives*, pp. 6–28 (Helsinki: Finnish Literature Society, 2006).

Löfgren, Orvar, 'Människan i naturen, in Jonas Frykman and Orvar Löfgren (eds), *Den kultiverade människan*, pp. 53–86 (Lund: Liber, 1979).

Nordiska ministerrådet, *Allemansrätten i Norden* (København, 1997).

Österlund-Pötzsch, Susanne, *Gångarter och gångstilar. Rum, rytm och rörelse till fots* (Göteborg: Makadam, 2018).

Österlund-Pötzsch, Susanne, 'Walking Nordic. Performing, Space, Place and Identity', in Peter Aronsson and Lizette Gradén (eds), *Performing Nordic Heritage. Everyday Practices and Institutional Culture*, pp. 27–52 (Abingdon, Oxon: Routledge, 2013).

Parga-Dans, Eva, 'Socio-Economic Impacts of the Camino to Finisterre', in Cristina Sánchez-Carretero (ed.), *Heritage, Pilgrimage and the Camino to Finisterre Walking to the End of the World*, pp. 121–34 (Cham: Springer International Publishing, 2015).

Macfarlane, Robert, *The Old Ways. A Journey on Foot* (London: Penguin Books, 2012).

Nash, Roderick Frazier. *Wilderness and the America Mind* (New Haven: Yale University Press, 2014).

Ronström, Owe, *Öar och öighet. Introduktion till östudier* (Stockholm: Carlssons, 2016).

Ronström, Owe, 'Remoteness, Islands and Islandness', *Island Studies Journal* **16** (2) (2021): 270–97.

6. Archipelagic Paths

Sandell, Klas and Sverker Sörlin (eds), *Friluftshistoria. Från 'härdande friluftslif' till ekoturism och miljöpedagogik. Teman i det svenska friluftslivets historia* (Stockholm: Carlsson, 2000).

Schama, Simon, *Landscape and Memory* (London: HarperCollins, 1995).

Thrift, Nigel, 'Still Life in Nearly Present Time. The Object of Nature', *Body & Society* 6 (3–4) (2000): 34–57.

Thurfjell, David, *Granskogsfolk. Hur naturen blev svenskarnas religion* (Stockholm: Norstedts, 2020).

Wilke, Inga, 'Wohlbefinden durch 'Hinspüren'. Reflexives und relationales Erzählen von Gesundheit im Kontext von Entspannungs- und Achtsamkeitsangeboten', in L. Dieckmann, J. Menninger and M. Navratil (eds), *Gesundheit erzählen. Ästhetik, Performanz und Ideologie seit 1800* (Berlin/Boston: De Gruyter, 2020).

Williams, John Alexander, *Turning to Nature in Germany. Hiking, Nudism, and Conservation, 1900–1940* (Stanford: Stanford University Press, 2007).

CHAPTER 7.

FUSION: CO-CREATED HERITAGE IN STORIES FROM THE CAMINO DE SANTIAGO

Camilla Brudin Borg

Stories from the Camino de Santiago de Compostela – sometimes known as 'Jacobean literature' – continue to inspire people to walk the old pilgrimage way to Santiago de Compostela. These stories become part of, and even direct, the pilgrim's understanding of the pilgrimage process; however, the stories also narrate the pilgrimage trail and create a narrative world in which the trail's environment is as important as the events of the story. This article will analyse how the Jacobean literature contributes to the immaterial heritage of the Camino by using an intertextual, historical method that deploys the concept of the palimpsest. This perspective is extended by co-reading the textual layers with the materiality of the trail itself to detect *natureculture entanglements* in stories of Swedish pilgrimage.

The *Liber Sancti Jacobi*, also called the *Codex Calixtinus* (c. 1140) is a very early text that tells of the pilgrimage road to Santiago de Compostela.[1] The Codex was probably written by the monk Aymeric Picaud, who was a chancellor of Pope Calixtinus II (1119–1124). It is a kind of guidebook for medieval pilgrims. However, in addition to describing the way, its dangers and possible lodgings, the author retells the myths and miracles of the pilgrimage trail. Book III, of the five books of the manuscript, tells the mythical Christian story of a bright star in the year 813 that shone above the Liberdón in Northern Spain, showing the hermit Pelayo the tomb of Saint James. It also recounts an even older medieval legend of the apostle's martyrdom and decapitation by King Herod in Jerusalem (44 AD) and of Saint James' miraculous journey in a boat of stone to the shores of Galicia, where his remains were buried. The same star was still shining in 835, when Bishop Theodemir of Iria was said to have found three bodies buried in a field. One was decapitated and bore the inscription 'Jacobus, son of Zebedeus and Salome'. The other two were said to be his disciples Theodorus and Athanasius. These legends, which promised miracles along the way, promoted the medieval interest in walking to Santiago de Compostela. It noteworthy that it was a set of stories that started

---

1   *The Miracles of Saint James.*

7. Fusion

the pilgrimages to Santiago de Compostela. This points to the importance of storytelling in creation and maintaining cultural heritage in connection to trails.

In modern times, including the last five decades, millions of people have made the pilgrimage to Saint James' tomb in the cathedral of Santiago de Compostela in Spain, after the rebirth of the old pilgrimage trail in the 1970s.[2] Although this modern movement is the result of official and conscious management and restoration, the popularity of the pilgrimage is also a result of uncountable stories in books, films and social media promoting the trails.[3] Just as 'all roads lead to Rome', there are several trails that go to Santiago de Compostela, and the stories told on these trails continue to inspire others to set out on a pilgrimage. The stories and legends together with the trail itself can be seen as an intertwined immaterial heritage that is important for the continuation of the tradition to walk. In the process of telling and retelling – as well as imitating and emulating – old and modern pilgrim myths, peoples' views and ideas on how to walk and behave on such a pilgrimage are co-created, contested and reshaped. In this way, literature is an important carrier of ideas and rituals that keep, transmit and transform the memories, history and perceptions of the pilgrimage trail and, in this sense, an important part of the immaterial heritage of the Camino de Santiago.[4] This process is of course also maintained by scholarly books and the ever-growing body of research on the Camino.[5]

Tangible and intangible heritage on the Camino

Historically, there were several ways to walk to St James's tomb in Santiago de Compostela, depending on where the pilgrimage began. The *Codex Calixtinus* describes four pilgrims' trails that converge in the small village of Puente de la Reina.[6] Since 1993, UNESCO has listed a network of four routes in Northern Spain as a world heritage 'serial site'.[7] The city of Santiago de Compostela was declared a world heritage site in 1985, and the old Spanish pilgrimage way to the city was appointed as the 'First European Cultural Route' by the Council of Europe in 1987. Tangible heritage comes to the fore on the trail, as the

---

2   For statistics, see the webpage of The Pilgrim's office in Santiago de Compostela: https://oficinadelperegrino.com/en/statistics/ (accessed 2 Dec. 2020).

3   Lois González and Lopez, 'Liminality Wanted'; Schrire, 'The Camino De Santiago'; L. Gemzöe, 'I skrivande pilgrimers fotspår'.

4   Margry, 'Imagining an End of the World'; Frey, *Pilgrim Stories*; Schrire, 'The Camino De Santiago'; Gemzöe, 'I skrivande pilgrimers fotspår'.

5   Frey, *Pilgrim Stories*.

6   *Vägvisare till Santiago de Compostela*, p. 23 [*Liber Sancti Jacobi*, Book 4, Chapter I].

7   https://whc.unesco.org/en/list/669/ (accessed 29 March 2021)

Figure 1.

'Roman road', Camino de Santiago de Compostela, Spain. Photograph by Camilla Brudin Borg.

pilgrimage way has a long history and harbours countless 'churches, hospitals, hostels, monasteries, calvaries, bridges, and other structures' – in other words, historically interesting individual sites along the trail.[8] But is the trail itself included as a world heritage site? And, if so, in what way? Dani Schrire asks an important question that seems to remain unsolved:

> It is not clear whether the space between the monuments is considered 'heritage material' as well: roads, modern buildings, etc. In other words, UNESCO's idea of a (linear) route is not very clear; is it like in a child's game – 'connecting the dots'?[9]

UNESCO's webpage still states that the Camino has 'outstanding natural landscapes' and an important and rich intangible cultural heritage that has survived to the present day.[10] The survival mode of this intangible heritage is

---

8   Ibid.
9   Schrire, 'The Camino De Santiago', 71.
10 The Camino made the list of UNESCO's World Heritage Sites for its 'Outstanding Universal Value' and due to its authenticity and integrity for having been outstandingly influential for faith, for having

7. Fusion

tied to cultural mediation, among other manifestations, through the narratives that circulate around and shape the Camino and how it is connected to the walking practice itself.

Nevertheless, part of the idea of the Camino's heritage does not seem to fall neatly into either the *material* category (i.e. the churches, hospitals, hostels, monasteries etc. stretching though Northern Spain) or the *immaterial* category (i.e. the memories and traditions). What is missing is a better understanding of the how the narratives and the trail itself are intertwined, tied and fused together. It is therefore worth investigating if it is possible to understand the trail itself as a *natureculture zone*, a storied space infused by narrative meaning, as well as, importantly, a material space that contributes to the creation of meaning and narrative structures in the stories 'along the trail'. In this article I will introduce the *palimpsest* as a metaphor to discuss how the interconnectedness of material trail and stories can be understood as a co-creation of tangible and intangible heritage.

The palimpsest

The *palimpsest* is a concept used in literary theory.[11] It attempts to capture how texts and narratives within a tradition imitate and emulate older texts, genres or themes, by reusing or sometimes opposing old motifs and introducing new ones in dialogue with earlier authors.

A palimpsest is also an old manuscript that is reused for new writing: a parchment that was once imprinted is wiped clean for reuse, although the old words remain somewhat visible. Similarly, in the world of stories, a parody or paraphrase can use an old story but reshapes it and tells it anew. The old story can be said to remain somewhat visible through the rewriting.[12] The idea of the palimpsest within literary theory invites scholars to a relational reading between texts. The concept of palimpsests has also been used within studies of historical geography, landscape- and urban studies to detect and 'read' the historical layers imprinted in the (urban) landscape. Andreas Huyssen in this way reads Berlin as text: 'historically, intertextually, constructively, and deconstructively', but also as materiality to 'be woven into our understanding of urban spaces as lived spaces that shape collective imaginaries'.[13] I will in this sense extend the textual

---

the most completely preserved material registry, for having played an important role as a cultural transmitter and for having outstanding natural landscapes. See UNESCO, 'Routes of Santiago de Compostela'.

11   Allen, *Intertextuality*, pp. 32–47; Genette, *Palimpsests*, pp. 3–6.
12   Dillon, *The Palimpsest*.
13   Huyssen, *Present Pasts*, p. 7 and Ch. 4: 'After the War: Berlin as Palimpsest', pp. 49–71.

Figure 2.

Material communication at the Camino de Santiago de Compostela, Spain. Photograph by Camilla Brudin Borg.

metaphor to include the relation between the text and the materiality of world.

The pilgrimage trail in the physical world is beaten by many feet, imprinted by human activity and performatively imitated by a steady stream of walkers. But the trail is also shaped by historical, literary, critical, theoretical, political and other cultural layers of text. In walking each step to Santiago de Compostela, the walker can loosely be compared to a pen imprinting another layer of words onto the stories already written on an old parchment, as the walker adds a new layer to the stories that already infuse the walking path with meaning (as also Benjamin Richard's contribution to this volume discusses). Tim Ingold prefers 'impress' to 'imprint', and thus makes a subtle distinction between the pen and the foot while still elaborating on the same metaphor when juxtaposing the lines of writing and traces of mobility that connect the past and the present in the landscape.[14] At any rate, this metaphor *fuses together* the images of layering,

---

14   Ingold, *The Life of Lines*, p. 60.

7. Fusion

imprinting, dialogue and deep history in a creative and continuous process that I would like to add to the discussion of the heritage of trails and paths. Like a palimpsest, the trail itself as well as old myths and narratives remain somewhat visible as the new Camino stories add new traditions, performances and practices on top of old ones.

Looking back, it is hard to find discussions of how the physical world contributes to the narratives. From the late 1970s, geographical perspectives began to be used to study landscapes as constructs made by human narrativisation and meaning-making.[15] Humans create narratives as a cultural activity to infuse their world with meaning – to both understand and shape their world.[16] Narratives have also been postulated to be the medium that carries memories, ideas, stories and legends between individual humans, cultures and generations; and after 'the semiotic turn', it has 'become common to "read" human action *as if* it were narrative; with "the spatial turn", "narrative" was stretched to include such things as cultural and spatial "hidden" patterns of modern culture'.[17] But, after 'the material turn', *matter* and the physical world is now considered to include its own *agency*.[18] This latest turn has opened up the possibility of reading matter itself (or as in this case, the trail) as a kind of narrative. The idea that *matter* contains its own agency, rather than being, as previously presumed, 'a passive substratum' or sheer background, can be found within the theoretical schools of new materialism, material feminism and material ecocriticism.[19] Serenella Iovino and Serpil Oppermann state that 'the world's material phenomena are knots in a vast network of agencies, which can be "read" and interpreted as forming narratives, stories'.[20] Following these recent accomplishments, it is possible to view narratives as part of – and integrated within – the trail and the materiality, producing the world but also being produced by the world. We can now talk about a *co-production* or *co-creation* of the trail as well as the narrative. The concept of the palimpsest can thus be used when investigating narratives as the medium infusing the pilgrimage trail with their cultural meaning and when stories are seen as important transmitters of immaterial heritage. Movement heritage can in this way be seen as including co-created material and immaterial dimensions.

To see how this works, it is useful to take a walk on the trail with which the

---

15 Tuan, *Space and Place*, pp. 38 ff; Tally, *Literary Cartographies*; González and Lopez, 'Liminality Wanted'; Duncan and Duncan, '(Re)Reading the Landscape'.
16 Lefebvre, *The Production of Space*.
17 Sinding Jensen, 'Narrative', p. 292.
18 Iovino and Oppermann, 'Introduction'.
19 Alaimo and Hekman (eds), *Material Feminisms*; Iovino and Oppermann (eds), *Material Ecocriticism*.
20 Iovino and Oppermann (eds), *Material Ecocriticism*, p. 1.

textual elements are entangled and co-created – in this case the trail stretching from Saint-Jean-Pied-de-Port on the French side of the Pyrenees to the Cathedral in Santiago de Compostela. I will therefore turn to some examples demonstrating a pattern whereby autobiographical Camino stories relate to the topographical structure of the trail.

Topographical agencies

Current eco-narratological theory points out that understanding a narrative as the sequence of events alone is insufficient because the reader also needs to create an idea *of the world* in which the events take place – a *storyworld*. The concept refers to the specific environment where the events unfold.[21] The topographical shape of the Camino Frances is an important part of the fictive created storyworlds of the pilgrimage stories taking place on the Camino Frances. The shape of the environment somehow influences the walkers' experience and, in this sense, makes the trail itself an active part of the narratives, thereby displaying its agency. The topography shining through in a Camino story, as in a palimpsest, would then be an agent that creates a similar narrative pattern in several instances of the Camino literature.

The first part of the narrative of most Camino stories focuses on the walker's body: blisters appear, and pain and discomfort must be dealt with. This coincides not only with the experience of walking twenty or thirty kilometres per day, which is probably new to many modern people, but also with a rather strenuous landscape, as the Pyrenees, with their high passes, must be crossed at the beginning of the trail. This part of the Camino Frances is often called 'the physical part'. The medieval guidebook the *Codex Calixtinus* tells of this first part of the Camino (including Navarra and the Basque country) being particularly hard.[22]

Modern pilgrims struggle and share their difficulties and have plenty of opportunities to help each other and connect with other Camino fellows. In *A Woman's Journey*, an autobiographical novel written by the Swedish author Agneta Sjödin, the protagonist gets such bad blisters that she has to walk backwards downhill, and it is at this point that she meets the group of pilgrims who will support her and accompany her to the end.[23]

After approximately two weeks walking, the pilgrims enter Burgos, the portal city of the plains to come. Here, the second stage of the Camino Frances begins,

---

21 Herman, 'Storyworld'; James and Morel, *Environment and Narrative*; see also James, *The Storyworld Accord*, p. xv.
22 *Vägvisare till Santiago de Compostela*, pp. 29–36 [in *Liber Sancti Jacobi*, Book 4, Chapter VII].
23 Sjödin, *En kvinnas resa*.

7. Fusion

Figure 3.

Walking and talking at the Camino de Santiago de Compostela, Spain. Photograph by Camilla Brudin Borg.

along with a new mode in the Camino stories. The landscape is characterised by the *Meseta Central* which is famous for being completely flat, with its neverending wheatfields and endless hot roads stretching forever under the burning sun. The second section ends at León. In between these two cities, the narrative structure shows a slightly different pattern. In many cases in the Camino literature, a meditative or introvert mode appears at this point. The walking narrative is now interrupted by a closer series of flashbacks, digging deep down into the walker's/narrator's personal history. The reader is transported to the pre-history of the pilgrimage, to a time or maybe occasion that motivated the walker to set out on a pilgrimage. Nowadays, the Camino is often called '*ruta de la terapia*', meaning 'therapy road' or 'the road to introspection'.[24]

The second part of the Camino Frances, with its monotonous landscape, particularly earns this epithet, as it seems to provoke the walker's inner worlds to surface. In Agneta Sjödin's story we become acquainted with the protagonist's low self-esteem and with situations in her past that constitute the source of

---

24 Frey, *Pilgrim Stories*, p. 45; see also Frey's webpage 'Walking to presence'.

her problems.²⁵ In another example, Camilla Davidsson's *Under the Stars of the Milky Way* (2014), we relive a destructive love affair and experience parts of a shameful childhood together with the main character, Emma, and her alcoholic mother.²⁶ At this point in the narrative of *I'm Off Then* (2008), written by the German comedian Hape Kerkeling, the author deals with the reasons why he suffered a burnout.²⁷ The examples are multiple.

Leaving Léon and entering the third and final stage towards Santiago de Compostela, the walker faces new mountains and what (in some narratives) is called 'the bewitched' Galicia.²⁸ In modern Camino literature, frightening stories of wild dogs are particularly common. In Coelho's *The Pilgrimage*, a big, wild, black dog is a hostile spirit the protagonist must fight as part of a spiritual trial and thus staging a metaphor to create the feeling of hostile and unsecure surroundings.²⁹ Somewhere on the last part on the trail, as it is often told in the modern Camino literature, a personal breakdown occurs, followed by an epiphany or insight that profoundly changes the walker's original way of seeing personal problems. This creates a pattern.. The idea here is that the mind has been prepared during the monotonous stretches of the *meseta*, and that the soul is ripe and open to accept new views or to receive a religious epiphany. The final steps towards Santiago are often walked in peace and happiness, together with the new friends that have been made on the way.

These coincidences in many of the narratives of the physical trail can be seen as a common pattern, indicating that the topography of the landscapes of this trail contributes to the creation of the stories, infusing an agency that pushes the way the stories are told in a common direction. The narrative structure is in this way like a palimpsest incorporating the structure of the landscape, i.e., of the trail itself. It seems as if the Camino is characterised not only by its cultural meaning and intertextual (textual) exchange, but also in this way by mixed *naturecultures* (Haraway) or *entanglement of matter and meaning*. The trail is in sense meeting the story 'half way', as in Karen Barad's view.³⁰

To further investigate how the narratives of Camino de Santiago are layered and co-created by the physical trail, I will now turn to the literary motif of the healing power of walking the pilgrimage.

---

25   Sjödin, *En kvinnas resa*.
26   Davidsson, *Under Vintergatans alla stjärnor*.
27   Kerkeling, *I'm Off Then*.
28   Mullen, *Call of the* Camino, p. 132.
29   Coelho, *The* Pilgrimage, pp. 95–96.
30   Haraway, *The Companion Species Manifesto*; Barad, *Meeting the Universe Halfway*.

7. Fusion

Figure 4.
Early morning at the Iron Cross, Camino de Santiago de Compostela, Spain. Photograph by Camilla Brudin Borg.

The healing powers of the Camino

The motif of the healing powers – whether energies or agencies – of the Camino is probably one of the most commonly represented in the Camino literature, both old and new. The idea of the healing energies of the Camino is collectively created by several texts that repetitively use the same idea while giving it a new shape over the years. We also find traces of the environment's importance here. As a final example, I will compare three different layers of the palimpsestic structure of the average Camino literature to show how an idea of the entanglement of the physical and spiritual world is represented by the stories of the Camino.

The Christian way

Old legends – as well as new Camino stories – tell of miracles occurring on the trail. In the essay book *The Starfield: An Essay of Saints and Blisters* (2003), for example, the Swedish author Ulrika Kärnborg experiences the trail opening to spiritual forces. She walks the Camino with her husband, trying to cross a cold, wet and windy Pyrenees, when the mountains hit the walkers with their full power. Ulrika collapses, totally exhausted, and turns to Saint James in prayer. She then experiences the sensation of a 'steady and kind hand' that firmly gets her on her feet again. Afterwards she remembers that her mind was sharpened and that she recovered her energy and was able to safely walk down to Roncesvalles.[31] The storyworld created in Kärnborg's narrative about this occasion is dependent on the harsh weather on the mountain, creating the need and opening for the 'helping hand'. It would have been quite a different story if the sun had been shining; but the stormy storyworld harbours the experience of a miracle and opens the way to other dimensions connecting to the medieval experienced world.

In medieval times, God, Saint James or Saint Egidius were (as they still are) imagined to be the helpers and executers of miracles on the Camino de Santiago.[32] Book II of the *Codex Calixtinus* contains a collection of legends and stories recounting miracles that were said to have occurred on the way to Santiago de Compostela. Stories are told in which the blind can suddenly see and the lame can suddenly walk after travelling the way to Santiago de Compostela or visiting certain monasteries.[33] One of the most famous is the miracle of the bread and wine turning to real flesh and blood on a – *nota bene* – stormy and snowy day in the church of the remote Galician mountain village of O'Cebreiro. Another story tells of how soldiers thrust their lances into the ground surrounding the town of Shaugun the night before an important battle, and then found that their lances had sprouted leaves, eventually growing into a forest encircling the city. Each lance or tree represented a fallen soldier who suffered martyrdom in the name of God and the soldier's soul was thus 'liberated'.[34] This legend, interestingly enough, literarily intertwines the material with the spiritual by means of the spirit-linked lance piercing though the physical soil. In recounting such powers of the pilgrimage trail, the storyworld is composed of a double-layered reality in which healing powers emanate from a divine source.

The esoteric way

In the 1970s, when pilgrimages to Santiago de Compostela slowly got started again, alternative ideas and myths were introduced into the Camino folklore: these stories described the Camino as an ancient path with a much older origin and said that the Christian Camino was built on an archaic, pre-Christian path

---

31   Kärnborg, *Stjärnfältet: En essä om helgon och skoskav*, p. 23.
32   *The Miracles of Saint James*, pp. 57–96.
33   Ibid.
34   *Vägvisare till Santiago de Compostela*, p. 23.

with strong energy fields. By these new stories, the Camino – and especially the stretch to its alternative trail-end of Finisterre at the Atlantic coast – was launched as an old Celtic place of Sun-worship. The stories now created the trail as a universal place of spiritualism, knowledge and initiation.[35] Some of these esoteric ideas of an 'alternative' and much older Camino can be traced to Louis Charpentier and his *Les Jacques et le Mystère de Compostelle* (1971). Charpentier's alternative version of history 'positioned the Camino within a new esoteric context. He also brought up ancient "secrets" by "revealing" – inventing – a thousand-year-old pre-Christian pilgrims' route to the west in Galicia'.[36] These esoteric ideas from the 1970s were reused in other spiritual or alternative novels, guidebooks and websites, such as Henri Vincenot's novel *The Prophet of Compostela: A Novel of Apprenticeship and Initiation* (1995).[37] Paulo Coelho's *The Pilgrimage* (1987) and Shirly McLain's *The Camino: A Journey of the Spirit* (2000) also connected to this 'new age' and esoteric vein, describing the 'powers of the place' and explaining the healing energies and mystical elements of the Camino within an esoteric context.[38]

The secular way

Today, the Camino's healing force is sometimes (or also) attributed to the trail itself – to nature, the universe and/or to the workings of the moving body – and the miracles are retold as a secular narrative with an explanation grounded in scientific findings such as exercise and time spent in nature being beneficial for one's health.[39] In this way, the old motif of the healing powers of the Camino that once motivated medieval pilgrims is transformed into new stories, in a continuous dialogue with the traditional understanding while being reshaped according to modern paradigms, creating historical hybrids and modern versions of old stories. The core idea contained in the literary motif of 'the healing powers of the Camino' still has an important function at a narrative level as the motivation for walking the trail, but the idea has taken on different explanations and different logics – even secular ones – in modern times. These stories still continue to motivate pilgrims to walk 800 kilometres in search of better health and, sometimes, to be restored by a miracle or by the healing environment of the Camino.

---

35 Margry, 'Imagining an end of the world'.
36 Margry, 'Imagining an end of the world', p. 37; Charpentier, *Les Jacques et le Mystère de Compostelle*.
37 Vincenot, *The Prophet of Compostela*.
38 Margry, 'Imagining an end of the world'; Frey, *Pilgrim Stories*.
39 Mullen, *Call of the Camino*, p. 11.

Figure 5.

'Keep going', Camino de Santiago de Compostela, Spain. Photograph by Camilla Brudin Borg.

7. Fusion

Bibliography

Allen, G., *Intertextuality* (Abingdon, Oxon & New York: Routledge, 2011).

Barad, K., *Meeting the Universe Halfway: Quantum Physics and the Entanglement of Matter and Meaning* (Durham, North Carolina: Duke University Press, 2007).

Charpentier, L., *Les Jacques et le Mystère de Compostelle* [The James' and the Mystery of Compostela] (Paris: Editions Robert Laffont, 1971).

Coelho, P., *The Pilgrimage. A Contemporary Quest for Ancient Wisdom*, A.R. Clark (trans.) [*O Diário de um mago*, 1986], (Stockholm etc.: Harper Collins, 2005).

Davidsson, C., *Under Vintergatans alla stjärnor* [Under the Stars of the Milky Way] (Stockholm: Bladh by Bladh, 2014).

Dillon, S., *The Palimpsest: Literature, Criticism, Theory* (London & New York: Continuum, 2007).

Duncan, J. and N. Duncan, '(Re)Reading the Landscape', *Environment and Planning. D, Society & Space* **6** (2) (1988), pp. 117–126.

Frey, N.L., *Pilgrim Stories. On and Off the Road to Santiago* (Berkeley: University of California Press, 1998).

Gemzöe, L., 'I skrivande pilgrimers fotspår'[In the footsteps of writing pilgrims], in L. Gemzöe and A. Bohlin (eds), *Fiktion och verklighet* [Fiction and Reality], pp. 123–146 (Makadam: Göteborg, 2016) [Author-translated title].

Genette, G., *Palimpsests: Literature in the Second Degree*. (Lincoln, Neb.: University of Nebraska Press, 1997).

Haraway, D., *The Companion Species Manifesto* (Chicago: Prickly Paradigm Press, 2003).

Herman, D., 'Storyworld', in D. Herman, M. Jahn and M.-L. Ryan (eds), *Routledge Encyclopedia of Narrative Theory* (London & NY: Routledge, 2005).

Huyssen, A., *Present Pasts: Urban Palimpsests and the Politics of Memory*. (Stanford: Stanford University Press, 2003).

Ingold, T., *The Life of Lines* (Abingdon, Oxon & New York: Routledge, 2015).

Iovino, S. and S. Oppermann, 'Introduction', in S. Iovino and S. Oppermann (eds), *Material Ecocriticism* (Bloomington: Indiana University Press, 2014).

S. Alaimo and S. Hekman (eds), *Material Feminisms* (Bloomington: Indiana University Press, 2008).

James, E., *The Storyworld Accord: Econarratology and Postcolonial Narratives* (Lincoln, NE: University of Nebraska Press, 2015).

James E. and E. Morel, *Environment and Narrative: New Directions in Econarratology* (Columbus: The Ohio State University Press, 2020).

Kerkeling, H., *I'm Off Then: Losing and Finding Myself on the Camino de Santiago* [*Ich bin dann mal weg: Meine Reise auf dem Jacobsweg*, 2008] (New York: Simon & Schuster, 2009).

Kärnborg, U., *Stjärnfältet: En essä om helgon och skoskav* [The Starfield: An Essay of Saints and Blisters] (Stockholm: Bonniers, 2003) [Author-translated title].

Lefebvre, H. *The Production of Space* [1974] (Oxford: Basil Blackwell, 1991).

Lois González, R.C. and L. Lopez, 'Liminality Wanted. Liminal Landscapes and Literary Spaces: The Way of St. James', *Tourism Geographies* **22** (2) (2019): 1–21. https://doi.org/10.1080/14616688.2019.1647452

Margry, P.J., 'Imagining an End of the World: Histories and Mythologies of the Santiago-

Finisterre Connection', in C. Sánchez-Carretero (ed.), *Heritage, Pilgrimage and the Camino to Finisterre: Walking to the End of the World* (Heidelberg, New York etc.: Springer International Publishing, 2015).

The Miracles of Saint James. Translations from the Liber Sancti Jacobi, T.F. Coffey and M. Dunn (trans.) (New York: Italica Press, 1996).

Mullen, R., *Call of the Camino: Myth and Meaning on the Road to Compostela* (Forres: Findhorn Press, 2010).

Schrire, D., 'The Camino De Santiago: the Interplay of European Heritage and New Traditions', *Ethnologia Europaea* **36** (2) (2006): 69–86.

Sjödin, A., *En kvinnas resa* [A Woman's Journey] (Stockholm: Bazar förlag, 2006) [Author-translated title].

Sinding Jensen, J., 'Narrative', in M. Stausberg and S. Engler (eds), *The Oxford Handbook of the Study of Religion* (Oxford Handbooks Online, 2016). [https://www.oxfordhandbooks.com/view/10.1093/oxfordhb/9780198729570.001.0001/oxfordhb-9780198729570] (accessed 31 March 2021).

Tally, R.T., *Literary Cartographies: Spatiality, Representation, and Narrative* (New York: Palgrave Macmillan, 2014)

Tuan, Y.-F., *Space and Place. The Perspective of Experience* (Minneapolis: University of Minnesota Press, 1977)

Vincenot, H., *The Prophet of Compostela. A Novel of Apprenticeship and Initiation* (Rochester, Vermont: Inner Traditions, 1995).

Vägvisare till Santiago de Compostela: Ur Codex Calixtinus [Directions to Santiago de Compostela: From the Codex Calixtinus] M. Nordberg (trans.) (Skellefteå: Artos, 2011*).*

Webpages

The Pilgrim's office in Santiago de Compostela: https://oficinadelperegrino.com/en/statistics/ (Accessed 2 December 2020).

UNESCO, 'Routes of Santiago de Compostela: Camino Francés and Routes of Northern Spain' (The United Nations Educational, Scientific and Cultural Organization, 2021). https://whc.unesco.org/en/list/669/ (accessed 29 March 2021).

'Walking to Presence'(N. Frey's webpage): https://www.walkingtopresence.com/home/component/k2/item/2-the-camino-de-santiago-and-walking-your-blues-away (accessed 2 April 2021).

CHAPTER 8.

TRACING MEMORIES. THE GUIDED TRAIL AS AN AID TO CULTURAL MEMORY IN ARTWORKS BY JANET CARDIFF

Laura M.F. Bertens

Guided trails can play an important role in the construction and maintenance of shared, cultural memory and, as such, they are part of a vast and ever-growing movement heritage. Leading their users along traces of historical events and landmarks that preserve memories, these trails present walkers with narratives that unfold as they are moving and following signposts.[1] Most historical paths are inherently tied to communal memories and the ability of trails to communicate stories and memories can be increased by the use of audio guides, which add information and meaning to the encountered surroundings.

As audio guides have become more common over the last decades, we have grown accustomed to navigating cultural trails with the help of disembodied voices, speaking to us through headphones and giving us directions and historical context. Nowadays, most museums, heritage sites and cities provide audio tours, sending their users on walks past memorable objects and locations. The ubiquity of smartphones and the continuous access to internet and GPS location services have made it possible for audio guides to be looked up and used practically everywhere.[2] Initially belonging to the domain of the museum space, the audio guide has become a varied and flexible medium, providing narration for walking trails all over the world.[3]

Although the medium belongs first and foremost to the realm of tourism, its popularity has resulted in experimental applications for scholarly and artistic purposes. Examples of the former include Michael Gallagher's *audio drifts* and Toby Butler's *memoryscapes*, both of which illustrate the use of audio walks in the field of

---

1   See for instance the 'trailscapes' discussed by Fagence, 'A Heritage "Trailscape"'.
2   Butler, 'Memoryscape', pp. 1–2; Dickinson et al., 'Tourism and the Smartphone App', pp. 84–87; Lee, 'A Review of Audio Guides', pp. 705–06; Marshall, 'Audio-based Narratives for the Trenches of World War I', pp. 28–29.
3   See also Morosini, this volume.

cultural geography.[4] Instances of artistic use are numerous, dating back over half a century, and include Max Neuhaus' sound work *LISTEN* (1966), a sonic journey led by the artist; the artwork *Linked* by Graeme Miller (2003), which provides an artistic perspective on urban innovation; and Christina Kubisch's *Electrical walks* (2004–2017), in which electromagnetic fields are made audible.[5] At present, the audio and video walks created by Janet Cardiff, in collaboration with her partner George Bures Miller, are among the most well-known artistic applications of the medium.[6] Since the 1990s, the couple has been creating site-specific artworks for locations all over the world. The guided walks resemble audio guides but take the format beyond its traditional form and purpose. In their relationship to the construction and preservation of cultural memory, as well as their intentional creation and repetition of trails, the walks become part of a movement heritage that allows the act of walking to attach meaning to the walkers' surroundings.[7]

Cardiff's artworks require active participation and can only be fully experienced by performing them.[8] Provided with headphones and an audio device (in the older works a cd-player, in the more recent ones an mp3-player or iPod), the participant sets out on a carefully choreographed, individual walk guided by the voice of the artist. While some of these works are designed for the enclosed space of a museum (e.g., *Ittingen Walk*, 2002), many take place in public urban environments, such as Central Park in New York or Edinburgh's Old Town. The participant makes her way through the mundane, everyday life of these spaces, partially aware of her surroundings and partially submerged in the audio of the artwork. In recent years, the artist has also started to create video walks, in which the audio track is combined with a video recording played on an iPod. The participant sees the walk through the eyes of the artist and is

---

4   Gallagher, 'Sounding Ruins'; Butler and Miller, 'Linked: A Landmark in Sound'; Butler, 'Memoryscape'. The use of walking methods in geography is discussed in Pink et al., 'Walking Across Disciplines'; Revill, 'El tren fantasma'.

5   These and other artistic uses of sound in general and the audio guide in particular are discussed in Butler and Miller, 'Linked: A Landmark in Sound'; Butler, 'Memoryscape', pp. 3–5; Fischer, 'Speeches of Display'; Labelle, *Background Noise*, pp. 119–216.

6   Although they often work together, Janet Cardiff is the main artist in most projects and on their official website she is listed as the only artist for several of the walks. Of the artworks discussed in this essay, *Her long black hair* and *The missing voice: case study B* are works by Cardiff and the *Alter Bahnhof video walk* is a collaboration between Cardiff and Bures Miller. In all works the main voice is Cardiff's; for the sake of simplicity, the essay will therefore refer to Cardiff as the artist.

7   The importance of guided walks in the process of assigning meaning to our surroundings is also discussed in the chapter by Petra Lilja in this volume.

8   It is of course possible to play audio and video of the works in locations other than those intended (from home, for instance) and this can certainly create a powerful experience, albeit a very different one from the experience *in situ*. In this article, the focus of the analysis will be on the performance of the walks in their intended locations.

8. Tracing Memories

invited to align the image on the screen with her surroundings.

Both the audio and the video walks are centred around the voice of the artist, who provides instructions on the route to take, while at the same time drawing the participant into a complex narrative that weaves together references to encountered landmarks in the built environment, cultural memory connected to the site, personal memories of the artist (genuine or invented) and elements of fictional stories. The paths traced by these artworks are followed by thousands of participants over periods of decades (*The missing voice: case study B*, discussed in this chapter, has existed for over twenty years), becoming cultural trails in their own right and forming part of the movement heritage of their surroundings.

The artist's voice, heard through headphones, is accompanied by a range of audio fragments, mostly recorded *in situ* and with the use of binaural recording technology; during recording, a dummy head, fitted with microphones on its ears, is used to capture sounds coming from all directions.[9] When listening to the final audio track, the participant is thus surrounded by a three-dimensional soundscape. The voice of the artist seems to speak inside one's head and the additional sound fragments blend in with reality so seamlessly, that it is only natural to occasionally take off the headphones to check whether the footsteps, birds and street noises are real or part of the artwork.

The combination of binaural audio, the hypnotic voice of the artist and the intricate layering of stories results in an immersive and highly personal experience. Although it is common for traditional audio guides to provide directions on a guided trail, the instructions in these works are more intimate. In *Her long black hair* (2004) the artist instructs us: 'Try to walk to the sound of my footsteps so we can stay together.'[10] Similar instructions are given in other artworks and throughout the walks we are told to wait for her as we cross streets, to note people and objects she points out and to join her in carrying out small experiments. We are in the presence of the artist, experiencing her thoughts, fears and memories.

At the centre of each work is the act of walking itself, following a trail set out by the artist. The importance of walking is emphasised in the works, for instance in *Her long black hair*, which takes place in Central Park, New York. While making our way through the park, the artist tells us:

> Walking is very calming, one step after another, one foot moving in the future and one in the past. Do you ever think about that? It's like our bodies are caught in the middle. The hard part is staying in the present, really being here, really feeling alive.[11]

---

9   Cardiff and Bures Miller, *Something Strange this Way*, p. 91.
10 Track 1, *Her long black hair* (2004).
11 Track 1, *Her long black hair* (2004).

Laura Bertens

An interest in the relationship between past and present is a frequent occurrence in Cardiff's artworks and seems to be concerned more with memory than with history. The works are not intended to convey historical information about the trails. Instead, they involve the participant in the emotional layers of meaning that have become attached to these locations. By using personal memories and making frequent allusions to the process of remembering and commemorating, the works make participants aware of the mnemonic significance of their surroundings and of the act of walking through them. As such they form part of, and add to the growing awareness of, movement heritage.

The distinction between memory and history is far from exact and is best understood as a difference of perspective. In Oren Baruch Stier's words, 'history is concerned with events in the past and their meaning *for* the present, while memory involves the impact of the events of the past and their meaning *in* the present'.[12] As such, cultural memory is not simply passed on as passive and immutable information, but is continuously produced by those individuals in the present for whom the past holds relevance; it is a performative construction.[13] Art can both actively add to this construction and help us reflect on its process. The walks by Janet Cardiff do both.[14]

In this essay, I will look at two of Cardiff's artworks to show that the artistic use of audio- or video-guided walks can be a powerful tool in the communication and production of site-specific cultural memory.[15] The audio walk *The missing voice: case study B* (1999) takes its participants through the Whitechapel neighbourhood in London. The second case study, the *Alter Bahnhof video walk* (2012), leads one through the train station in Kassel, Germany. While the two artworks differ in location, historical context and use of audio and video, they both explore the close relationship between the act of walking and the cultural memories of the traversed (urban) landscape. In the train station in Kassel, the artist tells us: 'It's hard for me to be in the present sometimes.' Performing Cardiff's walks, the participant experiences this same sensation of becoming caught in a confusing network of memories, connected to the trail.

By comparing the characteristics of the two walks to those of the traditional audio guide, idiosyncratic aspects of the artworks come to light. The analysis helps us understand why Cardiff's artistic strategy is a such powerful tool in the

---

12 Stier, *Committed to Memory*, p. 2, original emphasis.
13 Erll and Rigney, *Mediation, Remediation, and the Dynamics of Cultural Memory*, pp. 1–2.
14 Well-known examples of this dual nature can, for instance, be found in artworks by Christian Boltanski and Gerhard Richter.
15 On the importance of trails, with or without the aid of audio guides, for the construction and preservation of cultural memory, see also the chapter by Maria Piekarska.

8. Tracing Memories

communication of site-specific cultural memories. After introducing the two artworks in the next section, the following three characteristics of the artworks will be discussed: the refusal to create coherent narratives, the deliberately confusing nature of the artworks, and their performativity.

The footsteps of ghosts

The older of the two artworks, *The missing voice: case study B*, is performed in the Whitechapel district of London.[16] This area is well-known for the gruesome murders committed here in 1888 by the Whitechapel murderer, Jack the Ripper. Fascination with the unsolved crimes endures, as evidenced by the numerous books on the subject, the *Ripperologist Magazine*, boardgames and TV series like *Ripper Street*. From the very start, the site has been a tourist attraction; as early as 1888, unofficial tours visited the area in search of (the myth of) Jack the Ripper. And organised tours were already held by the Crimes Club (of which Arthur Conan Doyle was a member) at the start of the twentieth century.[17] Nowadays, commercial tourism companies take visitors on walks through the area and, in addition to these in-person tours by guides, audio guides can be downloaded which allow visitors to explore the area of the crimes on their own.[18] While the historical events have left no visible traces in the neighbourhood, the memories of the deaths are thus still strongly present and continue to attract tourists.

Cardiff's audio walk leads its listeners through the very streets in which the horrors took place but, like the neighbourhood itself, the artwork contains no direct references to these events. No mention is made of the historical importance of the area, and it is only through the work's focus on murder, disguise and detective investigation that Jack the Ripper is brought to mind. Reviews of the audio walk often mention the connection between the neighbourhood and the murders, but there is no reason to suspect that the artist intended an

---

16   The complete artwork (consisting of three audio tracks) can be found on the website of Artangel: www.artangel.org.uk/project/the-missing-voice-case-study-b. No description can truly do justice to the work and I recommend listening to (part of) it, to get a sense of the soundscape and the atmosphere. When listening, it is important to use headphones to be able to appreciate the effect of the binaural recording.

17   Blum, 'Murder, Myth, and Melodrama', pp. 242–44.

18   Blum ('Murder, Myth, and Melodrama', pp. 247–53) describes three of the most well-known tours with guides, by the companies London Walks (www.walks.com/our-walks/jack-the-ripper-walking-tour), Discovery Tours & Events (www.jack-the-ripper-tour.com) and Secret Chamber Tours (www.rippervision.com). Two examples of audio guides which can be downloaded are the tours by Guidigo (www.guidigo.com/Web/The-bloody-steps-of-Jack-the-Ripper/LMvHuGxYQnY/Stop/1/St.James-Passage) and by iAudioguide and BlueBrolly (www.iaudioguide.com/jack-ripper-london-audio-guide).

explicit connection.[19] Nonetheless, the audio walk addresses the sense of danger one might feel at night in an urban environment, and the famous Victorian murders form an undeniable part of the history of this present-day experience. Given the artwork's location and the lingering memory of the murders, it makes sense to consider the walk in the context of these historical events and the anxiety they caused.

The walk starts in the crime section of the former Whitechapel Library, currently the Whitechapel Gallery, where the voice of the artist asks us to pick up a crime thriller by Reginald Hill. After reading a few sentences from it, she tells us to put it back and follow her through the library. Upon finding a note in another book saying 'Someone is following you', the artist leads us out of the library and into the street. In between instructions on the route to take and remarks about people and things she encounters on her walk, we hear fragments from different narratives. A man, seemingly a detective, is on the trail of a woman with red hair who appears, herself, to be investigating something. Early on in the walk, the artist tells us: 'I started these recordings as a way to remember, to make life seem more real. I can't explain it. But then the voice became someone else, a separate person hovering in front of me like a ghost.' Is it this second person who is being trailed by the detective? The plot is purposefully ambiguous and the listener remains unable to untangle the different threads.

Throughout the walk, there are references to crime, investigation and surveillance. Passing newsstands, the artist reads out headlines related to an ongoing murder case – from 'Killer waited an hour' and 'Woman's body found in Thames' to 'Dead woman identified'.[20] Both the artist and the detective (and therefore the listener too) seem to be following the red-haired woman, whose picture was found by the artist near a photo booth and who may or may not be the victim from the news reports. References to crime fiction, the sensation of being followed and even attacked and the use of played-back voice recordings – crackling and distant – lend the artwork a mysterious air.[21] The arts organisation Artangel, which commissioned the audio walk, describes it as '[p]

---

19 A link is seen by, for instance, Boxer, 'An Artist Who Travels with You'; Gorman, 'Wandering and Wondering', p. 83; Preece, 'Janet Cardiff at Whitechapel Library'. Whyte ('"Lost in the Memory Palace"') goes so far as to assert that the artist is 'mapping the famous murderer's ancient paths.'

20 Track 1, *The missing voice* (1999).

21 The atmosphere and plot elements strongly reminded me of Paul Auster's *The New York Trilogy* (1987), another work in which the act of tracing paths through the city plays a central role; Pinder ('Ghostly Footsteps', p. 6) notes the same.

8. Tracing Memories

art urban guide, part detective fiction, part film noir'.[22] It is included in their series *Inner City*, intended to 'encourage writers and artists to excavate a range of urban places and contemplate the changing nature of city environments and the counterpoint between narrative and place; between language and location'.[23]

The second case study can be said to function in a similar way. Set in the train station in Kassel, it revolves around the deportation of Jewish citizens from this city to the camps. Their journey started at platform 13 of the train station and is commemorated in the building with a monument by Horst Hoheisel. While the first work was an audio walk and provided its participants with an audio track to follow, this one makes use of both audio and video, inviting the visitor to use an iPod and headphones in order to follow the artist's recording through the train station. Sitting on a bench outside the small office in which the iPods are provided, we are told by the artist to align the image on our screens with our surroundings and to follow her (see Figure 1).[24] She takes us through the main hall, past the monument, down to platform 13. Instructions and directions are woven together with personal recollections and fragments of collective memory and history: the artist talks about a friend's grandfather who survived deportation to Auschwitz and she recounts dreams and memories, both recent (from the day before) and older, vaguer ones. Much of the work is devoted to reflecting upon the notion of memory and the ways in which we experience it, both collectively and personally.

As in the last case study, the location of the walk bears few traces of its history. Rebuilt after the war, the only reminder in this modern building of the horrific events of 1941 is the monument.[25] As a functioning train station, the building exists first and foremost in the present moment; the layers of history are not readily discernible and most travellers are unlikely to dwell upon them. And just as the audio walk through Whitechapel never mentions Jack the Ripper, the video walk refers to the Holocaust in mostly indirect ways. Throughout the 26 minutes of the walk, there are only three explicit references to the event – a

---

22 Artangel, www.artangel.org.uk/inner-city/, section *The missing voice (Case Study B)*.

23 Artangel, www.artangel.org.uk/inner-city/, section *Inner City*.

24 A six-minute excerpt of the artwork can be seen on the Youtube channel of the artists: www.youtube.com/channel/UC4u0V-G5KTeWF5hnubp-lrA (accessed 29 November 2021). The video gives a good impression of what it is like to walk through the train station holding the iPod.

25 A complete account of the deportation from Kassel is provided on the website of Yad Vashem, the World Holocaust Remembrance Center: deportation.yadvashem.org/index.html?language=en&itemId=9442969 (accessed 29 November 2021). Tellingly, the only book about the history of the train station, Klee's *Hauptbahnhof Kassel*, describes only the bunkers built under the train station and square (discussed in purely positive terms as having saved many lives) and the bombing of the site in 1943; no mention is made of the role of the station in the deportation.

Figure 1.

'Alter Bahnhof Video Walk' (2012), by Janet Cardiff and George Bures Miller. On screen we see several people simultaneously and unexpectedly dropping their suitcases, a direct reference to an earlier remark by the artist: 'Memories are like a different form of travel. It's like filling a suitcase that we pull behind us and we open and close when we need to.' Photograph by Laura Bertens; original artwork © Janet Cardiff and George Bures Miller, courtesy of the artists and Luhring Augustine, New York; *re-use not permitted*.

8. Tracing Memories

description of the monument, an explanation of the significance of platform 13 and a story about an Auschwitz survivor. Nonetheless, the participant is constantly aware of this theme and all other stories, memories and observations are understood in light of this traumatic history. References made by the artist, to remembrance and to the suffering memories can cause, all point to the problem of commemorating an atrocity so gruesome that no representation can ever be emotionally truthful and complete.

As we wander through these sites, we are following in the footsteps of the ghosts of those who have contributed to the locations' identities: the murder victims (as well as the murderer) in Whitechapel and the Jewish deportees in Kassel. The imprint of their lives on these local cultural memories is invisible, intangible and faint, but Cardiff's walks allow participants to become temporarily aware of it. The next three sections will explore the peculiarities of the works that contribute to this effect, beginning with the persistent absence of a conventional, linear narrative.

An absence of narrative

The two artworks are not concerned with historical information – in fact, we learn very little about the sites and their history – but rather with the ways in which historical events have shaped, however slightly, our current experience of these sites. The Victorian murders have added to a collective sense of danger in big metropoles that is still with us today, especially for women walking alone late at night. As Judith Walkowitz asserts: 'the Ripper episode … established a common vocabulary and iconography for the forms of male violence that permeated the whole society'.[26] And in his analysis of theatrical histories of Jack the Ripper, Justin Blum explores how plays have helped create and consolidate a cultural myth around the murderer.[27] Modern-day references to the crimes – in books, films, boardgames etc. – further their relevance to the present moment. The memory of the horror lingers, although often based on a distorted image of the historical facts.

Likewise, in Kassel's train station we experience – always faintly and below the surface – the echoes of the meticulous bureaucracy and efficiency of deportation, which has tainted train stations, in Germany in particular. When De Certeau writes that '[t]here is something at once incarcerational and navigational about railroad travel',[28] I cannot help but think of the importance of

---

26   Walkowitz, *City of Dreadful Delight*, p. 220.
27   Blum, 'Murder, Myth, and Melodrama'.
28   De Certeau, *The Practice of Everyday Life*, p. 113.

railways during the Holocaust. As categories, both the city and the train station have seen their identities affected by these histories. Like palimpsests, these public places are suffused with layers of collective memories which shape our present-day experiences of them. As such, the history of each site is – in Stier's words – meaningful *in* the present, not just *for* the present. It is this emotional significance of the locations that Cardiff's walks bring to the fore, shifting our attention away from the facts of history to the experience of memory. While her guided walks may resemble traditional tours, the effect is markedly different.

Heritage audio guides usually provide clear and factual information connected to discrete points of interest encountered on a walk. The linear progression of the trail is matched by an unfolding, linear narrative, which gives the trail purpose and coherence. This is true for most Jack the Ripper tours, which try to match the series of locations to the chronology of events. In constructing the narrative, a strong emphasis is placed on the accuracy of the provided information.[29] One audio guide starts by saying that 'we should tell you exactly how events took place',[30] while another tells the listener to 'rest assured that, on our tour, you will be brought up to date on all the latest findings on the crimes'.[31] In addition to this, the guides often aim to transport their users back in time, for instance through old photographs.[32] They promise to 'paint a picture of each site to help you to visualise the area as it was back in the late nineteenth century',[33] or tell their users they will be 'spirited back to the mean streets of the 19th century East End'.[34] In these guided tours, trail and narrative are brought together: transported back to the historical period, the users 'watch' the events unfold as they make their way through the area.

Cardiff's walks are different, both in terms of the narrative and of the relationship to the past. The plot line of *The missing voice* is purposefully confusing, with answers to who is following whom and what mystery is being solved always out of reach; even the different characters in the recording cannot be clearly separated and the listener becomes lost almost immediately. Instead of a coher-

---

29   Blum provides a detailed discussion of the emphasis placed by tour guides on authoritative and truthful narratives ('Murder, Myth, and Melodrama', pp. 246–48).

30   Discovery Tours & Events, *Jack the Ripper Tour*, track 1.

31   'Guided by published authors', www.jack-the-ripper-tour.com

32   Blum, 'Murder, Myth, and Melodrama', p. 251-253; 'You'll peruse Victorian photographs', www.jack-the-ripper-tour.com; www.guidigo.com//Tour/London/United%20Kingdom/The-bloody-steps-of-Jack-the-Ripper/LmvHuGxYQnY. During the Secret Chambers Tour, historical photographs are projected directly onto walls during the walk, a method they promote as *Ripper-Vision* (rippervision.com/ripper-vision).

33   iAudioguide and BlueBrolly, *Jack the Ripper London audio guide*, track 2.

34   'Step into the autumn of terror', www.jack-the-ripper-tour.com

8. Tracing Memories

ent narrative, we are presented with fragments that work to communicate not facts but emotions. The artist tells us how she sometimes follows men, late at night when walking home, to feel protected. And there are references to people, including the artist (and thus the participant), being watched, followed and disappearing. Without ever referring to the violent history of the neighbourhood, the collection of incoherent fragments makes us aware of the danger of dark alleys, of being alone at night in the city, of encountering strangers. In the context of Whitechapel's history, it is easy to draw a connection to the fear felt by prostitutes wandering these streets at the time of the murders.

Secondly, the walks differ from standard audio guides in their relationship to the past. Instead of transporting the listener back to an earlier period, the echoes of these past events are brought to the present and are made relevant for the participant's current reality. After finishing the *The missing voice*, the participant is left with an acute awareness of her own presence in an area which held such danger. This refusal to transport the user back through time and present a narrative that is firmly in and of the past is also experienced in the *Alter Bahnhof video walk*. No linear narrative is provided and the recording consists of ambient noises from the train station, staged sounds accompanying things happening on screen and the voice-over of the artist, who recounts disjointed fragments of memories (hers and others'), dreams and philosophical questions concerning the phenomenon of memory. In this work, the oblique references to the Holocaust and the absence of a comprehensible narrative bring to mind our current understanding of trauma: while historical facts can help us gain a sense of control over an event, the experience of trauma is often described as the very inability to create such a narrative.[35] The video walk evokes this feeling through strange, incongruous images, which seem to take place in front of our very eyes. At some point an image appears of an underground tunnel, where a woman passes us, ominously counting in German. Later, this same woman is seen lying on the floor of the station, apparently having suffered a medical emergency. The nightmarish imagery is unsettling and brings the sense of traumatic memory, in need of processing, into the present-day train station. As in Whitechapel, both the video and the audio refuse to transport us back to a clear moment in history and, instead, allow us to feel the lingering effects of that history on our own reality.

This notable divergence from traditional audio guide practice is made explicit by elements in the works themselves; halfway into *The missing voice* we hear a tour guide in the background tell her listeners about the history of the area's

---

35   Erll, *Memory in Culture*, p. 87.

Jewish population. And in the *Alter Bahnhof video walk* the participant passes an old man recounting stories of the war and showing photos to a woman. In both cases these figures are noted by the participant as they relate what seem to be clear, coherent histories of the sites, so obviously missing from the artist's account. However, their stories remain just out of reach and the participant is pulled away and back into the present and onto the confusing trail set out by the artist.

What makes the artistic strategy particularly effective is the nature of the sites. Each can be understood as a location of dark tourism and, as such, emotion plays an essential role and memory comes to eclipse history.[36] The Whitechapel area represents a 'lighter' form, aimed mostly at entertainment and the enjoyment of sublime horror.[37] The station in Kassel, on the other hand, refers to one of the darkest forms, albeit through metonymy (the train station points indirectly to the camps it was connected to). Both sites are haunted by memories. In Kassel's train station, the artist tells us: 'Germany's like that for me, full of ghosts and history'. The artworks' refusal to control the sites through clarifying narratives magnifies this haunted atmosphere. It is further enhanced by the confusing design of the walks, discussed in the next section.

Anchored history versus unhinged memory

Much has been written about the ability of sound(scapes) to confuse our understanding, making a trail or site appear haunted and uncanny.[38] Gallagher describes it best when he writes:

> In a context where representations of space often involve images with strong truth claims attached – maps, photographs, architectural drawings, landscape paintings and so on – environmental audio recordings are prone to being more elusive in their meanings: unverifiable, referentially unstable, hinting at things which are never quite fully revealed

---

36   The relatively new phenomenon of dark tourism has been discussed and defined by various authors (for an overview, see Hartmann, 'Dark Tourism, Thanatourism, and Dissonance'; Sharpley and Stone, *The Darker Side of Travel*, pp. 9–12). The book *Dark Tourism* by Lennon and Foley has become fundamental in these discussions. Their definition of the concept concerns sites which are marked by: 1) the role of global communication (newspapers, TV etc.) in creating an initial interest in the history of the site; 2) a sense of anxiety and doubt about the project of modernity that the site induces; and 3) an educative element of the site that invites visitators (p. 11). Both case studies correspond to all three aspects of this definition of dark tourism.

37   A discussion of the spectrum of dark tourism, from dark to light, can be found in Sharpley and Stone, *The Darker Side of Travel*, pp. 20–22.

38   Marshall, 'Audio-based Narratives for the Trenches of World War I', pp. 29–30; Cox, 'Sound Art and the Sonic Unconscious'; Gallagher, 'Sounding Ruins'; Foreman, 'Uncanny Soundscapes', pp. 266–68.

8. Tracing Memories

... Environmental recordings are also ideal for amplifying the haunted qualities of sites, since by displacing the sounds of spaces they estrange, dislocate, render uncanny.[39]

The spectres that haunt our two sites are memories from past events. Since cultural memory is itself unstable and constantly in flux, it is fittingly represented through the unstable medium of Cardiff's walks, in which every repetition is different. The artworks reflect the shape-shifting nature of memory. While the traditional audio guide is an anchoring text in Barthes' sense of the word, intended on fixing the meaning of the object, Cardiff's walks do the opposite: they unhinge and upend.[40] Three distinct aspects of the walks contribute to this effect and will be addressed below: the complex soundscape around the artist's voice; the mismatch between the described reality and the participant's observed reality; and the purposeful deception that is introduced, in the video walk in particular.

Although the focus in the audio tracks is on the artist's voice, the complex network of surrounding audio fragments is experienced as a soundscape through which the participant travels. This experience is made more striking, as well as confusing, by the binaural recording technique, which makes it hard to distinguish between past sounds in the recording and present sounds on the walk itself. Both the artist's voice and the soundscape are continuous, following the continuous movement of the participant. Most audio guides create a series of small arcs of attention – taking you from one point of interest to the next. In Cardiff's walks, however, a constant level of attention is maintained throughout the walk and, as a result, the listener is kept aware of both her surroundings and her movement through them as she follows the artist's footsteps. No distinction is made between fore- and background, i.e. relevant versus irrelevant, in either the walk, the surroundings or the sounds. All streets, buildings and people become potentially significant and pervaded with memory and meaning, resulting in an estranging intensity.[41] As Pinder writes, the effect is 'to make you acutely aware of rhythm, pace, breath: of the practice of walking. It

---

39 Gallagher, 'Sounding Ruins', pp. 479–80.
40 Christensen, 'Four Steps in the History of Museum Technologies', pp. 17–20; Sohal ('Momentous Movement', pp. 55–57) discusses this estrangement in more detail, describing it as a result of a disturbance in the indexical relationship between the soundscape and the perceived reality of the participant; in other words, the sounds of the recording do not match up with the reality of the walking participant, which causes confusion.
41 Gorman ('Wandering and Wondering', p. 86) elaborates on the way in which the mundane everyday surroundings come to be seen through the eyes of the attentive tourist, using John Urry's theory of the 'tourist gaze' (*The Tourist Gaze*).

emphasizes the sensuousness of walking as a mode of apprehending the city.'[42]

Apart from estranging, the walks also disorient. Following a trail means navigating, finding the way, not getting lost. To this end, most guided tours (in books and audio guides) provide clear maps, photos and instructions – images with strong truth claims, in Gallagher's words. Cardiff's walks complicate the act of navigating by their unusually 'fuzzy' instructions: in *The missing voice* we try to align our footsteps with the sound of the artists' and look for informal landmarks like the convenience store with the Coca-Cola sign or the orange restaurant. In the constantly evolving city, however, these markers are unstable and several have changed beyond recognition.[43] Even the starting point has altered dramatically and the Whitechapel gallery has had to install a little bookshelf to mimic the presence of the old library, in order for participants to find their way. Besides landmarks, the artist is constantly describing people, parades and cars, most of which will have disappeared even a minute after the artist's passing them. In the video walk in Kassel, getting lost is less likely, due to the matching up of video and surroundings. But here, the addition of visual information makes the differences between the artist's reality and that of the participant all the more apparent. Far from being frustrating, these effects are intriguing and add to the mystery of the walks and the sensation of being surrounded by memories. It emphasises the perpetual and confusing evolution of the city and its layered identity, an observation made explicit by the artist: 'I wonder if the workers ever think about themselves as the changers of the city, the men that cover up the old stories, making room for new ones.'

Finally, the walk through Kassel's train station also contains moments of purposeful deception, playful inconsistencies that shatter the illusion that the participant is following a straightforward and consistent representation of an earlier reality. When standing at a railing, overlooking the platform, on which a woman can be seen walking away, the artist says: 'That's me in the white coat down there. I remember lying in the hotel room that night, alone, watching a German black-and-white movie.' Later, when we are looking out over the main hall, she points to a boy with headphones who is supposedly doing the video walk. These and other instances make the viewer aware of the constructed and contradictory nature of the video – how can the artist be seen on a platform, when she is supposedly recording the video, and how can the boy be performing

---

42   Pinder, 'Ghostly Footsteps', p. 5. Other personal descriptions of the effects on the participant's senses are found in Gorman, 'Wandering and Wondering', pp. 84 and 87; Petralia, 'Headspace: Architectural Space in the Brain', p. 107; Tubridy, 'Sounding Spaces', p. 6.

43   De Certeau discusses this relationship between walking and the memory of the city in his influential essay 'Walking in the City' (*The Practice of Everyday Life*, pp. 105–08).

8. Tracing Memories

the walk if he appears in the recording of that very walk? These incongruities make it impossible to truthfully reconstruct the artist's reality. We can never align our image, our experience, with hers. Every performance of the walk is an individual and unique one, following a fixed script but never able exactly to reconstruct previous performances. In this respect, the works mimic the nature of cultural memory: although the events form an unchanging script, the memory of the events is constantly reshaped by individuals relating them to their present realities. Over and over again, the same events become relevant to new people and the memory is shaped by these many iterations.

In the *Alter Bahnhof video walk*, the process of constructing memory is explicitly discussed by the artist on several occasions. As much as memories shape and define our identities, they also haunt us; the artist addresses this duality while leading us through the station:

> Memories are like a different form of travel. It's like filling a suitcase that we pull behind us and we open and close when we need to … What do other people do with memories they don't want? Do they just close the suitcase? Sometimes I imagine rolling bad memories into a ball, like a snowball, and throwing them away. It's only in the middle of the night they come back.

Performative memory

The process by which individuals perpetually (re)construct cultural memory is described by Astrid Erll and Ann Rigney

> as an active engagement with the past, as performative rather than reproductive. It is as much a matter of acting out a relationship to the past from a particular point in the present as it is a matter of preserving and retrieving earlier stories.[44]

As I have argued in more detail elsewhere, the active participation required in Cardiff's walks illustrates this construction of performative memory.[45] The memories attached to these sites are 'acted out' by the participants on both a personal, individual level and on a broader, public level.

Each performance of the walks is a personal and unique event. The many reviews and analyses of the walks attest to the transformative and intimate nature of this experience.[46] While following the trail, the participant has the sensation of being in multiple layers of time at once – the present moment

---

44 Erll and Rigney, *Mediation, Remediation, and the Dynamics of Cultural Memory*, p. 2.
45 Bertens, 'Doing Memory'.
46 Pinder, 'Ghostly Footsteps', p. 5. Other personal descriptions of the effects on the participant's senses are found in Gorman, 'Wandering and Wondering', pp. 84 and 87; Petralia, 'Headspace: Architectural Space in the Brain', p. 107; Tubridy, 'Sounding Spaces', p. 6.

of the performance, the moment of the artist's recording and the layers of older events – some fictional, some factual – to which the walks allude. The complex identity of the site is made explicit as its many ghosts and echoes of memory become almost palpable. The individual memory of walking through Whitechapel or Kassel's train station becomes contextualised in a wider network of cultural memory.

Apart from the personal experience of the individual performing the walk, the artworks also increase public awareness of the cultural memory of these locations. In both cases, few direct references to the events remain. Until 1988, Whitechapel boasted a pub called *The Jack the Ripper*, filled with Ripper memorabilia; it was one of the few tangible references to the events. Notably, it was pressured into changing its name, after a campaign against sensationalising the murders – a demonstration of the power still exerted by the memory of the events.[47] And in the Kassel train station only the Horst Hoheisel monument reminds travellers of the Jewish deportees from this town.

It is therefore mostly through intangible acts of remembrance that the memories are kept alive. Walking through Whitechapel at night, one is certain to come across guided tours about the Ripper murders and thus to be reminded of the area's history.[48] As in the case of right-of-way paths, discussed by Hickman and O'Hara in this volume, the act of walking is itself performative, adding to the identity and reality of the surroundings and keeping cultural memories alive.[49] Cardiff's walks function in similar ways. On each occasion that I have performed the video walk in Kassel, I have been approached by passers-by, wondering what these people with headphones and iPods were doing. The effect of the walks extends beyond the experience of individual participants. In both cases Cardiff's artworks add to the act of constructing and of maintaining cultural memory.

---

47 Begg, *Jack the Ripper*, p. 22; Hanlon, 'On the Ripper's Bloody Trail'. The reputation of the pub was based on the claim that it had been frequented by two of the murder victims.

48 A discussion of the active role of tourism in shaping the myth of Jack the Ripper and his importance to Whitechapel can be found in Blum, 'Murder, Myth, and Melodrama', pp. 240–46.

49 De Certeau's understanding of walking as an enunciative act is helpful in this respect: 'Walking affirms, suspects, tries out, transgresses, respects, etc., the trajectories it "speaks".' (*The Practice of Everyday Life*, p. 99). A discussion of this power of walking, taking De Certeau's thoughts as a starting point, can be found in Morris ('What We Talk About When We Talk about "Walking in the City"'). Sohal ('Momentous Movement', p. 69–72) considers the relevance of De Certeau's thoughts in direct relation to the audio walks by Cardiff, *The missing voice* in particular.

8. Tracing Memories

Conclusion

As a performative process, cultural memory is under perpetual construction and in need of constant and active attention. Individual actions help keep shared memories alive and these memories, in turn, alter the identities of the spaces that we pass through. While grounded in historical events, the memories take on constantly changing shapes and significances of their own, responding to the needs and desires of people in the present.

The complex process of cultural remembrance has been explored by artists through various methods. The audio and video walks by Janet Cardiff do so in the form of guided walks, emphasising the relationship between the act of following trails and the cultural memories attached to environments. This embodies what Caitlin DeSilvey has called 'kinetic memory', referring to the idea that memory is experienced and constructed through movement: 'kinesis, rather than stasis, creates the condition of possibility for the performance of memory'.[50]

The two artworks discussed in this chapter have illustrated the strength of this strategy; the experience of estrangement and confusion, as well as the active audience participation allow individual participants to explore the memories attached to the two trails as well as the phenomenon of remembrance itself. And in addition to their individual significances, the multiple performances of the trail, in turn, help perpetuate and shape site-specific cultural memory. The artist's seemingly arbitrary trails become explicit 'artefacts of movement', to borrow a phrase from this volume's introduction. By walking these trails, we carve paths through the built environment in which memory can live on.

Bibliography

Artangel, *The Missing Voice* (1999), www.artangel.org.uk/project/the-missing-voice-case-study-b (accessed 29 November 2021).

Auster, P., *The New York Trilogy* (London: Faber & Faber, 1987).

Begg, P., *Jack the Ripper* (London and New York: Routledge, 2005).

Bertens, L.M.F., 'Doing Memory: Performativity and Cultural Memory in Janet Cardiff and George Bures Miller's *Alter Bahnhof Video Walk*', *Holocaust Studies* **26** (2) (2020): 181–97.

Blum, J.A., 'Murder, Myth, and Melodrama: the Theatrical Histories of Jack the Ripper'. Ph.D. Thesis, University of Toronto, 2015.

Boxer, S., 'An Artist Who Travels with You (on Tape, That Is)'. *The New York Times*, 8 August 2000, https://www.nytimes.com/2000/08/08/arts/arts-abroad-an-artist-who-travels-with-you-on-tape-that-is.html (accessed 29 November 2021).

---

50   DeSilvey ('Memory in Motion', p. 493).

Butler, T. and G. Miller, 'Linked: A Landmark in Sound, a Public Walk of Art', *Cultural Geographies* **12** (1) (2005): 77–88.

Butler, T., 'Memoryscape: How Audio Walks can Deepen Our Sense of Place by Integrating Art, Oral History and Cultural Geography', *Geography Compass* **1** (3) (2007): 360–72.

Cardiff, J. and G. Bures Miller, *Something Strange this Way* (Ostfildern: Hatje Cantz, 2014).

Cox, C., 'Sound Art and the Sonic Unconscious', *Organised Sound: An International Journal of Music Technology* **14** (1) (2009): 19–26.

Christensen, J.R., 'Four Steps in the History of Museum Technologies and Visitors' Digital Participation', *MedieKultur* **50** (2011): 7–29.

De Certeau, M., *The Practice of Everyday Life* (Berkeley, CA: University of California Press, 1984).

DeSilvey, C., 'Memory in Motion: Soundings from Milltown, Montana', *Social & Cultural Geography* **11** (5) (2010): 491–510.

Dickinson, J.E., K. Ghali, T. Cherrett et al., 2014. 'Tourism and the Smartphone App: Capabilities, Emerging Practice and Scope in the Travel Domain', *Current Issues in Tourism* **17** (1) (2014): 84–101.

Discovery Tours and Events, *Jack the Ripper Tour* (London: Discovery Tours & Events, 2015), www.jack-the-ripper-tour.com (accessed 29 November 2021).

Erll, A. and A. Rigney, *Mediation, Remediation, and the Dynamics of Cultural Memory* (Berlin and Boston: De Gruyter, 2009).

Erll, A., *Memory in Culture* (London: Palgrave Macmillan, 2011).

Fagence, M., 'A Heritage 'Trailscape': Tracking the Exploits of Historical Figures –an Australian Case Study', *Journal of Heritage Tourism* **12** (5) (2017): 452–62.

Fischer, J., 'Speeches of Display: the Museum Audioguides of Sophie Calle, Andrea Fraser and Janet Cardiff', *Parachute: Contemporary Art Magazine* 94 (April–June 1999): 24–31.

Foreman, I., 'Uncanny Soundscapes: Towards an Inoperative Acoustic Community', *Organised Sound: An International Journal of Music Technology* **16** (3) (2011): 264–71.

Gallagher, M., 'Sounding Ruins', *Cultural Geographies* **22** (3) (2015): 467–85.

Gorman, S., 'Wandering and Wondering: Following Janet Cardiff's Missing Voice', *Performance Research* **8** (1) (2003): 83–92.

Guidigo, *The Bloody Steps of Jack the Ripper* (2021), www.guidigo.com/Web/The-bloody-steps-of-Jack-the-Ripper/LMvHuGxYQnY/Stop/1/St.Jame-s-Passage (accessed 29 November 2021).

Hanlon, M., 'On the Ripper's Bloody Trail: The 100th Year since Jack's Murderous Spree Means Big Business for London Tourism', *Toronto Star*, 9 May 1988.

Hartmann, R., 'Dark Tourism, Thanatourism, and Dissonance in Heritage Tourism Management: New Directions in Contemporary Tourism Research', *Journal of Heritage Tourism* **9** (2) (2014): 166–82.

iAudioguide and BlueBrolly, *Jack the Ripper London Audio Guide* (2018), iaudioguide.com/jack-ripper-london-audio-guide/ (accessed 29 November 2021).

Klee, W., *Hauptbahnhof Kassel: Bilder einer Station in der Mitte Deutschlands* (Paderborn: Bonifatius Druck, 2012).

LaBelle, B., *Background Noise: Perspectives on Sound Art*, second edition (London: Bloomsbury Academic, 2015).

8. Tracing Memories

Lee, S.J., 'A Review of Audio Guides in the Era of Smart Tourism', *Information Systems Frontiers* **19** (4) (2017): 705–15.

Lennon, J. and M. Foley, *Dark Tourism*, fifth edition (London: Cengage Learning, 2009).

London Walks, *Jack the Ripper Walking Tour* (London: London Walks, 2011), www.walks.com/our-walks/jack-the-ripper-walking-tour (accessed 29 November 2021).

Marshall, M.T., D. Petrelli, N. Dulake et al., 'Audio-based Narratives for the Trenches of World War I: Intertwining Stories, Places and Interaction for an Evocative Experience', *International Journal of Human-computer Studies* 85 (2016): 27–39.

Morris, B., 'What We Talk About When We Talk about "Walking in the City"', *Cultural Studies* **18** (5) (2004): 675–97.

Petralia, P.S., 'Headspace: Architectural Space in the Brain', *Contemporary Theatre Review* **20** (1) (2010): 96–108.

Pinder, D., 'Ghostly Footsteps: Voices, Memories and Walks in the City', *Ecumene* **8** (1) (2001): 1–19.

Pink, S., P. Hubbard, M. O'Neill et al., 'Walking Across Disciplines: From Ethnography to Arts Practice', *Visual Studies* **25** (1) (2010): 1–7.

Preece, R.J., 'Janet Cardiff at Whitechapel Library, London (1999)', *Artdesigncafé*, 15 September 2009, www.artdesigncafe.com/janet-cardiff-artist-1999 (accessed 29 November 2021).

Revill, G., 'El tren fantasma: Arcs of Sound and the Acoustic Spaces of Landscape', *Transactions – Institute of British Geographers* **39** (3) (2014): 333–44.

Secret Chamber Tours, *Ripper Vision* (2016), www.rippervision.com (accessed November 2021).

Sharpley, R. and P.R. Stone, *The Darker Side of Travel (Aspects of Tourism)* (Bristol: NBN International, 2009).

Sohal, R., 'Momentous Movement: Janet Cardiff's Audio Walk', Ph.D. Thesis, McGill University, 2007.

Stier, O.B., *Committed to Memory: Cultural Mediations of the Holocaust* (Amherst and Boston: University of Massachusetts Press, 2003).

Till, K.E., 'Artistic and Activist Memory-work: Approaching Place-based Practice', *Memory Studies* **1** (1) (2008): 99–113.

Tubridy, D., 'Sounding Spaces. Aurality in Samuel Beckett, Janet Cardiff and Bruce Nauman'. *Performance Research* **12** (1) (2007): 5–11.

Urry, J., *The Tourist Gaze: Leisure and Travel in Contemporary Societies* (London: Sage, 1990).

Walkowitz, J., *City of Dreadful Delight: Narratives of Sexual Danger in Late-Victorian London* (London: Virago Press, 1992).

Whyte, M., '"Lost in the Memory Palace": Janet Cardiff and George Bures Miller. April 6 to August 18, 2013'. *Galleries West*, 8 July 2013, www.gallerieswest.ca/magazine/stories/lost-in-the-memory-palace-janet-cardiff-and-george-bures-miller-april-6-to-august-18-2013/ (accessed 29 November 2021).

CHAPTER 9.

WALKING AND WORLDING: TRAILS AS STORYLINES IN VIDEO GAMES

Finn Arne Jørgensen

Video games have grown into a major industry, ranging across a variety of genres that appeal to many kinds of users. No longer a niche phenomenon, video games are part of mainstream popular culture. During the COVID lockdowns of 2020 and 2021, more people than ever turned to video games for entertainment and social interactions.[1] Confined to their homes by lockdowns and restrictions, many embraced video game worlds as complements to, not replacements for, the world outside their homes. Games are not only a way to pass the time, but also a truly meaningful activity to many.[2]

It is not uncommon for video games to feature expansive, nuanced, and lively three-dimensional worlds that serve as venues for storytelling, exploration, social interactions and shared memories. Players traverse and navigate video game landscapes, observe virtual scenes and vistas and come to attach meaning to places in the game worlds. Players interact with video game worlds through controllers, often represented by an avatar in the game world.[3] As players move through game worlds, they also proceed through the plot of the game. Avatar movement is key to the act of getting to know video game worlds; it is not only a mechanism for transporting the player from place to place, but also a way of gradually introducing players to stories, characters and places.

This chapter is concerned with the place of trails, movement and heritage in a popular – and growing – genre of games called 'walking simulators'. Such environmental narrative games tend to focus on movement through and immersive interaction with landscape, rather than gameplay mechanics centred on competition, puzzles, urgency and structured branching or linear narratives. The chapter considers walking as a narrative practice, in video games and beyond, as evidenced by the vast amount of nature writing that uses walking as a method for reflection.[4]

---

1   Bengtsson, Bom and Fynbo, 'Playing Apart Together'.
2   Shi, et al., 'Understanding the Lives of Problem Gamers'.
3   Wolf, 'World Design', 71.
4   E.g. Macfarlane, *The Old Ways*.

9. Walking and Worlding

In essence, walking simulator games create a world based on walking, and they use the act and mindset of walking as a way of facilitating the experience of this world. 'Paths and trails exist because there is walking', write the editors to this book in their introduction. While that is true, walking on paths and trails also stages the landscape through which they pass in particular ways, drawing the attention of the walker to particular features. Paths and trails bring into being relationships between the ones who walk, and the landscapes being walked through and upon. This chapter asks whether the mechanisms through which such world-making relationships develop are similar in video game worlds and 'the real world'.

The chapter develops an argument that games and virtual worlds can involve some form of movement heritage too. Building on Rodney Harrison's argument that heritage isn't something that *is*, but something that *does*, and which is thus dependent on continuous use or memory work to remain, the chapter argues that walking simulators can hold some lessons for the study of movement heritage, in particular when it comes to the relationship between walking and worldmaking.[5] If physical walking relationships can become heritage, as is the central argument in this volume, could the same be true for walking in virtual worlds? Walking simulator games direct our attention to particular gameplay mechanics, where paths and trails are used by designers to signal to a player the continuation of a story. Heritage is always articulated, represented, mediated and experienced in negotiations between different actors. Trails give the player direction and structure in an otherwise unstructured landscape. As such, these trails are traversed by players – in some games millions of them – who have shared experiences of these landscapes. Anthropologist Tim Ingold highlights the close connection between storytelling and movement, arguing that a story is a journey between locations and subjects.[6] Walking trails create storylines in digital game landscapes. This insight can apply to scholarship on trails and heritage: trails provide a common shared space for narratives about the landscape the trail passes through.

In this chapter, we will go on hikes through three games, framed by an introduction to 3D game worlds and a concluding discussion of heritage, walking and worlding in video games. The chapter discusses the interpretation and representation of movement heritage, but also the experience, and even enacting of, movement heritage in and through media.

---

5   Harrison, *Heritage*.
6   Ingold, *Lines*, p. 90.

Finn Arne Jørgensen

A brief history of virtual worlds

Most of us have, at some point in time, encountered some form of video game world, as a player or as a spectator. Many classic video games take place along two axes, X and Y. In such two-dimensional games, players can go left or right, up or down. Basic two-dimensional games generally do not require massive computational resources to run. Early 3D games, which introduced a Z axis as well, were severely limited by computer processing capabilities, so they were designed to be simple and empty, with as few objects as possible, so that they could run on low-powered computers. For example, *Battlezone* (1980), which is generally acknowledged as the first 3D game, uses simple wireframe vector graphics (Figure 1) to evoke a three-dimensional world. In *Battlezone*, players drive a tank around a simple, flat landscape, with mountains in the background, a moon in the sky, and various solid geometrical objects on the ground that players can hide behind while battling other tanks. 3D graphics of this type opened the way for an entirely different feeling of space to be navigated by players.

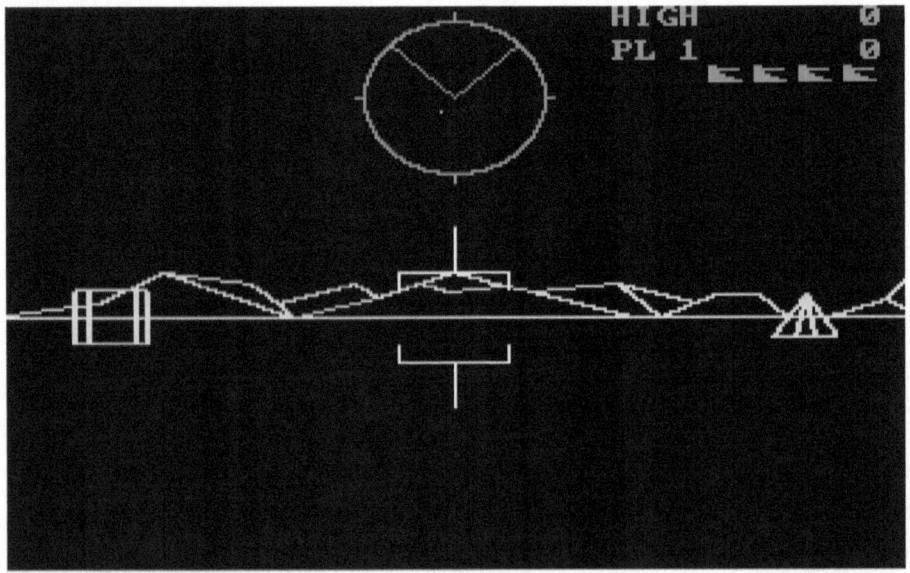

Figure 1.

Screenshot from *Battlezone* (Atari, Inc., 1980), captured by Finn Arne Jørgensen.

9. Walking and Worlding

As games moved from 2D to 3D, they allowed for freer navigation and exploration by players. The spaces of video games worlds changed, making movement in video games more similar to the way we orient ourselves in the physical world. As digital media scholar Michael Nitsche argues, while video game worlds are processed in particular ways, depending on algorithms and mathematical rules, the players' experience of video game spaces cannot be explained solely by the technology creating these spaces.[7] There are emergent qualities to the experience of players. Nitsche highlights how video games are often spatial, presenting the player with spatial environments to be interacted with through navigation, exploration, movement and manipulation. In games, '[s]pace is understood best through movement, and complex spaces require not only movement but navigation', argues media studies scholar Mark Wolf.[8]

With increasing computing capabilities over time, the 3D engines that power these game worlds became more and more powerful and sophisticated. Game worlds are now filled with detailed objects that can often be manipulated and not just observed by players. They exist as entities in space, reflecting light and casting shadow. These objects also exist in relation to one another, with physics and collision detection as an integrated part of the game engine. Common game engines like Unity, Unreal Engine or Source Engine games are software frameworks for game development that feature graphics rendering in 2D or 3D, a physics engine, game assets such as objects and sounds, and so on. Using the tools at their disposal, game world designers combine text, images, visuals, sounds and space to create and shape environments. In practice, 3D games are engines, settings, environments, experiences, all in one. The resulting game worlds vary tremendously in detail; some are small and bounded, not reaching much further than the immediate surroundings of the player. Others are vast and open, feeling like living breathing worlds where there is always something more to discover just around the corner. Some approach photorealism in style, whereas others are cartoonish. Some games pay close to attention to the physics of avatars moving through the world, with a field of view that bobs as the player walks, runs or jumps, at speeds that vary depending on the terrain, and player endurance that requires rest and recovery at regular intervals. In other games, the avatar feels strangely disconnected from the game world, with movement patterns that don't feel right, either floating effortlessly over the ground or feeling heavy and sluggish.

Within the broad category of 3D game worlds, many different genres exist

---

7   Nitsche, *Viteo Game Spaces*, 8.
8   Wolf, 'Theorizing Navigable Space in Video Games'.

and each features different mechanisms and purposes of movement within the game. This chapter will particularly focus on the 'walking simulator' genre. The term 'walking simulator' was initially a derogatory term, indicating that such games were not 'proper' games and that simply walking was not a sufficient gameplay mechanism, but game makers quickly embraced the term and made it their own.[9] The online game store Steam currently has more than 1,100 games categorised as Walking Simulators.[10] Notable popular games on this list are *Gone Home*, *Death Stranding*, *Firewatch*, *Everybody's Gone to the Rapture*, *Dear Esther* and *What Remains of Edith Finch*. There is a huge variety within this selection, but most games emphasise immersion and the experience of a place as major parts of the gameplay. Game studies scholar Alenda Chang, in her study in environmental games, characterises walking simulators by highlighting 'their slowness, their lack of action, the absence of people, their spatial storytelling'.[11]

In some games, your role as player is to make the narrative unfold and follow it to the end. For example, games like *Dear Esther*, *Gone Home*, and *What Remains of Edith Finch* build on exploration of limited spaces and scripted events, allowing players to take part in a story by exploring an environment. Media studies scholar Ian Bogost, in critique of walking simulators, notes that environmental storytelling in games 'invite[s] players to discover and reconstruct a fixed story from the environment itself'.[12] Despite the interactivity of these games, they are in essence linear experiences, as there is a set story to follow – to enact – and a strictly bounded space in which to experience them. In other games, such as *Red Dead Redemption 2*, you create the narrative, moving freely in open worlds between scripted or algorithmically-generated encounters with landscapes and stories. Some qualities and features of these worlds are emergent, whereas others are predetermined by the creator of the game.

Within these walking simulator games, the act of walking along a trail or path often plays a central role, though there is variation in how these relate to heritage. In the following sections, we will take three hikes on the paths and trails of different games, in order to discuss some of the forms of digital movement heritage in walking simulators.

---

9   Zimmermann and Huberts, 'From Walking Simulator to Ambience Action Game'.
10   Steam web store, 'Browsing Walking Simulator': https://store.steampowered.com/tags/en/Walking%20Simulator/ (accessed 12 April 2021).
11   Chang, *Playing Nature*, p. 43.
12   Bogost, 'Video Games Are Better Without Stories'.

9. Walking and Worlding

Hike 1: *Dear Esther* (no landscape is a blank slate)

Dear Esther – originally from 2008, released commercially in 2012 – is often labelled as the first walking simulator. In the game, the player walks repeatedly along a path on an island (Figure 2), listening to audio fragments from people who lived on the island. With each playthrough – or walk across the island – new fragments appear and add up to a more detailed story that explains why the player is on this mysterious island. But there is no ultimate goal or end beyond the gradual immersion in a story, something which characterises walking simulators. There are no opponents, no fights, no challenges to overcome. Yet, *Dear Esther* differs from later walking simulators in that there is less room for individual explorations. The game takes place along the path, in a linear fashion, with very little interaction with the game world itself. Even

Figure 2.

Screenshot from *Dear Esther* (The Chinese Room, 2012), captured by Finn Arne Jørgensen.

the player avatar feels strangely disconnected from the game world, hovering at eye-height from the ground, but never bobbing around or being jostled when moving through the landscape.

Walking in *Dear Esther* is an exploration of heritage. The audio clues from the past that appear through the act of walking reveal the path as a keeper of the past. In walking, the player discovers the existence of other stories, but never fully, only in fragments.[13] There is no complete and orderly storyline in the game but, by walking the path, the player figures out the story piece by piece. As observed by Rebecca Solnit, trails and paths cannot be experienced as a whole at the same time by a traveller, and so it is also in this game.[14] While players of *Dear Esther* are limited to the path and can't break out to explore other parts of the island, they are still reminded that walking is a cultural act, of experiencing, but also of reinforcing, the traces of those who have gone there before.

Walking the trail in *Dear Esther*, we are reminded that no landscape is a blank slate. If we glance over to some of the tropes of traditional travel writing, one can get the impression that the explorers of the nineteenth and early twentieth centuries, upon 'discovering' scenic mountain regions for the first time, considered them blank slates.[15] But we know that these landscapes were not undiscovered; the travellers used local guides who knew the mountains, and they often walked along paths made by people and animals, and so on. Trails remind us of those who have gone before us; they are incomplete traces of a past that we can't fully know.

Hike 2: *Firewatch* (modeling on real-world environments)

Firewatch is a 2016 game that puts the player in the position of a fire lookout named Henry in the Shoshone National Forest in Wyoming, one of the oldest national parks in the US. As such, the game world is modelled on a real place (though not actually replicating it). The game is also situated in time, taking place in 1989, a year after the largest fire in the history of the Yellowstone National park. Like in many other walking simulators, the game lets the player gradually uncover a story through snippets. The story features mystery and even some drama that is put into motion by the player's character, Henry, leaving a fire lookout to navigate the outdoors, using trails, maps, and a compass, as shown in Figure 3. In doing so, Henry discovers other sites and other people in the forest, and these discoveries propel the story along.

---

13   Şengün, 'Ludic Voyeurism and Passive Spectatorship'.
14   Solnit, *Wanderlust*.
15   Dolan, *Exploring European Frontiers*; Fjågesund and Symes, *The Northern Utopia*.

9. Walking and Worlding

Figure 3.

Screenshot from *Firewatch* (Campo Santo and Panic, 2016), captured by Finn Arne Jørgensen.

Firewatch puts great emphasis on the act of walking and navigating the outdoors, writes Alenda Chang.[16] Unlike in *Dear Esther*, players in *Firewatch* can choose to wander freely within the area of the game world, even though the story depends on the player locating particular places in the world to move the story forward. Rather than accurately copying landscape features from 'the real world' to the game, the game designers chose to instead evoke the feeling of the place through extensive place-based research. This feeling of 'place-ness' is central to many compelling game worlds, where visual style, narrative, game engine physics and landscape features come together to create an experience that feels right.

Firewatch shows us how the relationship between game worlds and the physical world is a complicated one. Place and location are never something that can be copied completely into a game – or into any heritage setting – so designers have to choose which characteristics are important to convey. It can be physical features – an iconic peak – or it can be a feeling. We can't say that one feature is better than the other, or more important to translate into a game setting. Maps like the ones featured so prominently in *Firewatch*, serve to mediate the relationship between the player, the physical world and the game world.

Henry uses a map and a compass to navigate the game world, matching up landmarks and environmental clues to features on the map. This game map draws heavily on conventions of real-world maps, serving as a representation of a physical space that highlights some things while leaving out others. The

16 Chang, *Playing Nature*, p. 44.

Firewatch map, which we see in Figure 3, is topographical, using contour lines to represent landforms and terrain, including bodies of water and forests. It shows both natural and man-made features, including roads and trails. Finally, the map is annotated with placenames and a compass rose that aligns the map with the cardinal directions. As the player moves throughout the game and its story, Henry scribbles notes on the map, contributing to further annotation of the landscape.

While maps are common in video games, they are often displayed as a part of the technical interface of the game, rather than as an object in the game that the avatar must handle, as is the case in *Firewatch*. Most video game maps also show the location of the player on the map, making navigation relatively easy. This is a convention most of us also know from using modern GPS units, where the user is always located at the centre of the map, while the rest of the world revolves around them. However, in *Firewatch*, players can choose in the settings whether to have their location displayed on the map or to only navigate in a more realistic way by using a compass and reading the landscape. In doing so, the game gives the player the option to engage with the game world in a different way.

Firewatch evokes heritage by allowing players to explore a game world that builds on real-world environments and real-world navigation conventions. As in *Dear Esther*, the story is revealed and experienced as the player moves through the game world, pieced together from small and incomplete components. The game directly addresses the ways in which the player makes sense of a landscape through annotating the map with notes about their experiences. The map becomes a form of heritage, a recollection of the journey the player has taken and the paths they followed.

Hike 3: *Red Dead Redemption 2* (immersion in vibrant worlds)

Even in games that feature more traditional gameplay mechanics, users can sometimes choose to disregard these aspects of gameplay and instead explore the world through walking and a gameplay approach that borrows heavily from walking simulators. In the high-profile action-adventure game *Red Dead Redemption 2* (2019), set in a fictionalised representation of the US southwest in 1889, the player is Arthur Morgan, an outlaw member of the van der Linde gang. While the game has a compelling, action-oriented and often violent plot, many players instead spend a considerable amount of time exploring the carefully crafted game world, through activities like birdwatching, animal spotting and walking or riding along trails. Through such activities, players develop a

9. Walking and Worlding

Figure 4.

Screenshot from *Red Dead Redemption 2* (Rockstar Games, 2019), captured by Finn Arne Jørgensen.

deep knowledge of and connection to the game world. A recent survey found that playing *Red Dead Redemption 2* increased players' knowledge of animal behaviours and interspecies interactions, as well as improving their ability to identify wildlife.[17] These connections are built through movement and experience of place.

The appeal of diverging from the main plot of the game in large part stems from the stunningly detailed game world of *Red Dead Redemption 2*. Unlike the early 3D games that had to take a minimal approach, this game environment is filled with rich details, where plants, trees, birds, animals, fish, weather and light makes the world feel alive (Figure 4). This makes the game more of an immersive environmental simulator than a walking simulator. The player has some freedom in deciding how far to follow the storyline and how much time to spend exploring the world, either through side quests or just enjoying

---

17   Crowley, Silk and Crowley, 'The Educational Value of Virtual Ecologies in Red Dead Redemption 2'.

landscapes, views and wildlife. This has to some extent been included in the game design. For example, the player keeps a log of all species encountered, and even makes little sketches of plants and animals. To get an animal entered into the log, the player has to study it for a little while. Many animals are wary and/or very mobile, so it is challenging to get close enough. For this, the player has binoculars, which let them study animals (and landscapes) at a distance. They can also sneak up on animals on foot, by crouching or hiding behind landscape features, and also by considering wind direction and scent. The player has to develop a very careful environmental sensibility, being aware of the relationship between their virtual body, the landscapes it moves through and the other virtual entities inhabiting this space.

Calling *Red Dead Redemption 2* a walking simulator is not entirely unproblematic, but it borrows many characteristics from the genre. One commentator notes how one of the quests in the game basically recreates the setup of *Gone Home*, another well-known walking simulator.[18] In this quest, Arthur, the game's protagonist, agrees to visit the seized home of an old man he meets to recover some valuables – his pistol, pocket watch and an old ledger. Upon visiting the house and breaking down the door with an eviction notice, Arthur finds various clues that reveals that the old man was a slave catcher in the south before the Civil War. This exploration of environmental clues to piece together a history is a common trope of the walking simulator genre, unveiling that any place encountered in the game can have hidden histories and a deep heritage. Furthermore, the walking in this game is clearly designed to be slow and deliberate, to stimulate immersion and attention to detail. Players who want more speed can run, but their stamina is limited. Players can also ride horses, which arguably is a major part of the game. Horses come in many different breeds with different characteristics, and over time the player builds a deeper relationship with the horses. But even though horses are faster than walking, their capacity to gallop is also limited by their stamina.

Like many open-world games and walking simulators alike, *Red Dead Redemption 2* requires exploration of the world in order to proceed in the story. The large game world of *Red Read Redemption 2* is navigable through an extensive network of paths and trails, ranging from large and well-used to small and sometimes hardly even noticeable. These paths and trails can be seen on the in-game map, where a fog-of-war mechanism also shows the player which areas have been explored (Figure 5). The existence of unexplored areas on the map is something that encourages players to seek out these areas, as

---

18 King, 'Is Red Dead Redemption 2 A Walking Simulator?'.

9. Walking and Worlding

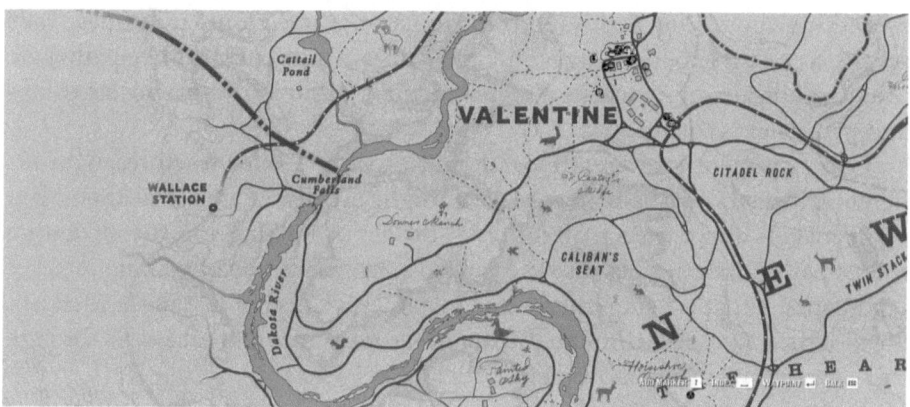

Figure 5.

Game map from *Red Dead Redemption 2* (Rockstar Games, 2019), captured by Finn Arne Jørgensen.

do the trails that lead there. Over time, previously explored landscapes can be accessed through fast travel, in this case by taking the railroad from one of the stations on the map.

The paths, trails, and roads in Red Dead Redemption 2 facilitate discovery and navigation in a very large and lively world that feels storied and inhabited, dense with characters, non-human life, varied landscapes and traces of a past that the player constantly must negotiate as Arthur Morgan. Over time, as the player gets to know the layout of the game world through constant movement and navigation, trails become familiar routes between key locations, taking on additional meaning. Players learn what kind of animals are common in particular areas and they figure out which areas are safe, and which are more risky to be around. Weather effects and regional climate differences also contribute to the lived-in feeling of game world of *Red Dead Redemption 2*.

Movement heritage in video games

We have seen three examples of games where walking, paths and trails play a central part. Video games have spaces that can become places. They can also have heritage, shared understandings of past and place. There is no doubt that trails and footpaths in physical landscapes represent some form of heritage – we have inherited them from longue durée uses of landscape. They represent modification through use. They structure a landscape as well as accommodate movement. They are a form of engagement with space, stretched over time. By making the detour (following the path) through video games, we can learn something about how paths and trails function as media in landscapes. They set the scene for experiencing landscape. Trails in particular (unlike paths) are often specifically designed to direct wanderers' attention to particular things and particular landscapes.

Games present interpretations of landscapes and infrastructures, with inherent expectations about how players might use and understand them. But game makers also pay such attention to the act of walking and the mediating role of paths and trails because they are an established way of making sense of landscapes. What is being interpreted in games is thus not just the landscapes, but also the movement through them, and the relationships that evolve through this movement. This is movement heritage, as I see it.

Rodney Harrison argues that we should consider heritage as 'a series of strategic sociotechnical and/or biopolitical assemblages composed of various people, institutions, apparatuses (*dispositifs*) and the relations between them'.[19] In games like the ones that have been discussed here, heritage exists as something we might call worlding or world-making, an emergent process where 'realities are built, designed and held together by observational and ordering practices'.[20] Geographer Yi-Fu Tuan wrote that 'When space feels thoroughly familiar to us, it has become place.'[21] This also happens in video games. Some game worlds are persistent over time, for example in series of games or in massive multi-player games like *World of Warcraft*, where imagined geographies are explored and shaped over time. As one of the best-known games in the genre, *World of Warcraft* launched in 2004 and is still receiving updates and expansion packs that extend the gameplay and develop the game world.[22] Like many other such games, *World of Warcraft* builds on even older games – the first in the series, *Warcraft: Orcs & Humans*, launched in 1994 – and generates sequels and spinoff games. Over their long lifespan, games like *World of Warcraft* gain a history, and become full of lore. Another famous franchise, the *Elder Scrolls* game series, does something similar, where a series of games developed over decades take place in the same world, gradually gaining more and more depth and identity – a heritage – that returning players continue to immerse themselves in over time, learning more and forming new attachments to the world. The time players invest in such game worlds is considerable, easily moving into hundreds or even thousands of hours.

---

19 Harrison et al., *Heritage Futures*, p. 37.
20 Harrison et al., *Heritage Futures*, p. 251.
21 Tuan, *Space and Place*, p. 73.
22 The last expansion pack, *Shadowlands*, was released in 2020, and received its last major patch in mid-2021.

9. Walking and Worlding

Questions about heritage in games and virtual worlds will only become more relevant as large corporate actors continue to commercialise virtual reality through initiatives like *Second Life* (which saw a big push in the mid-2000s and early 2010s) and the Metaverse (which is Facebook's 2021 big bet on the future). Such virtual worlds will not only require heritage that users can explore but will also become heritage over time, as Rodney Harrison argued in his study of museums, monuments and buildings in *Second Life*.[23] This has major implications not only for the ways in which we think about video games and virtual worlds, but also for how we conceptualise and manage heritage. Game worlds in particular are tied to software and hardware platforms that become obsolete over time, so either the games need to be actively maintained and transitioned to new platforms in order to remain usable or the platforms need to be preserved so that the game can run on them (a point explored in Raiford Guins' excellent study of the afterlives of video games).[24] Like many preserved heritage experiences, video game worlds can also be saved as snapshots, unchanging and frozen in time. Yet, like so much cultural heritage, a significant part of the heritage consists of active communities of people, who use, discuss, develop and change heritage. Perhaps here we can find a final paradox of movement heritage – in order for it to become heritage, it needs to remain in movement, never to be fully captured and frozen in time.

Acknowledgements

This chapter builds upon research from the FORMAS-funded project 'Experiencing Nature in the Digital Age' and the Research Council of Norway project 'Locative Technologies and the Human Sense of Place', #287969.

Bibliography

Bengtsson, Tea T., Louise H. Bom and Lars Fynbo, 'Playing Apart Together: Young People's Online Gaming During the COVID-19 Lockdown', *Young – Nordic Journal of Youth Research* **29** (4) (2021): 65–80.

Bogost, Ian, 'Video Games Are Better Without Stories', *The Atlantic* (2017), https://www.theatlantic.com/technology/archive/2017/04/video-games-stories/524148/

Chang, Alenda, *Playing Nature: Ecology in Video Games* (Minneapolis: University of Minnesota Press, 2019).

Crowley, Edward J., Matthew J. Silk, and Sarah L. Crowley, 'The Educational Value of Virtual Ecologies in Red Dead Redemption 2', *People and Nature* **3** (6) (2021): 1229–43.

---

23   Plunkett, 'On Place Attachments in Virtual Worlds', 174; Harrison, 'Excavating Second Life'.
24   Guins, *Game After*.

Dolan, Brian, *Exploring European Frontiers: British Travellers in the Age of the Enlightenment* (New York: Palgrave MacMillan, 2000).

Fjågesund, Peter and Ruth A. Symes, *The Northern Utopia: British Perceptions in Norway in the Nineteenth Century* (Amsterdam: Rodopi, 2003).

Guins, Raiford, *Game After: A Cultural Study of Video Game Afterlife* (Cambridge, MA: The MIT Press, 2014).

Harrison, Rodney, 'Excavating Second Life: Cyber-Archaeologies, Heritage and Virtual Communities', *Journal of Material Culture* **14** (1) (2009): 75–106.

Harrison, Rodney, *Heritage: Critical Approaches* (London: Routledge, 2013).

Harrison, Rodney et al., *Heritage Futures: Comparative Approaches to Natural and Cultural Heritage Practices* (London: UCL Press, 2020).

Ingold, Tim, *Lines: A Brief History* (London: Routledge, 2007).

King, Andrew, 'Is Red Dead Redemption 2 A Walking Simulator?', *PlayStation Lifestyle* (2018), https://www.playstationlifestyle.net/2018/11/14/red-dead-redemption-2-walking-simulator/

Macfarlane, Robert, *The Old Ways: A Journey on Foot* (London: Penguin Books, 2013).

Nitsche, Michael, *Video Game Spaces: Image, Play, and Structure in 3D Worlds* (Cambridge, MA: The MIT Press, 2008).

Plunkett, Daniel, 'On Place Attachments in Virtual Worlds', *World Leisure Journal* **53** (3) (2011): 166–78.

Şengün, Sercan, 'Ludic Voyeurism and Passive Spectatorship in Gone Home and Other "Walking Simulators"', *Video Game Art Gallery* (2017), https://vgagallery.org/vga-reader-articles/ludic-voyeurism-and-passive-spectatorship-in-gone-home-and-other-walking-simulators

Shi, Jing, Rebecca Renwick, Nigel E. Turner and Bonnie Kirsh, 'Understanding the Lives of Problem Gamers: The Meaning, Purpose, and Influences of Video Gaming', *Computers in Human Behavior* 97 (2019): 291–303.

Solnit, Rebecca, *Wanderlust: A History of Walking* (New York: Penguin Books, 2001).

Tuan, Yi-Fu, *Space and Place: The Perspective of Experience* (Minneapolis: University of Minnesota Press 1997).

Wolf, Mark J.P., 'Theorizing Navigable Space in Video Games,' in Stephan Günzel, Michael Liebe and Dieter Mersch (eds), *DIGAREC Keynote-Lectures 2009/10*, pp. 18–49 (Potsdam: Potsdam University Press, 2011).

Wolf, Mark J.P., 'World Design', in Mark J.P. Woolf (ed.), *Routledge Companion to Imaginary Worlds*, pp. 67–73. (London: Routledge, 2018).

Zimmermann, Felix and Christian Huberts, 'From Walking Simulator to Ambience Action Game: A Philosophical Approach to a Misunderstood Genre', *Press Start* **5** (2) (2019): 29–50.

CHAPTER 10.

ATTENTIVE WALKING: ENCOUNTERING MINERALNESS

Petra Lilja

Walking between contexts

This essay consists of insights gathered from a series of curated mineral walks in a disused limestone quarry in Limhamn, near the coast of the southwestern edge of Sweden.[1] The text is polyphonic in its structure, as I am walking between contexts and roles as design researcher (theorising my practice) and curator (practising theory). As an industrial designer by training, I have an inherently extractivist mindset and interest in physical materials, which is conflicted by an increasing unease over how 'design is central to the structures of unsustainability' and involved in intensive resource use and vast material destruction.[2]

As walkers as well as consumers and citizens – in the context of Occidental modernity – I suggest that we are all interconnected with extractivism, understood here as a mode of accumulation on massive scale by the capitalist system.[3] This mindset puts the interest of the human, perceived as a bounded subject, before and above the so-called nature we walk in or in other ways exploit as resource; 'a taking without caretaking'.[4] Our actions leave traces behind and, as this volume proposes; 'traces of people's movements can be regarded as a distinct kind of cultural heritage, a "*movement heritage.*"'[5] If, then, movement heritage is about creating trails and paths, the question that this text adds is: what traces should we be careful not to lose for heritage not to become entirely anthropocentric? Proposing that it matters *how* we walk in the world, *with whom* and *what for*, walking, framed through an ontology of mineral becoming, is used as a method to explore this question. Departing from Bennett's concept vibrant

---

1   The mineral walk is curated by designers Petra Lilja and Anette Væring and conducted with permission of the municipality of Malmö. The many collaborative group walks, undertaken here since 2019, are open to public and invited artists, designers and a transdisciplinary range of researchers and scholars.
2   Escobar, *Designs for the Plurivers*, p. 1; Lilja, 'Tracing Matters', 5.
3   Acosta, 'Extractivism', 62.
4   Klein, *This Changes Everything*, pp. 847–48. See also Klein's use of the notion 'extractive mindset'.
5   Svensson, Saltzman, and Sörlin, 'Introduction' to this volume, p. 5.

matter, as a way to think around the nature/culture dualisms underpinning the problem of the anthropocentric, extractivist mindset, I suggest an attentiveness to encounters with mineralness. In addition to the importance of maintaining pathways of the quarry's industrial pasts 'by continuous use or memory work', the insights from the mineral walks also suggest that we acknowledge more-than-human path makers and craft sensitivities to matter in order to start processes of unveiling and rethinking anthropocentrism.[6]

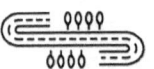 **Mineral walk-introduction at Limhamn limestone quarry, 30 September 2020:**

> We walk in the enduring company of rocks, so let us pay attention to their mineral stories, not just those that talk about human productivity, culture and politics, which presuppose that the mineral only exists for us. As you step onto this mineral-rich landscape of limestone, feel the kinship of the cosmic scales of calcium carbonate spread by dying stars that long-ago infiltrated life on Earth, building your bones, supporting your body's movements step by step. 'You are a walking, talking mineral', and here you are a path-maker among others, tracing the paths of industrial pasts as well as shaping the future by the traces you leave behind.[7] Pick a stone from the myriads of mineral compositions around you. Imagine the past soundscapes of crushing and grinding that has come to an end. Walk in silence. Sharpen your senses and attentiveness to the fossilised 'earth others' inhabiting this site in this moment.[8] The stone is your lithic co-walker, a figure to move and think with, when entering this archive of life, death and the fossils in between.

Walking with vibrant matter

The nature/culture divide is a prerequisite for extractivism, not only in the old quarry of Limhamn or elsewhere in Sweden but globally, and materially linked to the systems of energy, technology and products involved in our everyday lives. The problem, Jane Bennett argues, is that 'materiality is both too alien

---

6   Svensson, Saltzman, and Sörlin, 'Introduction' to this volume. For more on engaging the becoming of trails with other than human actors see Syse, this volume.

7   Margulis and Sagan, *What is Life?* P. 49. The authors are referencing Russian scientist Vladimir Ivanovich Vernadsky (1863–1945), in this quote. V.I. Vernadsky, 'The Biosphere', 44, 58; V.I Vernadsky, 'The Biosphere and the Noösphere', 1–12.

8   Plumwood, *Feminism*, p. 196.

10. Attentive Walking

Figure 1.

Walking in silence. Photograph by Petra Lilja.

and too close for humans to see clearly'.[9] With the concept of vibrant matter, Bennett wants to make us more sensitive to what she calls nonhuman forces and events, realise their powers in and on our bodies and surroundings and, by connecting this to ecological thinking, evoke a more ethically and ecologically sustainable relationship with nonhuman nature. Bennett theorises a vital materiality following the less dominant European tradition of philosophers spanning history from Democritus, Epicurus, Spinoza and Diderot to Deleuze and Guattari. Explaining vitality as the capacity to produce effects through movement, Bennett's vital view is importantly detaching 'materiality from the figure of passive, mechanistic, or, divinely infused substance'.[10] Rocks, stones and minerals are not often understood as a form of life; rather, they imply something abiotic, dead or inert.[11]

Perhaps the most accessible way of understanding matter as vibrant is through the extracted minerals' entanglement with the capitalist system

---

9   Bennett, 'The Force of Things', 349.
10 Bennett, *Vibrant Matter*, p. xiii.
11 Bennett, 'Artistry and Agency'.

capable of moving matter around the globe and processing it, mixing it into diverse compounds, manufacturing it into products, buildings, infrastructure and so on. Yet, the crucial question at hand, reading Bennett, is how minerals are vibrant outside of this capitalist system and how this can be perceived and valued without that anthropocentric framing? Inspired by Vernadsky, whose work broke boundaries between biology and geology by calling both living organisms and mineral 'living matter', one way this question has been explored in the curated walks in Limhamn is by introducing what I call mineralness.[12] *Mineralness* can in this context be understood as an attribute to help us think the mineral beyond the subject/object divide, which might be a first step for understanding the temporalities of 'natureculture'.[13] It considers the quality of the mineral as active subject rather than passive object but also its natureculture entanglement as the mineral constitution of bodies, including the human. By diffractively reading feminist new materialist and posthumanist perspectives with walking theory, the curation of the mineral walk attempts to transform the extractive site of the quarry by framing it through its mineralness, questioning the boundaries and onto-epistemologies of our own humanness, exploring ways to create different relationships to matter outside the extractivist mindset. Walking is a relational practice of movement and, for the curation of the mineral walk, the following themes in walking research identified by scholars Stephanie Springgay and Sarah E. Truman play a major role: sensory inquiry, embodiment, rhythm as well as attunement to geos and place.[14]

The beaten trails of Limhamn

The name of the location of the mineral walks is Limhamn which means lime-harbour, indicating the site's so-called natural resource. The quarry pit measures 1,300 by 600 metres, with a depth of 65 metres which makes approximately 50,700,000 cubic metres of limestone, displaced by the quarrying over the last century.

---

12   For more on Vernadsky, see Margulis and Sagan, *What is Life?* p. 51.
13   Haraway, *Companion Species*. For a historical overview of natureculture temporalities in terms of an articulation of environmental times and its current synchronisation with social times, see Sörlin, 'Environmental Times', 64–101.
14   Springgay and Truman, *Walking Methodologies*, pp. 1–163.

10. Attentive Walking

> **Fieldnotes from a research walk around the quarry, 20 November 2019:**
>
> From where I am standing, I have a good overview of the gigantic hole of the quarry. It is a void of displaced matter. Looking closer, though, I see that it is already filled; with plants, animals, insects and rocks or lithic earth others.-

Stepping down from the 'view from above', facilitates a closer look at the more than 1,500 plants, insects and animals that, in addition to the fossils and rocks, inhabit the quarry today.[15] Rather than a void or empty hole, this place can more accurately be described as a lively whole. In Limhamn, extraction of lime has occurred since the seventeenth century, when mortar and plaster were manufactured by hand. Back then, the area was full of small holes and mounds that covered more land area than the current location of the quarry. However, the cut in the landscape was less severe, as it was formed through small-scale, manual digging by farmers making an extra income from selling limestone to the owner of a kiln located at the nearby seaside. The lime processed at that time is traceable in different historical buildings in the local vicinity of Copenhagen and southern Sweden. Larger-scale quarrying started in 1866, with the inauguration of what was later to become one of Europe's largest open-pit quarries.[16] The extraction of limestone ended here in 1994 when the industry closed down and the headquarters relocated.[17]

The heritage historically associated with movement in this area has evolved from kettle trails to the industrial era of paved roads and iron rails for transporting the limestone to the cement factory in the harbour, connecting the local lime with a global network of markets. In terms of public trails for recreational purposes, the official one was landscaped in 2015 and is a four-kilometre-long trail for biking, fitness- and dog-walking encircling the quarry, following the fence that closes off the open pit. Acknowledging the past extractivist labour, the mineral walk follows parts of the already beaten tracks of animals and humans that formed the infrastructure which to this day can be traced in certain

---

15 Haraway, *Situated Knowledges*, p. 589; Rogowska-Stangret, 'Situated Knowledges'.

16 Emanuelsson et al., *Det skånska kulturlandskapet (The Scanian cultural heritage landscape)*; Malmö Stad, *'Kalkbrottets industrihistoria' ('The industrial history of the limestone quarry')*; Länsstyrelsen, 'Bevarandeplan' ('Conservation plan').

17 This quarry closed due to increasing energy costs and competition from other more cost-efficient production methods, by both national and international suppliers of lime, see Wickström, *Kalkstenen (The limestone)*, pp. 273–76.

roads that have been paved to permanency.[18] Movement as such produces place; however, these trails and roads are confined to a prescriptive and extractive way of thinking of animals and minerals as mere resources. Furthermore, this understanding of movement suggests linearity and direction, one conventional way of understanding walking as well; to move from point a to point b. In an attempt to resist this linear understanding of movement and a reductionist sense of place as mere dead matter or means for walking, the mineral walk attempts to walk otherwise by opening up to certain other paths, *off* the beaten trails. Namely, the ones that follow what has normatively been pushed to the wayside by a singular anthropocentric focus. To attempt this, the understanding of movement must be expanded to also include the dynamic force or vibrant movement inherent in all living matter, as outlined by Bennett and Vernadsky.

Walking as method

Walking has been the main method used to explore mineralness and it has been conducted on numerous occasions by myself walking alone; with my colleague; with geology students, as well as with larger groups of participants in the curated mineral walks. Important predecessors come from the arts, where a wide gamut of work demonstrating a range of artistic strategies can be found.[19] Scholarly work has established walking as a cultural practice and research method, often in conjunction with artistic methods.[20] Walking as place-making is used by artists and designers, for example in designing games and audio-walks.[21]

In the mineral walk, a relational understanding of place is fundamental; however, this does not imply walking in harmony with the landscape of the quarry, consuming the impressive sedimented limestone walls as a backdrop. There is no such thing as a frictionless world or 'an *a priori* reality– an extant, smooth "social space"' – rather, the '"social" is in the making, produced with every footstep', as Pope reminds us.[22] However, most understandings of social space uphold the nature/culture divide and do not take into consideration the more-than-human. The aim of the mineral walk aligns with Springgay's

---

18   The traces of two main kettle trails and ancient dirt roads in the area are today the streets of Hyllie Kyrkoväg, Kalkbrottsgatan and Limhamnsvägen – see map in Wickström, *Kalkstenen (The limestone)*, p. 67.

19   For a short overview of walking in art, see Pope, 'Walking Transformed'.

20   'Walking Lab'; 'Cultural Geographies'; 'The Walking Institute'.

21   Innocent and Dale, 'Heightened Intensity'. For more on art and audio walks, see Bertens in this volume.

22   Pope, 'Walking Transformed'.

10. Attentive Walking

Figure 2.

Mineral bones. Photograph by Petra Lilja.

and Truman's project of 'queering the trail' that – despite different contexts – 'demand[s] that we think otherwise about human and more-than-human entanglements'.[23] Understanding walking as entangled with the complex world enables critical inquiry into its political dimensions. Springgay and Truman's use of the notion of 'walking-with' captures this complex relationality of place and walking. As a research method, walking as practice connects to the discursive work of walking-with the lithic. This entanglement is nicely articulated by Jeffrey Jerome Cohen who states that:

> to tell a story with stone is intensely to inhabit that preposition *with*, to move from solitary individuations to ecosystems, environments, shared agencies, and companionate properties.[24]

---

23   Springgay and Truman, *Walking Methodologies*, pp. 25-30; Springgay and Truman, 'Stone Walks'.
24   Cohen, *Stone*, p. 11. Cohen draws in turn from Ingold, *Being Alive*, pp. 19–32.

> **Fieldnotes from group walk 30 May 2021:**
>
> The group gets up and starts walking through the gates into the quarry. We are walking in silence, in order to sharpen our senses and become attentive to what we may meet on the way. Starting off on the paved road enclosed by lush greenery, the expected quarry views are not yet in sight. Instead we meet a richness of plants, trees, insects and suddenly an unexpected sound of what might be a small water fall. The water seeping out from the rock, tells us the level of the groundwater, about five metres below ground. We follow the water as it flows across the asphalt in a tiny downward stream. Soon we spot some thick pipes mounted on the rocky wall, leading to the pump station at the bottom of the pit. It pumps the ground water out from the quarry, at the incredible speed and volume of seventy litres per second. The human entanglement in this place becomes obvious as the current formation of the quarry is completely dependent on the redirection and control of the trickling groundwater. Where the water runs off the edge of the road, the greenery withdraws and our view shifts towards the vastness of the pit in the other direction.

Attentive encountering

The silent part of the mineral walk is an attempt to become attentive to surroundings that are often taken for granted or overlooked when walking while chatting. Sensorial isolation aims to enhance specific senses in order to practice attentiveness, common for example in the walking meditations of Theravada Buddhism.[25] Respecting that level of refinement of attentive practice, the mineral walk rather aims to 'look around instead of ahead' as Anna Tsing puts it, following what she calls the 'arts of noticing'.[26] Thom Van Dooren has expanded noticing into attentiveness, to include cultivation of skills for both paying attention to others and meaningfully responding. Attentiveness he proposes, 'remind[s] us that knowing and living are deeply entangled and that paying attention can and should be the basis for crafting better possibilities for shared life'.[27]

In framing the rocks, stones and minerals of the quarry as vibrant matter, I am aware of the risk of anthropomorphising matter in the form of living, autopoietic systems – as an image of the human, or the 'human-all-too-human'

---

25   'Walking Meditation'.
26   Tsing, *The Mushroom*, pp. 17–25.
27   Van Dooren et al., 'Multispecies Studies', 17.

10. Attentive Walking

Figure 3.

Technofossil silos. Photograph by Petra Lilja.

– as framed in posthumanism.²⁸ Yet, the curation of sensorial and embodied movement opens up to forms of attentiveness beyond the form of the human altogether as we begin to encounter and learn from the mineralness of the place. To encounter is something that forces us to think otherwise, opposed to recognising which only reconfirms what we already know or believe, or presents a representation of what is always already in place.²⁹ Drawn from Deleuze, Simon O'Sullivan's delineation of the 'encounter' is helpful in articulating the aim of attentiveness in the mineral walk in terms of encountering the minerals anew, or rather the mineralness of everything in and connected to the quarry, instead of just recognising it from the singular perspective of its former industrial function as exploitable resource.

---

28   Important and interesting critical perspectives on theories like Bennett's have recently been put forth: see for example Colebrook, 'Death of the posthuman', suggesting that such posthumanisms are, ultimately 'human-all-too-human' or 'ultra-humanisms insofar as they attribute all the qualities once assigned to man – qualities such as mindfulness, connectedness, self-organizing dynamism – to some supposedly benevolent life in general that needs to be saved from the death of merely calculative systems', 162.

29   O'Sullivan, *Art Encounters Deleuze and Guattari*, pp. 1–4.

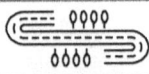 **Field notes from group walk 3 May 2021:**

Straight ahead from the water pumps the gigantic silos and crushing hall materialise themselves. We pass by some concrete modules that looks as if spray-painted red. As I come closer I realise that it is not paint but the concrete's entanglement with algae, creating a symbiotic relationship. In other words, when what we call concrete meets algae, both matters resist being bound entities and rather enter into ever changing relations. What we are encountering, is the entangled mineralness of biotic life and industrial heritage.

Fossils of kinds

Despite the nowadays thriving nature in terms of algae, plants, insects and animals, this specific location's anthropocentric heritage is inscribed in stone and concrete: more precisely, the industrial heritage built on extraction, separation and purification of the mineral calcite from its biotic and lithic entanglements. The concrete silo building presents itself like a worthy representative of the 'technosphere', a notion that spans not only the world's large-scale resource extraction systems – of which the Limhamn quarry is just one small part – but also the extraction of energy, and, as Peter Haff lists: 'power generation and transmission systems, communication, transportation, financial and other networks, governments and bureaucracies, cities, factories, farms and myriad other "built" systems, as well as all the parts of these systems, including computers, windows, tractors, office memos and humans'.[30] The main use of the quarried limestone is as a large component in concrete, which is one of the markers of the Anthropocene.[31] The building – a former crushing hall in the quarry – is abandoned by the industry as well as by its current owner, the municipality, who decided not to maintain it despite the advice that it is of 'great importance for the understanding of the lime quarry as an industrial environment'.[32] Among humans, it seems only to be the trespassing graffiti-painters who ignore the warning signs to make their mark on its concrete. As a 'technofossil', the exhausted building is in itself a mineralisation-in-becoming, a remnant of human labour in the past, present and anticipated future, which includes our own species memorialisation, and

---

30   Haff, 'Humans and Technology', 127.
31   Waters and Zalasiewicz, 'Concrete', 75–85.
32   Schlyter, *Limhamns kalkbrott (Limhanm limestone quarry)*, pp. 8–9.

10. Attentive Walking

Figure 4.

Processed minerals in the shape of buildings clinging on the brink of the quarry. Photograph by Petra Lilja.

our legacy in the rocks.³³ Walking in these spatial and temporal scales exposed by fossil strata intermingled with technofossils, not only raises questions linked to the urgency of our times of climate change and environmental destruction, but importantly also to geopolitical questions of the Anthropocene's connection to historical and ongoing social inequities around the world.³⁴

The Limhamn quarry's current status has been contested and the restricted access to the site today is the latest mode of many in the negotiations over the value and function of the quarry, ranging from public initiatives of motocross tracks to the nature reserve implemented by the municipality since 2011. All of which can be summed up as more or less anthropocentric in terms of cui bono, asking, who benefits from the initiatives? This becomes even more palpable when looking up at the new concrete buildings – the physical results of the processed minerals – clinging near the brink of the quarry. The apartment buildings stirred up a fuss when built and it is interesting to follow how the

33 Zalasiewicz, Williams, Waters et al., 'The Technofossil Record'.
34 For more on the racial and colonial patterns of the extractivist global industry, see Yusoff, *A Billion Black*, pp. xi–110.

anthropocentric function and value of the quarry has changed from raw extraction to exclusive backdrop view.[35] The real controversy perhaps rather lies in the coming plans to pave over every inch of the remaining natural habitat around the quarry, as reported in the local newspaper, leaving its other-than-human inhabitants stranded with no escape routes.[36]

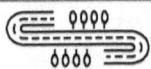 **Mineral walk-introduction 30 September 2020:**

You are walking through deep layers and thick deposits of sedimented matter. This is a strange archive displaying that which once was animal and then became stone during unimaginable 65 million years. A museum perhaps, of life, death and the fossils in between, but let us ignore museology and instead learn through musing, wondering, pondering, dreaming and loitering![37]

Walking back in time

Planetary large-scale extraction is anthropocentric action where swift economic growth is prioritised before biodiversity-measures relevant over generational time scales. Bennett suggests that thinking through evolutionary instead of biographical time might challenge this kind of short-sightedness and be helpful in claiming vitality intrinsic to matter.[38] It is difficult to grasp the deep timescales that are exposed in the vertical walls in the quarry. Drawing from walking methodologies that 'privilege an embodied way of knowing where movement connects mind, body and environment', the curation of the mineral walk aims to connect the walker with the quarry's fathomless scale of temporality, to make it more understandable.[39] The fact that the quarry measures 65 metres from top to bottom and the exposed sediments span 65 million years is an interesting numeric coincidence. Furthermore, the walking distance from the highest to the lowest level measures 650 metres. Hence, it is possible to calculate that each step we take, equals 50,000 years, turning the fossil layers into a kind of vertical

---

35 The first buildings were developed in 2008–09: see Wikipedia, 'Victoria Park' and Grundström, 'Grindsamhälle' (Gated community), pp. 18–39.

36 Thomasson, 'Så ska Kalkbrottet skyddas' (This is how the limestone quarry will be protected); Thomasson, 'Vi måste sluta med vårt invasiva sätt' (We have to stop our invasive ways). For a citizen initiative against the expansion, see, 'Bevara, Bunkeflo Strandängar' (Protect Bunkeflo beach meadows).

37 For the etymology of museum and muse, see 'Online Etymology Dictionary'.

38 Bennett, *Vibrant Matter*, p. 11.

39 Springgay and Truman, *Walking Methodologies*, p. 4.

10. Attentive Walking

Figure 5.

Pondering the exposed sediment layers. Photograph by Petra Lilja.

measuring tape. However, if walking provides a way of understanding place as always 'in flux', it must also question the logic of measuring.[40] This exercise in arithmetic is admittingly reducing time to linear spatiality. Nevertheless, it provides a tool – suitable for the extractivist mindset – that might bridge an instrumental and mechanistic world-view to a less anthropocentrically limited understanding of temporalities of the world.

Field notes from group walk 30 September 2020:

Keep walking, focusing on the fossil layers. Here, it has taken 50 years for every millimetre of limestone to form. The so-called Anthropocene, the human epoch, makes up only two millimetres of our very first step on this walk. As we descend down towards the bottom of the pit I notice my lithic co-walker stone that presses against the palm of my hand. How can I relate differently to this hard, cold composition of minerals?

---

40   Rendell, *Art and Architecture*, p. 189.

Petra Lilja

Trans-corporeal mineralness

Temporally, the limestone spans from biological animal to geological mineral which, if we look at it over very long durations of time, challenges taxonomies of lively and dead matter. As Elisabeth A. Povinelli writes, 'the perspective and scale from which we examine the relationship between Life and Nonlife creates and undermines the distinctions between Life and Nonlife'.[41] So, instead of a linear temporality supporting static and binary categorisations of animated (e.g. biology, algae, tree) or dead (e.g. geology, fossil, wood), what this walk puts focus on is an agency in nature beyond the limits of a passive resource.

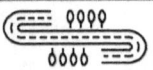 **Field notes from group walk 30 May 2021:**

> We leave the asphalt and concrete behind and the sound of our steps changes as we walk onto the bright white gravel, descending yet another level to the lowest reachable point in the quarry. Here, we meet a flock of cranes and hear the sound of the rare frogs dwelling in the water. I want to become invisible, but only succeed in walking a bit more quietly, in order not to disturb them. At a plateau, we all sit down in a circle prepared with mats, drinking glasses and pitchers of water. The feeling of the cold water entering my mouth and throat after a long walk is pleasing and I realise that water literally runs through this whole experience. We invite the participants to trace their skeletons on the skin of their hands with a watery mineral mix. Our stained skins become visual markers of the human-mineral-water entanglements and the process of sedimentation that also occurs within our human bodies.

Complex assemblages like human bodies need calcium to maintain strong bones and to carry out many important functions like moving muscles and speedy nerve communication. As this volume points out, 'our movements are also stored, and storied, in muscle memory … movement heritage thus includes traces on the ground, and in ourselves'.[42] Walkers are – along with all living bodies of animals, plants and water – connected to a dynamic cosmos of nonhuman forces and materialities that extends to the most remote parts of the galaxy, as recent scientific findings of calcium released from exploding stars indicate.[43] The attentive aim of the mineral walk is not only to address the

---

41 Povinelli, *Geontologies*, p., 44.
42 Svensson, Saltzman, and Sörlin, 'Introduction', p. 10.
43 Jacobson-Galan et. al., 'Transient Supernova'; 'Exploding Stars'.

10. Attentive Walking

Figure 6.

Encountering mineralness. Photograph by Petra Lilja.

lithic matter of the landscape, but also to begin an 'opening of subject positions to non/inhuman forces' or earth forces, layered also in our own bodies.[44] The painting exercise described in the fieldnotes above points at this kind of reconceptualisation of humans as inhuman subjects, following Yusoff's notion of the geosocial, and Stacy Alaimo's concept 'trans-corporeal', meaning 'that all creatures, as embodied beings, are intermeshed with the dynamic, material world, which crosses through them, transforms them, and is transformed by them'.[45] The mineral walk is about encountering the mineralness within both ourselves and the living matter of the quarry.

Towards attentive walking

Walking leaves traces, whether we stick to the beaten trails or not, and hence it also entails ethical implications. It matters *how* we walk in the world and this essay suggests walking-with as an affirmative ethico-aesthetic and politi-

---

44   Yusoff, 'Geologic Subjects', 389; Springgay and Truman, *Walking Methodologies*, p. 27.
45   Alaimo, 'Trans-corporeality', 435; see also Alaimo, *Bodily Natures*, pp. 11–25.

cal practice of attentiveness. Encountering becomes a tool for noticing *with whom* we walk, in other words, a tool for becoming attentive to the vibrant matter we, as trans-corporeal, inhuman subjects embody and in which we are embedded. Movement heritage is about creating trails and paths, and attentive walking opens up to encountering the human-inhuman, or more-than-human, as vibrant matter that might get lost in a heritage based on merely recognising an anthropocentric selection of natural or cultural artefacts or phenomena. Attentive walking can potentially disrupt our extractive mindsets and offer a creative moment of thinking and being differently in the world.

Bibliography

Acosta, Alberto, 'Extractivism and Neoextractivism: Two Sides of the Same Curse', in Miriam Lang and Dunya Mokrani (eds), *Beyond Development: Alternative Visions from Latin America*, pp. 61–86 (Quito: Fundación Rosa Luxemburg, 2013).

Alaimo, Stacy, *Bodily Natures: Science, Environment, and the Material Self* (Bloomington & Indianapolis: Indiana University Press, 2010).

Alaimo, Stacy, 'Trans-Corporeality', in Rosi Braidotti and Maria Hlavajova (eds), *Posthuman Glossary*, pp. 435–38 (London: Bloomsbury Academic, 2018).

Bennett, Jane, 'The Force of Things: Steps toward an Ecology of Matter', *Political Theory* 32 (3) (2004): 347–72.

Bennett, Jane, *Vibrant Matter: A Political Ecology of Things* (Durham N.C.: Duke University Press, 2010).

Bennett, Jane, 'Artistry and Agency in a World of Vibrant Matter', New School, New York: Youtube, 2011. https://www.youtube.com/watch?v=q607Ni23QjA&t=2964s.

Cohen, Jeffrey Jerome, *Stone: An Ecology of the Inhuman* (Minneapolis: University of Minnesota Press, 2015).

Colebrook, Claire, *Death of the Posthuman: Essays on Extinction*. Critical Climate Change. Edited by Tom Cohen and Claire Colebrook. Vol. 1 (Open Humanities Press, 2014) http://www.openhumanitiespress.org/books/titles/death-of-the-posthuman/.

Dooren, Thom van, Eben Kirksey and Ursula Münster, 'Multispecies Studies, Cultivating Arts of Attentiveness', *Environmental Humanities* 8 (1) (2016).

Emanuelsson, U., C. Bergendorff, M. Billqvist, B. Carlsson and N. Lewan, *Det Skånska Kulturlandskapet* (Lund, Sweden: Naturskyddsföreningen i Skåne, 2002).

Escobar, Arturo, *Designs for the Pluriverse, Radical Interdependence, Autonomy, and the Making of Worlds*, 2018 ed. (Durham and London: Duke University Press, 2017).

Grundström, Karin, 'Grindsamhälle: The Rise of Urban Gating and Gated Housing in Sweden', *Housing Studies* 33 (1) (2018): 18–39. https://doi.org/https://doi.org/10.1080/02673037.2017.1342774.

Haff, Peter K., 'Humans and Technology in the Anthropocene: Six Rules', *The Anthropocene Review* 1 (2014): 126–36. https://doi.org/10.1177/2053019614530575.

10. Attentive Walking

Haraway, Donna J., 'Situated Knowledges: The Science Question in Feminism and the Privilege of Partial Perspective', *Feminist Studies* **14** (3) (1988): 575–99. https://doi.org/10.2307/3178066. https://www.jstor.org/stable/3178066.

Haraway, Donna J., *The Companion Species Manifesto: Dogs, People, and Significant Otherness* (Chicago: Prickly Paradigm Press, 2003).

Ingold, Tim, *Being Alive* (London: Routledge, 2011) https://doi.org/https://doi-org.focus.lib.kth.se/10.4324/9780203818336.

Innocent, Troy and Dale Leorke, 'Heightened Intensity: Reflecting on Player Experiences in Wayfinder Live', *Convergence: The International Journal of Research into New Media Technologies* **25** (1) (2019): 18–39.

Instone, Lesley, 'Walking as Respectful Wayfinding in an Uncertain Age', in Katherine Gibson, Deborah Bird Rose and Ruth Fincher (eds), *Manifesto for Living in the Anthropocene*, pp. 133–38 (Brooklyn, NY: Punctum, 2015).

Jacobson-Galán, Wynn V., Abigail Polin, Ryan J. Foley, Georgios Dimitriadis, Charles D. Kilpatrick, Raffaella Margutti, David A. Coulter, et al., 'Ca Hnk: The Calcium-Rich Transient Supernova 2016hnk from a Helium Shell Detonation of a Sub-Chandrasekhar White Dwarf', *The Astrophysical Journal* **896** (2) (2020): 165. https://doi.org/10.3847/1538-4357/ab94b8.

Klein, Naomi, *This Changes Everything: Capitalism Vs. The Climate* (London: Allen Lane, 2014).

Lilja, Petra, 'Tracing Matters of Scale by Walking with Minerals', NORDES, Kolding, Denmark, Nordes, 2021.

Länsstyrelsen. Bevarandeplan För Natura 2000-Område, Limhamns Kalkbrott Se0430157 (Malmö: Länsstyrelsen i Skåne län, 2016).

O'Sullivan, Simon, *Art Encounters Deleuze and Guattari, Thought Beyond Representation* (Hampshire; New York: Palgrave Macmillan, 2006).

Plumwood, Val, *Feminism and the Mastery of Nature* (London, New York: Routledge, 1993).

Pope, Simon, 'Walking Transformed: The Dialogics of Art and Walking', *C Magazine*, no. 121 (2014). https://cmagazine.com/issues/121/walking-transformed-the-dialogics-of-art-and-walking.

Povinelli, Elizabeth A. *Geontologies: A Requiem to Late Liberalis* (Durham and London: Duke University Press, 2016).

Rendell, Jane, *Art and Architecture: A Place Between* (New York: Bloomsbury Publishing PLC, 2007).

Schlyter, Olga, *Limhamns Kalkbrott, Industrihistoriska Lämningar (Limhamn Limestone Quarry, Industrial Historical Remains)*, Kulturarvsenheten Malmö Stad (Malmö, Sweden: Malmö Museer, 2010). http://media.skanesmoderna.se/2016/02/Rapport_2010_011_low.pdf.

Springgay, Stephanie and Sarah E. Truman, 'Stone Walks: Inhuman Animacies and Queer Archives of Feeling', *Discourse: Studies in the Cultural Politics of Education* **38** (6) (2017): 851–63. https://doi.org/10.1080/01596306.2016.1226777.

Springgay, Stephanie and Sarah E. Truman, *Walking Methodologies in a More-Than-Human World: Walkinglab*, Routledge Advances in Research Methods (London: Taylor and Francis, 2019).

Sörlin, Sverker, 'Environmental Times: Historical and Scientific Temporalities from Annales to Anthropocene, 1920s–2020s', in Anders Ekström and Staffan Bergwik (eds), *Times of History, Times of Nature: Temporalization and the Limits of Modern Knowledge*, pp. 64–101 (New York: Berghahn Books, 2022).

Thomasson, Therese, 'Så Ska Kalkbrottet Skyddas – När Det Ringas in Av Bostäder', *Sydsvenska Dagbladet* (Sweden), 2020.

Thomasson, Therese, 'Vi Måste Sluta Med Vårt Invasiva Sätt Att Leva', *Sydsvenska Dagbladet* (Sweden), 2021.

Tsing, Anna Lowenhaupt, *The Mushroom at the End of the World: On the Possibility of Life in Capitalist Ruins* (Princeton: Princeton University Press, 2015).

Waters, C.N. and J. Zalasiewicz, 'Concrete: The Most Abundant Novel Rock Type of the Anthropocene', in Dominick DellaSala Michael Goldstein (eds), *Encyclopedia of the Anthropocene*, pp. 75–85 (Elsevier Inc, 2018).

Vernadsky, Vladimir I., 'The Biosphere and the Noösphere', *American Scientist* 33 (1)(1945): xxii–12.

Vernadsky, Vladimir I. *The Biosphere*, ed. by Mark McMenamin (New York: Springer Science+Business Media, 1998).

Wickström, Ingemar, *Kalksten Händelser Och Personer Kring Kalkstenen I Limhamn under 500 År* (Malmö: Kira Förlag, 2020).

Yusoff, Kathryn, 'Geologic Subjects: Nonhuman Origins, Geomorphic Aesthetic and the Art of Becoming in Human', *Cultural Geographies* **22** (3) (2015): 383–407.

Yusoff, Kathryn, *A Billion Black Anthropocenes or None* (Forerunners. Minneapolis: University of Minnesota Press, 2018).

Websites

Bevara, Bunkeflo Strandängar. Facebook, 2021.

'Cultural Geographies in Practice Walking and Looking', 2014: https://misshalfpenny26.wordpress.com/2014/03/23/cultural-geographies-in-practice-walking-and-looking-by-andrea-phillips/ (accessed 3 August 2021)

'Exploding Stars Created Calcium in Human Bones, Study Says' CNN / WVLT TV, 2020: https://www.wvlt.tv/2020/08/06/exploding-stars-created-calcium-in-human-bones-study-says (accessed 14 March 2021)

'Kalkbrottets Industrihistoria', Malmö Stad, 2020: https://malmo.se/Uppleva-och-gora/Natur-och-parker/Limhamns-kalkbrott/Kalkbrottets-industrihistoria.html (accessed 24 March 2021)

'Online Etymology Dictionary', 2021: https://www.etymonline.com/search?q=museum&utm_campaign=sd&utm_medium=serp&utm_source=ds_search (accessed 20 November 2021)

'Situated Knowledges', 2018: https://newmaterialism.eu/almanac/s/situated-knowledges.html (accessed 11 June 2021)

'The Walking Institute, the Deveron Projects': https://www.deveron-projects.com/the-walking-institute/tourism-and-economic-regeneration/ (accessed 30 March 2022)

'Walking Lab', 2021: https://walkinglab.org/ (accessed 26 August 2021)

'Walking Meditation in Theravada Buddhism' Drarisworld: https://drarisworld.wordpress.com/2020/04/22/walking-meditation-in-theravada-buddhism/ (accessed 3 August 2021)

'Victoria Park', Wikipedia: https://sv.wikipedia.org/wiki/Victoria_Park (accessed 3 August 2021)

Section III
Searching for New Path Heritage

CHAPTER 11.
KODAGU WALKING TRAILS AND INDIGENOUS HERITAGE MAKING: A BIOREGIONAL STUDY

Subarna De

Introduction

Kodagu, anglicised as Coorg, is situated on the eastern slopes of the Western Ghats in the present state of Karnataka in India. The Kodagu region, approximately 4,102 square kilometres, is the source of the significant Tala Kaveri watershed.[1] In the Kannada language, Kodagu means 'mountain', which geographically defines its rocky mountainous topography.[2] It is a wet hilly region with moist black alluvial soil, evergreen forests and rich biodiversity.[3] The people of Kodagu, also known as the Kodava people, were initially hunter–gatherers and forest dwellers with small acreages of land where they cultivated paddy, their staple diet.[4] Their indigenous identity and traditional belief system are therefore rooted in their forests.[5] With the advent of European colonisation in India in the final quarter of the eighteenth century, The Indian Forest Act of 1878 was established, which replaced Indian forest lands with cash crops such as tea, coffee, indigo, potato and rubber plantations.[6] Thus, Kodagu lost its dense mountain forests to colonial

---

1   Neilson, 'Environmental Governance in the Coffee Forests of Kodagu, South India', 187; also see Kadambi, 'Short Note on the Evergreen Forests of Mysore State'; Lewis, *Mysore and Coorg from the Inscriptions*; Richter, *Gazetteer of Coorg*.

2   Richter, *Gazetteer of Coorg*, p. 4.

3   Chisholm, 'Coorg', 91–92; Proctor, 'Notes on Evergreen Rainforests of Karnataka State, South-West India', 228; also see Kadambi, 'Short Note on the Evergreen Forests of Mysore State'; Karnataka Department of State Education Research and Training n.d.; Lewis, *Mysore and Coorg from the Inscriptions*; Ramachandrachar, *Kodagu Folk and Tribal Culture*; Richter, *Gazetteer of Coorg*; Thurston, *The Madras Presidency with Mysore, Coorg, and the Associate States*.

4   Poonacha, '*Rites de Passage* of Matrescence and Social Construction of Motherhood', 102.

5   I use the term 'indigenous' to refer to the people and their culture, heritage, knowledge system and lifeways that grew *in situ* prior to colonisation; see Shaw, Herman and Dobbs, 'Encountering Indigeneity', 268, and the terms 'tradition' and 'traditional' to refer to the historical practice, a 'central process of Indigenous survival and renewal'; see Clifford, *Returns*, pp. 28–29. Because the Kodava people were born in Kodagu, their ancestors owned the land prior to colonisation and they share a strong spiritual connection with their ancestral land, I call the Kodava people 'indigenous'.

6   Gadgil and Guha, *This Fissured Land*, pp. 99, 125. European colonisers burned the vast forested mountain slopes of Kodagu and introduced coffee monoculture and continuous cultivation. See Mandanna, *Tiger Hills*, p. 222; Nambisan, *The Scent of Pepper*, p. 57. For details on monoculture, see

coffee plantations.[7] The environmental degradation, topographical transformation and biodiversity loss threatened the Kodagu native ecology and their traditional knowledge, rooted in place.[8] To survive the cultural and existential crisis, the Kodava people began to practise agriculture as their livelihood, rather than hunting and gathering, and then gradually adopted the colonial coffee plantation culture.

The passing of time and the transformation of the Kodava society had significant impacts on the Kodagu landscape.[9] Until the late nineteenth century, Kodagu's walking trails offered the only effective means for communication among the Kodava forest dwellers.[10] These walking trails, which have always been an integral part of the forest land, are narrow linear tracks created by the footprints of humans and animals such as elephants, wild boars, jungle fowl, rabbits, jungle cats and wild cats.[11] These trails run through and across mountain

Shiva, 'Globalisation and the War against Farmers and the Land'; Wirzba, *The Essential Agrarian Reader*. For details on continuous cultivation, see Berg and Dasmann, 'Reinhabiting California'.

7   Before coffee was introduced in Kodagu, Ceylon had been the top coffee-growing country in the world since the mid-seventeenth century. Beginning in 1872, Ceylon's coffee production seriously declined because of the fungus *Hemileia vastatrix*, which caused a leaf disease known as leaf rust. Kodagu's dark-soiled mountainous region situated at an elevation of about 1,800 feet above sea level became an alternative for the European colonisers after Ceylon coffee production stopped in 1879. For a more comprehensive colonial history of the coffee plantations in India and Ceylon, see Lewis, *Mysore and Coorg from the Inscriptions*; McCook, 'Global Rust Belt'; Mendis, *Ceylon Under the British*; Richter, *Gazetteer of Coorg*; Thurston, *The Madras Presidency with Mysore, Coorg, and the Associate States*; Wenzlhuemer, *From Coffee to Tea Cultivation in Ceylon, 1880–1900*.

8   I use the term 'native' to indicate plant species that occur naturally in the region, without direct or indirect human actions, and that do not cause the environment any harm; see Guiaşu, *Non-Native Species and Their Role in the Environment*, p. 11; Morse, Swearingen and Randall, 'Defining what is Native', 12. With the use of 'traditional knowledge' and 'indigenous knowledge' interchangeably, I refer to the unique knowledge system of the Kodagu community that was developed around their immediate physical environment for generations; also see Grenier, *Working with Traditional Knowledge*, p. 1. I borrow the term 'place' from Cresswell, *Place*, pp. 7–8, to refer to the Kodagu 'spaces' that the Kodava people have 'made meaningful' and are 'attached to' in one or more ways.

9   I use the term 'landscape' to represent a cultural image of place, an individualist way of seeing and conjuring the natural scenery that separates the subject from the object by eliminating alternative modes of experiencing our relations with nature: see Cosgrove, *Social Formation and Symbolic Landscape*, pp. 13, 262; Pavord, *Landskipping*, p. 353; Stilgoe, *What is Landscape?*, pp. ix, 17–18, 31.

10 In this essay, I prefer to use the term trails rather than paths or pathways. This is because the Kodagu paths and pathways are man-made, broader, more common routes of transit among the community members which are, unlike the trails, often discoverable on maps and *Google Earth*, whereas the Kodagu trails are narrow linear tracks created by the footprints of both humans and nonhumans; also see Belliappa email correspondence, 15 Aug. 2021; Mandanna, *Tiger Hills*; Richter, *Gazetteer of Coorg*. Hereafter, I refer to the Kodagu walking trails as 'trails' or 'walked environments' where 'environment' represents the non-human world and signifies 'the knowledge-based representation' of nature in which 'humans and their actions are embedded'; see Castree, *Nature* p. 9; Sörlin and Wormbs, 'Environing Technologies', 103; Warde, Robin and Sörlin, *The Environment*.

11 Mandanna, *Tiger Hills*, Nambisan, *The Scent of Pepper*. I use 'land' to describe the ground within a particular place, the earth's solid surface distinguished by ownership, belongingness and emotional attachment, and understood by all human senses; see Syse, From Land Use to Landscape, 48.

11. Kodagu Walking Trails and Indigenous Heritage Making

Figure 1.

Kodagu walking trails on C.P. Belliappa's coffee estate. Photograph by C.P. Belliappa.

forests, agricultural lands, riverbanks, paddy fields and valleys. The trails have continually been produced and reshaped over time and, even today, they are not featured on maps or tagged on *Google Earth*.

This essay investigates how Kodagu's trails entered the colonial Kodagu landscape and evolved as sites of indigenous heritage making while reviving the nature–culture relationship. Rodney Harrison describes heritage as an 'all-pervasive aspect of contemporary life' that experiences 'the physical traces of the past in the present'.[12] Heritage foregrounds the cultural distinctiveness of the Kodava community by considering their past experiences and present interactions with the land and landscape of Kodagu.[13] I argue that Kodagu's trails evolve as the sites of heritage making as heritage determines the indigenous knowledge and cultural continuity of the Kodava community. In doing so, I explore the on-trail experiences which include Kodava indigenous knowledge, traditional practices and various kinds of movement practices such as walking, running, strolling, frolicking, playing.[14] To understand Kodagu's indigenous lifeways and worldviews, this essay draws on Sarita Mandanna's historical fiction, *Tiger Hills* (2010), which narrates the Kodava experience of the colonial coffee plantations and the sociocultural ecological transformations of place and people across four generations during the years 1878 to 1936.[15] A bioregional reading of this novel shows how Kodagu's trails defined the precolonial Kodagu landscape and continue to play a significant role in constructing 'a geographical terrain' and a 'terrain of consciousness', even after the transformation of the region's nature, landscape and the host society that came with the advent of European agency.[16]

---

12   Harrison, *Heritage*, pp. 1, 227.

13   I differentiate between land, which has ownership and can be encapsulated with all senses, and landscape, which remains a panoramic way of regarding nature through only the visual senses and cannot be owned; see Syse, From Land Use to Landscape, 48–49; Olwig, 'Performing on the Landscape Versus Doing Landscape', 81–83.

14   One of the editors of the present volume, Sverker Sörlin, the Swedish environmental historian, suggested in a review comment that playing, walking, frolicking and running are types of movement with a wider range than walking.

15   Sarita Mandanna is a Kodagu-born and raised investment banker and a private equity professional presently living in Toronto, Canada. Of her two novels, *Tiger Hills* and *Good Hope Road* (2014), only *Tiger Hills* is set in Kodagu. *Tiger Hills* has been translated into fourteen languages worldwide and was longlisted for the 2011 Man Asian Literary Prize. This essay will also refer to the anthropological and ethnographical works of Rev. Gundert Richter's *Gazetteer of Coorg* (1870), Lewis Rice's *Mysore and Coorg from the Inscriptions* (1909), E. Thurston's *The Madras Presidency with Mysore, Coorg, and the Associate States* (1913), and D.B. Ramachandrachar's *Kodagu Folk and Tribal Culture* (1991) as secondary sources to support the fictional and empirical observations.

16   Both terms 'a geographical terrain' and a 'terrain of consciousness' are taken from Berg and Dasmann, 'Reinhabiting California', 218. Here, nature refers to the 'entire physical world', both the humans and the non-humans; see Castree, *Nature*, p. 1; Habgood, *The Concept of Nature*, p. 4.

11. Kodagu Walking Trails and Indigenous Heritage Making

Bioregional possibilities in Kodagu

The term 'bioregion' refers to 'the geographical terrain and a terrain of consciousness – to a place and the ideas that have developed' about living in that place.[17] In precolonial Kodagu, the mountainous forest trails served as the region's natural barriers, making Kodagu a 'separate country'.[18] Peter Berg and Raymond F. Dasmann argue that, geographically, a bioregion should always be a 'separate whole' determined by 'climatology, physiography, animal and plant geography, natural history, and other descriptive natural sciences'.[19] Kodagu's colonial history and its unique native biodiversity, wet climate, black alluvial soil, mountainous topography, indigenous people and their cultural distinctiveness make Kodagu a bioregion. Berg and Dasmann argue that the inhabitants who live-in-place or reinhabit a bioregion best determine its final boundaries.[20] Living-in-place means 'following the necessities and pleasures of life as they are presented by a particular site and evolving ways to ensure long-term occupancy of that site', and reinhabitation means learning to live-in-place in an injured land – that is, damaged and exploited land that has been altered by human activities that consider land a commodity, such as clearcutting, monoculture and industrial agriculture, and natural calamities such as wildfires.[21] Reinhabitation helps restore the land and revive the lost nature and culture of a place by developing a bioregional lifeway, where the adjective 'bioregional' refers to the 'intellectually rich and culturally diverse way of thinking [about] and living' an ecological lifeway rooted in place.[22]

The walking trails in Kodagu have always played a significant role in defining a bioregional lifeway. Michael Vincent McGinnis argues that 'long before bioregionalism entered the mainstream lexicon', indigenous people had been practising many of the bioregional tenets.[23] In this sense, the Kodagu indigenous practices were bioregional. In *Tiger Hills*, Mandanna narrates that, as Kodava children around the late 1870s, the protagonists Devi and Devanna 'frolicked all day long, roaming the fields and adjoining woods,' creating trails with Tukra,

---

17   Berg and Dasmann, 'Reinhabiting California', 218.
18   Mandanna, *Tiger Hills*, pp. 4–6.
19   Berg and Dasmann, 'Reinhabiting California', 218; also see Berg, *Reinhabiting a Separate Country*.
20   Berg and Dasmann, 'Reinhabiting California', 218.
21   Ibid., 217.
22   McGinnis, 'A Rehearsal to Bioregionalism', 1–3, Snyder, 'Reinhabitation', 44. All the inhabitants of a place, including both the indigenous people and the settlers, can have a bioregional identity and reinhabit the land. However, in Kodagu, even today, only the indigenous Kodava people reinhabit the land.
23   McGinnis, 'A Rehearsal to Bioregionalism', 2.

their domestic helper.[24] 'Frolicking' and 'roaming' are types of movement practices that add to the children's on-trail experiences, which in turn helps them to know their land because Tukra taught the children to search for the 'juiciest mulberries' and 'thickest mushrooms' in Kodagu's dense forests and high mountains.[25] The children's search for the best native forest produce helped them discover and know the 'secret places' in their land.[26] Kirkpatrick Sale considers this way of 'knowing the land' and 'becoming conscious' of the availability of fruits and mushrooms to be a crucial part of bioregional living.[27] The trails, in turn, taught the children the 'realities of living-in-place' by raising their awareness about how to find both the means of survival and the pleasures of life.[28] The trails thus generated 'conscious ideas of how to live-in-place', which are the most crucial parameters for defining the 'final boundaries of a bioregion'.[29] Overall, Kodagu's walked environments came to be 'teachers' that taught the children to know their land and guided them to learn about their place.

Eventually, the trails evolved as cultural tools that introduced the children to the ecological lifeway connecting them to their land and taught them about long-term survival. From Tukra, they learned how to take 'the cattle to pasture', 'craft slingshots from the fibrous bark of the bairi tree and darts from porcupine quills', and catch crabs in the crab stream.[30] As a result, the Kodava children identified the trails as natural resource grounds that always served as powerful tools defining their indigenous bioregional lifeway. Their bare-footed movement practices, such as walking and running across valleys, pastures, river banks and mountain forests, contributed to the children's 'experiences of tactile, feet-first, engagement' with the land.[31] The trails they created connected them to nature, providing in-place experiences of 'doing' and 'practising' the wild.[32] Tim Ingold and Jo Lee Vergunst echo Pierre Bourdieu in arguing that such engagement with the land not only expresses thoughts and feelings, but also 'continually generates culture', with culture understood as the 'way of life' in a particular 'place' where

---

24   Mandanna, *Tiger Hills*, p. 18.
25   Ibid., p. 19.
26   Ibid., p. 19.
27   Sale, *Dwellers in the Land*, pp. 42–44.
28   Berg and Dasmann, 'Reinhabiting California', 218.
29   Ibid., 218.
30   Mandanna, *Tiger Hills*, pp. 18–19, 36–37, 278.
31   Ingold and Vergunst, 'Hunting and Gathering as Ways of Perceiving the Environment', 3.
32   Snyder, *The Practice of the Wild*, 'Reinhabitation'.

11. Kodagu Walking Trails and Indigenous Heritage Making

'the community meets and discovers itself'.[33] In precolonial Kodagu, culture developed from place-based on-trail experiences. These movement practices that configured the Kodava people's on-trail experiences generated feelings of attachment to the place by knowing the land through sensual experiences.

However, the place-based experiences in Kodagu and the Kodava people's emotional attachment to land changed with the colonial intrusion. *Tiger Hills* narrates the influence of the European coffee trade on the Kodava people, which made them clear hundreds of 'acres of underbrush from beneath their holdings of rosewood, and turn to coffee'.[34] The novel depicts Devi's changed attitude toward land on coming into possession of a hundred acres of untended coffee plantation. She began to look at land as a commodity, as something which can be 'assigned a value and exchanged', and she became one of the successful native coffee planters in Madikeri, Kodagu.[35] Assignment of an exchange value disrupts the emotional attachment to land, thereby turning more and more of the human lifeworld into something that can be bought and sold.[36] Kodagu's colonial plantations produced coffee as a commodity and destroyed all the place-based knowledge that had been available in its forests and trails, thus threatening Kodagu's indigenous culture.

As a result, to reconnect with the land, Kodagu's lost trails evolved as routes of remembrance, essential structures of place and memory. To redefine her spiritual connection to the land, Devi recollected how the trails served as natural resource grounds during her childhood. She remembered the trails that led to her favourite crab stream and her childhood days of catching crabs and bringing them home for Tayi (her grandmother) to cook 'crab chutney' (crab jam).[37] Recalling memories of place and ecology was the only way for Devi to feel rooted in the transformed place. Here the lost trails signified the 'cultural infrastructure of human memory'.[38] Devanna was also still deeply in love with Kodagu's lost ecology. Married to Devi, he lived in the farmhouse on the coffee plantation and recollected his childhood memories of native plants, his tactile senses of the land and wild smells.

---

[33] Appadurai, *Modernity at Large*, p. 76; Bourdieu, *Outline of a Theory of Practice*, pp. 93–94; Ingold and Vergunst, 'Introduction', 2; Innocenti, *Cultural Networks in Migrating Heritage*, p. 2; Williams, *Keywords*, p. 90.

[34] Mandanna, *Tiger Hills*, p. 222. Rosewood is native to Kodagu.

[35] Lane, 'Karl Marx: The Commodity', 319; Marx and Engels, *The Communist Manifesto*, p. 30.

[36] Allan, *Explorations in Classical Sociological Theory*, p. 77.

[37] Mandanna, *Tiger Hills*, pp. 19, 64, 225, 449.

[38] The editors of *Pathways* introduce the idea that trails evolve into the 'cultural infrastructure of human memory' in their introduction, p. 5.

Figure 2.

Human trails on Kodagu's forested coffee plantation. Photograph by Subarna De.

In the early 1920s, with an indigenous plan to recreate the lost place, Devanna proposed to Devi that growing coffee under native shade trees in Tiger Hills, their hundred-acre coffee plantation, would help recover Kodagu's forests and would also provide enough shade for the coffee bushes to produce more coffee.[39] Mandanna writes, 'It was months later that Devanna's theory was finally proven right'.[40] From then on, native paddy, cardamom and pepper became common native crops that every Kodava household grew in their backyards and estates.[41] The new trails established on the forested plantations eventually became the characteristic feature of the Kodagu region and 'contribute greatly to Coorg's [Kodagu's] image', providing a cultural identity for the local Kodava coffee-growers.[42]

---

39   Devanna stated that 'as years passed, the initial advantage of virgin soil had been eroded'. The European planters had followed Ceylon's coffee plantations too closely, which was a severe error in Kodagu because the 'coffee in Kodagu was exposed to too much sunlight'; see Mandanna, *Tiger Hills*, pp. 227–28.
40   Mandanna, *Tiger Hills*, p. 229.
41   Ibid., pp. 223–30.
42   Biénabe, 'Towards Biodiverse Agricultural Systems', 240. During my 2014–2017 ethnographic fieldwork in Kodagu, the coffee plantations were filled with shade trees such as jackfruit, mango, orange and silk cotton.

11. Kodagu Walking Trails and Indigenous Heritage Making

From a bioregional perspective, reforesting plantations with native trees meant reinhabiting Kodagu.[43] Kodagu's indigenous reforestation practice redefined Kodagu's 'geographical terrain' and helped the Kodava people remember and reconnect to the lost trails while creating new ones. The new trails in turn continue to engage the community's tangible and intangible place-based experiences, enhancing the development of their indigenous knowledge and their communication with the environment. Rodney Harrison describes heritage as an interdisciplinary approach to 'tangible' and 'intangible' things.[44] Here the tangible things are place-based nature-culture practices, while the intangible things include the sense of place, indigenous knowledge, a belief system, the emotional attachment to land and a sensual perception of the land and landscape. The new trails therefore connect the precolonial past with the colonial present and provide a cultural continuity for the future. 'Connectivity', Harrison argues, is a method for understanding heritage and its role in a society because heritage interlinks the 'old' and the 'new' while creating a 'modern sensibility'.[45] Below, I discuss how Kodagu's walked environments are essential places of connectivity as they link Kodagu's precolonial past with the colonial present in making indigenous heritage.

Kodagu's trails as sites of indigenous heritage making

In Kodagu, indigenous heritage is constructed through the interaction of people with nature and culture. Indigenous worldviews often include sociocultural behaviour, ecological knowledge, cultural practices, ancestors, the sacred and the supernatural.[46] I situate indigenous heritage making within the environmental geographies of place where indigenous communities have increasingly been engaged in restoring their environment and reviving the cultural practices that they consider traditional. I reorient 'indigenous heritage making' as an interdisciplinary theoretical approach to developing reinhabitory bioregional models of place-based experiences, practices and identity, and I identify Kodagu's trails as sites of heritage making.

Place-based experiences and practices, to quote Kenneth Olwig, involve 'doing' the land and/or landscape with 'feet, body, and both eyes', also, ears, and nose – which Olwig doesn't mention – to the extent that the sense of place is

---

43   Native trees help in land restoration. They balance the unsustainable practice of coffee monoculture, control topsoil erosion and increase the native biodiversity.

44   Harrison, *Heritage*, p. i; also see Harrison and Sterling, *Deterritorializing the Future*.

45   Ibid., pp. 227–29.

46   Reid, *Sorcerers and Healing Spirits*, Varutti, 'Crafting Heritage'.

Figure 3.
Elephant trails on C.P. Belliappa's estate. Photograph by C.P. Belliappa.

11. Kodagu Walking Trails and Indigenous Heritage Making

reinforced in the landscape.[47] Doing the land and/or landscape shares similarities with reinhabitation, as both require recreating the place.[48] Devanna's ecological practice of reforesting the colonial plantation was an act of doing the land. Accompanied by Tukra, he planted scarlet-tipped orchids, sampigé samplings, masses of wild roses, brilliant spumes of bougainvillaea, wild orchids and bamboo bushes alongside vegetable gardens in Tiger Hills, which soon turned into a bounty-rich forest filled with native trees, fragrant wildflowers, and birdsong.[49] Devanna and the children Nanju (Devi and Devanna's son) and Appu (Machu the tiger-killer's son) followed elephants' trails through the forests of Tiger Hills and made a natural birdhouse from gatherings of elephant-trampled coffee bushes and athi trees.[50] Renato Rosaldo and Lye Tuck-Po call this kind of ecological practice during the walks 'improvisation'.[51] Contextualising the Batek hunter–gatherer society of Malaysia, Tuck-Po has shown how improvisation becomes a context before a walk and along the walk and states that improvisation continues in the privacy of the trail and along the trail, which often results in new opportunities for connecting to place.[52]

From a bioregional perspective, Tuck-Po's 'improvisation' can be understood as a reinhabitory practice that helps to recreate place and develop a place-based identity. The Kodava people's identity as forest dwellers is fundamental for them. From his place-based experiences, Devanna knew that their indigenous knowledge emerged from Kodagu's trails. He therefore set up aviaries, a chicken coop, a cattle shed and a pigsty in Tiger Hills, where the children Nanju and Appu could stroll about with Tukra practising and learning the wild: catching bandicoot rats near the drumstick tree and chasing harmless grey rubber bugs, furry-legged caterpillars, and long-waisted centipedes.[53] The reintroduced wilderness on the forested plantation created a strong sense of place and identity for the children, engaging them in communicating with the environment. Like Devi and Devanna when they were kids, their children also created trails, and these also evolved as sites of participatory learning, teaching them the indigenous Kodagu lifeways. The trails thus became symbols of cultural continuity.

---

47 Olwig, 'Performing on the Landscape Versus Doing Landscape', 82, 87.
48 Ingold, 'Hunting and Gathering as Ways of Perceiving the Environment'; Olwig, 'Performing on the Landscape Versus Doing Landscape'; Snyder, *The Practice of the Wild, A Place in Space*; Thayer, *LifePlace*.
49 Mandanna, *Tiger Hills*, pp. 296–98.
50 Ibid., p. 283.
51 Rosaldo, *Culture and Truth*, pp. 109–26; Tuck-Po, 'Before a Step Too Far', 24.
52 Tuck-Po, 'Before a Step Too Far', 24.
53 Mandanna, *Tiger Hills*, pp. 281–82, 338.

Figure 4.

Gunflower bush in Rani Machaiah's coffee plantation. Photograph by Subarna De.

Similar to Marzia Varutti's concept of 'indigenous heritage', the trails 'hark back to the past of indigenous communities at the same time as [they open] new directions of future development'.[54]

Another way to understand how Kodagu's trails became meaningful places of cultural continuity and indigenous heritage making is through Kodagu's cultural practices. Mandanna writes that, around the 1890s, during Kailpodh, the festival of arms that marked the commencement of the hunting season, the Kodava people walked along the forest trails in search of the gunflower groves that grew in Kodagu's jungles.[55] The gunflower is an orange-yellow blossom that blooms one week each year around the time when Kailpodh is celebrated, on 3 September. In accordance with traditional Kodagu beliefs, this is the only flower used to decorate the ancestral hunting instruments and invoke

---

54   Varutti, 'Crafting Heritage', p. 11.
55   Mandanna, *Tiger Hills*, p. 54.

11. Kodagu Walking Trails and Indigenous Heritage Making

Figure 5.

Kodagu paddy fields and trails. Photograph by Subarna De.

their ancestors on Kailpodh.[56] The colonial plantation culture threatened the traditional Kodagu ritual and cultural practices, and Mandanna writes that the Kodava community created new trails on their estates in search of gunflower groves for the Kailpodh celebrations. Even today, the ceremony includes the forest walk, invoking ancestors with gunflowers, communal gatherings and a grand traditional meal.

During Puthari, the harvest festival, it is also a Kodava custom to walk on the traditional paddy fields and cut the first ripe sheaves while singing songs of rejoicing and praising their ancestral lord and protector of the Universe.[57] Another integral part of the Puthari celebration is the traditional grand feast, which entails collecting fruits, crops, grains, spices, fish and meat from the forests,

---

56   Ibid., pp. 54–55.
57   Ibid., pp. 188, 199, 205.

valleys, rivers and streams.[58] From a bioregional perspective, the Puthari walk on the traditional paddy fields resembles the celebration of pleasure and 'sufficiency', or maintaining and using the 'natural life-system continuities' of a place, such as water, soil, and forests, for long-term survival.[59] In fact, the Puthari walk continues to symbolise the abundance and the natural resources of the region.

More importantly, Kailpodh and Puthari both construct Kodagu's trails as sites of indigenous heritage making because the trails remain crucial to the symbolic cultural practices of walking, gathering and feasting. Walking the forest trails, valleys, agricultural lands and river banks helps develop indigenous ecological knowledge and advances place-based experiences. Gathering from the trails reminds the Kodava people of their identity as forest-dwellers, their hunter–gatherer ancestral past and the critical roles of the trails and landscape in providing their traditional food. Feasting adds to the sociocultural practice of togetherness as a communal value of forest-dwellers. Taken together, these two cultural practices enrich the Kodava people's indigenous identity and their place-based experiences and help present and future Kodava communities develop ideas about how to live-in-place. Overall, the bioregional lifeway explains how indigenous places are understood and maintained and how heritage is made along Kodagu's walked environments.

Conclusion

Throughout history, Kodagu's trails have played a significant role in every transformed landscape. In pre-colonial Kodagu society, the trails defined place and configured cultural practices. They continued to serve as vital indigenous ingredients for the Kodava people to remain rooted in their traditional culture in colonial times. In (post/de)colonial Kodava society, the trails, continue to enhance the human perception and understanding of indigenous ecology and culture of place and provide a bioregional lifeway. Though the trails remain an integral part of the Kodagu landscape and 'culturescape' in all the transformed Kodava societies, they did not however influence the transformation from hunting-gathering to agriculture to plantation societies.[60] Instead, the trails 'entail a reformed relationship' between human communities and the place and changing 'relationships between and within societies'.[61]

---

58 See Lewis, *Mysore and Coorg from the Inscriptions*; Mandanna, *Tiger Hills*; Nambisan, *The Scent of Pepper*; Ramachandrachar, *Kodagu Folk and Tribal Culture*; Richter, *Gazetteer of Coorg*.
59 Berg and Dasmann, 'Reinhabiting California', p. 219.
60 I borrowed the term 'culturescape' from Sörlin, 'Monument and Memory', 272.
61 Sörlin and Wormbs, 'Environing Technologies', 116.

11. Kodagu Walking Trails and Indigenous Heritage Making

Kodagu's trails are thus socially and culturally produced and articulated to reconnect with the land. The articulation of the trails finds expression in Kodava people's perception of their landscape. This becomes evident when they recollect childhood memories of on-trail experiences, enjoy movement practices such as frolicking, running, strolling and playing on the trails, forest walks, and cultural walking practices during communal ceremonies of Puthari and Kailpodh. Given by ecological, sociocultural and epistemological value structures of the place and people, the articulation of Kodagu's trails or walked environments is seen combined in the process of indigenous heritage making and trail-making. This collaborative process strengthens the attachment of Kodava sociocultural and ecological knowledge with the place. It emphasises that, for the continued existence of Kodagu's indigenous culture, Kodagu's trails, especially trail-making, need to be preserved.[62] In Kodagu, the presence of the indigenous ecologies in place is vital for the traditional Kodava culture to continue because their indigenous culture cannot survive without nature. Preserving trail-making practices ensures Kodava's cultural continuity, develops a bioregional sense of place and promotes a better understanding of Kodagu's environmental and socio-cultural history.

More so, the preservation of Kodagu's trails and trail-making moves beyond conventional frameworks of environmental narratives. Here, despite the presence of the European agency, trails were deeply embedded in the landscape, perceived and continued to be created. Looking at Kodava trail-making beyond conventional narratives prompts a decolonial interdisciplinary approach to heritage making. This is because heritage making helps the indigenous community to be understood from an indigenous perspective.[63] Also, it connects the pre-colonial past to the post-colonial future. It draws attention to how Kodagu's trails have evolved as reinhabitory tools for place-making. Thus, together, the bioregional approach of trail-making and heritage making becomes crucial to preserve the traditional meaning of place.

Finally, the future of indigenous heritage making on Kodagu's trails depends entirely on the preservation of trails and the trail-making practices. At present, the responsibility of preservation depends altogether on the contemporary Kodava people who are aware of the fact that, though European agency influenced them to reconnect with the land, in the present decolonial Kodava society, preservation of trails and trail-making would mean more indigenisation. For

---

62   Katarina Saltzman, one of the editors of the present volume, referred to my idea of preservation and suggested that it is the trail-making that ought to be preserved.
63   Shaw, Herman, and Dobbs, 'Encountering Indigeneity', 267; Sundberg, 'Decolonizing Posthumanist Geographies', 34–35.

environmental researchers, ethnographers, anthropologists and practitioners, it is essential to consider a deeper ecological and bioregional inquiry, drawing on diverse disciplinary sources such as the indigenous histories and geographies of place, nature, culture, art, folklore and ethnobotany to develop a decolonial interdisciplinary approach to disseminate knowledge about the preservation of trails and trail-making. Focusing on Kodagu's walked environments, the central research of this essay opens such interdisciplinary dialogues that may help preserve trails and trail-making in world indigenous environments.

Acknowledgements

Field research was made possible by grants from the Central University of Tamil Nadu, India. I thank C.P. Belliappa for the photographs from his coffee estate in Kodagu; and Rani Machaiah for being a wonderful friend and host, and for keeping her plantation gates always open for my fieldwork. I particularly thank Daniele Valisena for his constructive comments on my earlier draft; Karen Lykke Syse, Paul Readman, Laura M.F. Bertens for stimulating discussions on land and landscape in the virtual workshop; Susanne Österlund-Pötzsch for her exciting questions about the types of Kodagu walking practices; and Ben Anderson for his interest in Indian Land Rights. I am grateful to the editors for their comments on earlier versions of this essay. Any errors of interpretation are my own.

Bibliography

Allan, K., *Explorations in Classical Sociological Theory: Seeing the Social World* (Thousand Oaks, CA: Pine Forge Press, 2010).

Appadurai, A., *Modernity at Large: Cultural Dimensions of Globalisation* (New York: Routledge, 1996).

Berg, P., and R.F. Dasmann. 'Reinhabiting California', in P. Berg (ed.), *Reinhabiting a Separate Country: A Bioregional Anthology of Northern California*, pp. 217–20 (San Francisco, CA: Planet Drum Foundation, 1978).

Berg. P. (ed.), *Reinhabiting a Separate Country: A Bioregional Anthology of Northern California* (San Francisco: Planet Drum Foundation, 1978).

Biénabe, E., 'Towards Biodiverse Agricultural Systems: Reflecting on the Technological, Social, and Institutional Changes at Stake', in H. Étienne (ed.), *Cultivating Biodiversity to Transform Agriculture*, pp. 221–61 (New York: Springer, 2013).

Bourdieu, P., *Outline of a Theory of Practice*, trans. R. Nice (Cambridge: Cambridge University Press, 1977).

Castree, N., *Nature* (Oxon: Routledge, 2005).

Chisholm, H., 'Coorg', in H. Chisholm (ed.) *Encyclopædia Britannica*, Vol. 7, pp. 91–92 (Cambridge: Cambridge University Press, 1922).

11. Kodagu Walking Trails and Indigenous Heritage Making

Clifford, J., *Returns: Becoming Indigenous in the Twenty-First Century* (Cambridge, MA: Harvard University Press, 2013).

Cosgrove, D.E., *Social Formation and Symbolic Landscape* (Madison, Wisconsin: The University of Wisconsin Press, 1984).

Cresswell, T., *Place: A Short Introduction* (Oxford: Blackwell Publishing, 2004).

Gadgil, M. and R. Guha. *This Fissured Land: An Ecological History of India* (New Delhi: Oxford University Press, 2013).

Grenier, L., *Working with Traditional Knowledge: A Guide for Researchers* (Ottawa, Canada: International Development Research Center, 1998).

Guiașu, R.C. *Non-Native Species and Their Role in the Environment: The Need for a Broader Perspective* (Leiden: Brill, 2016).

Habgood, J., *The Concept of Nature* (London: Darton, Longman & Todd, 2002).

Harrison, R., *Heritage: Critical Approaches* (New York: Routledge, 2013).

Harrison, R. and C. Sterling (eds), *Deterritorializing the Future: Heritage in, of and after the Anthropocene* (London: Open Humanities Press, 2020).

Ingold, T., 'Hunting and Gathering as Ways of Perceiving the Environment', in R.F. Ellen and K. Fukui (eds), *Redefining Nature: Ecology, Culture, and Domestication*, pp. 117–55 (Oxford: Berg, 1996).

Ingold, T. and J.L. Vergunst, 'Introduction', in T. Ingold and J.L. Vergunst (eds), *Ways of Walking: Ethnography and Practice on Foot*, pp. 1–20 (Hampshire: Ashgate, 2008).

Innocenti, P., *Cultural Networks in Migrating Heritage: Intersecting Theories and Practices across Europe* (Surrey: Ashgate Publishing Limited, 2015).

Kadambi, K., 'Short Note on the Evergreen Forests of Mysore State', in *Proceedings of the all-India Tropical Moist Evergreen Forest Study Tour and Symposium*, pp. 99–113 (Dehra Dun: Forest Research Institute, 1960).

Karnataka Department of State Education Research and Training, 'Kodagu District Profile', http://dsert.kar.nic.in/dietwebsite/kodagu/DistrictProfile.htm (accessed 24 July 2021).

Lane, R.J., 'Karl Marx: The Commodity', in R.J. Lane (ed.), *Global Literary Theory: An Anthology*, pp. 319–28 (London: Routledge, 2013).

Lewis, R., *Mysore and Coorg from the Inscriptions* (New Delhi: Asian Educational Services, 1909).

Mandanna, S., *Tiger Hills: A Novel* (New Delhi: Penguin Group, 2010).

Marx, K. and F. Engels, *The Communist Manifesto*, trans. by S. Moore (London: Penguin, 1988).

McCook, S., 'Global Rust Belt: *Hemileia vastatrix* and the Ecological Integration of World Coffee Production since 1850', *Journal of Global History* 1 (2) (2006): 177–95. doi:10.1017/S174002280600012X

McGinnis, M.V., 'A Rehearsal to Bioregionalism', in M.V. McGinnis (ed.), *Bioregionalism*, pp. 1–10 (London: Routledge, 1999).

Mendis, G.C., *Ceylon Under the British* (New Delhi: Asian Educational Services, 2005).

Morse, L.E., J.M. Swearingen and J.M. Randall, 'Defining what is Native', in B-H. Lore and M. Wilson (eds), *Roadside Use of Native Plants*, pp. 12–14 (Washington, D.C: Island Press, 2000).

Nambisan, K., *The Scent of Pepper* (New Delhi: Penguin Group India, 1996).

Neilson, J., 'Environmental Governance in the Coffee Forests of Kodagu, South

India', *Transforming Cultures* **3** (1) (2008): 185–95. https://doi.org/10.5130/tfc.v3i1.680

Olwig, K.R., 'Performing on the Landscape Versus Doing Landscape: Perambulatory Practice, Sight and the Sense of Belonging', in T. Ingold and J.L. Vergunst (eds), *Ways of Walking: Ethnography and Practice on Foot*, pp. 81–92 (Hampshire: Ashgate, 2008).

Pavord, A., *Landskipping: Painters, Ploughmen and Places* (London: Bloomsbury, 2016).

Poonacha, V., '*Rites de Passage* of Matrescence and Social Construction of Motherhood: Coorgs in South India', *Economic and Political Weekly* **32** (3) (1997): 101–10. http://www.jstor.org/stable/4404990

Proctor, J., 'Notes on Evergreen Rainforests of Karnataka State, South-West India', *The Commonwealth Forestry Review* **65** (3) (1986): 227–32. https://www.jstor.org/stable/i40096676

Ramachandrachar, D.B., *Kodagu Folk and Tribal Culture* (Madras: Institute of Asian Studies, 1991).

Reid, J., *Sorcerers and Healing Spirits: Continuity and Change in an Aboriginal Medical System* (Canberra: Australian National University Press, 1983).

Richter, G., *Gazetteer of Coorg: Natural Features of the Country and the Social and Political Condition of its Inhabitants* (Mysore, Karnataka: [Mysore Government Press 1870] Delhi: Low Price Publications, 2010).

Rosaldo, R., *Culture and Truth: The Remaking of Social Analysis* (Boston: Beacon: 1993).

Sale, K., *Dwellers in the Land: The Bioregional Vision* (Athens, Georgia: The University of Georgia Press, 2000).

Shaw, W.S., R.D.K. Herman and G.R. Dobbs, 'Encountering Indigeneity: Re-imagining and Decolonising Geography', *Geografiska Annaler: Series B, Human Geography* **88** (3) (2006): 267–76. https://doi.org/10.1111/j.1468-0459.2006.00220.x.

Shiva, V., 'Globalisation and the War against Farmers and the Land', in N. Wirbza (ed.), *The Essential Agrarian Reader*, pp. 121–39 (Berkeley: Counterpoint, 2003).

Snyder, G., *A Place in Space: Ethics, Aesthetics, and Watersheds* (Berkeley, California: Counterpoint, 1995).

Snyder, G., *The Practice of the Wild* (New York: North Point Press, 1990).

Snyder, G., 'Reinhabitation', *Manoa* **25** (1) (2013): 44–48. https://doi.org/10.1353/man.2013.0010

Sörlin, S., 'Monument and Memory: Landscape Imagery and the Articulation Theory', *Worldviews: Environment, Culture, Religion* **2** (1998): 269–79. https://www.jstor.org/stable/43809666

Sörlin, S. and N. Wormbs. 'Environing Technologies: A Theory of Making Environment', *History & Technology* **34** (2) (2018): 101–25. https://www.tandfonline.com/doi/full/10.1080/07341512.2018.1548066

Stilgoe, J.R., *What is Landscape?* (Cambridge, Massachusetts: The MIT Press, 2015).

Sundberg, J., 'Decolonizing Posthumanist Geographies', *Cultural Geographies* **21** (1) (2014): 33–47. https://doi.org/10.1177%2F1474474013486067

Syse, K.V.L. From Land Use to Landscape: A Cultural History of Conflict and Consensus in Argyll 1945–2005 (Ph.D. Dissertation, University of Oslo, 2008).

Thayer, R.L. Jr, *LifePlace: Bioregional Thought and Practice* (Oakland, California: University of California Press, 2003).

Thurston, E., *The Madras Presidency with Mysore, Coorg, and the Associate States* (London: Cambridge University Press, 1913).

11. Kodagu Walking Trails and Indigenous Heritage Making

Tuck-Po, L., 'Before a Step Too Far: Walking with Batek Hunter-Gatherers in the Forests of Pahang, Malaysia', in T. Ingold and J.L. Vergunst (eds), *Ways of Walking: Ethnography and Practice on Foot*, pp. 21–34 (Hampshire: Ashgate, 2008).

Varutti, M. 'Crafting Heritage: Artisans and the Making of Indigenous Heritage in Contemporary Taiwan', *International Journal of Heritage Studies* **21** (10) (2015): 1–14. https://doi.org/10.1080/13527258.2015.1050055

Warde, P., L. Robin and S. Sörlin, *The Environment: A History of the Idea* (Baltimore, MD: Johns Hopkins University Press, 2018).

Wenzlhuemer, R., *From Coffee to Tea Cultivation in Ceylon, 1880–1900: An Economic and Social History* (Leiden: Brill, 2008).

Williams, R., *Keywords: A Vocabulary of Culture and Society* (Oxford: Oxford University Press, 1983).

Wirzba, N. (ed.), *The Essential Agrarian Reader* (Berkeley: Counterpoint, 2003).

CHAPTER 12.

HERITAGE TRAILS: PATHWAYS TO SUSTAINABLE DEVELOPMENT GOALS

John Martin, Joane Serrano, Jacqueline Nowakowski and Dominica Williamson

Introduction

Cultural and natural heritage are widely acknowledged as important components in the achievement of Sustainable Development Goals (SDGs, Figure 1). The 2030 Agenda for Sustainable Development, adopted by all United Nations Member States in 2015, provides a framework for improving health and education, reducing inequality and spurring economic growth, all while tackling climate change and working to preserve our oceans and forests. At its heart are the seventeen SDGs, which are seen as a call for action.[1]

Heritage, tangible and intangible, is increasingly being identified as a unique asset that can support the sustainable regeneration of rural areas across the world. Trails are often at the heart of the areas being investigated or developed. For example, the Lake District National Park and UNESCO World Heritage Site in the UK hosts 3,203 kilometres of accessible trails within an area of 2,300 square kilometres.[2] These features are generally identified as tourist or health and wellbeing assets and the true culture values are often overlooked. Complex relationships exist between protecting natural capital and local economic, social and cultural values.

The specialised agency of the United Nations, UNESCO (United Nations Educational, Scientific and Cultural Organization) has overlaid designations such a Global Geopark and World Heritage Site (WHS) upon landscape containing thousands of kilometres of trails. UNESCO define the designations as follows: 'Global Geoparks: are single, unified geographical areas where sites and landscapes of international geological significance are managed with a holistic concept of protection, education and sustainable development'; 'World Heritage Sites are designated because of their cultural, historical, scientific or other

---

1 UN, The 17 Sustainable Development Goals.
2 Lake District National Park, Web page.

12. Heritage Trails

form of significance. The sites are judged to contain "cultural and natural heritage around the world considered to be of outstanding value to humanity'".[3]

UNESCO sees the key role Global Geoparks play in contributing to the SDGs at a landscape scale. This chapter reviews the following SDGs at a fine level, examining them in the context of trails and movement heritage:

SDG 2: End hunger, achieve food security and improved nutrition and promote sustainable agriculture;
SDG3: Ensure healthy lives and promote well-being for all at all ages;
SDG4: Ensure inclusive and equitable quality education and promote lifelong learning opportunities for all;
SDG11: Make cities and human settlements inclusive, safe, resilient and sustainable;
SDG13: Take urgent action to combat climate change and its impacts;
SDG15: Protect, restore and promote sustainable use of terrestrial ecosystems, sustainably manage forests, combat desertification, and halt and reverse land degradation and halt biodiversity loss.

It focuses on heritage trails as pathways to SDGs, and explores the lessons learnt from communities using the trails as well as the benefits of the trails. It aims to illustrate how narrative trails and mobility are used to make sense of how heritage sites are socially and culturally constructed and how cultural values relate to SDGs. 'Heritage trail' is framed here both as a tool to reach or experience heritage and as part of the heritage in and of itself. Trails play an important role in understanding the landscape as they cut across environmental silos of agriculture, forestry, fisheries and conservation.

Methodology

This chapter employs a narrative trail of two heritage areas – the Ifugao Rice Terraces landscape in the Philippines and Carwynnen Quoit, Cornwall, UK. The case study areas were selected to highlight that, although the areas have very different landscape and cultures, the method used draws out common issues between the areas. The first landscape has been designated as a WHS by the UNESCO. The second landscape lies adjacent to a WHS.

The method used defines trails as paths taken by the researchers and communities as they make sense of their lived experiences in the two landscapes, one in the Philippines and the other in the UK. The first case study is a single walker navigating the trails and connecting SDGs with the experience gained

[3] UNESCO, Global Geoparks, Biosphere Reserves and World Heritage Sites: A Complete Picture

John Martin, Joane Serrano, Jacqueline Nowakowski and Dominica Williamson

Figure 1.

Sustainable Development Goals. Source: United Nations.[4]

from moving through the landscape. The second is a group of co-walkers who are embracing trails as method to connect with SDGs in order to set goals and address the language of policymakers to access support for Heritage (tangible and intangible).

Case study areas

The Case of Ifugao, Philippines

Ifugao is one of the provinces in the Cordillera Administrative Region (CAR), located in the northern portion of the Philippines. Situated within the Cordillera mountain range, it covers a total area of approximately 263,000 hectares (see Figure 2). The Ifugao province is generally mountainous, characterised by thick forests, creeks and streams that are tributaries to major rivers. Ifugao is a landlocked province with eleven municipalities and home to an approximate population of 208,000 people who mostly belong to the Ifugao ethnic group.[5] The term Ifugao also refers to an ethnolinguistic group that is subdivided into five major classifications, namely the *Tuwali, Ayangan, Kalanguya, Hapuwan* and *Henanga*.[6]

---

4   UN, The 17 Sustainable Development Goals.
5   PSA, Philippine Statistics Authority. Ifugao quickstat.
6   Fagyan et al., 'Pamaptok Tuh Binoltan Caring for our Heritage'.

12. Heritage Trails

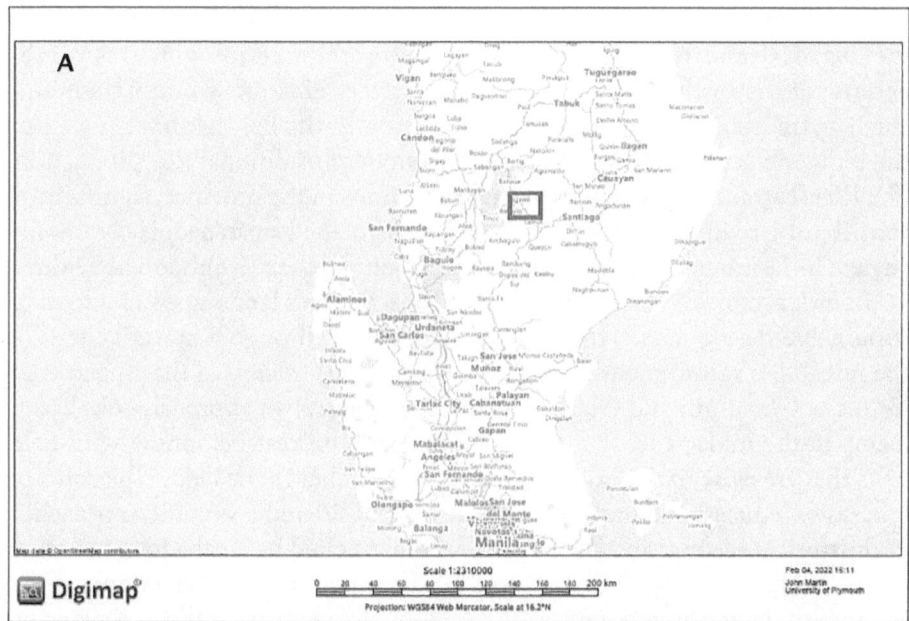

Figure 2 (A and B).

Location of Ifugao. Source: [A, top] Digimaps © Crown copyright and database rights 2022 Ordnance Survey (100025252); [B, bottom] Google maps.

John Martin, Joane Serrano, Jacqueline Nowakowski and Dominica Williamson

The Ifugao landscape is dominated by terraced rice fields, which are known as the Ifugao Rice Terraces. There are five rice terrace clusters recognised as WHSs because of their cultural importance. The terraces illustrate cultural traditions (such as traditional farming practices, beliefs and rituals) that have sustained the indigenous community's communal system of traditional rice production. The Rice Terraces are the main tourist attractions in the province, significantly contributing to its economy. Aside from tourism, the Ifugao people commonly engage in farming, wood carving, and weaving for their livelihood activities.

In order to make sense of the Ifugao Rice Terraces landscape in relation to sustainable development, this case was examined through a narrative trail of the researcher's movement along the physical trails (*dalan*) of the Ifugao Rice Terraces. Clandinin and Connely's concept of narrative approach talks about 'being in the midst' and of storying the research process beginning with field texts that are close to the experience of the researcher in the field.[7] The concept focuses on educational narrative, which was considered a suitable approach.

Historical accounts by Beyer[8] and Barton[9] as cited by Acabado[10] show that the rice terraces are over 2,000 years old and were carved out of the slopes of the mountains. However, a recent study by Acabado[11] shows that the rice terracing systems in the Philippine Cordillera were a response to Spanish colonialism, which makes the Ifugao Rice Terraces only around 500 years old. According to Acabado,[12] the rapid expansion of the terrace system is a result of the migration of people from the lowlands to avoid the Spaniards. Archaeological evidence suggests that, during the Spanish colonial period, there was an active and intense contact with lowland and other highland groups and that the rapid social differentiation coincided with the arrival of the Spaniards in the northern part of Luzon.[13] Acabado[14] noted the intense alteration and modification of the marginal landscape to suit rice production, a practice which he noted is viewed by anthropologists as 'complementary'. The intensification of the landscape meant lowland groups migrated to the highlands, and the development

---

7   Constantino, 'Review of Narrative Inquiry: Experience and Story in Qualitative Research; Personalizing Evaluation'.
8   Beyer, *The Origins and History of the Philippine Rice Terraces*.
9   Barton, *Ifugao Law*.
10 Acabado, 'Antiquity, Archaeological Processes and Highland Adaptation: The Ifugao Rice Terraces'.
11 Ibid.
12 Ibid.
13 Acabado et al., 'Ifugao Archaeology: Collaborative and Indigenous Archaeology in the Northern Philippines'.
14 Acabado, 'Antiquity, Archaeological Processes and Highland Adaptation'.

12. Heritage Trails

of social organisation and agricultural technological systems. The movements are assumed in this paper as the beginning of trails, which shaped the Ifugao Rice Terraces landscape.

The narrative trail described focuses on the relationships between cultural and natural landscapes, co-evolution across generations of human-nature, development of agricultural systems, and social organisation. It focuses on a physical trail or *dalan* of the Open Air Museum at the Nagacadan Rice Terraces, which is considered a living cultural landscape by UNESCO.[15] This assumption challenges the notion that trails 'themselves are *not heritage, but merely infrastructure* that enable transport, access and mobility between heritage sites', as put forward in the introductory chapter to this volume. The *dalan* of the rice terraces form part of the terrace structure as they serve as the top layer of the terraces. The capping stones on the top layer are usually the flattest and widest stones to provide a finished look to the stone wall and to serve as footpaths.[16] The rice terraces are structured in such a way that each terrace has stone walls that stabilise the soil surface, prevent soil erosion, conserve soil fertility, retain water and serve as trails for humans as they tend to the planted rice in their *payoh* (rice fields) which partly addresses SDG 15, as, through this structure, degraded land and soil are restored and reduce degradation of natural habitats. A typical Ifugao community, shown in Figures 3 and 4, consists of a *muyung* (community forest or private woodlot), *payoh* (rice terraces) and *boble* (village/residential area).

These components of an Ifugao community are harmoniously interrelated – the *muyung* provides water and nutrients to the *payoh*, which provides harvest to residents in the *boble*, and the residents must tend and maintain the *muyung* and *payoh* the whole year round for food production and biodiversity.[17] If one walks the trails from the *muyung* to the *payoh* and to the *boble*, one sees the harmonious relationship between humans and nature as evidenced by rich biodiversity, the abundant rice field cultivated by the Ifugaos and the unique irrigation system engineered by the Ifugao ancestors, a co-evolution across generations that results in a sustainable community that addresses SDG 11. This sustainable system passed on by the Ifugaos from generation to generation safeguards its cultural and natural heritage.

---

15 UNESCO, Global Geoparks, Biosphere Reserves and World Heritage Sites: A Complete Picture.
16 Ngohahyon, I'fugao Indigenous Knowledge (IK) Workbook'.
17 Serrano et al., 'Re(connecting) with the Ifugao Rice Terraces as a Socio-ecological Production Landscape Through Youth Capacity Building and Exchange Programs: A Conservation and Sustainable Development Approach'.

Figure 3.

Batad Ifugao community, showing forest, rice field and village. Source: Y4IRT project.

Figure 4.

Youths walking the Nagacadan Ifugao Rice Terraces trails. Source: Y4IRT project.

12. Heritage Trails

The Open Air museum (see Figure 5) was initiated by the Local Government Unit (LGU) of Kiangan, Ifugao to address the problem of abandoned rice terraces caused by outmigration. The Museum aims to showcase Ifugao cultural and natural heritage, revive the production of *Tinawon* or Ifugao heirloom rice and promote tourism as a source of livelihood for the Ifugaos. According to Nasser,[18] sustainable tourism can have positive attributes for conservation and development in heritage places, but it is important to be strategic, especially in management of cultural resources, the uses and activities that the built environment sustains and the integration of these factors with the sociocultural needs of the local community. The revival of *Tinawon* or Ifugao heirloom rice also addresses SDG 2, which targets increasing the agricultural productivity of indigenous peoples, but at the same time maintains ecosystem as well as genetic diversity and benefits from associated traditional knowledge. As one walks the trails, one can feel the ancestral character of the landscape through the worn out tracks that emerged as the terraces were constructed by the Ifugao ancestors and sustained across generations. These trails are unique in the sense that they serve as the top layer of the stone walls of the terraces, which were constructed through an ancient Ifugao engineering system considered advanced for that period. These trails served as pathways for the farmers and community members to traverse the rice terraces. The trails now allow visitors to experience this living cultural heritage as they see and encounter Ifugao farmers working on their rice paddies and members of Ifugao families helping out. This shows the strong family bond and kinship that is inherent in Ifugao culture, which is also one of the reasons why the sustainable practices of the communities are preserved as they are passed on from generation to generation.

In the kinship structure, the oldest offspring, regardless of sex, inherits the rice terraces, thus ensuring their continuity and sustainability. As one continues along the trails, one encounters traditional Ifugao houses or *baleh* that showcase artefacts such as hand-woven fabrics and wood carvings. Tourists can also experience first-hand Ifugao culture through rice planting and harvesting as well as Ifugao festivals and culture such as Ifugao dances and *Hudhud*.

Ifugao is also recognised for its rich oral literary traditions. Their *Hudhud* chants are considered one of the 11 Masterpieces of the Oral and Intangible Heritage of Humanity, with UNESCO formally inscribing it as Intangible Cultural Heritage in 2008. The Ifugao tugging rituals and games, locally called *Punnuk*, were also inscribed in the UNESCO Intangible Cultural Heritage List

---

18 Nasser, 'Planning for Urban Heritage Places: Reconciling Conservation, Tourism, and Sustainable Development'.

Figure 5.

One of the stops in the Open Air Museum is a traditional Ifugao house containing artefacts. Source: Y4IRT project.

in 2015. Through initiatives like the Open Air museum, indigenous knowledge is preserved. This rich cultural heritage is a result of Ifugao's commitment to harnessing its indigenous knowledge, which helps address SDG 4's target of ensuring that learners acquire knowledge and skills needed to promote sustainable development, including appreciation of cultural diversity and of culture's contribution to sustainable development. Zhang and Nakagawa,[19] in their review of literature,[20] noted that there are times when indigenous knowledge is observed to perform even better than modern science and technology.

The *muyung* system helps address SDG 13 since it is considered to be an effective climate change mitigation strategy by enabling greater carbon se-

---

19 Zhang and Nakagawa, 'Validation of Indigenous Knowledge for Disaster Resilience against River Flooding and Bank Erosion'.
20 Rasid and Paul, 'Flood Problems in Bangladesh: Is There an Indigenous Solution'; Zhang et al., 'Three Dimensional Flow around Bandal-like Structure's; Basak et al., 'Impacts of Floods on Forest Trees and Their Coping Strategies in Bangladesh'; Dewan, 'Societal Impacts and Vulnerability to Floods in Bangladesh and Nepal'.

questration, degradation prevention and co-benefit creation.[21] The continued maintenance of the *muyung* system ensures a safe habitat for various species which fosters biodiversity and addresses SDG 15.

In recent years, the movements of Ifugao youths as they out-migrate have created a different kind of trail. As Avta et al.[22] have noted, the mounting economic pressure on Ifugao communities results in societal changes that alter the perception of the youth about the importance of traditional practices, threatening the long-term sustainability of the Ifugao rice terraces. As fewer youths walk in the trails, there is no assurance that the Ifugao rice terraces will be sustained, and thus the co-evolution and harmonious relationship between human and nature will be threatened.

The Case of Carwynnen Quoit, Cornwall, Uk

This case study offers reflections on experiences obtained through the regaining of Carwynnen Quoit, and how this is being taken forward in seeking out the early medieval chapel of Fenton-Ia. By carrying out participatory walks and facilitating intergenerational exchange of memory and knowledge whilst reclaiming trails through walking and re-walking, movement heritage has become a vital tool in the restoration of these tangible heritage sites. For instance, the walks were chosen through democratic discussion and joint exploration, through the act of mapmaking and actually walking the land, ideas of what is heritage, and where is our heritage came to the fore. Different voices and interests shaped ideas and elicited questions like 'Where has that well gone?' 'Why has that pathway become blocked?' 'Why do we not know these and their Cornish names?' People wanted to find answers, and these answers were more often than not gained by re-walking the walks. The ambition of the project was that, through the restoration of these two sites, trails would be and are being remapped into memories and onto paper. As part of this mapping, SDG goals were mapped. This process has helped the realisation that movement heritage is a framework which can bring people powerfully together, to re-find and preserve heritage.

Since 2006 the village of Troon (see Figure 6) has been a designated area within the Cornish Mining WHS. Like many of the small industrial hamlets in the Cornwall Mining WHS, Troon's low terraced streets of small miners' houses reveal its industrial history, born out of metal mining in the eighteenth

---

21 Avtar et al., REDD+ Implementation in Community-Based Muyong Forest Management in Ifugao, Philippines.
22 Ibid.

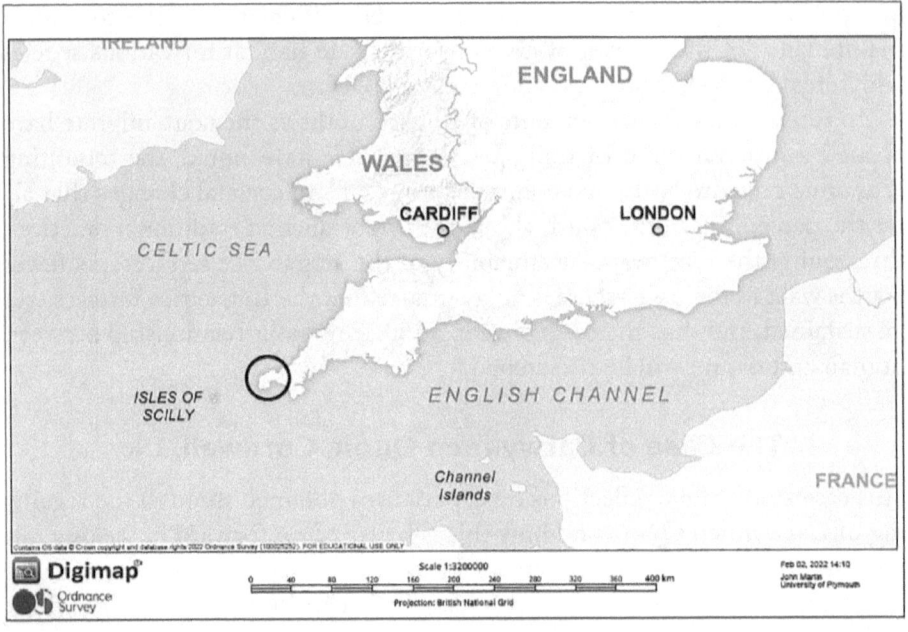

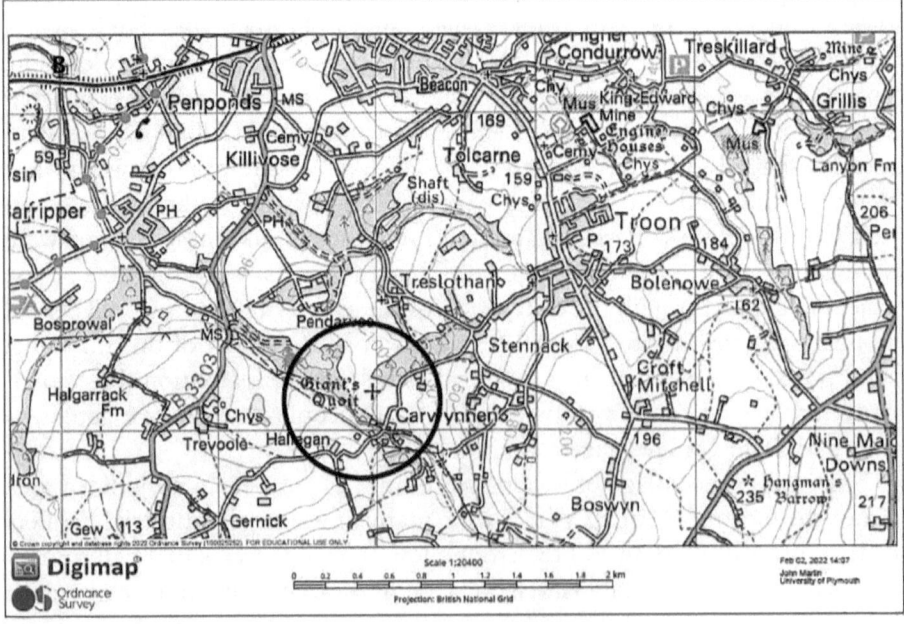

Figure 6 (A and B).

Location of Carwynnen Quoit. Source (both maps): Digimaps © Crown copyright and database rights 2022 Ordnance Survey (100025252).

12. Heritage Trails

and nineteenth centuries. On one side of the village lies King Edward Mine, with its scatter of chimneys and engine houses, which now show cases a unique collection of tin processing machinery to visitors. This open-air museum provides a documented account of the mining heritage. However, Troon's history is far older than the historic mining.[23] Although now there is little evidence of its much earlier human story, yet hidden to the south and west lie the sites Carwynnen Quoit and Fenton-Ia.

Regaining Carwynnen Quoit

In the early nineteenth century, Carwynnen Quoit stood on the edge of rough moorland within view of the Pendarves' family mansion. A major re-landscaping project in the mid-nineteenth century by Edward Pendarves removed the medieval farming hamlets and their small stony fields as well as the medieval settlement and pilgrimage chapel of Treslothan. The latter were replaced by a new church, schoolhouse and rectory, all built in Early English Gothic revival style rather than drawing on the Cornish vernacular[24]. The change marked a new chapter in Troon's history. Small fields were amalgamated into much larger ones, extensive woodland plantations were established and access to the landscape changed. The quoit withstood all these changes and it's likely that folk-memory, fear and superstition played its part in keeping the monument standing.[25] Nowakowski and Gossip,[26] suggest that when the monument fell down in the nineteenth century it was restored by the landowner because it had the power to exert and strengthen superstition and fear of retribution. The power of the ancestors was a palpable reaction in the Victorian past as it was in medieval and earlier times.

This 4,000-year-old monument is an open chamber which comprises a granite capstone finally balanced on three upright stones. In the late 1960s, the monument fell down and for many years laid abandoned. In 2009 The Sustainable Trust sought to bring it back to life with an ambition to drive social sustainability and shine a light on Troon's earlier pre-industrial human story.

The archaeological project provided an opportunity for hands-on participation and wider social inclusion which meant that everyone who had an interest and felt inspired by the common goal of *helping the Giants Quoit back on its feet* was invited to join the team and take part in events. The events inspired

---

23 Thomas, *Mrs Percival's Endowed School At Penponds and Treslothan Camborne 1761 to 1876*.
24 Ibid.; Nowakowski and Gossip, 'Regaining a Lost Cromlech: the Excavation and Restoration of Carwynnen Quoit'.
25 Lukis and Borlase, Prehistoric Monuments of the British Isles
26 Nowakowski and Gossip, 'Regaining a Lost Cromlech'.

experimental archaeology, artwork, poetry, storytelling and memory sharing with the free exchange of practical skills and local knowledge. Guided walks and talks in and around the site and landscape took place throughout the project. The spirit and whole ethos of the project was openness and the mission to share, collate and spread knowledge.

Through this outdoor educational experience, which immersed itself in the past and current use of the landscape, the project was reaching SDG 4 and 11. It has promoted intergenerational learning and restored pride back into the community. This has been achieved through multiple forms of local engagement, from welcoming local schools to walk through the woods down to the site and take part in workshops on site, to talking with the elders of Troon. The elders shared their memories of the Quoit, as well as helping to organise walks to and from the site by assisting a videographer to walk and record sights, places and observations along the way that meant something to them from their childhood. Such activities were archived on a website (www.giantsquoit.org) and a webapp (www.thegiantoutdoors.com).

Through these activities, the community gained pride in their local cultural heritage, looked with fresh eyes at their landscape and felt that something lost had been regained. As a consequence, their place in the world feels restored, not just the site, their pathways are back on the map. This sense of empowerment gives confidence that the future of their place is more resilient. This is evidenced with a conversation between elder Wendy Penberthy(WP) and Dominica Williamson (DW)

> WP: 'Well it is something to look at, isn't it! And I mean now we know some of the history of it, which years ago we didn't know.'
> DW: 'So when you were young you had no idea it was an ancient site?',
> WP 'No, no'
> DW: 'And what about Carn Brea hill?' [Neolithic site in the nearby town excavated 1970–73]
> WP: 'No, no. Carn Brea was Carn Brea.'

Revealing trails to and from the site

Beneath the soil a stone pavement and the socket holes for the stone supports were discovered; this meant that the original footprint of the stone chamber, was there for all to see (see Figure 7). The objects, broken bits of beach flints and pots made from gabbroic clays from the Lizard showed that people had travelled distances to visit the quoit and throughout different periods of time.[27]

---

27   Ibid.

12. Heritage Trails

Figure 7.

Finding quoit pathways. Left: Celebratory dance under the restored quoit. Right: The discovered Neolithic stone pavement, 2014. Source: The Sustainable Trust.

This helps to identify the heritage of the pathways leading to the site. The physical unearthing and revealing of this stone pavement was a visceral experience which gave everyone an immediate direct link to the very distant past; this physical pathway fired imaginations about how the Quoit stood in the landscape many thousands of years ago and how ancient communities approached it. The monument was aligned up towards a hidden valley and this sparked discussions about processions, pilgrimage and its place-making and landmarking role in the wider landscape. A viewshed analysis of the area links it to archaeologically important distant hills such as Carn Brea (HeritageGATEWAY)[28] and the seascapes of Gwithian Beach and St Ives Bay, which has encouraged further walking and finding of past routes to and from the site. The linking of these sites matched the elders' memories of storied-place.[29]

Placing the capstone back on its supports was an awesome spectacle and witnessed by over 600 people who gathered on Midsummer Day in 2014. Many people offered their memories and anecdotes about this place; all have contributed to a treasure chest of stories and memories unique to this place and now part of this monument's unique history and biography. These archived memories held on the project's web (www.thegiantoutdoors.com), are actively listened to and continue to form ideas on how cultural heritage can help this community to become healthier and more resilient through cultural herit-

---

28 Cornwall Heritage Gateway, Carn Brea – Neolithic tor Enclosure, Iron Age Hillfort.
29 Thomas, 'Elder Talks about the Gorsedh at Carwynnen Quoit in 1948'.

age. SDG 3 is therefore met, as healthy lives have been promoted for all ages through community engagement. Wellbeing has been enhanced and teamwork championed through the act of walking to and from the Quoit.

When Carwynnen Quoit was built, it must have been realised as a major community venture and undertaking, so it is striking to realise that the synergies of the original project must align with present-day experience.

Securing access on foot to Carywnnen Quoit

Until 2014, Carywnnen Quoit had stood on private land with no formal public access. Walks to the site were, however possible, through the woods down from Treslothan and it is from these starting places that the importance of the trails and their 'own' heritage began to emerge. Memories and stories shared with the restoration project revealed that, despite difficulties of access, the monument has always been part of Troon's wider mental map of the village, highlighting the fact that the pathways are part of the heritage of the area and recorded in community memories. The restoration of the monument also restored its accessibility, as The Sustainable Trust gained the funding to purchase the field and restore it to public greenspace.

Such feelings were no doubt affirmed by other special events such as the Cornish Gorsedd gathering held there in September 1948,[30] which strengthened the need for walking access. This annual gathering holds great distinction in celebrating Cornish language and identity. The procession of bards started from the heart of Troon down through the wooded lanes and on to the Quoit, with many local people joining in. These types of public events revealed just how much the Troon community identified the Quoit not only as a legitimate part of their village landscape and recognised its special significance.

In summary, there are no formal heritage trails created to the Quoit but four walking trails to the site have been co-developed and formalised with the Ramblers Association. These make up the future development of community engagement and interest. As a place and local landmark, the Quoit's restoration has ensured its rightful place back in the living village and landscape, the place is now open to all and the field is available for community gatherings and events. This has enabled SDG 11 to be met: a new green space has been created for the local community but also other communities nearby and further afield can visit and understand this often negated part of Cornwall which is actually rich in ancient, medieval and mining history.[31] The successful restoration of

---

30   Gorsedh Kernow, 'Gorsedh Kernow returns to Carwynnen / Gorsedh Kernow a dhehwel dhe Gerwynnen 1948–2015'.
31   CRCC, Rural Deprivation in Cornwall and the Isles of Scilly: Profile Report for Troon

12. Heritage Trails

the Quoit starts to fulfil the ambitions defined by the SDGs outlined, due to this leveraging of cultural heritage value in a rural landscape.

Seeking out Fenton-Ia

Since 2019 there has been a series of walks to further explore the surrounding area of the Quoit. Small groups (8–30) of walkers (co-developers), starting out from Camborne or from Treslothan chapel, have set out on local pathways to explore the trails already created for the Quoit restoration project.[32] The highly immersive events have shaped ambitions to build on the project's legacy with a focus on another unique place associated with Troon's early history – the medieval chapel site of Fenton-Ia which lies hidden under vegetation in the Reens (see Figure 8). The walks have involved pilgrimage routes, multi faith walkers, different disciplines/vocations, intergenerational exchanges and different rapid mapmaking activities.

On arrival at Fenton-Ia, mapmaking activities have often happened (see Figure 9). Examples of these are participatory mapmaking based on sensory ethnographic work;[33] plant recording and foraging; searching for medieval holy wells and identifying water catchment spots and, importantly, Green Map making activity based on matching Green Map Icon to SDGs;[34] as well as research into understanding historical common land use. Acknowledging that everyone's view of heritage is different, due to their values and backgrounds,[35] everyone was and is welcome and all knowledge/questions and ideas were and are encouraged, no matter how seemingly insignificant. Philip Hills (walking activist) captures the experience of walking with the group:

> When people come together to walk we bring our unconscious selves as much as our conscious selves; our memories inspired, we reflect and we meet in a state of increased awareness. Individually we take away with us those collective memories, new perceptions that enlighten our humanity. And such places as Reen Woods enhance and instill a reverence of care and compassion in our relationships with ourselves and nature.

---

32 Williamson, 'Shells, Wells, Saints and Saunterings: A Movement Heritage Project Centred on Fenton-Ia'.
33 Pink, *Doing Sensory Ethnography*; Martin et al., 'Development of the My Cult-Rural Toolkit'.
34 Green Map, Green Map System: Green Map System encourages communities to gather data about their green facilities and spaces. The result of this community process-orientated mapping is that Green Maps typically present a variety of ecology-related points of interest on a map. The points use a globally shared set of Green Map Icons, which have been co-produced through facilitation with Green Map System. In 2017 Green Map System matched the icons to the UN's 17 Goals for sustainable development. Both sets of icons are on the organisation's open mapping platform, and this enables Green Mapmakers to readily chart their work against this global framework.
35 Eugster, 'Evolution of the Heritage Areas Movement'.

Figure 8.

Walking the trail by Fenton-Ia in the Reens. Top: Guest co-developer Brother Petroc stands on the Reens in the summer, reaching the highest point of the trail. Bottom: Co-developers stall on the trail during the autumn to laugh over stories while some observe fungi and the view, 2021. Source: Peter Dewhurst.

12. Heritage Trails

Figure 9.

Participatory map-making by Fenton-Ia in the Reens. Top: Mapping of land use within the different categories of common land created by Philip Hills. Bottom: Using Green Map Icons to map movement heritage findings, 2021. Source: Andy Hughes.

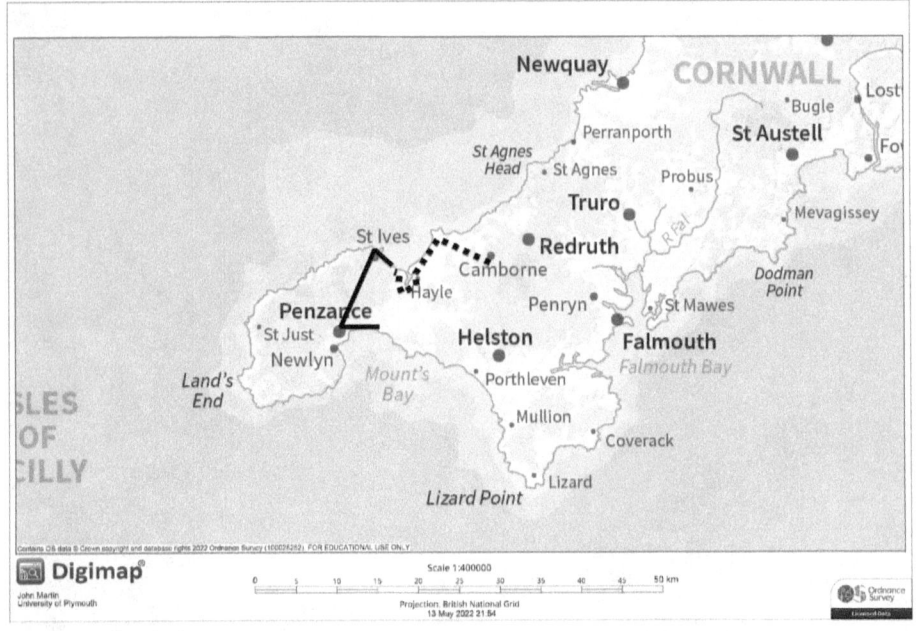

Figure 10.

Location of Pilgrimage line. Source: Digimaps © Crown copyright and database rights 2022 Ordnance Survey (100025252).

The medieval chapel site of Fenton-Ia would have been a distinctive feature within the early Christian landscapes of south-western Britain. These early sites lay on medieval paths and routeways deep into the Cornish countryside, many of which have disappeared. The chapel of Fenton-Ia is currently an overgrown ruin. It is difficult to access; however the woods and deep valley are visited by local walkers as well as young people from the village. Walkers must navigate ploughed fields, Cornish tumbled down hedges and rocky paths with carpets of leaves and flora.

While on private land, the chapel and the Reens have a history of public access within living memory. Present ambitions to make Fenton-Ia more visible and accessible are focused on safeguarding the site so it is not lost.

Fenton-Ia lies on the pilgrimage trail of St Michael. This informal trail is relatively unknown. Hence making the presence and knowledge of Fenton-Ia more visible in the landscape would bring wider community benefits. A future aspiration would be to connect Fenton-Ia to a long-distance walk to St Michael's Mount in West Cornwall as well as up from Troon to Gwithian and St Gothian's chapel, following the valley to the north Cornish coast (see Figure 10).

12. Heritage Trails

This would restore its original purpose as well as open up otherwise hidden places within the rural landscape which lie off the official historic trails connected with the adjacent WHS.

Over the past century, the landscape of the Reens has been accessible as a shared community asset, has played a greater part in the making of cherished childhood and family memories and like a local touchstone forged a sense of place for the people of Troon.[36] Public accessibility to Fenton-Ia by re-marking/making trails will ensure a deeper connection to place for present and future generations in Troon and will help display feelings of pride which can be harnessed in celebrating and promoting a shared cultural heritage. Providing access to all types of people and access to lesser-known heritage trails through this process of co-developing walks and restoration projects deepens and propels movement heritage as it builds on heritage justice.[37]

Conclusion

These two case studies highlight how trails are more than just infrastructural features that link destinations. They suggest that, as people walk the trails, whether they are members of the local community or researchers, they connect with the heritage of the trail and surrounding landscape but also more importantly with their sense of place and heritage. Evidence from the case studies also suggests that the trails underpin the sense of place, as walkers often relate trails to sensory experiences, memories and associations that are key elements of a sense of place. Issues such as land ownership, land use and time depth (heritage) are encountered by walkers, which again clearly influence the sense of place. Hence understanding the trails as an essential element of 'place making', rather than just a feature, allows a better understanding of the value and management of the natural and heritage landscape.

In addition, the 'place making' element of trails enables a deeper understanding of sustainability to be gained. The case studies show that walking trails in landscapes highlight the interconnectedness of histories, different habitats and socio-economic factors but also fragmentation, especially when walking pathways with people who hold indigenous knowledge. The loss of intangible and tangible heritage becomes clear when searching out a track, the state of a trail often indicating the status of heritage on route. Audible and visible indicators are experienced in real time on foot and in different seasons: flora

---

36 Penberthy, 'Elder Talks about Access to the landscape at the Reens'. Oral history video
37 Fincham, 'Justice and the Cultural Heritage Movement: Using Environmental Justice to Appraise Art and Antiquities Disputes'.

and fauna decline become sharpened when walking with elders as does the status of heritage. The socio-economic disparities are arguably more apparent too. The researcher or community sees who is walking and who has access to trails and who is living amongst trails. As walking progresses, further mobility questions will be explored, as suggested by Salazar.[38] Through the case studies, it can be seen that the act of walking trails deals with cultural values and so with the three pillars of sustainability – the complex interplay of social, economic and environmental knowledge is being formed and reformed; the past, the present and future often intertwined but also made more explicit through this embodied trailed process.

For instance, the Cornish walks have continued since the Covid-19 lockdowns and, as the co-walkers moved through post Brexit farmland, the values attached to the farmed landscape, largely geared to a supermarket all-year round demand economy, became disrupted. People's relationship with the access to the countryside is also in flux. A mound of dumped daffodils and the sight of a glut of wasted courgettes thrown against a Cornish stone hedge through farmland, both recorded during the post-lockdown walks, are reminders that attitudes to economy and land are changing and that, as we move forwards in this post-pandemic world, sustainability and valuing localism become even more pressing. This in turn may lead to more serious land use changes.

In the case of the Ifugao Rice Terraces, because of the Covid-19 lockdowns, many Ifugaos have been displaced. Many locals rely heavily on tourism as one of their sources of income. With the restrictions in tourism, other industries are also affected such as woodcarving, weaving and other crafts and specialities. These changes in economic activities also influence the nature of walks across the trails, with fewer foreign visitors and more locals accessing the trails. Access to the trails by locals come in various forms, from interacting with nature as a form of recreation, to family visits reinforcing strong Ifugao bonds and kinship, to doing work facilitated by the government, i.e. repairs to rice terraces.

The SDG diagrammatic language as used by Green Map System is an accessible way to introduce people to sustainable goal making. This can be enhanced with the use of Green Maps Icons.[39] The case studies illustrate the intangible and tangible heritage link to the trails and how these can support the understanding and successful achievement of SDGs. If walkers analyse, pool and gain support for their activities, SDGs act can act as a tool by which the community, designated landscapes and the researcher community can perhaps

---

38   Salazar, 'Key Figures of Mobility: An Introduction'.
39   Green Map, Green Map System.

12. Heritage Trails

sharpen their walking efforts and understand their landscape and trails better. It is also a way for funders to see that they can add value to trail restoration projects, showing that the concept of movement heritage provides a practical framework in which to work and that SDGs can therefore be harnessed from the bottom up and top down through the act of heritage trails.

Bibliography

Acabado, S., *Antiquity, Archaeological Processes, and Highland Adaptation: The Ifugao Rice Terraces*, (Manila: Ateneo de Manila University Press, 2015).

Acabado, S., M. Martin and F. Datar, 'Ifugao Archaeology: Collaborative and Indigenous Archaeology in the Northern Philippines', *Advances in Archaeological Practice* **5** (1) (2017): 1–11. doi:10.1017/aap.2016.7

Avtar, R., K. Tsusaka and S. Herath, 'REDD+ Implementation in Community-Based Muyong Forest Management in Ifugao, Philippines', *Land* **8** (2019): 164. https://doi.org/10.3390/land8110164

Barton, R., *Ifugao Law*. University of California Publications in American Archaeology and Ethnology, Vol. 15. (Berkeley and Los Angeles: University of California Press, 1919).

Basak, S.R., A.C. Basak and M.A. Rahman, 'Impacts of Floods on Forest Trees and Their Coping Strategies in Bangladesh', *Weather and Climate Extremes* **7** (2015): 43–48.

Beyer, H.O., *The Origins and History of the Philippine Rice Terraces*, Proceedings of the Eight Pacific Science Congress, 1953 (National Research Council of the Philippines).

Cornwall Heritage Gateway, Carn Brea – Neolithic tor Enclosure, Iron Age Hillfort (2012): https://www.heritagegateway.org.uk/gateway/Results_Single.aspx?uid=MCO37&resourceID=1020 (accessed 20 December 2021).

Costantino, T.E. 'Review of *Narrative Inquiry: Experience and Story in Qualitative Research; Personalizing Evaluation*, by D. J. Clandinin, F. M. Connelly, & S. Kushner', *Visual Arts Research* **27** (1) (2001): 107–11.

CRCC, Rural Deprivation in Cornwall and the Isles of Scilly: Profile Report for Troon (2009): http://www.cornwallrcc.co.uk/downloads/ruraldeprivation/west/troon_profile.pdf accessed 2021 (accessed 12 November 2021).

Dewan, T.H., 'Societal Impacts and Vulnerability to Floods in Bangladesh and Nepal', *Weather and Climate Extremes* **7** (2015): 36–42.

Eugster, J. 'Evolution of the Heritage Areas Movement', The George Wright Forum **20** (2) (2003): 50–59, Published by the George Wright Society.

Fagyan, V.G., M.L. de Castro, F. Basilio, V. Dulinayan, R. Baliao and N. Dimog, '*Pamaptok Tuh Binoltan* Caring for our Heritage', in S. Ngohayon, M. Delson-Fang-Asan and L. Dulawan (eds), *Voices from the Cordilleras Guardians of the Forest, Steward of the Land* (Philippines : Cover and Pages Publishing, Inc., 2015).

Fincham, D. 'Justice and the Cultural Heritage Movement: Using Environmental Justice to Appraise Art and Antiquities Disputes', *Virginia Journal of Social Policy and Law* (2012): 43.

Gorsedh Kernow, 'Gorsedh Kernow returns to Carwynnen / Gorsedh Kernow a dhehwel dhe Gerwynnen 1948–2015' (2015): https://gorsedhkernow.org.uk (accessed 1 November 2021).

Green Map, Green Map System (2017): https://www.greenmap.org/stories/sdgs-icons-un-sustainable-development-goals-green-map-icons/201 (accessed 1 December 2021).

Lake District National Park (2022): https://www.lakedistrict.gov.uk/visiting/things-to-do/rowupdates
(accessed 1 February 2022)

Lukis, W.C. and W.C. Borlase, *Prehistoric Monuments of the British Isles*, Vol. 1 (Published by London; Society of Antiquaries;, 1885).

Martin, J., D. Williamson, K. Łucznik andd J.A. Guy, 'Development of the My Cult-Rural Toolkit', *Sustainability* **13** (2021): 7128. https://doi.org/10.3390/su13137128

Nasser, N. 'Planning for Urban Heritage Places: Reconciling Conservation, Tourism, and Sustainable Development', *Journal of Planning Literature* **17** (4) (2003) https://doi.org/10.1177/0885412203017004001

Ngohahyon, S., A. Alcayna, M. Babang, M. Labhat and G. Valdez, *Ifugao Indigenous Knowledge (IK) Workbook* (Philippines: Ifugao State University, 2011).

Nowakowski, J. and J. Gossip, 'Regaining a Lost Cromlech: the Excavation and Restoration of Carwynnen Quoit, Camborne, Cornwall 2009–2014' (in press).

Penberthy, W., Elder talks about access to the landscape at the Reens. Oral history video (2020): http://thegiantoutdoors.com/#st_ia_chapel The Reens and St Ia Chapel (accessed 12 November 2021).

Pink, S., *Doing Sensory Ethnography* (London: Sage, 2015)

PSA, Philippine Statistics Authority. Ifugao quickstat – June 2018. https://psa.gov.ph/content/ifugao-quickstat-june-2018 (accessed 10 September 2021).

Rasid, H. and B.K. Paul, 'Flood Problems in Bangladesh: Is There an Indigenous Solution', *Environmental Management* **11** (1987): 155–73. http://dx.doi.org/10.1007/BF01867195

Salazar, N.B., 'Key Figures of Mobility: An Introduction', *Social Anthropology* **25** (1) (2017): 5–12.

Serrano, J.V., A.V. Lacaste, J.A.C. Belegal, C. Dl. Habito, and … V.K.B. Alag, 'Re(connecting) with the Ifugao Rice Terraces as a Socio-ecological Production Landscape Through Youth Capacity Building and Exchange Programs: A Conservation and Sustainable Development Approach', in UNU-IAS and IGES (eds), *Satoyama Initiative Thematic Review*, Vol. 5, pp. 149–68 (United Nations University, 2019). https://collections.unu.edu/eserv/UNU:7506/SITR_vol5_fullset_web.pdf

Thomas, A.C., *Christian Antiquities of Camborne, Warne, St Austell, Cornwall* (1967). Available online: https://map.cornwall.gov.uk/reports_cornwall_industrial_settlements_initiative/Troon.pdf (accessed 29 November 2021).

Thomas, A.C., *Mrs Percival's Endowed School At Penponds and Treslothan Camborne 1761 to 1876* (Institute of Cornish Studies, 1982).

Thomas, D., Elder talks about the Gorsedh at Carwynnen Quoit in 1948. (2020) Oral history video: http://thegiantoutdoors.com/#the_gorsedh_kernow (accessed 2 January 2022).

United Nations, *The 17 Sustainable Development Goals* (2015): THE 17 GOALS | Sustainable Development (un.org) (accessed 1 September 2021).

UNESCO, 'Global Geoparks, Biosphere Reserves and World Heritage Sites: A Complete Picture' (2021): https://en.unesco.org/global-geoparks (accessed 1 September 2021).

Williamson, D., 'Shells, Wells, Saints and Saunterings: A Movement Heritage Project Centred on

12. Heritage Trails

Fenton-Ia' (2022): https://padlet.com/dom108/bku5ybw111kj7yt4 (accessed 2 January 2022).

Zhang, H., Y. Nakagawa, K. Baba, K. Kawaike and H. Teraguchi, 'Three Dimensional Flow around Bandal-like Structures', *Annual Journal of Hydraulic Engineering – JSCE* **54** (2010): 175–80.

Zhang, H. and Y. Nakagawa, 'Validation of Indigenous Knowledge for Disaster Resilience against River Flooding and Bank Erosion', in R. Shaw et al. (eds), *Science and Technology in Disaster Risk Reduction in Asia*, pp. 55–76 (Cambridge, MA: Academic Press, 2018). https://doi.org/10.1016/B978-0-12-812711-7.00005-5

CHAPTER 13.

WALKING ON *TERRILS*. RUDERAL ECOLOGIES AND TOXIC HERITAGE IN WALLONIA, BELGIUM.

Daniele Valisena

Introduction

September, the time when autumn starts to colour up Wallonia. It was my second time in Liège, where I was concluding fieldwork in preparation for my Ph.D. dissertation. Leaving my room in the Carré neighbourhood, I got on a train at the Saint-Lambert station, right behind the Prince-Bishops' palace. It was a short ride to my destination in Jemeppe – ten minutes or so – but, after passing the last underground gallery, I gaped at the vision that presented itself. Exiting the train at Seraing Bridge (*Pont-de-Seraing*) I had entered the industrial *banlieue* of Liège, this in-between place sitting with one foot in the industrial revolution epoch and the other in the present post-industrial time. Rows of two-storied terraced houses with bricks blackened by centuries of air pollution and consumed by time, contoured the Meuse riverbeds on both sides. Clunky elevated conveyor belts and pipelines ran above the houses and crossed the river from side to side, connecting run-down giant steelworks and blast furnaces, most of which had been shut down or half-demolished. The sugary smell of gas and old car engines combined with the stinging odour of smelting iron that drifted from a nearby factory in Tilleur, one of the few still operating. The white soggy shade enveloping the sky was a familiar one to me: it was the same mixture of soot, humidity and smog that covers the sky where I grew up on the Po Plain in Northern Italy. It was at this moment in Liège that I began my walking ethnography through Pays de Terril Landscape Park.

Terril[1] is a French-Walloon word indicating a spoil tip made of coal waste and the various refuse materials resulting from coal mining. Currently over 1,200 *terrils* exist in Southern Belgium.[2] Together, these constitute a human-made

---

1   Pronounced *tèrrí* or *terríl*, the term has long since been widely used in all French-speaking countries, testifying to the inherent connection between Walloon culture and coal extraction.

2   According to the official survey conducted by Région Wallonie in 1995 there are over 1,200 terrils in Wallonia. Some 339 of those are considered as *terrils majeurs* and were produced between 1840

13. Walking on Terrils

Figure 1.

Liège-Seraing from one of the paths climbing Terril du Gosson, 2015. Source: Veronica Mecchia.

hill range that traverses three countries from Nord-Pas-de-Calais in France, through Belgium and proceeding into Germany towards the Ruhr basin. These coal slag heaps, born as landfills, are physical leftovers of the mining epoque and embody memories, stories, and affections pertaining to a prosperous industrial past that is now dead. At the same time, *terrils* are ecologically-rich sites where foreign and local species dwell in new lively ecologies concurring in the transformation of those wasted environments.[3] From frogs to dragonflies, rare flowers and exotic plants, as well as warblers and nesting birds, *terrils* constitute some of the most important reservoirs for biodiversity in Belgium. *Terrils*' twofold significance makes them a perfect example of 'post-industrial scars', to use the expression of heritage studies scholar Anna Storm.[4]

Trailing on the material and cultural topology of *terrils*, in this short essay I perform a geo-historical walk of Terril du Gosson, in the former industrial

and 1984. This calculation does not include French or German spoil tips. See *Moniteur Belge*, 22 June 1995, Arrêté du Gouvernement Wallon fixant la classification des terrils, 16 Mars 1995.

[3] In many cases, *terrils* have now turned into Sites of High Biodiversity Interest, *Site de Grand Intérêt Biologique*, according to the official Belgian classification.

[4] Storm *Post-Industrial Landscape Scars*.

periphery of Liège. With geo-historical walking, I intend an itinerant topian[5] trajectory meant to unfold and interpret the layered meanings and stories of *terrils* as storied-places.[6] By bodily sensing and moving through Walloon spoil tips, I conduct a walking ethnography of place, focusing on the interplay between industrialisation, ruderal ecologies, material heritage and memories that characterises the socio-environmental configuration of present-day Wallonia. Drawing upon Don Mitchell,[7] I adopt a layered theory of landscape meant to uncover the stories and the ecological relationships that produced *terrils* as geological, geographical and historical assemblages.[8] Focusing on *terrils* allows the retracing of the geo-historical, ecological and toxic legacy of coal extraction and industrialisation which produced *terrils* as material heritage and make this lineage visible. On the other hand, as Van Dooren and Rose wrote,[9] 'stories and meanings are not just layered over a pre-existing landscape. Instead, stories emerge from and impact upon the ways in which places come to be', and from the relationship between past layered histories and living multispecies actors and their ecologies. In order to narratively entangle this meshwork of histories, stories and ecologies, I use my walking body as an itinerant and sensorial instrument meant to retrace past, present and future geo-historical trajectories within *terrils*. Walking becomes a geo-historical practice[10] in that bodily itinerant topographies can elicit memories, sensorial knowledge and conflicting stories, and retrace ecological constellations through the unfolding of the various layered-stories hidden in the hybrid environments I traverse. By retracing with my own walking body the various itinerant trajectories that signified and made the industrial landscape of Wallonia, I render manifest the import as movement heritage[11] of those hu-

---

5   With 'topian trajectory', Tim Ingold refers to the place-making quality that a wayfarer exerts with his own bodily trajectory through the act of walking. This topian (or place-making) quality of walking originates from the active engagement that attentive wayfarers continually establish with the environment. Wayfarers might benefit from some kind of preemptive geographical, historical, and geological (geo-historical) knowledge of place. As a result, such preemptive knowledge turns into a geo-historical compass that guides geo-historical wayfarers and elicit their itinerant art of attentiveness. See Ingold *Lines*; Van Dooren, Kirksey and Münster 'Multispecies Studies: Cultivating Arts of Attentiveness'.

6   Van Dooren and Rose 'Storied-Places in a Multispecies City'; Van Dooren and Rose 'Lively Ethnography: Storying Animist Worlds'.

7   Mitchell *The Lie of the Land*.

8   Valisena 'Coal Lives'.

9   Van Dooren and Rose 'Storied-Places in a Multispecies City', 2.

10 de Certeau *L'invention du quotidien. 1. Arts de faire*; Canovi 'Pensare nella territorialità, abitare nel paesaggio'.

11 Svensson, Sörlin, and Salzman in the *Introduction* to this book, 'Pathways to the Trail'.

13. Walking on Terrils

man, non-human and more-than-human environments. Retracing past and present geo-historical trajectories and stories by moving through the environment is a form of performative rememorating, one that makes visible new and old relationalities and meanings in the landscape(s) we traverse.

Being alone, my geo-historical walking exploration turned out to be more focused on the ecological, bodily and non-human dimensions of the experience. Yet, as an abled white Italian man, my walking body did not simply unearth the manifold stories ensnared within the landscape, but rather brought about a particular account through my own 'politics, cultures, histories, and lived experiences',[12] which define my positionality and my relationship with the environment I traverse. Surely one could unearth other stories from the same landscape, for instance by focusing on environmental justice[13] or on environmental history of migration.[14] As Tim Ingold wrote: 'in storytelling and travelling, one remembers as one goes along'[15] and retraces new and old trajectories within landscapes.

Given their material, ecological and cultural import, spoil tips as hybrid socio-natures are nodal points both as place-making entities and as material and memorial legacy of industrialisation, hence constituting key signifiers in the coal-driven ecology of Wallonia. Nonetheless, as ruderal ecologies scholar Bettina Stoetzer has recently suggested, former wasted sites 'are not passive environments, but developed their own lives'.[16] Ruderal ecologies (from the Latin term *rudus*, meaning rubble) refers to ecosystems which prosper in severely polluted and disturbed environments. Following critical heritage scholar Caitlin DeSilvey,[17] I argue that ruderal thinking, with its focus on instability, ruination, decay and disturbed environment as the norm, might work as a socio-ecological compass for building new senses of place in Wallonia. Walking on *terrils*, one might equally encounter coal, mining debris, industrial wreckage, toxic waste, alien flowers, rare butterflies, *lieux de mémoire*, touristic trails, forgotten stories of labour and pieces of art. By retracing the geological, geographical and historical trajectories that produced such hybrid

---

12   Macpherson 'Walking Methods in Landscape Research', 426.
13   Thoreau and Zimmer 'Croisières toxiques'.
14   While in this essay I describe a solitary walking exploration, there exists a quite lively group of walkers and even sailors who are collectively exploring the former industrial landscape of Wallonia. See, for instance, La boucle noir (https://www.cm-tourisme.be/en/a/gr412-boucle-noire) in Charleroi, or the Croisières Toxiques group in Liège (https://www.entonnoir.org/2019/10/24/croisiere-toxique-derniere-edition/). See also Valisena 'Coal Lives'.
15   Ingold *Lines*, p. 17.
16   Stoetzer 'Ruderal Ecologies', 304.
17   DeSilvey 'Ruderal Heritage', 294–98.

ecologies, I want to unfold the ways in which industrialisation and its ruderal ecologies historically signified the environment, the history and the material memory of Wallonia through the concurrence of human and non-human storied-places.[18]

Drawing from environmental humanities, environmental history and memory and heritage studies, this text wants to contribute to the ongoing discussion on critical heritage studies arguing for a historical understanding of (post-)industrialisation that includes ruination, ecological continuities and toxicity as key elements of the Anthropocene. In that respect, I contend that geo-historical walking explorations can nurture new arts of noticing[19] and foster new senses of place through multispecies encounters and ruderal thinking.[20]

Walking towards Terril du Gosson, Liège

From the mining town of Jemeppe it was hard to miss the spoil tip. Terril du Gosson dominates the industrial *banlieue* beyond the Meuse river bend southwest of Liège. Standing 165 metres above sea level, Gosson's green silhouette is sullied now and then by a few dark spots. Sitting between the municipalities of Seraing and Saint-Nicolas, the coal waste hill is actually composed of two spoil tips, Gosson 1 and Gosson 2. The *terril* originated from the slag and debris produced by Société Anonyme Charbonnière de Gosson-Lagasse, which was active between 1877 and 1966. As a consequence of such long coaling activity, the Gosson area now gathers some 9,500 m^3 of coal mining and industrial waste, occupying an area of 41.2 ha.[21] On my way towards the hill I encountered several mining rowhouses (*corons*), many of which hosted well-kept vegetable gardens in which I could recognise big orange pumpkins, tomatoes, lettuce, and even some free-roaming chickens. Vegetable gardens are important places in many working-class communities around the world,[22] and especially in mining communities.[23] In the case of former industrial areas, vegetable gardens often play the function of an identity reservoir signified with different cultural and ecological practices, through which communities can re-appropriate their own environments and inscribe new relationships with the

---

18 Van Dooren and Rose 'Storied-Places in a Multispecies City'.
19 Tsing *The Mushroom at the End of the World*.
20 DeSilvey 'Ruderal Heritage'.
21 Fédération Wallonie-Bruxelles, La biodiversité en Wallonie, Sites de Grand Intérêt Biologique, Terril du Gosson, http://biodiversite.wallonie.be/fr/1854-terril-du-gosson.html?IDD=251659927&IDC=1881.
22 Cabedoce and Pierson 'Cent ans d'histoire des jardins ouvriers 1896–1996'.
23 Valisena 'Coal Lives', 297–302.

13. Walking on Terrils

land.²⁴ In the hamlet of Mabotte, those vegetables were literally growing less than a couple of metres away from the coal slag heap flanks, and the number of animals that thrived around them were eating grass and seeds which had probably mixed with and spurred from the coal waste. It was an uncomfortable thought to hold on to. On my way to the top of Gosson, I also crossed the old railway line, now turned into a cycling and pedestrian lane as part of a transnational touristic route of industrial heritage.²⁵ As in the case of cities like Paris, Stockholm and Berlin, former industrial infrastructures had been turned into a greening pathway within the heart of the spent industrial sprawl. While the architectures of the area were a living testimony of nineteenth-century's coal workers' towns, the public memory of the place also seemed to be filled with it through the toponymy: rue des Mineurs, rue Germinal; everything spoke of the legacy of coal mining. These ghostly trajectories are part of the material and cultural heritage of coal in Wallonia. These coal-produced assemblages are embedded traces – the mobility heritage – of the flows of materials, commodities, energy and infrastructure that informed and signified the landscape of Southern Belgium throughout the Modern era.

I reached the spoil tip's base level by walking a good twenty minutes north past Seraing Bridge. White birches were holding onto the hill flanks together with ruptureworts and coltsfoots. The orderly trees stood next to one other almost identical in height. I figured it was probably a sign of the fact that they had been planted in the same period of time as part of the *terril* reforestation project between the 1960s and 1980s.²⁶ Many of the *terrils* that were not worth exploiting are thus now covered in greenery and, in the case of Liège province, are part of the *Route des Terrils*: a transnational touristic and natural route which unites former Belgian and German coal basins (Aachen).

Standing at the feet of Gosson was Maison des Terrils, a coalmining museum (*Centre d'interprétation du site minier de Saint-Nicolas*) inaugurated in 2008. Maison des Terrils occupies the old building of the Gosson mine's *lavoir*, the washing place where coal was cleaned right after pitmen dug it out from mine shafts. The museum hosts a *bistrot*, a small but well-equipped environmental library and a tourist centre from where excursionists and conservationists begin their trips in the natural park. The most striking feature of the centre is the *salle des pendus*, the changing room of the old coalmine. *Pendus*

---

24   Valisena and Armiero, 'Coal Lives'.
25   Actually, two touristic routes merged there: the Liège province-based *Route du Feu* (the fire route) and the European Route of Industrial Heritage. See https://www.laroutedufeu.be/la-route-du-feu.php; https://www.erih.net/.
26   Raes and Boostels *Terrils*.

Daniele Valisena

Figure 2.

Terril du Gosson, 2015. Source: Veronica Mecchia.

in French-Walloon mining jargon both refers to coat hangers and to hanged men, perfectly embodying the perilousness and precariousness of coalminers' lives. The same precarious condition now survives in the environment of the landscape park. *Terrils* are very unstable techno-natural assemblages. The coal and industrial waste that constitutes the large part of spoil tips' mass is held together artificially through the reforestation projects that interested Wallonia from the 1960s onwards. Wind action, massive rains, the cumulation of snow or simply walking in the wrong place might result in landslides modifying the unstable structure of the hills. Perhaps the roots of the orderly birch trees I noticed were holding the whole hill flank. Also, the very ground on which Wallonia stands is very unsteady. As I discovered during an interview with some second-generation Italians living in Saint-Nicolas,[27] it is not uncommon for new-build houses or roads to suddenly collapse into one of the thousands of abandoned underground mine shafts piercing the region.

---

27   Interview with Anna Gagliardelli and William Ferrari, Saint-Nicolas 5 March 2018. Valisena 'Coal Lives', 302–03.

13. Walking on Terrils

Exiting the visitor center, Gosson 2 hillside emerged in the background. A big part of the hillslope was completely free of any verdure, revealing a black ruler-cut lining of seemingly burnt material. In fact, the *terril* is still burning: the internal combustion of coal-waste materials has not ceased yet, nor will it for the next few decades. *Terrils* internal temperature can reach up to 1,000°C and 1,300°C at their apex.[28] As a result, *terrils*' surfaces have a slightly higher temperature than the surrounding areas and a different microclimate. As one of the visitor centre's workers told me, it was not uncommon to see *terrils* smoking, especially in the early years after their formation. In the nearby French mining region of Nord-Pas-de-Calais, it has been calculated that one out of three *terrils* used to combust, as did many others in Polish Silesia, Russia, Portugal and Wallonia.[29] The same process can even lead to the bursting of spoil tips. In 1975 *terril 6* in Calon-Ricouart in Nord-Pas-de-Calais exploded, provoking the fall of 11,000 m³ of burning schists and ashes onto the nearby mining town, killing five Polish workers and injuring of four more.[30]

In front of the *lavoir* some scrap metal had been repurposed to make a dragonfly sculpture, whose legs turned into a rusty rail track with a few wagons crammed full of coal briquettes. The sculpture symbolised the ecological continuity between the coaling landscape and the natural park environment. This would not be the only dragonfly I encountered that day. Right behind the *lavoir* I found two trails. They were carved out in the coal rubble of Gosson hill. For the first time I could clearly see the layers of coal waste the spoil tip was made from. A reshuffling of geological and human history materialised right in front of me. Fossil plants dating back to the carboniferous era had been dug out from the coal seams and the shale layers in which they had been enclosed for millions of years. Mixed with those, I could see the orange shades of baked shale minerals, glass-like elements and pyrite nodules scattered along the slope. The complex aesthetic of the minerals signalled different temporal and material stages of the elements' transformation inside the hill. The presence of old cracked bricks and scraps of metal tools signalled the transient moment in which the industries of Southern Belgium were massively excavating coal through the labour of thousands of mine workers.

Together with the spoil tip's flank, I saw layers of soil and wasting materials with roots, blades of grass and flowers. Among those I spotted quite a large plant

---

28   Thierry et al. 'La combustion des *terrils*', 23–25.
29   Ibid.
30   See Archives de l'INA, Médiathèque, 'Explosion d'un terril à Calonne-Ricouart, FR3, Journal Télévisé, 26 août 1975', https://fresques.ina.fr/memoires-de-mines/fiche-media/Mineur00151/explosion-d-un-terril-a-calonne-ricouart.html.

with yellow flowers, reminding me of a big yellow daisy. The name of the plant was *seneçon du Cap*, or *Senecio* — as one of the guides working at the museum kindly told me. *Senecio inaequidens* had travelled across oceans and continents to put its roots in that greening landfill. The common name for *Senecio inaequidens* is in fact *Seneçon du Cap* in reference to its origin in the area of Cape Town, in South Africa. The alien plant is believed to have travelled to Belgium via the fleece of South African sheep that used to be worked by local textile industries. Furthermore, *Senecio inaequidens* is toxic to most insects, herbivores and even to many native plants in Wallonia. Coal miners were not the only migrants in the layered history of Wallonia, nor were humans the only species exposed to the *longue durée* of the coaling business' hazards.

Continuing my walk, I was enticed by the numerous brown and black spots that I encountered now and then along the trailside. Was this coal or not? How could I tell? Deceived by my sight, I opted for my other senses, starting from smell. Yes, it smelled like wet coal. But the more I touched the fine grains of coal sand emerging amid the grass, the less I was sure about the odour of coal. The fact that I wanted to find coal might have worked as an unconscious form of autosuggestion, sabotaging my genuine sensorial experience of place. But was it really so? Does such a genuine sensing of place exist at all? Of course not. As environmental historians such as Bill Cronon[31] have rightfully pointed out, the environments we live, dwell and move in are always social and natural, cultural and material at once. Although coal was clearly part of the materials composing *terril* du Gosson, it amounted to only around twenty per cent, as I later discovered.[32] Most of what I saw, smelled and touched was thus elicited by what I wanted to find. While the geo-historical layers that make *terrils* – as well as any other landscape – are the result of complex geographical, geological and historical processes which are immediately there to be seen, smelled, touched and traversed by all wayfarers, there is an inherently subjective component to those landscapes. In fact, as per all sites of memory, the post-industrial scars[33] embedded in *terrils* might elicit very different memories, senses and significance depending on the relationship between those who are traversing those sites and the stories they convey. It is not so much a matter of singular or collective experiences, but rather a question of positionality towards the memories unearthed through the geo-historical wayfaring.

Reaching the plateau that divided the two peaks of the *terril*, the black

---

31   Cronon *Uncommon Ground*.
32   Bedoret et al. 'Le site du Gosson'.
33   Storm, *Post-Industrial Landscape Scars*.

13. Walking on Terrils

surface of the hill became more distinct. Human and animal footprints marked the path, as well as the chirping of Eurasian blue tits (*mésange bleue*) and blue-winged grasshoppers. Following the trail, I could not help but notice many little balls of dung. Trying to avoid stepping on those, I began to ponder about what kind of animals could have produced them. A hare maybe? A little dog? For sure it was not a horse. After spending a good five minutes trying to figure it out, I heard a bleating, or at least, I thought I did. In the very instant that I heard the animal's sound I realised that the trail was fringed by a fence, a long stockade that encircled all the table land. A few seconds later, I saw them. '*Moutons!*' I said out loud. Sheep here? Yes, they were. Those were Luciano Casanova's sheep. Casanova is an *enfant de mine*, a mine's son as they are called in Wallonia. His father came to the Walloon coalfields in the late 1940s following the 'men in exchange for coal' agreement between Italy and Belgium that brought over 300,000 Italians to Southern Belgium.[34] In 2008, the municipality of Saint-Nicolas asked him to bring his sheep onto the *terril* as part of its transformation into a natural park and, since then, the flock has been spending half the year up there. Thinking about the example of *seneçon du Cap*, I began to wonder about the kind of plants that Luciano's sheep could eat. Apart from poisonous flowers, even normal grass and other weeds would probably be filled with toxins dug under the surface of the *terril*. Covering a landfill with greenery did not suffice to remediate centuries of highly toxic wasting practices. That hay might be dangerous to sheep, as it probably was for many other animals living in that deceptively green wasteland ecology. Under a shallow layer of organic soil and plants sit tons of scrap materials, heavy metals, spent oils, industrial soot, rubber, ashes and various other wastes. While metallophyte and non-native plants such as *seneçon du Cap* and their companion insect species prosper in such a disturbed ruderal environment, *milieux calaminaires* (calamine landscapes) are hazardous for many other native species. Green *terrils* did not mean salubrious parks for all species.

Leaving Casanova's sheep behind, I reached the peak of the spoil tip. Before me, lying at the centre of a stage-like plateau, another giant dragonfly installation was dominating the flat top of the hill. The body of the sculpture was built from the same shale stone that for millions of years enfolded the coal deposits that made the economic fortune of the region. The black crag of the half-forested coal slagheap still rimmed the schist stones, as it did underground for millennia. The four wings of the insect worked as rainwater recovery pools, forming four small ponds in which the pale blue sky was reflecting. Frogs and dragonflies

---

34   Morelli 'L'appel à la main d'oeuvre italienne pour les charbonnages'; Valisena 'Coal Lives'.

Figure 3.

'Libellule' by Daniel Steenhaut, Terril du Gosson, 2015. Photograph by Daniele Valisena.

crowded the sculpture, using the gutters as watery roads that disappeared within the edgings of the tableland. Slowly moving around the edge of the cliff separating the dragonfly from the promontory, my gaze encompassed the city of Liège: its southern industrial hub strewn around the industrial periphery of Seraing; the coal power plants and the rusty blast furnaces of Ougrée; the Ardenne forest before the bend of the Meuse river and the medieval old town; and the forested *terrils* that intersperse the scattered mining towns encircling the *métropole*. There it was, the socio-ecology of coal that is Wallonia.[35] I was still there, in the industrial hub of Liège, but I was also somewhere else, in a natural park with sheep and alien metallophyte species thriving in the polluted terrain, and somewhere else once more, in a continuously transforming environment on the top of a burning landfill.

35 Valisena 'Coal Lives'.

13. Walking on Terrils

Conclusions

The ruderal ecology of post-industrial Wallonia is not the result of a free re-appropriation by nature of the former coaling region of Belgium. Rather, it is a material testimony of the long-lasting heritage of the toxic legacy of industrial activity, even in a time when industrial buildings and infrastructures are mostly crumbling away in Wallonia. Furthermore, this process is not happening aside from human control, since most *terrils* have been purposely reforested by the same coaling companies that created them as landfills, or by Région Wallonie, mostly to improve the *terrils*' structural stability and for aesthetic reasons. What I find extremely valuable in those liminal places is that they never tell a single story, but rather embody the often-contradictory storying of very different actors, be they capitalist coaling companies, mine workers, sheep, ruderal flora blooming in toxic (for humans) environments, or insects engaged in a lively relation with those species and otherwise wasted places. The heterogeneity and the richness of ruderal ecologies is given by the crossing of different trajectories of inhabiting these liminal spaces which have been left behind by capitalist exploitation as wasted areas. But in order for these places to work as a sort of compasses in the history of industrialisation, they need to account for all the processes and the materials that produced them. By relating with the various narrative, material and ecological layers that compose *terrils*, it might be possible to apprehend the complex entanglement of those changing landscapes in their lively relation with their industrial past and their ruderal present. By bodily immersing oneself in an itinerant exchange with *terrils*, the geo-historical assemblage of industrial and post-industrial history might acquire a new meaning, one where non-human actors and more-than-human affections and stories matter.

Understanding post-industrial sites in less anthropocentric ways does not imply revaluating positively the meaning of toxicity and capitalist-driven extractivist activities. The repercussions of slow violence,[36] in its unfolding between invisibility and temporal discrepancies, still emanates from the legacy of industrial activities in Wallonia. Although some species might prosper in such polluted environments, many other animals and plants are threatened by the soil contamination and the new ecological regimes produced through the reforestation of *terrils*. At the same time, *terrils* are places of amazement; material and cultural testimonies to the continual ecological transformation of urban and industrial sites' environments. New relationalities spur from *terrils* in that new stories push forwards the apparently blocked historical narra-

---

36   Nixon *Slow Violence and the Environmentalism of the Poor*.

tive of de-industrialisation, but not in a historicist and clearly delineated way. In order to make visible the historical geographies of toxicity, industrialisation, and ecological transformation that inform the environmental history of Wallonia, I argue that we need denser accounts,[37] narratives that make visible the contradictory and conflating historical trajectories of industrialisation. With this essay, I wanted to show how following the industrial toxicity embodied within *terrils* as a geo-historical trail enables various subjects to unfold, allowing a retracing of the layered meanings, stories and ecologies of industrialisation. The significance as movement heritage of the paths I walked and retraced in the essay lies in their undefined and ambiguous heritagisation value[38], and in the latent ecological toxic continuity of an industrial past that is still haunting as an Anthropocene ghostly presence the memory, the human and non-human bodies and the environment in Southern Belgium.

While coal mines might be dead in Wallonia, *terrils* are very much alive. If we want to understand how so-called post-industrial processes affect societies and environments, we need to change the traditional historicist narrative of progressive economic and social history, making space for non-anthropocentric narratives accounting for permanence, ruination and toxicity.[39] The material and cultural heritage of industrialisation and its complex history can be mobilised as storied-places that counter the historicist narration of industrial progress by showing its inherent linkages with toxicity. At the same time, the more-than-human ecologies that have surged in the former industrial interstices of Wallonia can help in rethinking the heterogeneity of techno-natural assemblages in the ruins of European capitalism, mobilising place-making practices of conviviality,[40] caring and multi-species lively ethnology.[41] To travel back and through the history and the geographies of post-industrialisation in Wallonia means to retrace the *longue durée* of the capitalist-driven ecology of coal extraction in Southern Belgium and to merge it with the present and future history of ruderal ecologies now populating and resignifying *terrils*.

---

37 Zimmer *Brouillards toxiques*.
38 Storm *Post-Industrial Landscape Scars*.
39 DeSilvey *Curating Decay*.
40 Ibid., p. 20.
41 Van Dooren and Rose 'Lively Ethnography'.

13. Walking on Terrils

Bibliography

Bedoret, Julie, Émile Crespin-Noël, Fanny Saint-Viteux and Symi Nyns, 'Le site du Gosson, de la friche minière à un parc urbain et pédagogique nature admise?', in Viorel Chirita and Serge Schimtz (eds), *Les friches minières: paysage culturel et enjeu de développement rural. Regards croisés entre Bucovine et Wallonie* (Liège: Atelier de Presse, 2017).

Cabedoce, Béatrice and Philippe Pierson (eds), *Cent ans d'histoire des jardins ouvriers 1896–1996* (Ivry-sur-Seine: Créaphis, 1996).

Canovi, Antonio, 'Pensare nella territorialità, abitare nel paesaggio: introduzione alla geostoria', in Antonio Canovi, Lorena Mussini, and Sandra Palmieri (eds), *Fare geostoria nel tempo presente*, pp. 1–14 (Reggio Emilia: Comune di Reggio Emilia, 2009).

de Certeau, Michel, *L'invention du quotidien. 1. Arts de faire* (Paris: Gallimard, 1980).

Cronon, William (ed.), *Uncommon Ground. Rethinking the Human Place in Nature* (New York: Norton, 1996).

DeSilvey, Caitlin, *Curated Decay. Heritage Beyond Saving* (Minneapolis: University of Minnesota Press, 2016).

DeSilvey, Caitlin, 'Ruderal Heritage', in Rodney Harrison and Colin Sterlin (eds), *De-territorrializing the Future. Heritage in, of and after the Anthropocene*, pp. 289–309 (London: Open Humanities Press, 2021).

Ingold, Tim, *Lines. A Brief History* (London-New York: Routledge, 2007).

Macpherson, Hannah, 'Walking Methods in Landscape Research: Moving Bodies, Spaces of Disclosure and Rapport', *Landscape Research* **41** (4) (2016): 425–32.

Mitchell, Don, *The Lie of the Land. Migrant Workers and the California Landscape* (Minneapolis: Minnesota University Press, 1996).

Morelli, Anne, 'L'appel à la main d'oeuvre italienne pour les charbonnages et sa prise en charge à son arrivée en Belgique dans l'immédiat après-guerre', *Revue Belge d'Histoire Contemporaine* **19** (1–2) (1988): 83–130.

Nixon, Rob, *Slow Violence and the Environmentalism of the Poor* (Cambridge MA: Harvard University Press, 2011).

Raes, François and Emmanuel Boostels, *Terrils. De l'or noir à l'or vert* (Brussels: Racine Lanno, 2006).

Stoetzer, Bettina, 'Ruderal Ecologies: Re-Thinking Nature, Migration, and the Urban Landscape in Berlin', *Cultural Anthropology* **33** (2) (2018): 295–323.

Storm, Anna, *Post-Industrial Landscape Scars* (New York: Palgrave Macmillan, 2014).

Svennson, Daniel, Sverker Sörlin and Katarina Salzman, 'Pathways to the Trail – Landscape, Walking and Heritage in a Scandinavian Border Region', *Norwegian Journal of Geography* (2021): https://doi.org/10.1080/00291951.2021.1998216.

Thierry, Vincent, Ellina Vladimirovna Sokol, M. Naze-Nancy Masalehdani and Bernard Guy, 'La combustion des terrils', *Geochronique* 127 (2013): 23–25.

Thoreau, François and Alexis Zimmer, 'Croisières toxiques. Décontenancer l'histoire industrielle de la vallée de la Meuse', *Panthère Première* 4 (2019), https://pantherepremiere.org/texte/croisieres-toxiques/.

Tsing, Anna, *The Mushroom at the End of the World: On the Possibility of Life in Capitalist Ruins* (Princeton NJ: Princeton University Press, 2015).

Daniele Valisena

Valisena, Daniele and Marco Armiero, 'Coal Lives: Body, Work and Memory Among Italian Miners in Wallonia, Belgium', in Marco Armiero and Richard Tucker (eds), *Environmental History of Modern Migration*, pp. 88–107 (London: Routledge, 2017).

Valisena, Daniele, 'Coal Lives. Italians and the Metabolism of Coal in Wallonia, Belgium 1945–1980', Ph.D. dissertation, KTH – Royal Institute of Technology, Stockholm, 2020.

Van Dooren, Thom and Deborah Bird Rose, 'Lively Ethnography: Storying Animist Worlds', *Environmental Humanities* **8** (1) (2016): 77–94.

Van Dooren, Thom and Deborah Bird Rose, 'Storied-Places in a Multispecies City', *Humanimalia* **3** (2) (2012): 1–27.

Van Dooren, Thom, Eben Kirksey and Ursula Münster, 'Multispecies Studies: Cultivating Arts of Attentiveness', *Environmental Humanities* **8** (1) (2016): 1–23.

Zimmer, Alexis, *Brouillards toxiques. Vallée de la Meuse, 1930. Contre-enquête* (Paris: Zones sensibles, 2017).

Other Sources

Archives de l'INA, Médiathèque, 'Explosion d'un terril à Calonne-Ricouart, FR3, Journal Télévisé, 26 août 1975', https://fresques.ina.fr/memoires-de-mines/fiche-media/Mineur00151/explosion-d-un-terril-a-calonne-ricouart.html.

Moniteur Belge, 22 June 1995, Arrêté du Gouvernement Wallon fixant la classification des terrils, 16 Mars 1995

Fédération Wallonie-Bruxelles, 'La biodiversité en Wallonie, Sites de Grand Intérêt Biologique, Terril du Gosson', http://biodiversite.wallonie.be/fr/1854-terril-du-gosson.html?IDD=251659927&IDC=1881

CHAPTER 14.

WALKING, REMEMBERING, AND ENUNCIATING THE PLACE: JEWISH-ISRAELI MEMORIAL TRAILS IN NATURE

Maria Piekarska

Among all their other possible interpretations, trails in nature can at times be conceptualised as embodied memorials – a phenomenon inviting memory studies to deliberate on trails as heritage. 'Heritage and memory are similar in that they are productively synergistic by way of myriad forms of communication', being 'shared and produced through narratives, engagement with landscapes, performance and other endeavours'.[1] Trails themselves can act as such a communicative form. Designed with memorial qualities, they introduce an alternative to static commemoration – where 'body and place memory conspire with co-participating others in ritualized scenes of co-remembering',[2] challenging existing ideas on memorials' solemnity. Their intertextual qualities, though, make them difficult to detach from the socio-political contexts in which they are deliberately established. As such, they remain deeply entangled with existing discourses on memory and landscapes, evoking the political aspects of the term 'heritage'.

Memorial trails in the context of Jewish-Israeli hiking

The 'path dependency' of Jewish-Israeli movement heritage closely connects modern leisure and memorial culture in nature with early nation-building practices. Walking outdoors as an ideologically-saturated practice refers to, among other things, the nineteenth/twentieth century developing national discourses that found natural landscapes useful for identity-building. Indeed, an important element of the pre-state Zionist imaginary was the culture of walking the land. Through consciously produced connection between hiking and Zionist values of knowing and loving the land, walking served as a manifestation of early nationalism directed towards the physical earth. Long hikes to remote locations, often guided with help of biblical stories and focused

---

[1] Sather-Wagstaff, 'Heritage and Memory', 191.
[2] Casey, *Remembering*, p. xi.

on focal points of symbolic Zionist geography, aimed to create an embodied bond between immigrants and the land. Emphasising its ritualised character, it was described as 'a native-Israeli form of secular pilgrimage'.[3] Hiking soon became a formative socialisation ritual and an element of the educational system, institutionalised today as annual school trips advised by the Ministry of Education and excursions to Jewish heritage sites within the mandatory army service. Subsequently, Israel today has one of the most developed hiking networks in the region,[4] with its crowning achievement of trail marking being the *Shvil Israel* (Israel National Trail – INT) which crosses the country from North to South, including diverse heritage sites on its route.[5] Although today hiking as one of the most popular pastimes is seemingly devoid of its original explicitly ideological dimensions, contemporary research confirms its ritualised significance as an element of the Israeli 'civil religion' – for over three quarters of those hiking the INT, motivation is still *ahavat ha'aretz* – love for the land.[6]

In the last two decades, the established practice of walking the land has been engaged for directly commemorative purposes, and among the dense Israeli network of marked trails a subgroup of memorial character can be distinguished. While the majority of trails, including the INT, are marked by the Society for the Protection of Nature in Israel, the initiative behind establishing a memorial trail tends to be linked to a body concerned with commemoration of an event, person or group. Examples of such initiatives are *Shvil HaBanim* (Trail of the Sons) – over 200 kilometres devoted to the memory of Druze soldiers fallen in the Israeli army; or *Shvil Golani* (Golani Trail), a trail stretching over 1,200 kilometres connecting Golani Brigade battle sites and major Jewish-Israeli heritage sites. Shorter memorial trails are often established by Keren Kayemeth le'Israel-Jewish National Fund (JNF),[7] often following donors' initiatives. The purpose of their existence is not only to facilitate and popularise hiking in nature, but also to evoke certain recollections of the past in a natural environment, using tools like commemorative toponyms, routes narratively linking particular sites of interest,[8] or interpretive plaques placed

---

3   Katriel, 'Touring the Land'.
4   Rabineau, *Marking and Mapping the Nation*.
5   Hermann, *Shvil Israel*.
6   Collins-Kreiner and Kliot, 'Why do People Hike?'
7   JNF was founded in 1901 in order to buy and develop land in Palestine for the sake of the Zionist movement. From its creation to this day, it focuses on land development for the Jewish people and forestry. Although officially not a governmental body, it remains one of the decisive bodies regarding land management.
8   Feldman, 'Between Yad Vashem and Mt. Herzl'.

14. Walking, Remembering and Enunciating the Place

along trails.⁹ The commemorative character of such trails distinguishes them from regular hiking trails, as well as from traditional memorial structures typically comprising a static spatial form located on a square. Furthermore, nature's role in this mnemonic context comes to the fore as not only a pleasant background, but also a particularly useful narrative medium and even an active force influencing commemorative outcomes (e.g. bushes overgrowing plaques, fallen tree trunks limiting a trail's accessibility).

Generally, memorial trails may be identified as purposive cultural heritage trails, according to Timothy and Boyd's classification – 'collaborative networks developed between individual nodes'.¹⁰ Yet the Israeli case does not fall easily into pre-existing categories, as memorial trails are at times set up in 'blank' natural spaces – not locations of any particular event and without any previous objects to be connected by a trail.¹¹ In such 'empty canvases', memorial trails recall both collective and individual stories, serving as a universal vehicle of the Jewish-Israeli memory culture. A 'sense of place'¹² here stems not simply from directly echoing events that happened in situ, but from purposefully experiencing the place through the practice of walking. More important than the objects they connect, then, are the trails themselves, referring to the long-lasting Jewish-Israeli walking culture, and constantly co-creating the movement heritage of this group. The Martyrs' Trail has been selected as a prominent example as it offers a direct nexus of two crucial, yet very distinct, elements of the Jewish-Israeli 'civil religion': hiking as the basis of modern recreational culture, and the Holocaust as one of the foundations of cultural memory. This site additionally highlights the blurred division between natural and cultural heritage, as its landscapes are constructed outcomes of mass afforestation conducted in the last seventy years.

The spatial configuration of the Martyrs' Trail

The Martyrs' Trail (*Shvil HaKedoshim*) is a three-kilometre path that crosses *Ya'ar HaKedoshim*, the Martyrs' Forest. Among the growing body of Israeli trails, it holds an ambiguous position between a typical trail facilitating safe hiking through one of many forests of the Jerusalem Hills, and a trail purposefully connecting the most significant sites of particular commemorative meaning

---

9   Greenberg and Greenberg, 'Shvil haPtzuim'.
10   Timothy and Boyd, *Tourism and Trails*, p. 18. See also Miles, 'Remembrance Trails of the Great War'.
11   An example is the 2017 *Shvil HaBricha*, the Escape Trail, commemorating post-war illegal Jewish immigration to Palestine in the not-obviously-related Carmel Forest in northern Israel.
12   Collins-Kreiner and Kliot, 'Why do People Hike?'.

Figure 1.

The Martyrs' Trail information sign by the Scroll of Fire memorial. Photograph by Maria Piekarska.

scattered through a forest – despite being placed in a site unrelated to the recalled event. Created as the first state-wide memorial for Shoah victims, the Martyrs' Forest was a direct use of Zionist tree planting symbolism to promote urgent mass commemoration, responding to a major trauma present in the developing society.[13] The first of a symbolic six million saplings took root in the barren Jerusalem Hills in 1951, and collectively led to tremendous changes in the existing landscape. Plans for the Martyrs' Forest as a central green memorial complex were significantly scaled-down with the development of Yad Vashem in the second half of the 1950s,[14] yet the forest as a site of memory grew – due to maturing trees and new saplings, as well as additional memorials placed on its premises. The most notable structures added to this organic-commemorative complex, aside many individual stone markers, are connected today via the Martyrs' Trail.

According to the JNF Community and Forest Coordinator, the Martyrs' Trail

---

13   For more on the Martyrs' Forest as a memorial, see Piekarska, 'Instead of Tombstones'.
14   Bar, "'Le'an nifne be-yom ha-shoah?'".

14. Walking, Remembering and Enunciating the Place

in its current shape was established around the year 2013 in order to facilitate hiking through the whole complex.[15] It starts near the village of Ksalon, right behind the Scroll of Fire memorial (1972). Shaped like a Torah scroll, this largest bronze sculpture in the state is covered with pictorial depictions of Jewish history, separating the past into two parts – exilic destruction during Roman times and the Holocaust, and national rebirth in the Land of Israel. Since the Scroll of Fire, as the most renowned element of the forest, forms the beginning of the trail, visitors start their hike with focus not on the commemorated European event, but on the following events in the state of Israel – the triumph of the Jewish nation. Following this monument, the trail pursues a steep off-road path down. While hiking the green-marked trail, visitor encounters smaller stones dedicated to the memory of particular perished individuals and communities. Some markers are covered in weeds, damaged or even fully fragmented, which accentuates nature's agency as the living substance of this mnemonic assemblage. Additionally, near the trail some historical sites are located – winepress, cistern and stones used for oil production – referencing ancient Jewish roots in the land. Visitors, however, will not find interpretive markers describing experiences or messages to be gained from the walk as typically found in interpretive trails, leading walkers between plaques providing accounts of historical events or explanations on encountered objects.

After descending a large number of wooden stairs placed on a steep slope, the trail reaches the Martyrs' Cave (1959) next to Ksalon river. Inside this natural cave, slightly expanded to create a gathering area, there is a big stone funded by B'nai B'rith to remember the six million victims. Considering the tradition of holy caves utilised for sacred purposes, this part of the trail references a form of pilgrimage. This was reflected in the words of Yosef Weitz, director of the JNF Land and Afforestation Department, at the cave's dedication ceremony: 'Whoever crosses the threshold of the shrine frees himself from the cares of material everyday existence and enters into communion with these souls in deep silence. And this is its holiness.'[16] This reflection-inviting character of the site is non-existent today as it is generally closed with a barred gate, making it impossible to access its interior. At this point the Martyrs' Trail crosses the Israel National Trail, which is not unusual for local memorial trails. A result of such a strategy is a potentially higher number of unintentional visitors – *shvilistim*[17] can detour and explore such commemorations as a way of diversifying their hike.

---

15   Personal interview, Jan. 2020.
16   Quoted in Weiss, 'To Plant is To Remember', 205.
17   People hiking the INT.

Maria Piekarska

Figure 2.

Crossing of trails by the Martyrs' Cave. The green-marked Martyrs' Trail leads towards the Scroll of Fire.
The orange–blue–white mark signifies the INT. Photograph by Maria Piekarska.

The final stretch of the trail is the Anne Frank memorial (2011) situated near the cave. This rusted steel construction of an open cube recalls Anne's hiding place, with a chair overlooking a cut out tree shape – the horse chestnut mentioned in her diary. Even though the tree was brought up in the diary only three times, it was socially recognised as a symbolic object, containing meanings of redemption and hope.[18] This 'memorial to the tree' is supposed to invoke feelings of the discomfort of a hiding place, but more importantly refers to the comfort that nature offers as a space of freedom. As a 1944 diary excerpt cited at the memorial stands: 'I firmly believe that nature brings solace in all troubles.' Two pathways leading to the memorial, lined with plaques holding nature-focused diary quotes, form a circular end to the Martyrs' Trail.

18   Kirshenblatt-Gimblett, 'Epilogue'.

14. Walking, Remembering and Enunciating the Place

Merging recreation and commemoration

The recreational infrastructure of the trail follows the ambiguousness of the entire Martyrs' Forest which, despite its original commemorative character, serves today as one of the most popular places for recreation, offering cycling and 4x4 routes, as well as picnic and camping areas. The physical properties of the Martyrs' Trail in fact indicate its function for advanced hiking rather than easily accessible memorial performances. In physical effect, the path appears a typical hiking trail, clearly identified with a professional colour marker like many others throughout the country. The altitude between the Scroll of Fire monument and the mid-part of the trail is 300 metres, while the descent towards the Martyrs' Cave is steep and fits one person only. It is therefore the opposite of a neat park with alleys accessible for everyone willing to experience site for commemorative reasons, or a pilgrimage kind of walk. Engaging in such activity requires a higher level of mobility, excluding certain groups of users[19].

Alongside its obvious recreational features, the Martyrs' Trail simultaneously encompasses directly commemorative qualities. Proper place names 'carve out pockets of hidden and familiar meanings',[20] and in Israeli natural landscapes are often outcomes of intentional naming decisions made in the recent past. Although lacking direct interpretation in situ, the trail is marked with a name originating from the forest in which it resides – a commemorative toponym in itself. In this way, the trail connects not only to the territory of the forest, its inherent physical element, but also to the forest's commemorative nature, and beyond that – to further symbolic connotations of its name. By ascribing the term *kedoshim* (martyrs, saints) to the memory of those perished in the Shoah, a purposeful meaning of sacrifice for God is attributed to their deaths, referencing the religious concept of *kiddush ha-Shem* (sanctification of God's name). Although the trail's name is a reflection of the complex in which it is placed, it repeats afresh these religious undertones.

The trail's commemorative character is most clearly reflected in its route, connecting three main memorials located in the forest's extensive grounds. Its existence, then, creates a physical and narrative connection between these objects, which without it are rather separate in shape and meaning. Moreover, this route offers possibilities for constructing new commemorative practices: around *Yom HaShoah* (Holocaust Memorial Day) articles appear proposing the idea of

---

19   Preparing for the seventieth anniversary of the planting of the Martyrs' Forest, JNF announced changes in the infrastructure to make this site a 'Holocaust education centre', accessible for visitors with physical limitations. No changes in the formation of the Martyrs' Trail itself have been announced, maintaining its challenging character.

20   de Certeau, *Practice of Everyday Life*, p. 104.

Figure 3.

The Martyrs' Trail makes a narrow descent towards the Martyrs' Cave. Photograph by Maria Piekarska.

metaylim ve-zochrim, walking and remembering.²¹ Walking here is endorsed as a modern, yet very traditional-Israeli, alternative to the customary *yizkor* services. Indeed *tiyulim* (trips), with their ideological roots, have been called in literature a 'commemorative practice'.²² The overall Israeli remembrance culture in natural spaces is based on corporeal connections to land – planting trees by hand, moving on foot, immersing in outdoor recreation associated with territorial belonging. This ongoing emphasis on physicality sustains the early Zionist idea of a model citizen: bodily fit, experiencing their land in an active way by knowing it, dwelling in it and eventually being ready to defend it²³ – or, to use Hermann's conceptualisation, an ideal of a 'hiking Israeli' against a 'wandering Jew' without their own land, and a 'not-walking Jew' detached from their physicality.²⁴

21 Zakhai, *Metaylim ve-zochrim*.
22 Zerubavel, 'Ha-chazarah el ha-tanakh'.
23 Almog, *The Sabra*.
24 Hermann, *Shvil Israel*, 127.

14. Walking, Remembering and Enunciating the Place

Walking as a space of enunciation

The sense of place in the case of memorial trails is not a simple sum of the connections they provide between sites or objects. Memorials, as intertextual devices, serve 'as repositories of much more than the creators' intentions, as they include the variety of possible references to the existing historical, cultural, and social contexts'.[25] Adopting such an approach places in the sphere of deliberation not only the content found in situ, but also in that brought to the site by its visitors. While each visitor brings to the site their own experiences, 'recognizing that each story is unique and unrepeatable does not mean that it is therefore impossible to find the regularities or patterns that make the narratives similar'.[26] These regularities often result from socialisation and educational formation that provide individuals with a patterned set of 'imprinted' tools for interpreting encountered sites.[27]

According to de Certeau, the act of walking in a place is similar to the practice of reading a text – practising it, and therefore making it a significant space. Walking, then, is a way of realisation of place – just as language is realised during the act of speech:

> at the most elementary level, it [walking] has a triple 'enunciative' function: it is a process of appropriation of the topographical system on the part of the pedestrian (just as the speaker appropriates and takes on the language); it is a spatial acting-out of the place (just as the speech act is an acoustic acting-out of language); and it implies relations among differentiated positions ... It thus seems possible to give a preliminary definition of *walking as a space of enunciation*.[28]

Although writing about walking in the city, de Certeau devotes attention to the connections between walking and utterance, describing how 'spatial stories' take shared narrative-embodied forms. Through the act of walking, then, a place is simultaneously being acted-out and written again, reconstituting relations between its tangible and intangible elements.

Considering such 'rhetorics of walking', what does the Martyrs' Trail enunciate? Announcing news of the renovation of the Scroll of Fire memorial, JNF quoted the words of a 22-year-old Jewish-Israeli visitor: 'during the Holocaust, Jews marched to death, while today we have the privilege of walking through the Land of Israel'.[29] The acts of walking are sharply juxtaposed – death marches

---

25 Lähdesmäki, 'Narrativity and Intertextuality', 62.
26 Trzeszczyńska, *Pamięć o nie-swojej przeszłości*, p. 28.
27 Sörlin, 'The Articulation of Territory', 109.
28 de Certeau, *Practice of Everyday Life*, pp. 97–98.
29 JNF, *Making the Scroll of Fire Memorial Accessible*.

during World War II in Europe contrasted with physical exploration of the Jewish state's territory. Walking in the latter context is understood as freedom, as opposed to walking as slavish submission. The March of the Living, annually attracting participants from around the world, can be recalled as a similar example of this walking dichotomy. Yet its most iconic element, the three-kilometre walk between Auschwitz I and Auschwitz II-Birkenau, holds a very different character as a mass urban event leading over 10,000 participants along paved roads. A more relevant context is found at the Anne Frank memorial forming the end of the Martyrs' Trail. Here an opposition between slavery and nature is emphasised, where the latter is a source of endurance: 'Mother Nature makes me small and ready to bravely take every blow!', as one of the presented excerpts states. It should be noted that almost every diary entry mentioning nature was used in the site – and so visitors may get an impression that Anne's connection to nature was one of the main motives of her journal. Such a strategy once more evokes the ideal of a person for whom being in and knowing nature are sources of strength. It also forms a contrast between Israel as an open place of safe nature, and a diasporic confinement where nature is unobtainable – and whose most dramatic event peacefully dissolves in the lush and inviting Israeli natural landscape. The focus is again not on the European tragedy, but on the following Israeli victory, confirming the placement of this site in the meta-narrative of *mi-shoah li-geula*, 'from Holocaust to redemption'.

Following this understanding, being in nature is a sign not only of freedom as absence of oppression and limitations, but of freedom as sovereignty. In such a way, walking in nature is an active expression of Jewish self-determination, thus acquiring political meanings. Indeed, 'in the process of hiking the trails, the land becomes an object that people can have and which they claim by using it'.[30] This possessive significance of walking is a clear continuation of its pre-state roots, when distant hiking was a form of almost military-style border-making conducted by the Jewish civilians.[31] On the other hand, one of the most universal motifs of hiking is escapism from everyday life, including its conflicting socio-political realities, through direct contact with nature.[32] Nature in such a framework serves as a neutral place in which one can achieve peace and get closer to the pure 'organic' order of things. Yet such romantic pastoralism is problematic within the natural-cultural circumstances under consideration. As already noted, the current landscapes of Jerusalem Hills are outcomes of

---

30 Jaffe-Schagen, *Having and Belonging*, p. 3.
31 Almog, *The Sabra*, pp. 171–78.
32 Hermann, 'The Israel National Trail as a Place of Refuge'.

14. Walking, Remembering and Enunciating the Place

mass afforestation executed in the early period of Israeli statehood. This end of wildness – a situation of dominance in which even seemingly unspoiled nature is constructed (or 'restored') by humankind – is questioned from an eco-critical perspective, especially when the group responsible for such transformation attributes to itself a sense of righteous nativeness.[33]

Trail as an 'open form'?

Examining the trail as an enunciative form requires recognising it in a broader context of interpretive strategies employed at other Holocaust heritage sites. A particular repository of Holocaust memory bears resemblance to the studied site – the famous yet never realised 'Road' Monument by Oskar and Zofia Hansen, winner of the 1957 international competition for the victims of fascism monument at the site of Auschwitz-Birkenau camp. The essence of the project was a 1,000-metre-long road running across Auschwitz II-Birkenau, with the camp's remains located by its sides left to undergo gradual decay and overgrowth. Hansens' unrealised memorial is sometimes regarded as one of the first counter-monuments – a category introduced by Young over thirty years later[34] to refer to memorials that give up monumentality and reification in favour of spatiality and transformability. The project followed Hansen's theory of an Open Form that assumed objects' changeability, no top-down narrative, and focus on individual experience.[35] Regarding its materiality, the 'Road' would transform over time with the camp area becoming overtaken by untamed vegetation – in Hansen's words, 'woods surrounding the "Road" are a "clock" measuring the passage of time following the tragic events, a symbol of life being stronger than death'.[36] Nature's agency was also a symbolic element of the continued present and the future: 'when we reach the end of the "Road," we enter the open space of the fields. We return to life, to appreciate its value and to see our everyday problems in a different light.'[37] It was also an Open Form in terms of its meaning. Visitors were to fill it with their subjective experience – emotions, thoughts and possibly material additions, as the creators foresaw that spontaneous markers could be raised along the road, commemorating particular communities – an element bringing this design even closer to the Martyrs' Trail.

33 Katz, 'Anne Frank's Tree'.
34 Young, 'The Counter-Monument'.
35 Maliszewska, '*The Road* Monument by Oskar Hansen'.
36 Hansen, *Towards Open Form*, p. 130.
37 Ibid.

The Open Form perspective proves useful when analysing the Martyrs' Trail as a form of commemoration – eventually exposing limitations crucial for a full picture of the site's character. Just like the 'Road', which eliminated the 'problem with the traditional style of monuments ... you arrive by coach, lay a bouquet of flowers, and leave',[38] the Martyrs' Trail provides an alternative counter-way of commemorating Shoah. The role of nature is also crucial – through the surrounding vegetation that has flourished only in the last decades, the focus of the trail is not on what was, but what is – the continued Jewish life. Yet comparison to the Open Form becomes unsustainable once we consider the local-specific context that the Martyrs' Trail exists in. Socialisation in the values of knowing and loving the land provides immediate associations for any Jewish-Israeli visiting the site, and leaves little space for possible alternative receptions – though certainly individual reinterpretations are conceivable. Furthermore, the focus on monuments that open and close the trail guide visitor's attention to dominant tropes of Holocaust memory. Moreover, similarly to the 'Road', nature in situ overran past events – but dissolved in this landscape was not only the commemorated tragedy, but also Palestinian heritage and its destruction. Israeli afforested landscapes often hold a palimpsestic character, covering previous layers that included pre-1948 Palestinian villages.[39] Nature management and its conceptualisations, not limited to the issue of forests, are integral parts of the Israeli-Palestinian conflict,[40] and, not coincidentally, many spaces that served as centres of Palestinian life are today areas of nature – including some of the vast grounds of the Martyrs' Forest. To those aware of the site's past, it also enunciates this unaddressed heritage – even if through such subtle signs as a clump of unattended olive trees growing between the pines, indicating a former grove near a today-non-existent village.

Returning to de Certeau's idea of walking rhetorics, two 'pedestrian' stylistic figures are particularly important in his deliberations – synecdoche and asyndeton.[41] Synecdoche denotes the whole by addressing its part, while asyndeton connects sentences by omitting conjunctives. Put together, 'synecdoche makes more dense: it amplifies the detail and miniaturizes the whole. Asyndeton cuts out: it undoes continuity and undercuts its plausibility.'[42] Relating these

---

38 Ibid., p. 193.
39 See among else Kadman, *Erased from Space and Consciousness*, pp. 112–40; Grunebaum, 'Landscape, Complicity and Partitioned Zones'; Zerubavel, 'Forest as a National Icon'.
40 See among else Bardenstein, 'Threads of Memory and Discourses of Rootedness'; Abufarha, 'Land of Symbols'; Braverman, *Planted Flags*; Galai, 'Narratives of Redemption'.
41 Thanks to Laura Bertens for pointing my attention to this part of de Certeau's discussion.
42 de Certeau, *Practice of Everyday Life*, p. 101.

14. Walking, Remembering and Enunciating the Place

conceptualizations to the Martyrs' Trail, it can be noticed how a forest trail cutting through picturesque hills stands for the whole Jewish state, understood as a blooming, inviting, safe haven for Jews. At the same time, it bypasses the Palestinian heritage, visible in the site's flora alone, through focusing solely on the Jewish story in situ. These figures of (spatial) speech make the application of the positively-perceived category of counter-monument to the Martyrs' Trail beyond the bounds of possibility, as counter-monument's primary objective is to oppose any cultural reifications of national discourses. Comparing the Martyrs' Trail to the seemingly similar memorial design of the 'Road', then, highlights its intense site-specificity, questioning the possible perception of trails as a universally positive alternative to more traditional memorial forms.

Conclusion

The hybrid of walking and remembering created in the Martyrs' Trail offers a reconceptualisation of the collective founding event via a culturally-embedded practice of walking the land. Since memorials reflect both past experiences and the current lives of their communities, they become a fusion of group's present values and needs expressed in relation to the displayed past. The analysed trail is not a simple pathway to the past; in this framework, the 'path dependency' moves the trail's users from the painful past to the celebrated present and onwards – to quote JNF, 'this sacred space bears witness to Israel's complex reality, in which bereavement and the celebration of life are closely intertwined'.[43] Still, the marriage of recreation and plaques commemorating victims of extermination camps creates a certain level of cognitive dissonance in an outsider. Investigating such sites is even more important, as they challenge the idea of cosmopolitan memory cultures, pointing to the prominence of separateness in heritage practices.

As it is not a unique case of trail merging memory and recreation in Israel's natural landscapes, this locally developed commemorative form is characteristic of particular socio-cultural conditions. Despite seemingly pure recreational dimensions, these trails encapsulate identity discourse emerging from the historical and contemporary nexus of hiking, landscape production and power relations in Israel. Their transparency is precisely what makes them a vehicle in the ongoing co-creation of tangible and intangible heritage. Yet the issue of an ever-growing heritage assemblage in this region (already marked with a crisis of accumulation of the past) points strongly to matters of ontological politics, in which 'heritage

---

43   JNF, *The Holocaust Memorial*.

is rarely deployed innocently', and this fact serves 'to normalize and historicize inequalities of many kinds'.[44] The ongoing Jewish-Israeli movement heritage undeniably constitutes a remarkable material-semiotic phenomenon of its own. Featuring it, though, comes with the risk of suppressing landscape traces of the not very remote in time, yet today very intangible, heritage (including its dark and painful renditions) of another group, whose movement is exceptionally curbed. Following Harrison's stance, explorations of trails as heritage in Israel thus need to be conducted with 'a simultaneous sense of critical reserve and a creative engagement',[45] recognising multiple meanings woven together within them, and serving as a reminder of an unavoidable contestedness that comes with the category of heritage.

Bibliography

Abufarha, Nasser, 'Land of Symbols: Cactus, Poppies, Orange and Olive Trees in Palestine', *Identities: Global Studies in Culture and Power* 15 (2008): 343–68.

Almog, Oz, *The Sabra: The Creation of the New Jew* (Berkeley: University of California Press, 2000).

Bar, Doron, '"Le'an nifne be-yom ha-shoah?" Ya'ar ha-kedoshim ve ha-hitlabtut be-she'elat hantzahat zecher ha-shoah', *Cathedra* 140 (2011): 103–30.

Bardenstein, Carol, 'Threads of Memory and Discourses of Rootedness: of Trees, Oranges and the Prickly-pear Cactus in Israel/Palestine', *Edebiyat* 8 (1) (1998): 1–36.

Braverman, Irus, *Planted Flags: Trees, Land and Law in Israel/Palestine* (New York: Cambridge University Press, 2009).

Casey, Edward, *Remembering. A Phenomenological Study* (Bloomington: Indiana University Press, 2000).

Collins-Kreiner, Noga and Nurit Kliot, 'Why do People Hike? Hiking the Israel National Trail', *Tijdschrift voor economische en sociale geografie* **108** (5) (2017): 669–85.

de Certeau, Michel, *Practice of Everyday Life* (Berkeley: University of California Press, 1984).

Feldman, Jackie, 'Between Yad Vashem and Mt. Herzl: Changing Inscriptions of Sacrifice on Jerusalem's "Mountain of Memory"', *Anthropological Quarterly* **80** (4) (2007): 1147–74.

Galai, Yoav, 'Narratives of Redemption: The International Meaning of Afforestation in the Israeli Negev', *International Political Sociology* 11 (2017): 273–91.

Greenberg, Zeev and Irit Greenberg, 'Shvil haPtzuim beyn chatzar Tel Hai li-Kfar Gil'adi: ha-sipur ha-ishi ke-emtza'i le-havnayat sipur histori', *Cathedra* 142 (2011): 131–46.

Grunebaum, Heidi, 'Landscape, Complicity and Partitioned Zones at South Africa Forest and Lubya in Israel-Palestine', *Anthropology Southern Africa* **37** (3–4) (2014): 213–21.

Hansen, Oskar, *Towards Open Form*, ed. Jola Gola (Warsaw: Foksal Gallery Foundation and Warsaw Academy of Fine Arts Museum, 2005).

---

44   Harrison, 'Beyond "Natural" and "Cultural" Heritage', 38.
45   Ibid.

14. Walking, Remembering and Enunciating the Place

Harrison, Rodney, 'Beyond "Natural" and "Cultural" Heritage: Toward an Ontological Politics of Heritage in the Age of Anthropocene", *Heritage & Society* **8** (1) (2015): 24–42.

Hermann, Tamar, 'The Israel National Trail as a Place of Refuge', *Strategic Assessment: A Multidisciplinary Journal on National Security* (2020): 1–17.

Hermann, Tamar, *Shvil Israel: darka shel ha-israeliyut ha-chadashah-yeshanah* (Haifa: University of Haifa Publishing House, 2019).

Jaffe-Schagen, Judy, *Having and Belonging. Homes and Museums in Israel* (New York: Berghahn Books, 2016).

JNF, *Making the Scroll of Fire Memorial Accessible* (2019): http://www.kkl-jnf.org/about-kkl-jnf/green-israel-news/may-2019/scroll-of-fire-memorial-accessibility/

JNF, *Keren Kayemet le'Israel ve-B'nai Brit yekadmu et hangashat ya'ar hakedoshim le-ba'alei tzrahim meyuhadim ve-hafihato le-atar hinuhi al ha-shoah* (2020): https://www.kkl.org.il/new_in_kkl/sali-bein-commemorated-in-yaar-haksoshim.aspx

JNF, *The Holocaust Memorial that Breathes and Whispers in the Jerusalem* (2021): https://www.kkl-jnf.org/about-kkl-jnf/green-israel-news/january-2021/martyrs-forest/

Kadman, Noga, *Erased from Space and Consciousness. Israel and the Depopulated Palestinian Villages of 1948* (Indianapolis: Indiana University Press, 2015).

Katriel, Tamar, 'Touring the Land: Trips and Hiking as Secular Pilgrimages in Israeli Culture', *Jewish Ethnology and Folklore Review* 17 (1995): 6–13.

Katz, Eric, 'Anne Frank's Tree: Thoughts on Domination and the Paradox of Progress', *Ethics, Place and Environment* **13** (3) (2010): 283–93.

Katz, Eric, *Anne Frank's Tree: Nature's Confrontation with Technology, Domination and the Holocaust* (Knapwell: The White Horse Press, 2016).

Kirshenblatt-Gimblett, Barbara, 'Epilogue: A Life of Its Own – the Anne Frank Tree', in Barbara Kirshenblatt-Gimblett and Jeffrey Shandler (eds), *Anne Frank Unbound: Media, Imagination, Memory* (Bloomington: Indiana University Press, 2012).

Lähdesmäki, Tuuli, 'Narrativity and Intertextuality in the Making of a Shared European Memory', *Journal of Contemporary European Studies* **25** (1) (2016): 57–72.

Maliszewska, Marta, '*The Road* Monument by Oskar Hansen – Critical Narration and Commemoration Discourse', *The Polish Journal of Aesthetics* **47** (4) (2017): 129–42.

Miles, Stephen, 'Remembrance Trails of the Great War on the Western Front: Routes of Heritage and Memory', *Journal of Heritage Tourism* **12** (5) (2017): 441–51.

Piekarska, Maria, '"Instead of Tombstones – a Tree, a Garden, a Grove": Early Israeli Forests as Environmental Memorials', *Colloquia Humanistica* 9 (2020): 101–20.

Rabineau, Shay, *Marking and Mapping the Nation: The History of Israel's Hiking Trail Network* (Ph.D. Thesis, Brandeis University, 2013).

Sather-Wagstaff, Joy, 'Heritage and Memory', in Emma Waterton and Steve Watson (eds), *The Palgrave Handbook of Contemporary Heritage Research* (New York: Palgrave Macmillan, 2015).

Sörlin, Sverker, 'The Articulation of Territory: Landscape and the Constitution of Regional and National Identity', *Norsk Geografisk Tidsskrift – Norwegian Journal of Geography* **53** (2–3) (1999): 103–12.

Timothy, Dallen and Stephen Boyd, *Tourism and Trails: Cultural, Ecological and Management Issues* (Bristol: Channel, 2015).

Trzeszczyńska, Patrycja, *Pamięć o nie-swojej przeszłości. Przypadek Bieszczadów* (Kraków: Wydawnictwo Uniwersytetu Jagiellońskiego, 2016).

Weiss, Amy, 'To Plant is To Remember: The B'nai B'rith Martyrs' Forest and American Jewish Fundraising Customs for an "Evergreen" Holocaust Memorial', in Joseph Isaac Lifshitz, Naomi Feuchtwanger-Sarig, Simha Goldin, Jean Baumgarten and Hasia Diner (eds), *Minhagim. Custom and Practice in Jewish Life* (Berlin: de Gruyter, 2020).

Young, James, 'The Counter-Monument: Memory Against Itself in Germany Today', *Critical Inquiry* **18** (2) (1992): 267–96.

Zakhai, Dubi, *Metaylim ve-zochrim: tiyul be'in shoah le-gvura*, Makor Rishon (2012): https://www.makorrishon.co.il/nrg/online/55/ART2/358/694.html.

Zerubavel, Yael, 'Forest as a National Icon: Literature, Politics, and the Archaeology of Memory", *Israel Studies* **1** (1) (1996): 60–99.

Zerubavel, Yael, 'Ha-chazarah el ha-tanakh: ha-tiyul ve-zichron he-avar ba-si'ah ha-tayaruti be-yisrael', in Meir Hazan and Uri Cohen (eds), *Tarbut, zikaron ve-historia: be-hokara le-Anita Shapira*, volume 2 (Tel Aviv: University of Tel Aviv, 2012).

CHAPTER 15.

WALKING THE KALDERIMI: EMBODIED KNOWLEDGE AND HERITAGE NARRATIVES IN A PARTICIPATORY BUILDING WORKSHOP AT ZAGORI (NW GREECE)

Faidon Moudopoulos-Athanasiou and Ionas Sklavounos

> *Standing on the kalderimi, I already felt the fever of departure.*
> (Lymberopoulos, 1972)

Walking heritage is a new, growing field in heritage studies.[1] Although pathways are ephemeral and difficult to handle within heritage management systems, they constitute the physical and cultural infrastructure of human memory and past practices.[2] In that sense, pathways not only reveal how cultural landscapes are shaped through the activities of (more-than) humans, through historically defined taskscapes[3] but they may also function as analytical tools to understand and interpret change.

The Zagori (NW Greece) is a mountainous cultural landscape including 46 traditional and protected settlements. The region possesses more than sixty Ottoman-style early modern stone-arched bridges, the result of large-scale mobility mainly towards Wallachia and Central Europe in the later phase of the Ottoman period (eighteenth, nineteenth and early twentieth centuries). This large-scale mobility, ethnographically known as 'the travels', or 'travelling', shaped the cultural landscape of Zagori; wealthy emigré merchants were channelling the surplus of their entrepreneurial activities back into their homeland for the creation of private mansions and commonwealth structures (e.g., bridges, schools, churches).[4]

---

1 Solnit, *Wanderlust: A History of Walking*; Macleod, 'Cultural Routes, Trails and the Experience of Place'; Hall et al., *The Routledge International Handbook of Walking*.
2 Svensson et al., 'Introduction'.
3 *Sensu* Ingold, 'The Temporality of the Landscape'.
4 Dalkavoukis, *Γράφοντας Ανάμεσα. Εθνογραφικές Δοκιμές με Αφορμή το Ζαγόρι* [Writings in between. Ethnographic Essays Emerging from Zagori]; Μετοικεσίες Ζαγορισίων *(1750–1922)* [Zagorisian Relocations (1750–1922)]; Stoianovich, 'The Conquering Balkan Orthodox Merchant'.

On the other hand, intensive regional-scale mobility shaped the internal peasant landscape of Zagori.[5] Pathways in the microscale of the communities connected the core of the village with the wider agropastoral taskscapes,[6] while trails passing through the same famous bridges linked the nexus of settlements, weaving together a set of culturally defined taskscapes, trans-communal resources (e.g., watermills), and more-than-human actors such as the rivers and their sometimes annually-changing courses.

Consequently, the mountainous cultural landscape of Zagori is better appreciated through walking, trekking and hiking. However, there are various ways of walking and only a few of them result in the reenactment of this cultural landscape in the present.[7] Post-Civil War abandonment and subsequent permanent migration of the local population, following the trends of the *Gastarbeiter* and the wider urbanisation of the 1970s, led to large-scale afforestation covering the imprint of the agropastoral cultural landscape.[8] Contrastingly, the monuments that emerged as a by-product of the large-scale mobility of 'travelling' have become commemorative tropes of a canonical history addressing the importance of Zagori in the national narrative (i.e., prosperous Orthodox communities within a sea of Ottoman-Turks). Local mobility (taskscapes) is gradually being forgotten, and the touristic development followed a strict division into cultural (settlement) and natural (everything else) landscape. Such an understanding leaves no space for hillside cultivation, terraces, threshing floors, pens and various other traces of more-than-human activities in the wider landscape beyond settlements. This polarisation between loci of the cultural and natural landscape follows the constitution of modernity[9] and has affected pathways, walking and understanding the cultural landscape of Zagori. 'Traditional' swimming pools are emerging, while tourists gaze at the young dense forests of prickly oak and perceive timeless woodlands.

At present, the Greek Ministry of Culture and Sports is drafting the application to inscribe Zagori in the UNESCO World Heritage List, as a Cultural

---

5   Moudopoulos-Athanasiou, *The Early Modern Zagori of Northwest Greece. An Interdisciplinary Archaeological Inquiry into a Montane Cultural Landscape*.
6   For the neighbouring area of Konitsa, see Nitsiakos, *Peklari: Social Economy in a Greek Village*.
7   Moudopoulos-Athanasiou, 'Pathways to Remember, Sidetracks to Forget: Walking and the Archaeological Landscape of Zagori'.
8   Stara, Tsiakiris and Wong, 'Valuing Trees in a Changing Cultural Landscape: A Case Study from Northwestern Greece'; Moudopoulos-Athanasiou, 'Woodland Values in Zagori, NW Greece (19th–21st Century): Between Heritage and History'; Green et al., 'Landscape Perception in Epirus in the Late 20th Century'; Nitsiakos *Χτίζοντας τον Χώρο και το Χρόνο* [Constructing Space and Time]; Dalkavoukis, *Γράφοντας Ανάμεσα. Εθνογραφικές Δοκιμές με Αφορμή το Ζαγόρι* [Writings in between. Ethnographic Essays Emerging from Zagori].
9   Latour, *We Have Never Been Modern*.

15. Walking the Kalderimi

Landscape.[10] UNESCO promotes community engagement within World Heritage Sites and local stakeholder inclusion in the decision-making processes is deemed important – if not compulsory.[11] In this context, we organised the First Participatory Stone Masonry Workshop in Zagori, entitled 'Reappearances: New Kalderimi (cobbled pathway) in Aristi, Zagori',[12] abiding by our approach committed to grass-roots heritage management.[13] In a settlement with less than fifty permanent inhabitants, we explored the notion of places of origin as a foundation for the development of participatory models in the heritage management of cultural landscapes. Drawing from our fieldwork, this contribution reflects on the potencies of the kalderimi in rekindling communal memories, histories and modes of craftsmanship, through embodied practices such as, but not limited to, walking.[14]

The case of 'reappearances': walking between dwelling and the touristic gaze

'Reappearances' emerged beyond the context of strict disciplinary and formative boundaries. Our backgrounds[15] lay in archaeology, architecture and civil engineering, while our positionalities in the field presented radical differentiations, increasing the potential of the project, and facilitating the fusion of different approaches resulting in one methodology, as the subsequent sections reveal. The archaeologist of our group (Faidon Moudopoulos-Athanasiou), while vice-president of the local cultural club (Aristi Youth Club) and Ph.D. researcher at the Department of Archaeology at the University of Sheffield, invited the interdisciplinary research collectivity 'Boulouki'[16] to survey the current status of the existing kalderimia (plural) at the village of Aristi and co-organise a participatory workshop.

---

10   Moudopoulos-Athanasiou, 'Woodland Values in Zagori'.
11   Ripp and Rodwell, 'Governance in UNESCO World Heritage Sites: Reframing the Role of Management Plans as a Tool to Improve Community Engagement'.
12   More information available at https://www.boulouki.org/projects-reapperances (accessed 22 March 2021).
13   Sklavounos et al., 'Kalderimi X2, Tzoumerka, Epirus: Paving the Way for a New Generation of Craftspeople'; Moudopoulos-Athanasiou, 'Τοπικά Αφηγήματα, Τοπική Ιστορία και Αρχαιολογία' [Local narratives, local history and archaeology].
14   See Acknowledgements for the full list of collaborators in this endeavour.
15   See Acknowledgements.
16   In Greek, Boulouki means 'gaggle', a travelling group; a word evoking the tradition of itinerant companies of stone masons and craftsmen. See Sklavounos et al., 'Kalderimi X2, Tzoumerka, Epirus: Paving the Way for a New Generation of Craftspeople', p. 101.

Figure 1.

A mixture of different techniques, from dry-stone kalderimi (left) to concrete-paved slabs (right). Source: © Ionas Sklavounos / Boulouki.

The study of the archaeological landscape of Zagori, full of pre-and early modern dry-stone structures, had led the local researcher to argue that current trends in regional touristification, as described above, significantly alter the cultural landscape both within and beyond the settlements (Figure 1). The researchers of 'Boulouki', having deep knowledge of the values and variations of the dry-stone technique had reached the same conclusion through their exposure to the making of such structures and through critically observing the places they had worked previously.

In that sense, critical ethnography combined with hands-on approaches and an autoethnographic sensibility[17] proved in practice to surpass the unproductive division between insider/outsider;[18] and, through the unifying themes of *time* and *landscape*,[19] we identified two different modes of walking in Zagori. The

---

17 After Chang, *Autoethnography as Method*.
18 As hinted by Reed-Danahay, 'Bourdieu and Critical Autoethnography: Implications for Research, Writing, and Teaching'.
19 Ingold, *Making: Anthropology, Archaeology, Art and Architecture*, p. 11.

15. Walking the Kalderimi

first way of walking abides by the rules of single-visits and weekend expeditions[20] in line with the infamous tourist gaze,[21] while this model of development generates new pathways.[22] In contrast to the above, our research regards walking as a fundamental aspect of dwelling,[23] thus having the potential to rekindle memories, histories and knowledge of forgotten beliefs and activities.

Walking as a primary expression of dwelling

Walking the kalderimi is situated within the context of dwelling. The name of the kalderimi itself (turk. kildirim) means causeway or footway.[24] Pathways of this sort in their original sense were linguistically related to a vagabond mobile life in the pre-and early modern Ottoman world of the Balkans; leading the life of the kalderimi (turk. kaldirim üstünde sürün) means to lead a vagabond life of poverty, while kildirimcilik is the profession of a paver but also the action of picking pockets[25] and the expression 'dağa kaldir' is translated as 'to seize and take to the mountains'.[26] Consequently, the ontology of the dry-stone kalderimi is bound with a heritage of dwelling and mobility especially in, but not limited to, the mountainous landscapes of the Southern Balkans and the various modes of mobility occurring in that space.

Kalderimia articulated connections within the settlements, but also linked the inhabited spaces with their surrounded taskscapes. Subsequently, in the present, they have the potential to rekindle memories of past practices and generate histories forgotten due to the advent of the touristified modernity, as discussed previously. 'Reappearances' evolved around the notion of place. While working 'in place' – that is a fixed point within the settlement – our work facilitated movement, reestablishing a forgotten connection between two

---

20 Stara, Tsiakiris and Wong, 'Valuing Trees in a Changing Cultural Landscape: A Case Study from Northwestern Greece'; Moudopoulos-Athanasiou, 'Woodland Values in Zagori'; Nitsiakos, *Χτίζοντας τον Χώρο και το Χρόνο* [Constructing Space and Time].

21 Dalkavoukis, *Γράφοντας Ανάμεσα. Εθνογραφικές Δοκιμές με Αφορμή το Ζαγόρι* [Writings in between. Ethnographic Essays Emerging from Zagori]; Urry, *The Tourist Gaze*.

22 New pathways have emerged following global trends: the Zagori Mountain Running (80 km) https://zagorirace.gr/en/ and Epirus Trail, a network of new hiking pathways in the region of Epirus (370 km total) http://www.epirustrail.gr/en/. Furthermore, the ecological movement against the creation of new dams in the river of Aoos (Vjose in Albanian) resulted in the creation of the annual Protect Aoos Mountain Bike Ultra, through an initiative of the local community of Vovousa http://aoosmtbultra.gr/?page_id=3318 (accessed 22 March 2021).

23 For example Ingold, 'Culture on the Ground: The World Perceived through the Feet'; Ingold and Vergunst, 'Introduction'.

24 Avery, *New Redhouse Turkish-English Dictionary*, p. 585.

25 Ibid., p. 585.

26 Ibid., p. 265.

different neighbourhoods (mahalle) of the village. Furthermore, our practice directed us towards 'the road' – practically, as raw material for the construction came from small forgotten quarries located in the wider landscape, and metaphorically, following the stories of place as the following sections reveal.

Reconstructing the kalderimi

'[W]hile we academics are fond of convening so-called "workshops" to discuss our ideas,... apart from much earnest tapping on keyboards ... no handwork ever gets done'.[27] Such was the conclusion of Tim Ingold in a chapter expressing his thoughts on the embodied dimension of knowledge and its transmission.[28] Our team formed a heterogeneous community including stonemasons, beekeepers, ceramists, Ph.D. researchers in archaeology and architecture, undergraduate students and locals.[29]

Our workshop immersed in an affective field, in which our group reconstructed the kalderimi within an environment of 'communal' labour closely linked to the past practice when paving the cobbled pathways was a manifestation of dwelling, through bodily immediacy and by taking on active roles in the shaping of the local cultural landscape. Far from a folkloric revival, or the quest for the discovery of an idealised past, we aimed to approach dwelling and placemaking through the lens of embodied and collective action. That is why we opted for the term affective field (collective), rather than sensorial (individual), as our group formed a new community within the village and our practice aimed at different temporalities than the dominant (albeit quasi dormant due to the pandemic) touristic gaze.

We framed our own taskscape, which included walking and working in place, with a quite strict working schedule (08:00–16:00), shared meals, and jaunts in the wider landscape. Following the lead of three experienced craftsmen, day by day, our group (of apprentices and volunteers) moved deeper into the knowledge of drystone building, as well as the knowledge of the landscape itself. Engaged in such multisensorial fieldwork, we witnessed first-hand the

---

27 Ingold, *Making: Anthropology, Archaeology, Art and Architecture*, p. 124.
28 Ibid., pp. 109–24.
29 The reception of the local community in Aristi was far from singular. Community engagement always requires time, and although we presented our project in two open discussions long before the implementation, we did not manage to secure unanimous support. This could be partly due to the advent of COVID-19 and relevant reluctance to welcome a large group of people in a small village with mostly elder inhabitants, despite the strict health and safety measures implemented and communicated with local stakeholders. Nevertheless, the volunteers and discussants from Aristi, as well as the support of all the local businesses, point towards a successful engagement, given the circumstances.

15. Walking the Kalderimi

tacit nature of traditional craftsmanship, as our fellow stonemasons could articulate, and transmit, more knowledge than their verbal instructions. Furthering this thought, feeling the cobblestones, and tuning with the repetitive movements and sounds produced by hammers and chisels and the echo of this action in the silent neighbourhood, provided the more-than-human 'milieu' of our work and learning experience.

Such affective energy gradually became part of the material and mnemonic history of the neighbourhood[30] bringing us closer to the latent rhythms of the local community. Thus, alongside the sensorial assemblages generated by the work taking place, it was the participatory ethos of this workshop that allowed it to move beyond the revival of dead practices, or the simulation of an idealised past. As we argue below, it is this *atmosphere* that brought new interpretations of the place to the fore, while rekindling the memories of locals in relationship to the pathway and the forgotten regional ways of walking.

The narrative of the topsoil

As topsoil, we define the surface where walking was occurring before our intervention and the very textures that we disturbed to level the ground for the reconstruction of the kalderimi.[31] This thin layer of soil, and the past layers of walking it entailed, bridged our different backgrounds, methodologies and aspirations. For the archaeologist, topsoil is the layer to be removed, often in haste, to dive into the deeper layers of the human past buried underneath, while, for the architect and the civil engineer, it is the debris in need of riddance in order to lay the foundations of a structure. Although the soil in general bears great significance in branches of archaeology (e.g., geoarchaeology and soil chemistry) and material science, topsoil is broadly neglected in both. Hence, our interest in this layer imposed a level of sincere awkwardness, challenging our practice and institutional knowledge.

Walking the path of decay and oblivion

While dealing with this layer and levelling the ground, we collected evidence of material culture dating to the nineteenth and twentieth centuries from the surface. As in some instances we uncovered the stone-paving layer of the original

---

30 Hamilakis, 'From Fields of Discourse to Fields of Sensoriality: Rethinking the Archaeological Record', p. 247.

31 Petra Lilja (this volume) also puts the soil – mineral in her case – at the core of the argument. Our cases suggest that the soil and its qualities (composition, stratigraphy, etc) offer another layer to reflect on the 'feet first engagement with the world' (Ingold and Vergunst, 'Introduction', p. 8).

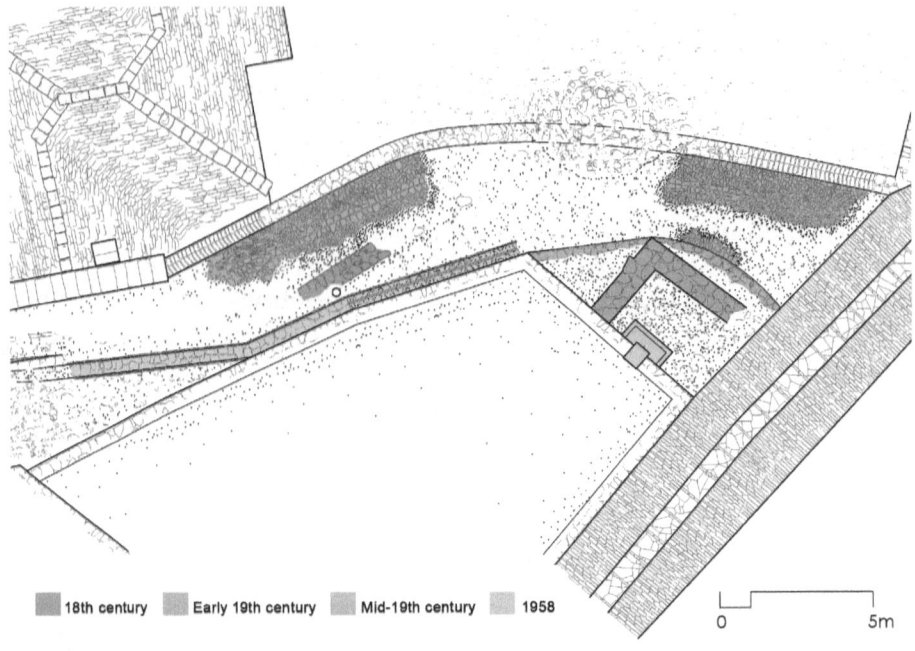

Figure 2.

The architectural drawing of the eastern side of the pathway, showing the remains uncovered during the project. The surviving patches of the nineteenth century paving layer are visible among other structures. The suggested chronologies are preliminary and relative, based on the combination of a) the material culture retrieved from each area, b) archival research and c) oral histories. Source: © Grigoris Koutropoulos / Boulouki.

Figure 3.

Left: imported nineteenth and early twentieth century potsherds from Apulia and Corfu. Right: A material culture assemblage of the Anthropocene. Photograph by Faidon Moudopoulos-Athanasiou.

15. Walking the Kalderimi

kalderimi we reconstructed (Figure 2), nineteenth and twentieth-century fragments of imported wares from Apulia and Corfu, with their fairly recognisable linear and flower decorative motifs pointing to the time this kalderimi passed into oblivion. The topsoil bore more indications of decay, forming an assemblage of the Anthropocene (Figure 3). On top of the forgotten kalderimi, we uncovered a set of unwanted, deposited, twentieth-century trash: metal parts of wooden doors, medicine injections for sheep and goats, gun cartridges and pill-boxes of one of the most commonly used painkillers. As these objects were uncovered above the nineteenth-century stone-paving layer, they portrayed a picture of forgetting and neglect, evolving in parallel to the gradual decay and depopulation of the local mountainous communities of the Zagori, Greece, and the Mediterranean, over the course of the twentieth century.[32]

Despite this image of abandonment, the pathway continued to be walked, but without any elder inhabitant remembering the existence of the paved kalderimi. This prolonged neglect of the village infrastructure coincides with the shift from dwelling to the touristic perception of this landscape: the shift from kalderimia linking neighbourhoods and taskscapes to asphalt roads facilitating the needs of single-visit tourists, as outlined in the introduction. Our pathway is situated very close to the (touristified) village centre, but its main value derives from its placement within the local taskscape. This dual characteristic played a significant role in choosing the location of our intervention, aiming to enhance the local taskscape and present an alternative to mass tourism, through potentially reiterating part of the visitor's movement away from the village square.

Topsoil and the memory of the elite 'travelling' mobility

On the western side of the pathway, we reconstructed the collapsed dry-stone wall of a private courtyard, a necessary step to pave the new kalderimi. While piling the old stones, we discovered at the foundation of the wall a small hoard of coins placed in between the stones. This practice, a rite for good fortune, transcends the borders of Zagori and is also empirically recorded in Southern Yorkshire (UK) and plausibly in other areas with a dry-stone tradition. The coins discovered were from Russia, China and Korea, dating to the final quarter of the nineteenth century (Figure 4). Like all objects, these discoveries have their

---

32 For some cases in Epirus, see, *inter alia*, Nitsiakos, *Η Κόνιτσα και τα Χωριά της* [Konitsa and its Villages]; Damianakos et al., *Εξουσία, Εργασία και Μνήμη σε Τρία Χωριά της Ηπείρου. Η Τοπική Δύναμη της Επιβίωσης* [Power, Labour and Memory in Three Villages of Epirus: The Local Power of Survival]; Green, *Notes from the Balkans: Locating Marginality and Ambiguity on the Greek-Albanian Border*. For a Mediterranean synthesis, see McNeill, *The Mountains of the Mediterranean World*.

Figure 4.

The small assemblage of coins from Russia, China and Korea. Photograph by Faidon Moudopoulos-Athanasiou.

peculiar itineraries,[33] being the tangible proof of the entrepreneurial activities of that family. From a common destination for the elites of Zagori, such as Russia, to the Chinese provinces of Fujian and Hubei, the nexus of mobility would have emerged on foot at our very own kalderimi. At the porch, they would have performed a ritual securing the ties to their homeland and then the procession of the 'travellers' and their families would have walked the kalderimi up to the liminal point of the village, at the location called 'Pigadouli'. That liminal location, spiritually represented by a shrine, is the final point to which families were allowed to follow the procession of the 'travellers', who then

---

33 Bauer, 'Itinerant Objects'.

15. Walking the Kalderimi

would continue their journey on foot to Thessaloniki, the main railway town, to continue their entrepreneurial journeys.

Walking the kalderimi, therefore, unites different modalities of past dwelling. Those striding along the local agropastoral taskscapes and those wandering the entrepreneurial pathways of the globalised 'long nineteenth-century' world-system. The reconstruction of the kalderimi and the attitude of researchers towards the potentialities of the topsoil to generate historical narratives of walking, albeit awkward at first, led to some profound observations, otherwise described in theoretical network analyses.

Beneath the topsoil: rekindling the memory of place

The eastern edge of the pathway is marked by the existence of a fountain established in 1958. This fountain is a manifestation of the communal effort to distribute flowing water in all the neighbourhoods, through the installation of permanent water tanks within the settlement. Villages in the Zagori mostly suffer from aridity[34] and Aristi is not an exception. Consequently, when this fountain was established, our pathway became the focal point of the neighbourhood: all households would walk the path to obtain drinking water from its edge. However, by that time the nineteenth-century kalderimi was already covered with debris.

While clearing the topsoil at this part of the pathway, we uncovered a decent part of the nineteenth-century kalderimi. We also discovered that the fountain was established on top of a collapsed structure, tangentially linked with another dry-stone wall, a courtyard defining that long-forgotten private property buried beneath the public fountain and pathway (Figure 5). Underneath the foundations of the twentieth-century wall attached to the fountain, we uncovered a copper coin of Sultan Abdulmecit I (1823–1861), thus establishing the approximate date for the ruination of the nineteenth-century courtyard. Topsoil on that part of the pathway contained a lot of charcoal and bones of sheep and goats. Inside the collapsed structure we uncovered a decorative part of the lower arm of a flintlock pistol (in use during the eighteenth and nineteenth centuries, Figure 6).

These newly discovered archaeological layers triggered a round of ethnographic inquiry from the locals that participated in our project. This way, we learned that elders had heard of the hut and, although destroyed before their time, they knew that it collapsed after it accidentally caught fire. This narrative would partially explain the concentration of charcoal in the area adjacent to the ruined structure.

---

34   Dalkavoukis, *Γράφοντας Ανάμεσα. Εθνογραφικές Δοκιμές με Αφορμή το Ζαγόρι* [Writings in between. Ethnographic Essays Emerging from Zagori].

Figure 5.

The eastern edge before (above) and after (below) the intervention. Photographs by Faidon Moudopoulos-Athanasiou.

Furthermore, our activity rekindled childhood memories, producing histories of past uses of space around the pathway. The area above the fountain, for example, was called 'the grove' and, as it was situated next to the school, children would play there during weekdays in the pre-and immediately afterwar period.

15. Walking the Kalderimi

Figure 6.

Left: a coin with the value of 10 Para, printed in year 19 of Sultan Abdulmecit I's reign (1858). Right: the decorative part of the flintlock pistol, partly preserved. Photographs by Faidon Moudopoulos-Athanasiou.

Scraping the surface of modernity

Having in mind the above, 'Reappearances' highlighted how working on – and around – a kalderimi facilitates the discourse of movement and pathways as heritage. One might suggest that this is partly because, in the case of a cobbled pathway, the footpath takes on the stability and permanence of a cultural artefact.[35] Paved and maintained by a community's own hands, kalderimia emerge as structures carefully – and laboriously – woven into the landscape, laden with meanings and evocative potential. However, as we saw earlier, this status as tangible object is not sufficient to recognise the cobblestone as a cultural artefact worth preserving, as its ties with practices, memories and narratives fade: kalderimia follow similar processes of abandonment to other 'natural' pathways, due to the occurring shifts in the cultural landscape.

---

35   Tuan, 'The Significance of the Artifact'.

Beyond modernity: the memory of place

A kalderimi is usually perceived as a humble structure, produced by non-experts and their communal labour, which, fortunately, does not easily qualify it for monument status. Such 'ordinary'[36] structures placed at the thresholds of institutionalised heritage are highly advantageous for exploring a direct, affective relationship with inherited artefacts and landscapes and developing an experimental approach to the potentialities of local memory.[37] Even more, they invite us to rethink the modern paradigm of 'heritage making': rather than arguing for the consideration of the kalderimi as yet another static artefact of heritage, we may reconsider heritage as a dynamic body of place-making practices, such as restoring or building a kalderimi anew.

Such a claim is supported by observing how the process of constructing the cobbled pathway – and engaging in the related affective field – has a multidirectional effect. In this case, 'Reappearances' created a short-lived and diverse community whose members engaged bodily and laboriously with a pathway belonging to the realm of the commons, tracing the outlines of a collective ethos that is similar in principle, but not identical, to the traditional forms of social solidarity and communal labour, of the mountainous communities of Epirus in the past.[38]

It is this very process that rekindled local memories of the place, from the time Aristi was densely populated and functioning within the context of the cultural landscape – that is, up to the 1970s. It is the ripple effects of a slow rediscovery of local knowledge, reverberating across the working site, as well as the sounds of chatter, chisels and laughter during communal meals, that encouraged the memories of elder inhabitants to resurface. Such rhythmical movements appeared to trigger aspects of a habitus[39] that was dormant, due to the ways modernity forgets: caught up in a flight to the future, in a radical denying of tradition, while obsessively turning to the past in nostalgia.[40] Is it not such an antinomy that also drives the superhuman speeds at which we are

---

36 For the category of 'everyday heritage', see Pendlebury and Townshend, *Conservation in the Age of Consensus*; Mosler, 'Everyday Heritage Concept as an Approach to Place-Making Process in the Urban Landscape'. The absence of grand narratives and legal protection regimes leaves room for a given community to step in and claim the appropriation of its own heritage, as well as to assume the responsibility for its protection, exploring the right to use, repair and even reshape it, according to practical and symbolic needs.

37 After Connerton, *How Modernity Forgets*, pp. 4–5.

38 For a case study on such laborious practices, see Nitsiakos, *Peklari: Social Economy in a Greek Village*.

39 After Bourdieu, *Outline of a Theory of Practice*.

40 Benjamin, 'Theses on the Philosophy of History'; Connerton, *How Modernity Forgets*.

15. Walking the Kalderimi

called to visit places that have since become 'destinations' and capture them through the detached gaze of the driver-tourist? (a gaze that persists even when s/he leaves the automobile behind).

Bridging social and disciplinary memory

If 'the narrative of the topsoil' suggested that our affective field was stretching backwards in time, the multitemporal narratives of mobility (from elite 'travelling' to the walks of subsistence) as represented by the different layers of uncovered kalderimi guided our practice in the present. This is manifested on the eastern edge of the pathway, which provided the most fruitful configuration during 'Reappearances'. Our team treated the uncovered remains of the old kalderimi, the discovered ruins of the mid-nineteenth century dry-stone hut beneath the topsoil and the superimposed fountain of the 1950s synthetically, assembling them into a new composition (see Figures 2 and 5). More specifically, we converted an area associated with many different ways of walking into a resting place: we elevated the contour walls of the ruined hut and reshaped its interior to form a small square and drystone seating around the fountain. The cognitive and affective value of such an experimental approach, elaborated on the borderlines of established restoration standards, can be assessed when seen to mediate between 'social' and 'disciplinary' memory, as follows.

Practices of additive transformations based on the reuse of building material and architectural spolia are rooted in the history of both 'vernacular' and 'pedigreed' architecture,[41] while the attenuation of this tradition seems to keep pace with the rise of the authoritative figure of the modern architect. In archaeology, an equivalent case can be found in the legacy of the 'cultural historical' approaches to the discipline, or in the ways some 'processual' archaeologists have interpreted the past through a static set of evidence, the archaeological record. John Barrett illustrated well the problem for both disciplines in 1988: time and space, he argued, are not merely descriptive and they constitute a field occupied by the practice of a particular discourse that is not devoid of the agency of the people.[42]

Indeed, the development of such discourses and their reiteration into society produced a profound cultural gap between the collective memory of communities and the disciplinary memory of knowledge systems that were constituted as modern 'scientific' fields. In the words of Stanford Anderson, 'vernacular architecture represents at least a close cohesion of social and dis-

---

41   Rudofsky, *Architecture without Architects: A Short Introduction to Non-Pedigreed Architecture*.
42   Barrett, 'Fields of Discourse: Reconstituting a Social Archaeology', p. 11.

ciplinary memory [while] it is the advent of writing and history that invited the increasing distinction between these memory systems'.[43]

In this connection, the emphasis on disciplinary memory encourages a literate way of reading the past through systems of precedents and references, codes and conventions, thus tending to fix it in irrevocable narratives. On the other hand, social memory collocates with an oral culture allowing for a perpetual reinterpretation carried out through processes of collective remembering as well as forgetting.[44] Importantly, in the case of social memory, this dynamic relationship with the past is consistent with the systematic reuse and adaptation of architectural artefacts; with a 'workable' – and 'walkable' – conception of the built environment, rather at odds with our modern historical sensitivity inviting us to 'protect' cultural landscapes and 'admire' them from afar.

In the context of Anderson's scheme, the layered affinities between Ottoman-era stone-arched bridges and their surrounding kalderimia would describe the proximity of social and disciplinary memory, manifested in vernacular architecture. However, things get more complicated when we think of which category *is officially recognised* as a monument in the present. With the advent of modernity, many such bridges were annexed into monuments, perceived as vessels communicating the values of the affluent early-modern historical past and the wealthy benefactors that financed their constructions. These names are carved in stone, placing the bridges within the modern disciplinary genealogy. In contrast, the 'humble' kalderimia *are not* considered monuments, although the processes of their collective creation and the stories of mobility they entail evoke critical aspects of the same heritage. Thus, if monuments, in general, appear to be cut off from modern societies, the artefacts of this 'modest' heritage are even more marginalised, fading away along with the practices and memories that held them in place and which evolved with – and through – them.

'Reappearances' opened a multitemporal and transdisciplinary field aiming to reestablish the links between academics, communities and volunteering participants, from the bottom up. In this connection, we tried to explore 'hands-on' the values of the – often praised but rarely studied – modalities of vernacular building, while opening new ways for their reinterpretation. The successful engagement of various stakeholders argues that the time has come for serious and deep community engagement, co-creation and reconfiguration of heritage beyond the social and disciplinary divide.

---

43   Anderson, 'Memory without Monuments: Vernacular Architecture', 15.
44   Le Goff and Nora, *Constructing the Past : Essays in Historical Methodology*.

15. Walking the Kalderimi

Heritage as the process of the kalderimi

Through specific episodes of 'Reappearances', we aimed to show how our practice invited a profoundly embodied engagement with heritage. This we explained through the intertwined practices of walking, working and narrating. As the affective field of our engagement with the place was multidirectional, we suggest that oral histories and ethnographic and archaeological inquiries are not to be set apart from the beats of the chisels or the sound of strides along the kalderimi, but rather that they should be seen (or heard) as elements of the same multi-sensorial ambience that enveloped this community of knowledge. Through this analysis, we also recognised the importance of enactment and orality as key concepts for alternative understandings of heritage that put forth the embodied aspect.

Our approach derived from the very 'nature' of kalderimi as a footpath, which invites us to walk and explore the settlement and its surrounding landscape. Such a 'feet-on' approach evokes a different temporality than the passing tourist, also emphasising the *depth* of the world, accessible primarily through bodily movement.[45]

By the same token, the manual labour involved in the restoration of the kalderimi empowers the embodied relation with heritage, already promoted by walking. This way, multisensorial engagement with heritage generates the affective field(work) of presence. The footpath not only invites us to explore the landscape with all our senses but also 'comes into our hands' and is placed at the centre of our creative work. The perspective of craftsmanship which focuses on the dialogue 'between hand and head'[46] builds on the perspective of walking and is thus presented as the key to further discussing heritage in terms of bodily engagement.

Our practice pointed to the idea that the various landscapes of developed societies are neither continuous nor homogenous, but hybrids including, in varying degrees, both orality and literate culture, myth and history, tradition and modernity. Such landscapes appear as 'patches' where different realities of the Anthropocene survive, interbreed and evolve.[47]

Thus 'Reappearances', as a project centred around hands-on reinterpretations of heritage, encouraged the community to (claim its right to) engage in an effective dialogue with its past. The affective field of our workshop reached,

---

45 Merleau-Ponty, *Phenomenology of Perception*; Koch et al., *Body Memory, Metaphor and Movement*.
46 Sennett, *The Craftsman*.
47 Tsing et al., *Arts of Living on a Damaged Planet*; Tsing, 'Contaminated Diversity in "Slow Disturbance": Potential Collaborators for a Liveable Earth'.

to an extent, its goal, rekindling memories and discourses of a past when communities were responsible, and proactive, in the interpretation and appreciation of their common cultural heritage. This was made possible through the sensorial assemblages emerging at our taskscape, and the welcoming reception of some local actors.

However, the conceptual depth of embodied knowledge becomes more apparent when it incorporates the act of speaking, as inextricably twined with our breath, tongue and body; our habits, customs and culture.[48] In this sense, the stories of the 'travels' from the Zagori to China and their material culture footprint are part of the embodied and affective multitemporal expression of dwelling, observed through its pathways.

Acknowledgements

The research was organised by 'Boulouki' and the Aristi Youth Club. Our team consisted of Panagiotis Kostoulas, Grigoris Koutropoulos, Christophoros Theocharis, Mina Kouvara and the authors. Four experienced craftsmen, Kostas Tarnanas, Pavlos Vichas, Michalis Besiris and Christos Tsekas, guided the three apprentices and introduced twenty volunteers to the craft of the drystone walling and kalderimi-making. The Ministry of Culture and Sports, the District of Epirus, and the Greek National Committee for UNESCO endorsed the project, and we received grants from the White Rose College for the Arts and Humanities (AHRC - Grant No. AH/L503848/1) and the Technical Chamber of Epirus, while 199 individuals contributed to our crowdfunding campaign. The former public school in Aristi, hotels and companies hosted the team and the volunteers, while the stone-masons and their apprentices lived in the neighbouring village of Ano Soudena, at the research facilities Lambriadeios School (Ano Soudena Cultural Foundation & PALASE, the University of Ioannina). The Aristi Youth Club, together with local restaurants and Agrifarm Premium Products, provided the meals for the team. We thank them all for their support.

Bibliography

Anderson, Stanford, 'Memory without Monuments: Vernacular Architecture', *Traditional Dwellings and Settlements Review* (1999).

Avery, Robert, *New Redhouse Turkish-English Dictionary* (Istanbul: Istanbul Press, 1968).

Bauer, Alexander, 'Itinerant Objects', *Annual Review of Anthropology* **48** (1) (2019): 335–52.

---

48   Durt et al., *Embodiment, Enaction, and Culture, Embodiment, Enaction, and Culture*.

15. Walking the Kalderimi

Barrett, John, 'Fields of Discourse: Reconstituting a Social Archaeology', *Critique of Anthropology* **7** (3) (1988): 5–16.

Benjamin, Walter, 'Theses on the Philosophy of History', in *Illuminations*, trans. Harry Zohn (New York: Schocken, 1968).

Bourdieu, Pierre, *Outline of a Theory of Practice* (Cambridge: Cambridge University Press, 1977).

Chang, Heewon, *Autoethnography as Method*, vol. 1. (Abingdon/New York: Routledge, 2016).

Connerton, Paul, *How Modernity Forgets* (Cambridge: Cambridge University Press, 2009).

Dalkavoukis, Vassilis, *Γράφοντας Ανάμεσα. Εθνογραφικές Δοκιμές με Αφορμή το Ζαγόρι* [Writings in between. Ethnographic Essays Emerging from Zagori] (Thessaloniki: Epikentro, 2015).

Dalkavoukis, Vassilis, *Μετοικεσίες Ζαγορισίων (1750–1922)* [Zagorisian Relocations (1750–1922)] (Thessaloniki: Rizareios, 1999).

Damianakos, Stathis, Ersi Zakopoulou, Charalambos Kasimis and Vassilis Nitsiakos (eds), *Εξουσία, Εργασία και Μνήμη σε Τρία Χωριά της Ηπείρου. Η Τοπική Δύναμη της Επιβίωσης* [Power, Labour and Memory in Three Villages of Epirus: The Local Power of Survival] (Athens: Plethron, 1997).

Durt, Christoph, Thomas Fuchs and Christian Tewes (eds), *Embodiment, Enaction, and Culture*, *Embodiment, Enaction, and Culture* (Cambridge MA: The MIT Press, 2017).

Green, Sarah, *Notes from the Balkans: Locating Marginality and Ambiguity on the Greek-Albanian Border* (Princeton: Princeton University Press, 2005).

Green, Sarah and Sander van der Leeuw, 'Landscape Perception in Epirus in the Late 20th Century', in *The Archaeomedes Project: Understanding the Natural and Anthropogenic Causes of Land Degradation and Desertification in the Mediterranean Basin*, pp. 330–59 (Luxembourg: Office for Official Publications of the European Communities, 1998).

Hall, Colin, Yael Ram and Noam Shoval (eds), *The Routledge International Handbook of Walking* (Abingdon: Routledge, 2017).

Hamilakis, Yannis, 'From Fields of Discourse to Fields of Sensoriality: Rethinking the Archaeological Record', in Michael Boyd and Roger Doonan (eds), *Far from Equilibrium: An Archaeology of Energy, Life and Humanity: A Response to the Archaeology of John C. Barrett*, pp. 239–57 (Oxford: Oxbow Books, 2021).

Ingold, Tim and Jo Lee Vergunst, 'Introduction', in Tim Ingold and Jo Lee Vergunst (eds), *Ways of Walking: Ethnography and Practice on Foot* (Aldershot: Ashgate, 2008).

Ingold, Tim, *Making: Anthropology, Archaeology, Art and Architecture* (Abingdon/New York: Routledge, 2013).

Ingold, Tim, 'Culture on the Ground: The World Perceived through the Feet', *Journal of Material Culture* **9** (3) (2004): 315–40.

Ingold, Tim, 'The Temporality of the Landscape', *World Archaeology* **25** (2) (1993): 152–74. https://doi.org/10.1080/00438243.1993.9980235

Koch, Sabine, Thomas Fuchs, Michela Summa and Cornelia Müller (eds), *Body Memory, Metaphor and Movement*, Advances in Consciousness Research vol. 84 (Amsterdam: John Benjamins Publishing Company, 2012).

Latour, Bruno, *We Have Never Been Modern* (Cambridge, MA: Harvard University Press, 1993).

Le Goff, Jacques and Pierre Nora (eds), *Constructing the Past : Essays in Historical Methodology* (New York: Cambridge University Press, 1985).

Lilja, Petra, 'Attentive Walking: Encountering Mineralness', in Daniel Svensson, Katarina Saltzman and Sverker Sörlin (eds), *Pathways: Exploring the Routes of a Movement Heritage*, pp. 201–18 (Winwick, Cambridgeshire: The White Horse Press).

Lymberopoulos, Giannis, *Ορεινοί και Μεθόριοι* [Mountainous and Liminal] (Athens, 1972).

Macleod, Nicola, 'Cultural Routes, Trails and the Experience of Place', in Melanie Smith and Greg Richards (eds), *The Routledge Handbook of Cultural Tourism*, pp. 369–74 (Abingdon: Routledge, 2013).

McNeill, John, *The Mountains of the Mediterranean World* (New York: Cambridge University Press, 1992).

Merleau-Ponty, Maurice, *Phenomenology of Perception* (Oxon: Routledge, 2014).

Mosler, Saruhan, 'Everyday Heritage Concept as an Approach to Place-Making Process in the Urban Landscape', *Journal of Urban Design* **24** (5) (2019): 778–93.

Moudopoulos-Athanasiou, Faidon, *The Early Modern Zagori of Northwest Greece. An Interdisciplinary Archaeological Inquiry into a Montane Cultural Landscape* (Leiden: Sidestone Press, 2022).

Moudopoulos-Athanasiou, Faidon, 'Woodland Values in Zagori, NW Greece (19th–21st Century): Between Heritage and History', *PLURAL* **8** (2) (2020): 103–19.

Moudopoulos-Athanasiou, Faidon, 'Τοπικά Αφηγήματα, Τοπική Ιστορία και Αρχαιολογία' [Local narratives, local history and archaeology] *Ηπειρωτικό Ημερολόγιο [Epirote Diary]* **93** (2018): 235–50.

Moudopoulos-Athanasiou, Faidon, 'Pathways to Remember, Sidetracks to Forget: Walking and the Archaeological Landscape of Zagori', *Presentation. Theoretical Archaeology Group Conference* (Cardiff: University of Cardiff, 2017).

Nitsiakos, Vasilis, *Peklari: Social Economy in a Greek Village* (Münster: LIT Verlag, 2015).

Nitsiakos, Vasilis, *Η Κόνιτσα και τα Χωριά της* [Konitsa and its Villages] (Ioannina: Epirus S.A, 2008).

Nitsiakos, Vassilis, *Χτίζοντας τον Χώρο και το Χρόνο* [Constructing Space and Time] (Athens: Odysseas, 2003).

Pendlebury, John and Tim Townshend, *Conservation in the Age of Consensus* (London: Routledge, 2009).

Reed-Danahay, Deborah, 'Bourdieu and Critical Autoethnography: Implications for Research, Writing, and Teaching', *International Journal of Multicultural Education* **19** (1) (2017): 144–54.

Ripp, Matthias and Dennis Rodwell, 'Governance in UNESCO World Heritage Sites: Reframing the Role of Management Plans as a Tool to Improve Community Engagement', in *Aspects of Management Planning for Cultural World Heritage Sites*, pp. 241–53 (Cham: Springer, 2018).

Rudofsky, Bernard, *Architecture without Architects: A Short Introduction to Non-Pedigreed Architecture* (Albuquerque: University of New Mexico, 1965).

Sennett, Richard, *The Craftsman* (London: Penguin Books, 2009).

Sklavounos, Ionas, Panos Kostoulas, Grigoris Koutropoulos, Christoforos Theocharis and Mina Kouvara, 'Kalderimi X2, Tzoumerka, Epirus: Paving the Way for a New Generation of Craftspeople', *Journal of Traditional Building, Architecture and Urbanism* **1** (2020): 100–11.

Solnit, Rebecca, *Wanderlust: A History of Walking* (London: Verso, 2002).

Stara, Kalliopi, Rigas Tsiakiris and Jennifer Wong, 'Valuing Trees in a Changing Cultural Landscape: A Case Study from Northwestern Greece', *Human Ecology* **43** (1) (2015): 153–67.

15. Walking the Kalderimi

Stoianovich, Traian, 'The Conquering Balkan Orthodox Merchant', *The Journal of Economic History* **20** (2) (1960): 234–313.

Svensson, Daniel, Katarina Saltzman and Sverker Sörlin, 'Introduction' in Daniel Svensson, Katarina Saltzman and Sverker Sörlin (eds), *Pathways: Exploring the Routes of a Movement Heritage*, pp. 1–29 (Winwick, Cambridgeshire: The White Horse Press).

Tsing, Anna, Heather-Anne Swanson, Elaine Gan and Nils Bubandt (eds), *Arts of Living on a Damaged Planet* (Minneapolis: University of Minnesota Press, 2017).

Tsing, Anna, 'Contaminated Diversity in "Slow Disturbance": Potential Collaborators for a Liveable Earth', *Why Do We Value Diversity? Biocultural Diversity in a Global Context* **9** (2012): 95–97.

Tuan, Yi-Fu, 'The Significance of the Artifact', *Geographical Review* **70** (4) (1980): 462–72.

Urry, John, *The Tourist Gaze* (London: Sage, 1990).

CHAPTER 16.

FORMING PATHS WITHIN POST-INDUSTRIAL LANDSCAPES

Benjamin Richards

Introduction

By introducing the idea of movement heritage, instead of, say, walking heritage, this book encourages the inclusion of the more-than-human forms that make up a particular landscape. But what does it mean to include such a perspective and how can this contribute toward thinking sustainably?

Movement includes walking without being about human movement exclusively. It rather implies the intra-relational quality of human movement within a larger moving whole, opening for an awareness of the multitude of interwoven forces at play, and the notion that the landscape itself is moving across a vast array of different yet overlapping temporalities.[1] This way of thinking about and engaging with landscapes is what I call intra-play.[2] We do not move in a vacuum, isolated from or unaffected by our surroundings, I propose that we are rather moved by the landscape as we move through it, moving it.

This chapter is a reflective essay, drawing on the experiences of doing research in the World Heritage area of Rjukan-Notodden in south-eastern Norway and the concepts and renderings that formed. The area is known for the harnessing of waterpower used for producing electricity and was subject to rapid industrialisation at the turn of the last century, particularly the production of chemical fertiliser. The former power station at Vemork has been turned into an industrial heritage museum. During the Second World War, heavy water, a by-product of this process, drew the attention of the Nazis as they sought to develop an atom bomb. The famous story of the Heroes of Telemark, where a group of saboteurs prevented the transportation of heavy water back to Germany, is marked by an

---

1   Ingold, 'The Temporality of the Landscape'.
2   Richards and Haukeland, 'A Phenomenology of Intra-play for Sustainability Research within Heritage Landscapes'.

16. Forming Paths within Post-industrial Landscapes

Figure 1.
Desire Path, Rjukan-Notodden World Heritage Site. Photograph by Benjamin Richards.

adventure trail called the 'saboteur route'.[3] Yet, despite its prominence and popularity, the story of the saboteurs is not yet part of the world heritage designation.

In this chapter I will first consider trails and paths as part of a wider *commons*, where use is an essential part of their continuous re-forming. Secondly, reflecting on experiences within Rjukan-Notodden, I will introduce and distinguish between *valued trails* and *paths of meaning*, that represent two different ways of moving and thinking within heritage landscapes. Finally, through the phenomena of *desire paths* and the concept of *drift*, I discuss what the process of forming paths can show us as visitors, inhabitants and researchers about relating sustainably to landscapes.

Paths of meaning

Following Rebecca Solnit, who says that 'exploring the world is one of the best ways of exploring the mind, and walking travels both terrains', I will now consider two different ways of moving within landscapes.[4]

The distinction made in this book between trails and paths is important. It helps us to distinguish between a more controlled or curated movement (an 'authorised' movement), as illustrated in the distinction between a 'public right of way' more prevalent in England, and the 'right to roam' or 'allemansretten' that is more broadly applied in Norway.[5] The former is often presented as a constant battle between public rights of way and private landowners or technical law changes that threaten their closure.[6] The latter represents a broader and more encompassing right to move in the landscape, with only a few exceptions such as private gardens and fields during crop season. Some of this can be explained by social and cultural differences, for example that in a country such as England the notion of private property is more strongly entrenched. Geographic differences also play a role, with England being far more densely populated than a country like Norway, with a far greater concentration of farmland and less wild space suitable for roaming, particularly in the south. In Norway, however,

---

3   Visit Norway (2020) Tracking the heroes of Telemark https://www.visitnorway.com/listings/tracking-the-heroes-of-telemark/211925/ (accessed 30 Nov. 2021)

4   Solnit, *Wanderlust*, p.13.

5   'Authorised Heritage' from Smith, *Uses of Heritage*. Regjeringen (2021) Allemannsretten https://www.regjeringen.no/no/tema/klima-og-miljo/friluftsliv/innsiktsartikler-friluftsliv/allemannsretten/id2076300/ (accessed 30 Nov. 2021); Government Digital Service (2021) Rights of way and accessing land https://www.gov.uk/right-of-way-open-access-land (accessed 30 Nov. 2021)

6   C. Davies (2015), 'Countdown begins to prevent loss of thousands of footpaths and alleyways', https://www.theguardian.com/environment/2015/dec/25/countdown-begins-to-prevent-loss-of-thousands-of-footpaths-and-alleyways (accessed 30 Nov. 2021)

16. Forming Paths within Post-industrial Landscapes

efforts to erode or exclude access also occur with, for example, attempts to form private beaches and the illegal building of cabins along the southern coastline.[7]

The differences go deeper though. The public right of way remains embedded in the Anglo-American political-economic model, where the relationship between public and private entities, in the modern period, has strengthened the rights of private ownership over the public good through law.[8] The walker, under such as system, has the right to pass through the landscape along specific, often fenced-off paths. The right to roam, conversely, through a number of well-established rules and conventions, limits the ability of private landowners to reduce access to only pre-determined paths, while still protecting their commercial interests. The landowner has the right to farm, hunt, graze animals and fell trees without interference, but not to limit access for other reasons such as walking, camping, mushrooming and wild berry picking. The right to roam has, as such, a much closer connection to the idea of the commons or a way of 'thinking like a commoner', where access to and use of the landscape was not determined by laws but through vernacular knowledge and the agreed behaviours that had formed within a specific landscape. The idea of the commons, then, does not simply refer to land or nature, nor the cultural codes and traditions around land use, but to the intra-play between people and landscapes.[9] As Peter Linebaugh describes, 'there is no commons without commoning' and equally no commoners without commons; the land and its inhabitants (as with path dependence) are co-dependent and cannot be separated.[10]

Looking back at the industrial period in Britain, the story of the commons is often referred to as an enclosure, where commoners were driven from the lands into 'wage slavery, urban poverty and inequality', losing their sense of 'community identity'.[11] While this is a part of the story, and enclosures are particularly relevant in relation to paths and trails, the history is always more nuanced. The fact that the early industrial period in Britain coincided with the privatisation of common land should not romanticise the life of commoners before that. While large scale industrialisation came later to Norway, as exemplified by the World Heritage site of Rjukan-Notodden, when labour

---

7   M. Dæhlen (2018), 'Kan du bade hvor du vil i Norge?', https://forskning.no/miljovern/kan-du-bade-hvor-du-vil-i-norge/1191986 (accessed 30 Nov. 2021).

8   D. Bollier (2011), 'The Commons, Political Transformation and Cities' http://www.bollier.org/commons-political-transformation-and-cities (accessed 30 Nov. 2021); Bollier, *Think Like a Commoner*; Ostrom, *Governing the Commons*, pp.12–15.

9   Bollier, *Think Like a Commoner*; Weber, *Enlivenment*.

10 Bollier, *Think Like a Commoner*, p. 19.

11 Ibid., pp. 41–45

jobs formed in the area, people travelled from all over the country and Europe to fill them without such forced enclosures being necessary. The 'dark satanic mills' of William Blake is a phrase often used to paint a picture of the terrible and dangerous conditions during the early industrial period.[12] Yet an overt focus on those aspects from the perspective of today overlooks the sense of pride and inclusion also felt by many of the workers, including children. Prior to the industrial period, in the lives of peasants and commoners, child labour and poverty were also a part of everyday life, but this is often looked upon as being natural and good, from a romantic perspective, compared with the labour and poverty of the factories and mines.[13]

What is interesting for this chapter, with regards to the commons, heritage and sustainability, is not the idea of returning to some romantic utopian idea of the past, but a way of thinking and behaving within the landscape that can be brought forth again in relation to living and thinking sustainably, and in how we form heritage today and in the future.

Heritage is often referred to as a commons, or a common, accumulated inheritance of that which has formed throughout history. But it is always in the present that it is considered, valued and given meaning and is as such subject to continual change. Following Rodney Harrison, I extend Linebaugh's description of the commons to heritage, that there is no heritage without 'heritaging'.[14] From this understanding, of heritage as an active process, I define heritage(ing) as 'a continual, creative intra-play between traces from the past and the present, forming futures'.[15]

The changes brought about by the processes of industrialisation have had profound implications on our relationships to the landscapes we inhabit. Moving human life into an ever-expanding urban environment, where working and living moved more and more inside or underground, severed further those ways of thinking and living that still remained from the commons. The release of previously unknown energy sources, the development of technologies and new modes of transportation and movement created enormous benefits and solved urgent problems. At the same time, these developments also created

---

12 The term 'dark satanic mills' appeared in William Blake's 1808 poem 'And did those feet in ancient time'. It is contested as to whether he referred to industrial mills or to the Church of England. It was however popularly used as a critique of the conditions in factories and the social class inequalities alongside the writings of William Wordsworth and Charles Dickens. Griffin, E., *Liberty's Dawn*, p. 11; Bollier, *Think Like a Commoner*, p. 43.

13 Schrumpf, 'History of Child Labor in the Nordic Countries', pp. 575–79.

14 Harrison, *Heritage: Critical Approaches*

15 Richards and Haukeland, 'A Phenomenology of Intra-play for Sustainability Research within Heritage Landscapes', p. 32.

16. Forming Paths within Post-industrial Landscapes

Figure 2.

Paths, Trails and Traces, Rjukan-Notodden World Heritage Site. Photograph by Benjamin Richards.

many, often unseen, consequences, most notably the polluting and poisoning of the air, land and water. But equally as important it has altered how we move in and subsequently interact with and think about the landscapes we inhabit. Within post-industrial heritage landscapes I am therefore interested in how paths are forming. Not only official heritage paths and trails, but new paths that are reconnecting these former industrial areas with the wider landscape again.

Heritage is to a great extent formed of what I am calling valued trails, as part of a heritage industry directed at tourism and regional identity building. These are predetermined, maintained routes through a region, often involving coaches, that help to shape and curate an authorised understanding and experience of the history, identity and values of a particular place. Such trails can be understood as part of a network connecting separate, definable objects that remain more-or-less fixed. The idea of paths of meaning, on the other hand, incorporates a landscape view of heritage. Here landscapes are understood to consist of an 'intra-play' of 'forms' (rather than objects, subjects, things), that are both forming and being formed by other forms. The notion of forms I find helps to dissolve the dichotomy between the human and more-than human world and points to the temporalities that bind them across scales.¹⁶ Humans are, then, also just forms within a landscape and a part of forming that landscape, as are building forms, migrating bird forms or calcite rock forms. Nor are they separate in any useful sense, humans are not just human but also more-than-human, in that they are formed of and by their surroundings, by other forms – both in terms of the tangible materiality of their bodies within the landscape (air, water, their 'mineralness'), but also in how thoughts, feelings and understandings are formed through sensory encounters within that landscape.¹⁷

As with Tim Ingold's concept of lines, paths of meaning can be understood as both the forming of physical traces, however temporary within the landscape, and the effect this movement has on how we think and feel.¹⁸ This could include a gust of wind, the slow growing of a branch on a tree, the long path of a building through time or the wandering movement of a researcher. All are part of that landscape within particular yet overlapping space-times, all are a part of the intra-play and what is forming. For Ingold, places 'are like knots' where lines converge and become entangled in their passing through; places are not enclosed nodes where life unfolds, connected within a network by pathways – it is rather that life is lived along these pathways.¹⁹ While Ingold does not speak of lines in a linear sense, there remains a certain degree of separateness that differs from what I wish to convey with paths of meaning.

While moving through a landscape, we participate in both a bodily and an emotive exchange with the world around us, that I call intra-play, causing both effects and affect. Our path is visible through the effects our movement has on other forms. The smell of the pollen released from a kicked flower, a footprint pressed into the mud on a rainy day, the snapping of a branch that had been slowly growing from a tree, the movement and chatter of birds aware of our presence. As such, rather than a line, our paths are perhaps better understood as the forces of movement that resonate out and are felt by other forms, the effects of which overlap in time and can still be felt within the landscape even after the physical traces have vanished.

Such paths are not only material but also constitute the forming of thoughts, ideas, feelings, memories, and meanings. There is a forming going on inside us as we move. Our thoughts and feelings, for example, do not come from inside us alone, as separate subjects, but are formed within the world around us. A

---

16   Richards and Haukeland, 'A Phenomenology of Intra-play for Sustainability Research within Heritage Landscapes'.
17   Our "mineralness", see Lilja in this volume.
18   Ingold, *The Life of Lines*.
19   Ingold, *Being Alive*, p. 149

16. Forming Paths within Post-industrial Landscapes

combination of a smell, a texture and a colour may trigger a feeling or emotion, which might later stir a memory, which is itself partly imagination, and then later still a thought or idea may form.[20] Such creative intra-plays are a part of what forms along paths of meaning and reflect a different way of ordering space-time within the landscape. It is not just that these paths are non-linear, they are also nonsequential. The e/affects of our movement are ephemeral, resonating out, merging, blending, fading and reappearing as new forms in another time.

This, I find, is best captured with the rendering *echo*, and the imaginary of heritage as the echoes of e/affective movements through time.[21] Some are repeated and amplified and persist, others fade and are forgotten, but all participate in the forming of the landscape. We could think of the landscape in this sense as being similar to a piece of music performed by an orchestra. You cannot grasp or absorb it – as a whole – all at once, and individually the notes played on each instrument lack context, but the experience is held together in its wholeness as a mood or feeling, an ambience. Even though we move through it in a particular order, the meaning that forms, that wholeness, is made up of all the individual parts, the rhythms and repetitions and combinations of moments as they are layered upon one another, we carry the echo of what came earlier into what comes later and together they form our meaningful experience of it. And as with music, the pathways and experiences that can be had within a landscape are both unique and potentially infinite.

Such meaningful experiences can form along valued trails, as we are always sensing, affected bodies, but part of what moving more freely within a landscape opens for is an attentiveness to the other forms making up that space-time with us and a new way of thinking about and viewing heritage as a landscape, beyond the curated routes and objects. While such an approach does not form a complete historical story that is easily communicated (or represented) in the way walking a valued trail might, it can form a more complex experience, drawing out new and strange perspectives of landscapes and what they are becoming, of which those authorised (hi)stories can also become a part.[22] Moving freely through a heritage landscape also includes moving along valued trails and through museums. As such, paths of meaning and the landscape view of heritage do not reflect an either-or critical perspective on valued trails or

---

20 Keightley and Pickering, *The Mnemonic Imagination*.
21 As used by a/r/tographer Rita Irwin who, instead of speaking of concepts, that she finds too defined, fixed and final, uses renderings. Renderings are rather in flux and may change and evolve, they are 'performative concepts of possibility'. Irwin, 'A/r/tography' p.8.
22 In reference to ruins, discarded and decaying traces from the path, forgotten heritage, DeSilvey, *Curated Decay*; DeSilvey and Edensor, 'Reckoning with Ruins'; Edensor, *Industrial Ruins*.

Figure 3.

Valued and forgotten forms, Rjukan-Notodden World Heritage Site. Photograph by Benjamin Richards.

the heritage industry, but rather an inclusion and enrichment of the experience of them. Here the remembered and the forgotten, valued and discarded, authorised and unauthorised, natural and cultural forms are experienced to be flowing through one another, intra-playing across multiple temporalities and extending beyond the delineated notion of authentic heritage and pre-assigned, authorised values.

Forming paths

Artist Richard Long emerged in the space created by early conceptual artists (including John Cage) with his 1967 art piece 'A Line Made by Walking'.[23] This artwork was part of a growing land art movement considering the temporality of art and the inclusion of the everyday in art and art in the everyday, proposing that walking itself could be an artistic practice. The piece was performed in an unknown field where Long, walking back and forth repeatedly,

---

23   Tate (2007) A line made by walking https://www.tate.org.uk/art/artworks/long-a-line-made-by-walking-p07149 (accessed 30 Nov. 2021)

16. Forming Paths within Post-industrial Landscapes

trod a visible straight line into the grass. He photographed it, and this black and white photograph is the only lasting evidence of the 'intervention'. As a self-declared sculptor, his work suggested the idea of walking as an act that sculpts the landscape,[24] whereby our very movement shapes cultural values and knowledge into the landscape. By not focusing on representing or altering the landscape permanently, though, Long's approach differed from other land artists of the time; he was instead more concerned with 'experiencing' the landscape.[25]

The landscape is full of such spontaneous interventions in the form of what are often referred to as *desire lines* or *paths*, a term credited to Gaston Bachelard in reference to 'the psychological, physical need to get from one place to the next'.[26] Desire paths *are* 'also known as cow paths, pirate paths, social trails, kemonomichi (beast trails), chemins de l'âne (donkey paths), and Olifantenpad (elephant trails)'.[27] These are unofficial paths that have formed through the continual, repetitive movements of humans and other animals within a landscape.

Desire paths can be understood as a form of protest or trespass, a movement against a more controlled and designed environment. Such unauthorised movements may represent a short-cut between two unforeseen connections, a desire to reach a particular place or form of interest, or an attempt to get away from surveilled spaces.[28] While you can speculate on their origin or uses, or try to deduce this from your observations, such lines can also be seen as meaningful forms of embodied knowledge that have formed and been formed through movement, between the 'affordances' of the landscape and the 'response-ability', attention and needs of the wanderer.[29] Following such paths in turn requires an attentiveness to what might unfold; the very act of moving along an unknown path attunes your senses to the world in a different way, making them stand-on-end. There is no map to look at beforehand, no expectation of a new information board appearing around the next bend explaining another part of the story. This 'heightened state' we experience draws us into the intra-play of forms, the 'living play of forces' that is movement, in a visceral way.[30] We

---

24 Roelstraete, *Richard Long*, pp. 5–9.
25 Ibid., pp. 18–19.
26 Furman, 'Desire Lines', p. 23.
27 R. Moor (2017), 'Tracing and erasing New Yorks lines of desire', https://www.newyorker.com/tech/annals-of-technology/tracing-and-erasing-new-yorks-lines-of-desire (accessed 30 Nov. 2021)
28 Luckert, 'Drawings We Have Lived'; Smith and Walters, 'Desire Lines and Defensive Architecture in Modern Urban Environments'.
29 'Affordance' from Gibson, *The Theory of Affordances*. 'Response-ability' from Essay one, J. Cage, *Silence: Lectures and Writings* (Middletown, CT: Wesleyan University Press, 1961).
30 Menke and Jackson, *Force*, pp. 81–98.

become aware of our intra-play with the world, by which I mean we are opened to the forms around us, we no longer know what to expect or what will form through our encounters and the landscape becomes mysterious and complex again through this experience, even as it forms meaning. This self-directed attunement and sensitivity (and the resulting feelings and moods) we carry with us when our movement continues along a valued trail, through a museum or back onto the bus, providing a wider context to the official route and adding to the layers of meaning that form our whole, unique experience.

The future of desire paths is uncertain: they could be the early stages of a valued trail forming, where, once established and popularised, they may be maintained and marked as official routes (a popular technique in architectural planning today).[31] In this sense, they contain the potential for becoming valued heritage trails in the future, a heritage forming. Alternatively, many will fade from view, either from a lack of use or through successful attempts to block or divert this unauthorised movement.

Everyone simply roaming around the landscape can of course cause a great deal of damage to the other forms there. Moving freely in a landscape therefore requires a responsiveness and care in how we are moving. As with the right to roam, such movement is only viable alongside a corresponding duty of care that is broadly adhered to. It is not a self-centred desire free from responsibility, and desire paths, in a way, bear witness to this care, in that they remain – people tend to follow a path if it is going in the direction they want. This indicates a concern to do less harm, but also a recognition of the knowledge and experience paths embody, that it may be a 'good way to go'.

You may not be led along a pre-made path all the way, but again that does not mean your movements are carefree. The reason you move off a trail or a desire path or deer track is because you are drawn towards some other form or you become directed toward a particular way. To get there or move in that direction requires a 'co-respondence' between yourself and the landscape you are within.[32] You would not necessarily move in a straight line (as Long does), and Long's work is far from a straight line conceptually, being strongly rooted in rhizomatic thought, nomadism and Guy Debord's theory of the dérive, or *drift*, that rather reflects a getting off the beaten track.[33]

Moving freely within the landscape is rather about forming a way with the

---

31 Turner, Tom (2018) Desire Lines are a key principle in landscape architecture (Accessed 30 Nov. 2021) http://www.landscapearchitecture.org.uk/desire-lines-key-principle-landscape-architecture/

32 Richards and Haukeland, 'A Phenomenology of Intra-play for Sustainability Research within Heritage Landscapes'.

33 Roelstraete, *Richard Long*; Smith and Morra, *Visual Culture*, pp. 77, 81.

16. Forming Paths within Post-industrial Landscapes

other forms around you, a 'co-forming'.[34] You might consider how the land is shaped, what plants, insects, animals, and bushes there are, what dangers there might be, how other forms might respond to your movements, your direction. Forming such a path can take all sorts of directions and ways of moving, bending under, climbing or stepping over and squeezing through. You may never be able to find or repeat that path again, or it may open for a new direction that others will later follow, leading to something new.

If we are to move from the idea of heritage as isolated things or objects, as in a defining of what heritage is, toward heritage as a process through which things become or form, then the question of how and why we form paths and trails is important. In that sense, the heritage of paths and trails is not only found in their reforming and maintenance, but in how new paths (future heritages) are being formed today.

What desire paths show us, and I speak here especially as a researcher, is the possibility to form our own paths, new paths that open for new thoughts, questions and directions along the way. New paths not only lead us to unexpected places, but they remind us that it is we who are experiencing. As with Long's intervention, there is a desire to make our own paths of meaning in the landscape too. Long reminds us of the effect we have when forming our own paths in the landscape, from physical trampling to the effect this can have, through time, on how we and others feel, think, and move.

Path of research

Drift is interesting to think about here in relation to the forming of paths of meaning. Situationist Guy Débord, whose notion of drift inspired Long, helped to develop an experiential method called psychogeography.[35] This method attempted to examine how the natural forces of the geographic environment shape the 'structures of society', the conception societies have of the world and 'the emotions and behaviour of individuals'. Despite the shortcomings of this method, the idea of psychogeographic drift remains useful; here the drifter seeks out new encounters through a playful movement while remaining aware of how they are being e/affected by the other forms around them. While drift, or the 'transient passage through varied ambiences', lacks a 'clear destination', it does have a purpose, which distinguishes it from the more submissive wander-

---

34   Richards and Haukeland, 'A Phenomenology of Intra-play for Sustainability Research within Heritage Landscapes'.

35   An organisation of social revolutionaries in Europe consisting of artists, intellectuals and political theorists between 1957 and 1972, Coverley, *Psychogeography*.

ing of the flaneur. The purpose of drift is to seek out and experience particular moods and ambiences within a landscape that can help form new aesthetic understandings and perspectives of that place.[36]

If heritage is not a definable object or story from the past but rather something that forms through a performative engagement within the landscape, then drift perhaps offers a way of thinking about, researching and experiencing such phenomena, where our less determined movement hints at the more complex whole that forms and sustains the landscapes around us and the viability of life within them.

Þóra Pétursdóttir considers the possibility of driftwood itself as heritage 'in and of the Anthropocene', highlighting the potential of forms that might normally be considered waste to become relevant and central to our way of thinking.[37] From Karen Barad, she highlights the 'radical' openness of matter where processes never end or close, 'things don´t simply add up' into neat stories.[38] By thinking metaphorically with driftwood, as a product of drift, we can re-evaluate heritage research as something formed by our movements, by how we move and how we become directed. Driftwood is perhaps the ultimate drifter, but even driftwood is not helpless, it has weight and length and shape and density, it has a body that has an effect and in that sense co-forms its drift. It does not start out as driftwood, however; along the way a piece of wood or a branch that had ended up in the water is slowly formed, it is shaped and smoothed by its journey into what we call driftwood.

As researchers and visitors, we can choose, in a sense, to be – more or less – driftwood-like in our approach, where our desire to make our own paths of meaning in the landscape is realised through an intra-play within it; that is to say, we co-form our path within that we seek to understand. Like driftwood, we have weight and length and density (a purpose), we have an effect, but like driftwood we are also shaped by our movements – we and our research are formed and changed along the way.

We can choose to pre-determine our route through a landscape with a theoretical and methodological map showing the direction our movement should take and what we wish to find out, but this is a way of moving that does not co-respond; it is to 'look but not see'.[39] Alternately we can form a path of meaning along the way, through experiencing the territory, where our

---

36   Coverley, *Psychogeography*, p.88-96.
37   Pétursdóttir, 'Anticipated Futures? Knowing the Heritage of Drift Matter'.
38   Ibid., p.99.
39   Thoreau and Searls, *The Journal 1837–1861*, p. 373.

drifting might traverse valued trails, museums, desire paths, as well as forming interventions of its own.[40] Such a way of moving and experiencing perhaps comes closer to what Solnit refers to as 'writing the landscape'.[41]

Summary

This essay has considered experiences within an industrial heritage landscape and introduced two distinct yet overlapping ways of moving within them: valued trails, where your movements are more curated toward the representation of an authorised story for the purposes of tourism, education and identity building; and paths of meaning, that open for a movement that is formed along the way by attending to what you encounter, a drift that seeks out new and unexpected encounters. Desire paths, in this scenario, do not represent a third form of movement but are rather a result of both. They may form either through the right to roam or a desire to drift from the marked footpath and they hint at the potential for our movements to become valued in the future. Equally, what valued trails teach us is not only the (hi)story of that trail, but that it is possible to make paths within the landscape with the forms we encounter. The experience of trails such as the Saboteurs' route can be enriched by the experience of having moved freely and formed our own paths within the landscape too, as the saboteurs once did. As such, the heritage of paths and trails is not a fixed thing, but the process of forming paths that has echoed across time, across generations and across epochs. Between humans and the landscapes, they are embedded.

By allowing ourselves to drift, we are made attentive to our surroundings, where our movements are actively shaped through an intra-play with the other forms, directions and ambiences we encounter. Such a way of moving forms a less precise but more complex experience, where heritage can be understood as part of an ongoing open process of co-responding within the landscape, where echoes from the past, the present and the potential of the future become entangled, in a continuous negotiation of how we can sustain ourselves amongst the other forms we are dependent on and with whom we form meaning.

---

40 Dr Alfred Korzybski is quoted as having said 'the map is not the territory ... the word is not the thing'.
41 Solnit, *Wanderlust*.

Bibliography

Bollier, D., *Think Like a Commoner: A Short Introduction to the Life of the Commons* (Canada: New Society Publishers, 2014).

Bowers, C.A., *Revitalizing the Commons: Cultural and Educational Sites of Resistance and Affirmation* (Lanham, Md: Lexington Books, 2006).

Coverley, M., *Psychogeography* (Harpenden: Oldcastle Books, 2010).

DeSilvey, C., *Curated Decay: Heritage Beyond Saving* (Minneapolis: University of Minnesota Press, 2017).

DeSilvey, C. and T. Edensor, 'Reckoning with Ruins', *Progress in Human Geography* **37** (4) (2012): 465–485. https://doi.org/10.1177/0309132512462271

Edensor, T., *Industrial Ruins: Spaces, Aesthetics and Materiality* (Oxford: Berg, 2005).

Furman, A., 'Desire Lines: Determining Pathways through the City', *WIT Transactions on Ecology and The Environment* **155** (2012).

Gibson, J.J., *The Ecological Approach to Visual Perception* (Boston: Houghton Mifflin, 1979).

Griffin, E., *Liberty's Dawn: A People's History of the Industrial Revolution* (London: Yale University Press, 2013).

Haraway, D.J., *Staying with the Trouble: Making Kin in the Chthulucene* (Durham, North Carolina: North Carolina: Duke University Press, 2016).

Harrison, R., *Heritage: Critical Approaches* (London: Routledge, 2013).

Hindman, H.D. and H. Hindman, *The World of Child Labor: An Historical and Regional Survey* (Armonk: Taylor & Francis Group, 2009).

Ingold, T., 'The Temporality of the Landscape', *World Archaeology* **25** (2) (1993): 152–74.

Ingold, T., *Being Alive: Essays on Movement, Knowledge and Description* (London: Routledge, 2011).

Ingold, T., *The Life of Lines* (Place: Taylor and Francis, 2015).

Irwin, R., *'A/r/tography': The SAGE Encyclopedia of Qualitative Research Methods* (Thousand Oaks, California: Publisher, 2008).

Keightley, E. and M. Pickering, *The Mnemonic Imagination: Remembering as Creative Practice* (London: Palgrave, 2012).

Luckert, E., 'Drawings We Have Lived: Mapping Desire Lines in Edmonton', *Constellations* **4** (1) (2013). https://doi.org/10.29173/cons18871

Menke, C. and G. Jackson, *Force: A Fundamental Concept of Aesthetic Anthropology* (New York: Fordham University Press, 2013).

Ostrom, E., *Governing the Commons: The Evolution of Institutions for Collective Action* (Cambridge: Cambridge University Press, 2019).

Pétursdóttir, Þ. 'Anticipated Futures? Knowing the Heritage of Drift Matter'. *International Journal of Heritage Studies* **26** (1) (2019): 1–17. https://doi.org/10.1080/13527258.2019.1620835

Richards, B. and P.I. Haukeland, 'A Phenomenology of Intra-play for Sustainability Research within Heritage Landscapes'. *Forskning & Forandring* **3** (2) (2020): 27–46. https://doi.org/10.23865/fof.v3.2406

Roelstraete, D., *Richard Long: A Line Made by Walking* (London: Afterall Books, 2010).

Schrumpf, E., 'History of Child Labor in the Nordic Countries', in Hugh D. Hindman (ed.),

16. Forming Paths within Post-industrial Landscapes

The World of Child Labor: An Historical and Regional Survey, pp. 575–79 (Abingdon: Taylor & Francis Group, 2009).

Smith, L. *Uses of Heritage* (Oxon: Routledge, 2006).

Smith, M. and J. Morra, *Visual Culture: Critical Concepts in Media and Cultural Studies: Vol. 3: Spaces of Visual Culture* (London: Routledge, 2006).

Smith, N. and P. Walters, 'Desire Lines and Defensive Architecture in Modern Urban Environments', *Urban Studies* 55 (13) (2018): 2980–95. https://doi.org/10.1177/0042098017732690

Solnit, R., *Wanderlust: A History of Walking* (London: Granta, 2014).

Thoreau, H.D. and D. Searls, *The Journal, 1837–1861* (New York: New York Review Books, 2009).

Weber, A., *Enlivenment: Towards a Fundamental Shift in the Concepts of Nature, Culture and Politics*, Heinrich Böll Stiftung Ecology Series **31** (2013): https://www.boell.de/en/2013/02/01/enlivenment-towards-fundamental-shift-concepts-nature-culture-and-politics

INDEX

A
Åland archipelago, Finland 20, 131–50
access (to land) 3, 8, 12, 17, 18, 19, 33, 35, 36, 39, 43, 45, 47, 49, 51, 58–62, 64, 67, 72, 74–93, 138, 211, 245, 251, 254, 258–60, 283, 319
Access to Mountains Act (1939), UK 45, 49, 61
Access to Mountains Bill, UK 74
accessibility 114, 119, 125, 133, 240, 259, 281, 285
Adamello Park, Italy 19, 114, 119, 125
affect; affective 46, 149, 300–01, 308–09, 311–12, 322–23, 327
afforestation 281, 283, 289, 290, 296
agent; agency 49, 102, 103, 111, 157, 158, 160, 214, 235, 240, 283, 289, 310
agriculture 35, 36, 48, 63, 75, 77, 82, 100, 101, 110, 111, 222, 224, 225, 234, 241, 245, 247
Alaimo, Stacy 23, 215
Alps; Alpine 74, 80–82, 86, 88–91, 114–15, 122–25
    Eastern Alps 76–77, 79–80, 85–86, 93
    Italian Alps 19
Alpini 121–24
Alter Banhoff video walk 170, 177–78, 181
amenity 33, 343, 60, 67, 71, 79
animal 18, 22, 56, 97–100, 103–04, 107–11, 125, 194–97, 205, 206, 214, 225, 269, 273, 275, 319, 327
    path 2, 8, 10, 18, 56–57, 97–100, 103, 107–11, 125, 192, 222, 273, 325
Anthropocene 1–3, 23, 125, 210, 211, 213, 268, 276, 303, 311, 328
Anthropocentrism 22, 202, 204, 206, 210–13, 216, 275
antiquarian; antiquarianism 41–42, 77, 90
archaeology 16, 23, 297, 300–01
    experimental 252
Aristi, Greece 23, 297, 305, 308, 312
Arnold, Edwin 46

artefact 4, 15, 67, 117–19, 125, 183, 216, 248, 307, 308, 310
articulation 3, 4, 9, 11–12, 15, 18, 19, 20, 187, 209, 235, 300–01
    of territory 14–15
attentive walking 22, 24, 201–18, 325
audio walk; audio guide 21, 119, 167–73, 176–80, 183, 191–92, 207
Austro-Hungarian army 114–16, 121, 122, 124
avatar 186, 189, 192, 194

B
Baldwin, Stanley 60
Balkans 300
Baker, E(rnest) A. 83
Barad, Karen 160, 328
Barnes, Phil 87
Battlezone 188
Bauernbefreiung 76, 80
becoming 7–8, 13, 15, 201, 210
behaviour 37, 39, 51, 52, 58, 81–83, 85, 134, 195, 229, 319, 327
Belgium 23, 264–78
Benesch, Fritz 82
Bennett, Jane 201–04, 206, 212
bioregion; bioregional 22, 222–39
Blühnbachtal, Austria 85
Boulouki, Greece 297, 298, 212
Britton, Lionel 86–87
Bryce, James 74

C
calamine landscapes 273
Camino de Santiago de Compostela 11, 21, 137, 143, 152–66
Camino Frances 158–59
Canterbury, UK 40
capitalism; capitalist 34, 35, 36, 52, 201, 203, 204, 275, 276
CAR (Cordillera Administrative Region), Philippines 242
Cardiff, Janet 21, 167–85

Carwynnen Quoit, Cornwall, UK 22, 242, 249–51, 254
Central Park, New York, USA 168, 169
Central Rights of Way Committee (CROW), UK 60, 62–66, 70, 71
Centre d'interprétation du site minier de Saint-Nicolas 269
De Certeau, Michel 23, 99, 175, 287, 290
Chubb, Lawrence 49
child; childhood 35, 39, 63, 70, 82, 97, 125, 147, 160, 225–27, 231, 235, 252, 259, 306, 320
city 52, 75, 81, 87, 91, 173, 176, 177, 180, 274, 287, Clare, John 35, 53, 67
Clarion Club Ramblers 77, 81
climate 5, 19, 105, 114, 197, 225
    change 117, 125, 211, 240, 241, 248
coal 23, 88, 264–76
coast 165, 201, 319
cobbled path *see also* kalderimi 22, 297, 300, 301, 307, 308
co-creation 14, 17, 18, 21, 98, 111, 152, 155, 157, 158, 160, 281, 292, 310
coffee plantation 22, 222, 224, 227–78, 231, 236
Colley Hill, Kent, UK 43
Collingwood, R.G. 43
colonialism; colonial 22, 81, 221, 222, 224, 225, 227, 229, 231, 233, 244
    decolonial 235, 236
    precolonial 224, 225, 227, 229, 234
    postcolonial 234, 235
commemoration 65, 170, 173, 175, 279–86, 289–91, 296
commodification 6, 70
commons 35, 43, 76, 78, 79, 80, 93, 308, 319, 320
Commons, Open Spaces and Footpaths Preservation Society, UK 60, 65, 79, 93
Commons Preservation Society, UK 39, 70
computer 188, 210
    game 16
concrete 210, 211, 214
concreteness 2, 17, 19, 20, 102, 131, 137
conservation 8, 119, 125, 241, 247
conservatism 45, 47–49, 52, 74, 76
Council of Europe 137, 140, 153
counter-monument 289–91

Country Life 50, 51
Countryside and Rights of Way Act (2000), UK 45, 51
county council, UK 50, 58, 59, 62, 69
COVID-19 6, 10, 17, 20, 21, 186, 260
Cow 2, 48, 97, 105, 107–11, 325
Cronon, William 272
cultural continuity 22, 224, 229, 231–32, 235, 247
culture 2, 4, 5, 6, 9, 13, 14, 15, 22, 34, 36, 37, 38, 42, 49, 66, 75–78, 80, 82, 85, 87, 92, 99, 100, 103, 142, 149, 157, 186, 202, 206, 222, 224, 225–27, 229, 223–36, 240, 241, 247, 248, 267, 279, 281, 286, 291, 301, 310–12

D

dairymaid 97, 105, 109, 110
Dear Esther 190–94
Débord, Guy 326–27
Derbyshire, UK 33
Denecourt, Claude 133
design 2, 3, 5, 14, 15, 17, 24, 57, 168, 178, 187–89, 193, 196, 198, 201, 206, 279, 289, 291, 325
designation 6, 51, 61, 137, 142, 240, 241, 250, 260, 318
DeSilvey, Caitlin 183, 267
desire path 2, 24, 57, 317–18, 325–29
Deutsche und Oesterreichische Alpenverein 74, 81, 82
Deutsche Nationalbewegung (German National Movement) 79
Deutsche Nationalpartei (German National Party) 79
digital 3, 16, 19, 21, 111, 187, 189, 190
DNT, The Norwegian Trekking Association 11, 106, 110
Van Dooren, Thom 209, 266
drift 4, 24, 318, 326–29
dwelling 286, 297, 299–300, 303, 305, 312

E

Earle, Timothy 56–57
education 22, 24, 87, 89, 240, 241, 252, 280, 287, 329
educational narrative 244
Elliot, Charles Boileau 97, 99, 104

Index

embodied 43, 45, 51, 71, 100, 107, 110, 111, 183, 204, 210, 215, 261, 276, 279, 280, 287
  encounter 39
  experience 42, 45, 52, 101
  knowledge 212, 296–313, 325
emulation 153, 155
enclosure 33, 35–36, 77–78, 91, 92, 319, 320
encounter 22, 39, 41, 52, 77, 83, 85, 87, 97, 100, 114, 123, 167, 169, 172, 176, 177, 190, 196, 200–18, 247, 259, 267, 268, 271, 272, 283, 287, 322, 326, 327, 329
Englishness 17, 33, 39, 46, 52, 60,
entanglement 18, 72, 152, 158, 160, 161, 203, 204, 207–08, 210, 214, 266, 275, 279, 322
environing 13–16
environment; environmental 6, 9, 10, 13, 14, 15, 19, 22, 23, 75, 76, 77, 83, 86–89, 91, 92, 114, 115, 119, 123, 125, 136, 142, 144, 152, 158, 161, 168, 169, 172, 173, 178, 179, 183, 189, 190, 192–96, 207, 210, 211, 212, 222, 226, 229, 231, 234, 235, 236, 241, 260, 265, 266–68, 270–76, 280, 300, 310, 320, 325, 327
erosion 2, 19, 36, 110, 245
ethnography 12, 23, 131, 236, 255, 264, 266, 295, 298, 305, 311
experience *see also* embodied 3, 6, 12, 18, 19, 21, 22, 23, 39, 42, 52, 56, 57, 63, 67, 69, 70, 71, 82, 87, 88, 99, 125, 131, 133, 134–36, 138, 140, 141–44, 149, 158, 161, 162, 169, 170, 173, 175, 176, 177, 179, 181–83, 187, 189–90, 192, 193, 194, 198, 199, 214, 224, 241, 244, 247, 249, 252, 254, 255, 259, 267, 272, 283, 285, 286, 287, 289, 291, 301, 316, 318, 323–29
  on-trail 20, 224, 226, 227, 235
  place-based 226, 227, 229, 231, 234
exploration 24, 42, 43, 186, 188, 190–92, 196, 249, 267, 268, 288
extractivism 201–02, 204, 205, 213

F
farmer 36, 45, 49, 51, 53, 59, 64, 76, 88, 90, 91, 100, 104, 205, 247
feminism 157, 204

Fenton-Ia, Cornwall, UK 249, 251, 255–59
Fetterappa Sandri, Carlo 123, 124
Field, The 47, 49, 50,
Finland 131–51
Finn Forest Trail 11
Firewatch 190, 192–94
footpath 33–55, 60, 62, 64–67, 69, 71, 79, 86, 93, 98, 121, 122, 137, 197, 245, 307, 311, 329
footprint 1, 143, 222, 273, 312, 323
forest *see also* afforestation; reforestation 2, 11, 15, 23, 40, 80, 84, 86, 89, 97, 133, 138, 144, 147, 162, 192, 194, 221–22, 224, 225–228, 231–35, 240, 241, 242, 274, 281–83, 285, 290–91, 296
Forest Ramblers 37
fossil 202, 205, 210–14, 272

G
Galicia, Spain 121, 152, 160, 162, 163
game *see* computer game; video game
gamekeeper 33, 45, 53, 84, 87, 91–92
Global Geoparks 240–41
Glyndŵr's Way 67
Gosson 265, 268–69, 271, 272
grazing 18, 40, 93, 99–100, 104–06, 108, 110, 111, 319
greening 269, 272, 273
Green Map System 255, 260
guide *see also* audio walk 81, 85, 141, 143, 144, 171, 192, 226, 252, 272
guidebook 11, 36, 42, 46, 62, 66, 133, 135, 152, 158, 163
Gustafsson, Lars 2

H
Hadrian's Wall Path 67
Hammarskjöld, Dag 11
Hansen, Oskar 289
Happisch, Leopold 88–90
Hardangervidda, Norway 97
Harrison, Rodney 8, 187, 198, 199, 224, 229, 292, 320
Hayes, Nick 52–53
Hayfield 78–79
Hayfield, Kinder Scout and District Ancient Footpaths and Bridlepaths Association 78

healing 24, 160–63
health 5, 6, 10, 17, 22, 36, 51, 78, 87, 104, 134, 147, 163, 240, 241, 253–54
Her long black hair 169
heritage 1, 3, 6–17, 19, 21, 24, 43, 66, 67, 71, 75, 76, 77, 78, 80, 84, 88, 92, 99, 125, 131, 134, 135, 136–37, 138, 140, 141–43, 144, 149, 187, 192, 193, 194, 198, 199, 201, 229, 241, 249, 251, 254, 255, 259, 260, 265, 266, 268, 275, 280, 289, 290, 291, 299, 307, 310–11, 318, 320, 321, 323, 326–29
  anthropocentric 201, 211
  cultural 4, 8, 137, 141, 153, 154, 199, 245, 247, 248, 252, 253, 269, 276, 281, 312
  immaterial 9, 11, 131, 152, 157
  industrial 210, 269, 316, 321, 329
  industry 321, 324
  intangible 152, 154, 155, 242, 259, 291, 292
  making 11, 13, 15, 16, 19, 20, 21, 224, 229, 232, 234, 235, 308
  management 5, 9, 111, 297
  movement xi, 5, 9, 10, 12, 14, 18, 19, 20, 21, 23, 39, 41, 42, 48, 52, 53, 98, 100, 106–11, 125, 157, 167, 168, 169, 170, 186–87, 190, 197, 198, 201, 205, 214, 216, 259, 266, 276, 280, 316
heritagisation 3, 23, 136, 137, 149, 276
hiking 6, 10, 11, 16, 21, 37, 38, 45, 49, 88, 89, 90, 120, 121, 125, 131, 134, 138, 141, 143, 144, 147, 188, 190–93, 279–81, 283, 285, 286, 288, 291, 296
Hill, Octavia 33, 39, 46, 52, 70
historian; history-writing 23, 33, 35, 38, 41, 42, 84, 91, 103, 115, 122, 272, 310
histories 23, 57, 70–72, 75, 76, 175, 176, 178, 196, 236, 259, 266, 267, 297, 299, 306, 311
Hobhouse Report (1947), UK 58
Holocaust 23, 173, 176, 177, 281, 283, 287–90
Hoheisel, Horst 173, 182
horizontality 2, 3, 7, 106
Hunter, Sir Robert 33, 47
hunting 8, 74, 80–85, 8, 89–92, 104, 222, 232, 234
hybrid 5, 14, 15, 163, 266, 267, 291, 311

I
Icknield Way 66, 67
identity 2, 66, 76, 176, 180, 181–83, 198, 221, 28, 229, 231, 234, 254, 268, 279, 291, 319, 321, 329
  place 132, 136, 142, 175, 231, 321
  national 34, 39, 45, 71, 79, 141
Ifugao, Philippines 242, 247, 248
  ethnic group 242, 244, 245
  Rice Terraces 22, 241, 244, 245, 249, 260
imitation 153, 155, 156
improvisation 231
India 22, 221–39
indigenous (people) 19, 221, 225, 226, 227, 234, 235, 236, 244, 247
  heritage making 22, 221, 224, 229, 232, 234, 235
  knowledge 224, 229, 231, 248, 259
individual 5, 13, 18, 19, 38, 57, 61, 71, 72, 74, 85, 137, 142, 149, 157, 168, 170, 181–83, 191, 281, 287, 289, 290
industrialisation 17, 33, 104, 266–68, 275–76, 319–20
Ingold, Tim 10, 39, 102, 156, 187, 226, 267, 300, 322
insect 205, 208, 210, 272, 273, 275, 328
intertextuality 152, 155, 160, 279, 287
intra-play 316, 319–326, 328, 329
island 20, 131–51, 191–92
Israel 23, 279–94
Israel National Trail (INT) 280, 283
Italy; Italian 80, 114–127, 267, 270, 273

J
Jack the Ripper 171, 173, 175, 176, 182
James, Saint 21, 152, 153, 162
Jemeppe, Belgium 264, 268
Jerusalem, Israel 152
  Hills 281, 282, 288
Joad, C.E.M. 84

K
Kailpodh 232–35
kalderimi 295–315
Kassel 21, 170, 173, 175, 178, 180, 182
Kastner, J.V. 86, 87, 92
Kent, UK 40–41, 43, 64

Index

Keren Kayemeth le'Israel-Jewish National Fund (JNF) 280, 282, 283, 287, 291
Kinder Scout 78, 85
  trespass 33–34, 49,
King's Trail (*Kungsleden*) 11
Kinship 247
Kipling, Rudyard 48–49
Kodagu, India 22, 221–39
Koselleck, Reinhart 5

L

labour; labourer 36, 39, 63, 88, 99, 102, 205, 210, 267, 271, 300, 308, 311, 319, 320
Lake District, UK 39, 41, 71
  National Park 240
land 2, 3, 17, 18, 19, 23, 34, 35, 36, 39, 40, 45–53, 56, 60, 62, 70, 72, 75, 77, 78, 83, 87, 100–04, 108, 111, 133, 138, 221, 222, 224, 225–27, 229, 231, 234–36, 245, 249, 254, 258, 260, 280, 283, 286, 288, 290, 291, 327
  art 324
  politics 33
  reform 45, 47
  rights 19, 236
  use 9, 18, 19, 49, 75, 77, 255, 259, 260, 318
landfill 265, 272–75
landmark 138, 144, 167, 169, 180, 253, 254
landowner; landlord ; land ownership 34, 35, 39, 46, 47, 49, 50, 51, 52, 58, 60–64, 77, 79, 81, 84, 86, 89, 90, 93, 138, 149, 251, 259, 318
landscape 2–23, 33, 38, 39, 41–43, 45, 46, 52, 56, 57, 65, 70, 71, 72, 75, 77, 78, 79, 83, 85, 87, 88, 91, 92, 98–104, 107, 111, 119, 122, 125, 133, 134, 135, 143, 144, 154, 155–60, 170, 178, 186–88, 190, 192–94, 196–98, 202, 205, 206, 216, 222, 224, 229, 231, 234–36, 240–42, 244–45, 247, 251, 252–54, 255, 258, 259, 260, 261, 266–67, 269–73, 275, 281–82, 285, 288, 290, 291–92, 295–300, 303, 307, 308, 310–11, 316, 318–23, 325–29
Law of Property Act (1924), UK 74, 79, 93
layers 1, 3, 5, 10, 11, 15, 17, 18, 21, 22, 23, 134, 144, 152, 155–56, 160–62, 169, 170, 173, 176, 180–82, 212–13, 215, 246, 247, 266, 271–73, 275, 276, 290, 301–03, 305, 309, 310, 323, 326
leisure 36, 60, 62, 63, 65–67, 69, 71, 74, 76, 82, 83, 89, 279
León 159, 160
Liber Sancti Jacobi 152
Liège 264–66, 268, 269, 274
Limhamn limestone quarry, Sweden 201, 202, 204, 205, 210, 211
line; linear 2, 3, 10, 12, 17, 23, 42, 45, 58, 122–24, 134, 154, 156, 175–77, 190–91, 194, 206, 213, 214, 222, 322–26
living-in-place 225–26, 234
local government *see also* county council; parish council 45, 50, 59
Long, Richard 324–26
Löwy, Arthur (Arthur Lenhoff) 74

M

Macfarlane, Robert 43, 108, 111
Maison des Terrils 269
Manchester, UK 78, 93
Manchester Ramblers Federation 81
Mandanna, Sarita 224, 225, 228, 232, 233
manliness; masculinity 77, 81, 83, 84, 85
map; mapping 15, 16, 38, 45, 50, 51, 57–59, 61–64, 67, 71, 103, 111, 119, 134, 135, 137, 141, 178, 180, 192–94, 196, 197, 224, 249, 252, 254, 255, 325, 328
marketisation 71
Martyrs' Trail (Shvil HaKedoshim) 281–85, 287–91
Martyrs' Forest (Ya'ar HaKedoshim) 282, 285, 290
materiality; matter 1, 2, 4, 8, 9, 12–17, 19, 20, 21, 22, 97–98, 100, 101, 103–04, 106, 131, 152, 155–57, 160, 162, 201–04, 205, 206, 208, 210, 212, 214–16, 265–67, 269, 271–72, 275, 283, 289, 292, 301, 312, 322
  vibrant matter 202, 203, 208, 216
Matless, David 45
meaning 1, 5, 6, 16, 18, 20, 21, 24, 60, 65, 67, 69–72, 103, 133, 142, 155–57 159–60, 167, 168, 170, 176, 178, 179, 186, 197, 208, 232, 235, 266–67, 275–76, 281, 284, 285, 288, 289, 292, 307, 318, 320–23, 325–29

Medieval 35, 40, 152, 158, 162–63, 249, 251, 254, 255, 258, 274
memorial 72, 267
    trail 280–94
memory 5, 9, 10, 13, 18, 22, 23, 80, 121, 167–70, 172–73, 175–83, 187, 202, 227, 249, 251, 252, 258, 268, 269, 272, 276, 279–83, 285, 289–91, 295, 303, 309, 310, 323
    collective 9, 173, 309
    disciplinary 309, 310
    kinetic 183
    muscle 10, 214
    performative 181
    of place 305, 308
Meseta Central, Spain 159–60
metaphor 4, 10, 21, 83, 84, 88, 155–56, 160, 300, 329
methodology 90, 100, 119, 242
    walking as 12, 23
migration, human 93, 247, 267, 296
miner 90, 249, 270, 272
mineral 22, 201–18, 271
mineralness 202, 204, 206, 209, 210, 214, 215, 323
Ministry of Housing and Local Government, UK 62, 66
Missing voice: case study B, The 169–71, 176, 177, 180
moorland 78, 82, 84, 86, 91, 93, 251
more-than-human 4, 19, 22, 86, 87, 206, 207, 216, 267, 275, 276, 296, 301, 316
mountain 15, 18, 19, 22, 33, 62, 71, 80–81, 83, 85–91, 93, 97, 100, 102, 104–06, 108, 110, 114, 115, 119, 124, 125, 160, 162, 188, 192, 221, 222, 225, 226, 242, 244, 295, 296, 299, 303, 308
multimedia 114, 118, 123, 125

N
Nagacadan Rice Terraces, Philippines 245–46
narrative 16, 19, 20, 21, 23, 57, 60, 69, 77, 78, 88, 89, 90, 115, 131, 133, 134, 136, 138, 140–42, 144, 147, 149, 152, 155, 157–60, 162, 163, 167, 169, 171–73, 175–78, 186, 187, 190, 193, 235, 241, 244, 245, 266–76, 279–81, 285, 287, 288, 289, 296, 301, 305, 307, 309, 310
National Footpaths Preservation Society, UK 43, 47, 65, 70
National Park 19, 33, 49, 115, 116, 119, 125, 192, 240
National Parks and Access to the Countryside Act (1949), UK 45, 58
National Trust, UK 33 47, 70
natureculture 152, 155, 160, 204
negotiation 58, 60, 62, 63, 71, 93, 187, 211, 229
Neolithic 252–53
Nitsche, Michael 189
New Zealand 8, 9, 66
Nord-Pas-de-Calais, France 265, 271
Norway 9, 17, 18, 19, 24, 97–113, 316–31

O
Oesterreichische Touristenklub 85, 89
Offa's Dyke 42, 67
Olwig, Kenneth 101, 229
Open Form 289–90
Open Spaces Society, UK 43, 62
Ordnance Survey 61

P
Pacific Crest trail 11
Palestine; Palestinian 290–91
palimpsest 3, 21, 152, 155, 157, 158, 160, 161, 176, 290
parish Council, UK 50, 58, 59, 62, 63, 65, 79
participatory 114, 231, 249, 255, 297, 301
past 2–5, 8, 10, 11, 16, 20–22, 36, 39, 40–43, 60, 65, 67, 71, 78, 85, 99, 100, 103, 136, 156, 169–70, 176–77, 179, 181, 192, 197, 202, 205, 210, 224, 229, 232, 234, 235, 251, 252, 253, 260, 265, 266–67, 269, 275, 276, 280, 283, 285, 290, 291, 295, 299–301, 305–12, 320, 328, 329
pasture 89, 91, 99, 110, 226
path dependence 10, 320
Ward, G.H.B. 71, 78, 85
Pays des Terrils Landscape Park, Belgium 264
Peak District, UK 14, 78, 79, 81, 85, 87, 91, 92, 93
    Footpaths Preservation Society 78–79

Index

Pennine Way 66
performance; performative 13, 20, 21, 24, 83, 84, 88, 91, 119, 131, 149, 156, 157, 168, 170, 171, 180–83, 265, 267, 285, 304, 328
Pétursdóttir, Þóra 328
phenomenology 102
Philippines 22, 240–63
pilgrim; pilgrimage 6, 11, 12, 20, 21, 40, 71, 137, 138, 140–43, 147, 149, 152–66, 251, 253, 255, 258, 280, 283, 285
Pilgrims' Way 43
place making 106, 259, 300
plant 8, 22, 123, 195, 196, 205, 208, 210, 214, 225, 227, 265, 271–73, 275, 327
metallophyte 273–74
play 93, 180, 186–200, 224, 235, 306, 327
poaching 76, 80, 83, 86, 87, 91–92
posthumanism 204, 209
post-industrial 264–64, 272, 275, 276, 316
Povinelli, Elisabeth A. 214
power 17, 35, 50, 59, 65, 84, 88, 136, 160–63, 170, 182, 203, 251, 252, 291
Powicke, F.M. 41–42
practice 3, 5, 6, 7, 8, 11–17, 19–22, 35, 36, 41, 42, 60, 75, 83, 89, 90, 92, 98, 111, 131, 134, 140–42, 144, 155, 157, 177, 179, 186, 189, 198, 201, 204, 206–08, 216, 224–227, 229, 231–36, 244, 247, 249, 266, 268, 273, 276, 279–81, 285–87, 291, 295, 297, 298–301, 303, 307–11, 324
preservation; preservationism 14, 33, 34, 39, 43, 45–48, 50, 58, 65, 67, 70, 79, 92, 93, 134, 137, 142, 167, 168, 181, 199, 235–36, 240, 247–48, 249, 307
property, property rights *see also* landowner; land rights 34, 36, 47, 48, 50–52, 62, 77, 80, 83, 86, 90, 305, 318
protest 17, 33, 47, 74–77, 82, 91, 325
Puthari 233–35
Pyne, Stephen 14
Pyrenees 159, 162

R

Ramblers Association, UK 38, 43, 49, 59, 78, 254
recreation *see also* leisure 5, 6, 12, 15, 17, 18, 20, 23, 33, 35–38, 42, 49, 51, 69, 74–75, 77, 79, 81, 87, 93, 110, 133, 205, 260, 281, 285, 286, 291
Red Dead Redemption 2 190, 194–97
Reens, The, Cornwall, UK 258–59
reforestation 229, 231, 261, 270, 275
reinhabiting 225, 229, 231, 235
rendering 5, 16, 190, 316, 323
resources 18, 20, 22, 75, 76, 79, 93, 100, 188, 201, 204, 206, 209, 210, 214, 226, 227, 234, 247
revolution 50, 76
rice cultivation 22, 244–45, 247, 260
heirloom 247
Ridgeway Walk 66
Right of Public Access 141
rights of way 18, 48, 50, 56–73, 76, 78, 79, 318
Rights of Way Act (1932), UK 59–60
right-to-roam 33, 318, 319, 326, 329
Rjukan-Notodden World Heritage Site, Norway 316–31
Roads Used as Public Paths (RUPPs) 65
rock *see also* mineral 8, 121, 122–24, 203–03, 205, 208, 211, 322
von Rosthorn, Oskar 89
Route des Terrils 269
ruderal ecology 23, 265–78
ruin 258, 267, 268, 276, 305, 309, 323

S

Saboteurs' trail 329
Saint Cuthbert's Way 67
Saint Michael Trail 258
Saint Olav Waterway 20, 137, 138, 140, 144, 146, 147
Saints Way 69
Santiago de Compostela, Spain 20, 21, 71, 137, 152–53, 156, 158, 160, 162
Scandinavia 12, 17, 133, 141
Schmiedl, Georg 89–90
Scorluzzino, Mount, Italy 117, 121, 122, 123
Scorluzzo, Mount, Italy 114, 116–25
Scotland 9, 66, 67
Seraing, Belgium 265, 268, 269, 274
Severn Way 70
sheep 40, 42, 91, 92, 97, 106, 108, 109, 272–75, 303, 305
Sheffield, UK 77, 78, 92
Clarion Ramblers 36

shieling 99, 100, 104, 105, 106, 109, 110, 111
Silkin, Lewis 58, 63
Sinclair, Iain 67
Snake Pass, UK 78–79, 93
Social Hiking 88–90
Société Anonyme Charbonnière de Gosson-Lagasse 268
soldier 19, 40, 119, 121–25, 162, 280
Solnit, Rebecca 192, 318, 329
soundscape 21, 169, 171, 179, 202
South West Coast Path 67, 70
spirituality 2, 4, 6, 11, 38, 69, 137, 147, 149, 160–63, 227, 304
spoil tip 264, 266–71, 273
Springgay, Stephanie 204, 206, 207
Standschützen 121–23
Steinwender, Otto 79–80
Stelvio National Park, Italy 19, 116–27
Stelvio Pass 117, 120
Stephen, Leslie 36, 53, 83
stories; storied *see also* narrative 9, 10, 19–21, 23, 43, 57, 91, 92, 97, 131, 133–34, 136, 140, 144, 147, 149, 152–66, 167, 169, 175, 180, 181, 186, 190, 192, 197, 202, 214, 253, 254, 265–68, 272, 275, 276, 279, 281, 287, 300, 310, 312, 323, 328
storyworld 158, 162
Strayed, Cheryl 11
suburbs 57, 81, 87
Sunday Tramps 36, 38, 53, 83
Sustainable Development Goals (SDGs) 23, 240–42, 245, 247–49, 252, 254, 255, 260, 261
sustainability; sustainable 2, 6, 9, 10, 17, 22, 125, 143, 149, 203, 241, 244, 245, 247–49, 259, 260, 316, 318, 320
Sustainable Trust, UK 251, 254
Sweden 9, 11, 17, 22, 104, 133, 137, 201–18
Switzerland 117, 123

T

tactile 23, 102, 226, 227
technofossil 210–11
temporality 56, 71, 100, 204, 211–14, 271, 275, 300, 309–12, 316, 322, 324
terril 254–78
Tiger Hills 224, 225, 227, 228, 231
Tilley, Christopher 71, 102

Tilly, Charles 10
time *see also* temporality 1, 2, 5, 7, 8, 9, 15, 18, 24, 42, 57, 59, 60, 70, 114, 122, 136, 144, 149, 176, 177, 181, 189, 192, 197–99, 212–14, 222, 224, 259, 264, 289, 292, 298, 309, 322, 323, 327, 329
Tirano battalion 123, 124
topography 21, 119, 158, 160, 221, 225
toponym 269, 280, 285
tourist; tourism 5, 6, 7, 9, 10, 12, 17, 18, 19, 22, 24, 33, 36, 37, 42, 48, 60, 66, 67, 69, 74, 76, 77, 81, 82, 90, 97, 99, 100, 104, 125, 133–34, 137, 143, 149, 167, 171, 179, 240, 244, 247, 260, 267, 269, 296–99, 300, 303, 309, 311, 321, 329
dark 178
sustainable 125, 143, 149, 247
Touristenverein 'Die Naturfreunde' (Naturfreunde) 74
toxicity 268, 275–76
trailscape 12, 15, 111
transhumance 57, 108, 110
trekking 8, 38, 104, 110, 296
trespass 17, 18, 33, 35, 36, 47–50, 52, 53, 75, 77–78, 83–88, 90–93, 136, 210, 325
Trevelyan, Charles 74, 84
Trevelyan, G.M. 38, 41, 42
Truman, Sarah E. 204, 207
Tucker, James Walker 37

U

urban *see also* city 6, 18, 21, 33, 36, 38, 45, 49, 52, 57, 71, 74–79, 80, 81, 82–83, 84, 85, 87, 92, 93, 144, 155, 168, 170, 172–73, 276, 288, 319, 320
urbanisation 17, 104, 296
UNESCO (United Nations Educational, Scientific and Cultural Organization) 11, 22, 23, 141, 142, 153, 154, 240–41, 245, 247, 296, 297, 312

V

Vemork, Norway 316
Der Verbotene Weg 74
verticality 2, 3, 7, 106, 312
video walk 168, 170, 173, 174, 177–83
Vienna, Austria 76, 86, 88, 89, 93, 94
virtual (world) 21, 22, 186–88, 196, 199

Index

W
Wales 18, 46, 51, 57, 58, 66, 69, 74
walked environment 226, 229, 234, 235, 236
    enunciation, walking as 23, 287
walking rhetorics 287, 290
walking simulator 21, 186, 187, 190–92, 194–96
Wallonia, Belgium 23, 264–78
Weber, Max 5
wellbeing 22, 134, 137, 147, 149, 240, 254
Western ghats, India 221
Whitechapel, London, UK 170–73, 175, 177–78, 180, 182
White War 114, 117, 119Winter, Max 90
woodland 33, 52, 90, 251, 296

world-making 187, 198
World Heritage Site 11, 22, 137, 153, 154, 240, 296–97, 316, 318, 319
World War One 19, 49, 85, 88–91, 114, 115, 119, 122, 125
World War Two 23, 40, 49, 67, 288, 316

Y
Youth Hostels Association (YHA), UK 37, 38
Yusoff, Kathryn 215

Z
Zagori, Greece 295–315
Zionism 23, 279–80, 282, 286

www.ingramcontent.com/pod-product-compliance
Lightning Source LLC
Chambersburg PA
CBHW021931290426
44108CB00012B/805